# BASEL II
# IMPLEMENTATION

# BASEL II IMPLEMENTATION

## A Guide to Developing and Validating a Compliant, Internal Risk Rating System

### BOGIE OZDEMIR

### and

### PETER MIU

New York   Chicago   San Francisco   Lisbon   London
Madrid   Mexico City   Milan   New Delhi
San Juan   Seoul   Singapore   Sydney   Toronto

1 2 3 4 5 6 7 8 9 0   DOC/DOC   0 1 0 9 8

ISBN   978-0-07-159132-4
MHID 0-07-159132-X

Part of set

ISBN   978-0-07-159130-0
MHID 0-07-159130-3

This publication is designed to provide accurate and authoritative information in regard to the subject matter covered. It is sold with the understanding that neither the author nor the publisher is engaged in rendering legal, accounting, futures/securities trading, or other professional service. If legal advice or other expert assistance is required, the services of a competent professional person should be sought.
            —*From a Declaration of Principles jointly adopted by a Committee*
                *of the American Bar Association and a Committee of Publishers*

McGraw-Hill books are available at special quantity discounts to use as premiums and sales promotions, or for use in corporate training programs. To contact a representative, please visit the Contact Us pages at www.mhprofessional.com.

This book is printed on acid-free paper.

*This book is dedicated to Johnny, Cecilia, Chun-Yen, Mei-Yu, and KJ.*

—Peter Miu

*To Angela, Ariel, Erem, and my parents.*

—Bogie Ozdemir

# CONTENTS

**Chapter 3**

# Validation of Internal Risk Rating System   183

**Chapter 4**

# Pillar II, Challenges, and Dealing with Procyclicality   281

# ACKNOWLEDGMENTS

We would like to thank Stuart Brannan of BMO Financial Group for contributing the section of EAD Estimation. We are indebted to Brooks Brady of Zions, Peter Chang of Standard & Poor's Risk Solutions, and David Schwartz of the Federal Reserve Bank of Richmond for their contributions to the empirical study on LGD discount rate. We would also like to thank Michel Araten, Christine Brown, Mark Carey, Michael Gordy, Andrea Resti, and Emilio Venezian for their valuable feedback on the same empirical study. We also acknowledge the helpful comments of Michael Ong and Stuart Turnbull, who served as chief editors of the *Journal of Credit Risk*, and two anonymous referees of the journal. We also benefited from insightful discussions with Rocky Ieraci and Jong Park of Standard & Poor's Risk Solutions. We are particularly grateful to Peter F. J. Heffernan, Annie Hung, and their team in Scotiabank for many valuable discussions. Finally, we thank McGraw-Hill for its professional contributions, including Jeanne Glasser, our editor, Herb Schaffner, the publisher, and especially Morgan Ertel of McGraw-Hill's business book division.

# INTRODUCTION

Implementation of the Basel II Accord has been one of the major risk management initiatives during the past few years for many financial institutions globally. Although the purpose of implementing internal risk rating systems (IRRS) for many banks is Basel II compliance, it also serves to enhance risk management practices and competitiveness.

We have been actively involved in the implementation of IRRS on many fronts. On the theoretical front, we have conducted research and written a number of research papers; on the practical front, we have globally helped many financial institutions implement and validate their IRRS. We would like to share our experiences with risk management practitioners.

This IRRS implementation handbook incorporates our published research papers, supplemented with practical *case examples* based on our hands-on experience.

## BACKGROUND

Basel II is a regulatory requirement for risk quantification for capital allocation purposes. It is the second of the Basel Accords, which are recommendations on banking laws and regulations issued by the Basel Committee on Banking Supervision (BCBS). It aims at:

1. Ensuring that capital allocation is more risk sensitive;
2. Separating operational risk from credit risk, and quantifying both;
3. Attempting to align economic and regulatory capital more closely to reduce the scope for regulatory arbitrage.

Basel II has profound implications for the financial industry as a whole, as well as for rating agencies and regulators. Basel II is implemented along its three pillars. Under Pillar I, banks are required to satisfy the minimum capital requirement, which determines the ratio of capital (Tier 1 or total) to risk-weighted assets. Pillar I describes the different approaches that may be taken to calculate the risk-weighted assets, namely the standardized approach and the foundation and advanced internal rating based (IRB) approaches. In the standardized approach, risk weights are assigned using rule-based methods supported by external rating assessments (e.g., those of Standard & Poor's, Moody's, and Fitch). In the IRB approach, using IRRS approved by national regulators, banks produce their own estimates of risk components [e.g., probability of default (PD), loss given default (LGD), and exposure at default (EAD)], which serve as inputs in the calculation of risk weights. Under the supervisory review process of Pillar II, national regulators ensure banks are in compliance with the minimum standards in fulfilling Pillar I. It can be achieved through examinations of the IRRS, methodology, risk oversight, internal control, monitoring, and reporting adopted by the banks in fulfilling the Basel II requirements. Finally, disclosures of the risk management process under Pillar III allow market participants (e.g., creditors, shareholders) to decide for themselves whether risks have been appropriately measured and managed by the banks.

Under the IRB approach, banks are allowed to develop, validate, and use their IRRS for the computations of minimum capital requirements and capital allocation purposes, subject to regulatory approval. Banks will have to demonstrate the soundness of their risk rating system to the regulators. It is a global initiative, and currently many banks and other financial intuitions have been very busy implementing Pillars I and II. Their motivation is threefold:

1. It is a regulatory requirement;
2. It could lead to a reduction in required capital, thus lowering the cost of capital;
3. It is perceived as a competitive advantage (banks believe that they cannot afford not to be Basel II compliant when the competitors are).

## THE CONTENT, THE INTENDED AUDIENCE OF THE BOOK, AND OUR VALUE PROPOSITION

The intended audience of the book is risk management professionals, particularly those involved in Basel and the IRRS implementations. These people are the practitioners working for the financial institutions and the regulators and academicians, as all three groups are actively involved in Basel implementation. The audience is seeking practical and implementable solutions that are

1. Academically credible, and thus defendable to their regulators;
2. Practical and that can be implemented within data, resource, and time constraints.

Our purpose for this Basel implementation handbook is to cover all aspects of IRRS implementation especially with respect to Basel II, which meets both requirements above. Our papers provide the theoretical foundation, and we have incorporated our hands-on practical experience with *case studies*.

The following papers are incorporated into the book:

- "Practical and Theoretical Challenges in Validating Basel Parameters: Key Learnings from the Experience of a Canadian Bank," Peter Miu and Bogie Ozdemir, *The Journal of Credit Risk*, 2005.
- "Basel Requirement of Downturn LGD: Modeling and Estimating PD & LGD Correlations," Peter Miu and Bogie Ozdemir, *The Journal of Credit Risk*, 2006.
- "Discount Rate for Workout Recoveries: An Empirical Study," Brooks Brady, Peter Chang (S&P employee), Peter Miu, Bogie Ozdemir, and David Schwartz, working paper, 2007.
- "Estimating Long-run PDs with Respect to Basel II Requirements," Peter Miu and Bogie Ozdemir, *Journal of Risk Model Validation*, Volume 2/Number 2, Summer 2008, Page 1–39.
- "Conditional PDs and LGDs: Stress Testing with Macro Variables," Peter Miu and Bogie Ozdemir, working paper, 2008.

## STRUCTURE OF THE BOOK

The book is structured parallel to the IRRS development under Basel II. In Chapter 1, we cover IRRS design, where designing of PD, LGD, and EAD risk rating systems is discussed. We continue in Chapter 2 with IRRS quantification, where PDs, LGDs, and EADs are assigned to the risk ratings. In Chapter 3, we discuss validation in detail. Lastly, in Chapter 4 we discuss some of the Pillar II issues. A number of Excel Spreadsheet applications of the methodologies considered throughout the book are provided in the CD which comes with the book.

# BASEL II
# IMPLEMENTATION

## CHAPTER 1

# Risk Ratings System Design

## OVERVIEW

Pillar I of the Basel II Accord requires the development of internal risk rating systems (IRRS). The purpose of IRRS is the estimation of probability of default (PD) under foundation internal rating-based approach (F-IRB) and also loss given default (LGD) and exposure at default (EAD) under advanced internal rating-based approach (A-IRB). Pillar II requires the demonstration of capital adequacy (using IRB parameters). The very first step of implementing Basel II under the IRB approach is therefore the design of IRRS. The objective is to categorize the obligors into homogeneous risk groups to establish *risk ratings* so that they rank order correctly in terms of their credit risks. For example, all obligors in the first pool (i.e., risk rating 1) have the same (default, LGD, or EAD) risk. Similarly, all obligors in the second pool (i.e., risk rating 2) have the same (default, LGD, or EAD) risk among themselves, and the obligors in risk rating 2 are riskier than those in risk rating 1. As illustrated in Figure 1.1, the first step is to establish a discretized categorization (or risk ranking/scoring) of the obligors.

 If we were to use a PD model, for instance, obligors would first be assigned to a *continuous* value of PD. This process involves both risk ranking (an obligor with a higher PD is riskier than the one with a lower PD) and risk quantification (the absolute level of PD assigned to each obligor). In a typical Basel II IRRS, risk ranking and risk quantification processes are likely to be separated. In other words, we first pool risk-homogeneous obligors into risk ratings so that they rank order, and then we assign risk measures (PDs, LGDs, EADs) to these risk ratings. As will be discussed in

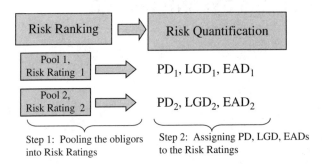

**Figure 1.1** Risk ranking/scoring of the obligors.

Chapter 3, the following three components of the overall design need to be validated:

1.  Are the obligors assigned to each risk rating in fact risk-homogeneous?
2.  Are the risk ratings rank-order?
3.  Are the levels of risk measures (PDs, LGDs, EADs) assigned to the risk ratings accurate?

## THE USE OF CREDIT RISK ASSESSMENT TEMPLATES IN IRRS

For low default portfolios (LDPs), it is usually impossible to build quantitative models based on (the inexistence of) historical default rate data. Many financial institutions (FIs) use expert judgment systems called credit risk assessment templates (or risk rating templates or matrices or score cards) for risk rating/scoring the obligors in LDPs. These templates score (i.e., rank order) the obligors based on fundamental credit risk factors/drivers. Figure 1.2 depicts the risk factors considered in a sample template

| Qualitative Inputs | Quantitative Inputs |
| --- | --- |
| - Resilience of Premium Volumes<br>- Stability and Quality Performance<br>- Asset Profile<br>- Competitive Strengths and Weaknesses<br>- Quality of disclosure | - Liabilities / Adjusted Liquid Assets<br>- Invested Assets – (Bonds + Cash) / Total Adjusted Capital<br>- Net Premiums Written / Adjusted Shareholders Funds<br>- Net Premiums Written / Gross Premium Written<br>- Combined Ratio |

**Figure 1.2** Examples of qualitative and quantitative risk factors used in a Credit Risk Assessment Template for insurance companies.

| Business Risk | Score | | Financial Risk | Score |
|---|---|---|---|---|
| **Industry Risk** | | | Operating Income to Sales | 8.5 |
| Industry Position | 6 | | FFO to Total Debt (%) | 4.5 |
| **Competitiveness** | | | EBITDA Interest Coverage (x) | 3.5 |
| Market Share Trends and Prospects | 2 | | Total Debt to Capital | 8.0 |
| Geographical Diversity of Operations | 2 | | Sales Turnover | 2.5 |
| Diversity Products & Services | 6 | | Financial Flexibility | 1.0 |
| Customer Mix | 1 | | | |
| Aftermarket Presence | 1 | | | |
| Cost Position and Flexibility | 2 | | | |
| Distribution System | 1 | | | |

|  | | Internal Rating | S&P Equivalent |
|---|---|---|---|
| Business Risk Score | 3.60 | a | A |
| Financial Risk Score | 4.31 | a- | A- |
| Standalone Rating | 3.99 | a | A |
| Final Rating | 3.99 | a | A |

| Business Risk (cont.) | Score |
|---|---|
| **Management** | |
| Quality and Depth | 4 |
| Continuity8 | |
| Style and Tolerance for Risk | 4 |
| Existence/Clarity/Focus/Track Record | 5 |
| Success/Viability/Feasibility | 4 |
| Counterparty Credit Risk | 8 |
| Market Risk | 6 |
| Off-balance Sheet Risk | 7 |
| Operational Controls | 2 |
| Executive Board Oversight | 2 |

* For Illustrative Purposes Only

**Figure 1.3**  An example of scoring of a company.

for insurance companies. Typically, both quantitative and qualitative risk drivers are captured, and each risk driver has a preassigned weight. We score an obligor based on each of the risk drivers and then use the weights assigned to the risk factors to arrive at an overall score for the obligor. Figure 1.3 outlines an example of scoring a company.

Templates are designed differently for different industries, and the ensuing scores are mapped to internal and (typically) external risk ratings, each of which is assigned a distinct value of PD (as will be discussed in Chapter 2).

Essentially, these expert judgment methodologies have been used by external rating agencies for many years. Not surprisingly, the risk advisory arms of these agencies have been among the major providers of these templates leveraging their expertise and experience as well as historical default data and statistics. Availability of the historical default data is particularly important. At the final step, we need to assign PDs to the risk ratings. Using rating agencies' rating methodologies directly has the important advantage that the rating agencies' historical default rate data can be used in assigning PDs to the internal risk ratings, given that these are default rates of the obligors that were rated by consistent methodologies. In Figure 1.4, suppose the Standard & Poor's BBB rating corresponds with internal risk rating 4. We also know the historical default rate for the Standard & Poor's

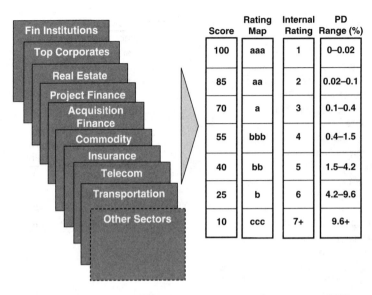

**Figure 1.4** Mapping of score to internal rating, external rating, and PD range.

BBB-rated companies. If our internal rating methodology is consistent with the Standard & Poor's rating methodology, we can use Standard & Poor's default history for BBB-rated companies when we assign a PD to our internal risk rating 4 (naturally, the same principal applies to all other ratings). In other words, internal and external ratings are mapped methodologically, and thus external default rates can be used robustly in assigning PDs to the internal ratings. If the internal and external methodologies are inconsistent, the use of the external default rates for internal ratings would not be robust, at least it would not have been proved historically. With the use of the external rating methodologies, internal ratings would have been effectively calibrated to external default rates. In the absence of internal default rates, especially for LDPs, use of methodologies of the rating agencies and thus the corresponding default rate time series has clear benefits over use of alternative methodologies. This is because these alternative risk rating methodologies have not been around long enough to produce sufficiently long default rate time series to allow for robust PD-risk rating mapping.

When a FI first adopts an external rating agency's templates in developing its IRRS for Basel II implementation, its internal ratings are effectively calibrated to external default rates. The change of the rating methodology from the old one (typically not appropriate for Basel II as it is not transparent, replicable, and auditable) to the new one (used by the external rating agency) may result in a sudden shift in the internal ratings.

For some FIs, this shift in risk ratings is not desirable considering the organizational change (cost). One way to resolve this concern is to calibrate the external rating agency's templates directly to the existing internal ratings (rather than to the external default rates). In this approach, whereas external rating agency's risk factors are still used, their weights are modified so that the new ratings under the new methodology would be as close as the ratings assigned under the existing methodology.[1] A level of consistency of as high as 95% can usually be achieved within plus and minus of two notches. This allows for the minimization of shifts in ratings despite the use of the new methodology while still making the new IRRS transparent and replicable as required by Basel II. The drawback, however, is the loss of the strong link between the resultant internal ratings and the external default rates, as the new rating methodology and the external rating agency's rating methodology is now less consistent because of the change in the weights on the risk factors. A typical development and calibration process is illustrated in Figure 1.5.

The templates typically allow for overrides and exceptions that are (when the templates are hosted in appropriate IT platforms) electronically captured and analyzed periodically (see Chapter 3).

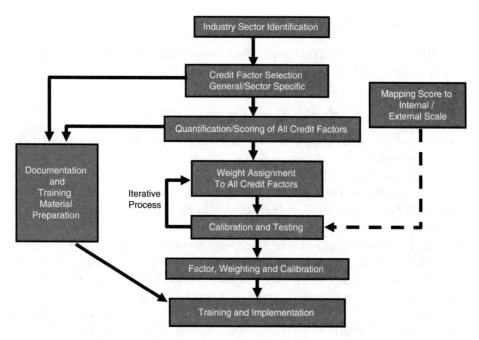

**Figure 1.5** Typical development and calibration process.

Although these templates provide an efficient, transparent, and replicable framework for capturing quantitative and qualitative credit risk factors, it is after all a credit scoring methodology driven by expert judgment. They therefore do not replace credit analysts' expert judgment but instead provide a transparent and replicable framework for it. The use of the templates consistently over time and among different credit analysts is essential in achieving consistent scores. The implementation of the templates must therefore include objective scoring guidelines for each material credit factor together with comprehensive training.

We have observed at times that some FIs try to reverse-engineer rating agencies' methodologies by conducting regression analysis on the external agencies' ratings and the financial ratios. This approach has the shortcoming that the qualitative factors and confidential information used in the external rating process, which play an important role, cannot be captured in the empirical analysis. Moreover, it is difficult to cater for the differences in the rating methodologies between the rated universe, which is typically made up of large corporate entities, and the nonrated universe of smaller companies. Even if we could reverse-engineer the methodologies for the rated universe, these methodologies would not necessarily be appropriate for the smaller companies.

## THE USE OF QUANTITATIVE MODELS IN IRRS

When there are sufficient historical data, quantitative models can be developed and used in IRRS. There are a number of alternatives.

### Models for Large Corporate Entities

Commercially available, off-the-shelf models can be used for publicly traded companies. The Moody's KMV Credit Monitor generates expected default frequencies (EDFs) based on a modified Merton model where distance-to-default (DD) is mapped to historical default rates. Similarly, the Standard & Poor's Credit Risk Tracker (CRT) Public Firm Model, originally designed to be used as a surveillance tool by its rating group but recently being made commercially available, generates one-year point-in-time (PIT) real-life PDs based on stock market information (e.g., DD) combined with macroeconomic factors as leading indicators and obligors' financial ratios. Whereas these two represent structural models, there are also reduced-form models (e.g., Kamakura Public Firm Model) in which credit spread that contains information on risk-neutral expected loss is used to infer PDs. From our experience, the quantitative models used for large corporate portfolios within IRRS are largely limited to commercially available off-the-shelf models, due to data limitations in building quantitative models internally by the FIs. We have seen some models (typically built by consultants in a one-off basis and not otherwise commercially available) where risk-neutral PDs are inferred from credit default option (CDO) or credit default swap (CDS) spreads under some assumptions and are then converted into real-life PDs and in turn explained by financial ratios via regression analysis. If we assume the relationship between the spread-implied PDs and the financial ratios established within the calibrated sample (i.e., obligors with traded CDO/CDS) also holds for the rest of the universe (i.e., obligors without traded CDO/CDS), we can generate PDs by simply entering the financial ratios into the calibrated model. This approach has the obvious advantage that the lack of default rate history is substituted by market-implied PDs. However, in our experience, one needs to be cautious with the robustness of these models due to the large number of assumptions that would have to be made and especially the limited sample data set of the relevant traded instruments.

The commercially available models mentioned in the prior paragraph produce a continuous value of PD—in theory every obligor can have a different PD—however, the assigned PDs under IRRS are discrete. That is, every obligor in a certain risk rating has the same unique PD as per the master scale. A mapping system therefore needs to be designed where the continuous PDs obtained from the model are mapped to the internal ratings based on a prespecified PD range assigned to each risk rating (Figure 1.6). For example, any obligor whose continuous PD from the quantitative model falls into the range provided for risk rating 1 (RR1) would have the same assigned PD (i.e., PD 1), corresponding to RR1. Effectively, in this process, we convert the continuous PD output from the quantitative model to a score (or internal rating) and then back to a discrete PD value assigned to the risk rating. In our experience, if a FI chooses to use a commercially available PD model in its IRRS, typically it is within a hybrid framework where continuous PD output is blended with other risk factors, as discussed later in this chapter in the section "The Use of Hybrid Models in IRRS."

Standard & Poor's also has a credit rating estimation model called CreditModel, which generates Standard & Poor's letter-grade rating symbology denoted in lowercase, indicating quantitatively derived estimates of Standard & Poor's credit ratings. The model is tailored to specific industries and regions and is applicable to publicly traded and privately owned medium and large corporations in North America, Europe, and Japan.[2] The fact that this model's output is a rating as opposed to PD can actually be

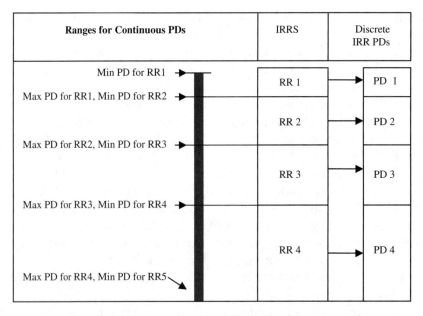

**Figure 1.6** Mapping of continuous model-implied PD to discrete PD value.

quite useful. Many FIs use available rating agency ratings in risk rating assessment. CreditModel allows FIs to obtain comparable ratings for the unrated obligors. The model is also very useful in the validation of the mapping between external and internal ratings (i.e., we can compare the internal ratings and CreditModel ratings to examine the performance of the mapping between internal and external ratings).

### Models for Small and Medium Enterprises (SME)

FIs have more choices available to them for middle-market (SME) portfolios where historical default data are much more readily available. FIs can use one of the commercially available models or they can build their own quantitative models should they have sufficient data. Sometime, they can even build a quantitative model based on a consortium of data among a group of FIs with similar SME portfolios.

Commercially available models include, for example, the Moody's KMV RiskCalc, where financial ratios and equity market–based information (average distant to default of public firms) are used to explain PDs of private firms. The Standard & Poor's Credit Risk Tracker (CRT) North America Private Firm Model generates forward-looking one-year PD estimates based on time series of relevant macroeconomic, financial, and industry-specific variables for middle-market (SME) firms (>$100,000 in assets). The model incorporates equity price information at the industry sector level.

An FI that wishes to use a commercially available model within its IRRS needs to be comfortable with the following factors:

- Performance of the model: Performance comparison studies have been conducted on the commercially available models.[3]
- Representativeness of the training data set: The training data set should be representative of the internal portfolio, in terms of the characteristics of the obligors and the average default rates.
- Definition of default used for the training data set should be reasonably consistent with that of Basel II.
- Models should be accompanied by sufficient methodology documentation and developmental evidence: This can be difficult because, most of the time, at least parts of the model methodologies and the training data are considered to be proprietary by the model vendor.

If an FI builds a quantitative model (or has it built) based on its own data or a consortium of data among a group of FIs with similar SME portfolios, all of the above factors are still relevant. The most critical issue is to ensure there is sufficient model documentation and developmental evidence. If they engage a subcontractor to build the models, they need to make sure model methodology and all developmental evidence are fully disclosed and documented.

If an internal model is built, the model output can be a continuous value of PD (like the commercially available models) or a score (i.e., discrete risk rate). If the output is continuous, this would need to be converted to risk ratings to which discrete values of PDs are assigned. The advantage of having a model in which the output is in the form of a continuous value of PD is that the continuous PDs may be used in other applications, for example in pricing, in which the ability to pinpoint the exact PD level of an obligor is important; a continuous spectrum of PD values is particularly essential for pricing deals of obligors with relatively high PD.

As there will be a calibration process among continuous PDs, risk ratings, and discrete value of PD assigned to each risk rate, we can make adjustments dynamically without recalibrating the continuous PD model.

The advantage of having discrete risk ratings as the output of the quantitative model is that no conversion of the continuous PDs to risk ratings is required. We, however, cannot obtain continuous value of PD; for example, all obligors in a certain risk rate are assigned a PD of 25%, even though individual PDs may vary considerably within the risk rate.

## THE USE OF HYBRID MODELS IN IRRS

Hybrid solutions incorporating a core quantitative model together with a qualitative overlay are frequently used by FIs. *Qualitative overlay* considers the expert judgment–based qualitative factors (such as industry risk, competitiveness, and management quality) that are not captured by a quantitative model. To ensure the industry-specific characteristics can be captured, FIs usually use different overlays for different sectors (e.g., real estate, services, retail, manufacturing, trading). Incorporating the qualitative factors enables a more complete risk assessment in the view of many FIs. The hybrid framework also allows FIs to have some control over the risk assessment despite the use of a quantitative model. It should also enhance the accuracy and forward-looking-ness of the model. Many FIs consider the qualitative factors are forward-looking, which therefore should make the overall risk assessment more PIT, especially for SME portfolios where quantitative forward-looking factors are limited.

   If the core quantitative model is a PD model, the continuous values of PDs generated by the model are converted into a discrete quantitative score, for example by means of the process described later in this chapter in the use of the quantitative models in IRRS. This score is then blended with the scores arrived at from the evaluation of the qualitative factors to come up with an overall risk rating as depicted in Figure 1.7. This approach has

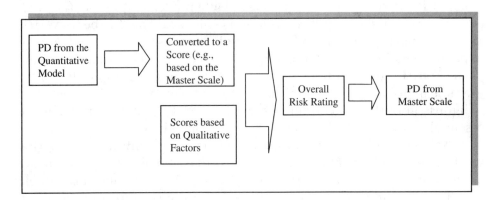

**Figure 1.7** Quantitative model together with qualitative overlay.

the benefit that we can separately backtest the PDs generated by the quantitative model and the PD generated by the whole hybrid model to assess the value-added of the qualitative overlay. We expect the addition of the qualitative overlay should increase the overall model performance.

The hybrid model illustrated in Figure 1.7 is quite typical where we use a commercially available PD model as the core quantitative model. When we determine the weights for the quantitative score (converted from the continuous PD generated from the PD model) and the qualitative scores (generated by assessing the qualitative risk factors), we can set our calibration objective to explain either the historical default rates or the current risk ratings. The former is analytically preferred, but it may result in significant shifts in the assigned risk rates when a new hybrid model is used. The latter avoids shifts in the assigned risk rates but makes the assumption that the current risk rates prior to the use of the new hybrid model are correct. If there are no historical data available for the calibration of the weights of the quantitative and qualitative scores, the weights are determined based on expert judgment.

In Figure 1.7, the quantitative PD model is first developed and then the qualitative overlay serves as an add-on module. If the FI has sufficient internal time series data including both quantitative and qualitative factors for both defaulted and survived obligors, an overall model can be developed in a single step by using, for example, logistic regressions incorporating both quantitative and qualitative explanatory variables. This integrated model development process is, however, not always preferred considering the subjectivity of the historical qualitative scores used in the regression analysis.

We have observed in some FIs that a continuous PD output from a core quantitative PD model is blended with not only qualitative factors but also some financial ratios. One needs to be careful with the potential of putting too much weight on the financial ratios in this approach, especially when the core quantitative PD model also directly uses financial ratios as inputs. The other overlap and thus potential double counting is in the quantitative factors, which are used as a direct input as well as implicitly within the agency ratings.[4] Another drawback of this approach is that direct calibration of the assigned risk rates (and thus the assigned PDs) to the historical default rates is usually unavailable. In this approach, usually only the core quantitative PD model is calibrated but not the overall model. The relative weights assigned to the continuous PDs, financial ratios, and other inputs used in determination of the overall risk rates are therefore not established based on actual default experience. An example of this approach is depicted in Figure 1.8.

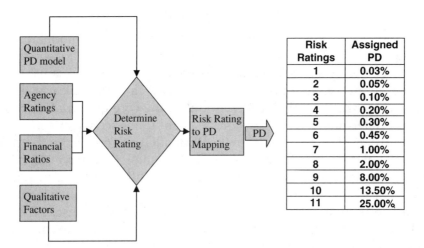

| Risk<br>Ratings | Assigned<br>PD |
|:---:|:---:|
| 1 | 0.03% |
| 2 | 0.05% |
| 3 | 0.10% |
| 4 | 0.20% |
| 5 | 0.30% |
| 6 | 0.45% |
| 7 | 1.00% |
| 8 | 2.00% |
| 9 | 8.00% |
| 10 | 13.50% |
| 11 | 25.00% |

**Figure 1.8** An example of a hybrid model.

The main advantage of adopting a framework likes the one presented in Figure 1.8 is the use of the alternative information available. However, our experience shows that this design is prone to consistency and stability issues as discussed below. The first issue is how to deal with the unavailability of some information for some of the borrowers, most notably PDs (or expected default frequencies (EDFs)) from quantitative models and/or agency ratings. The weights of the individual factors (PDs, financial ratios, agency ratings, and qualitative factors) are assigned under the assumption that all of these factors are available. If one (or more) of these factors is unavailable, then the weights of the remaining factors need to be increased accordingly. This means we are, in fact, talking about alternative models under the above design (one being if all risk factors are available, the other one being if PDs/EDFs are unavailable, another one being if agency ratings are unavailable, etc.). It is difficult to ensure these different models are consistent with each other. Some FIs using the above design have believed that the risk ratings produced under different scenarios (PDs [EDFs]/agency ratings are available or not) are not necessarily consistent, which indicates that the alternative models discussed above are not consistent with each other. In practical terms, we are in effect using two different risk rating philosophies under the same design thus the same risk rating system. For example, internal ratings assigned to the obligors will be more PIT when PIT PDs/EDFs are used than when they are not available.

One way to examine the consistency of the alternative models is the following. We examine the internal rating of a well-known borrower with both PD/EDF and agency rating available. It is desired that when we re-rate this company by ignoring the PD/EDF and agency rating, one at a time, the resultant internal rating would still be consistent with the original rating. This is a cross-calibration exercise among the alternative models where all factors are available or when one or some of them are missing. However, as discussed below, this cross-calibration is not a static one but a dynamic one as it changes over the course of the credit cycle.

The other issue is the stability of the ratings under this design over time. PDs (or EDFs) (e.g., produced from commercially available models) are more PIT than the agency ratings that are close to through-the-cycle (TTC). This creates a mismatch among the different risk factors, which can compromise the stability of the internal ratings over the course of the credit cycle (refer to Chapter 2 for a full discussion on risk rating philosophies). PIT PD/EDF is in effect *conditional PD* on current information.[5] The overall PD assigned to the internal risk rating (based on the master scale), on the other hand, is intended to be an unconditional PD (see the section "Long-run PDs" in Chapter 2). We need to distinguish PD assigned to the risk rating from PDs assigned to the obligors. Note that although PDs assigned to the risk ratings are unconditional, FI can still adopt a more PIT risk rating philosophy for the PDs assigned to the obligors via continuous re-rating of the obligors (or remapping between internal ratings and PDs or a combination of the two).

So in Figure 1.9, we use conditional (PIT) PD/EDFs and mix them up with more TTC agency ratings to arrive at a risk rating that is mapped to an unconditional (long-run) PD assigned to the risk rating. This process is

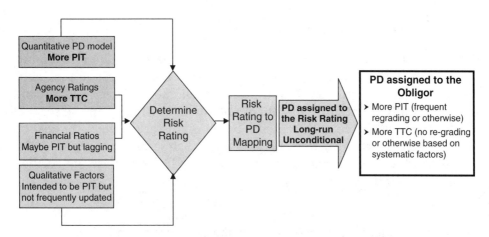

**Figure 1.9** A hybrid model using both PIT PD/EDFs and TTC agency ratings.

convoluted and prone to producing unstable results over the course of the credit cycle. Consider the following example: assume we are at a good part of the credit cycle and the PDs/EDFs are low (as they are more PIT than are agency ratings), but agency ratings, due to their more TTC nature, are presenting a more conservative picture. First of all, due to the conflicting information, it is difficult to arrive at an accurate internal risk rating mapped to an unconditional (long-run) PD. To further complicate the matter, suppose there are two otherwise identical borrowers where we have the PD/EDF for one but not for the other. For the one we have the PD/EDF; we will most likely arrive at a more favorable risk rating during a credit upturn.

We may try to correct this bias by correcting the PIT-ness of PD/EDF used as a factor (i.e., the first box on the left in Figure 1.9). To ensure stability, some FIs dynamically adjust the PD/EDF bands of their risk ratings based on the current state of the credit cycle. During a credit upturn (downturn), the values of the bands (i.e., maximum, mid-point and minimum) will be downwardly (upwardly) adjusted so as to match the decreasing (increasing) PIT PD/EDF. As an alternative, we can more formally estimate and use the unconditional PD/EDF implied from the PIT PD/EDFs. Lastly, in order to eliminate the inconsistency, we can replace the obligor-specific PD/EDF estimates with the sector (i.e., industry, size, etc.) average PD/EDF estimate.

In summary, despite the appealing benefits of using all available information, producing consistent and stable internal rating from the above rating framework is difficult. It requires a complicated design to adjust for the differences among the different rating philosophies of the inputs used. Moreover, this adjustment most likely needs to be a dynamic one over the course of the credit cycles.

## THE USE OF RETAIL MODELS IN IRRS

Retail models are usually built based on internal data that are much more readily available. More often, FIs use a two-step process. In the first step, they determine the statistically significant explanatory variables and identify statistically different segments of obligors accordingly. In the second step, they assign PD to each segment based on historical default rates for each segment. By construction, all obligors in each segment are assumed to be homogeneous and thus assigned the same PD. The following further elaborates on this two-step process:

### Step 1

- Select a list of variables (e.g., variables assessing individual net wealth, financial leverage and stability, also credit bureau scores when available, etc.) via cohort/tree building/cluster analysis based on defaulted and survived obligors (default = 1, nondefault = 0); both dummy variables (i.e., variables with yes/no outcomes) and continuous quantitative variables may be used.

- Determine the statistically significant ranges for the variables selected, when applicable. For example, assuming loan to value (LTV) is recognized as an important factor in step 1. Now we need to determine what ranges of LTV help to differentiate the different levels of risk.
- Conduct logit/probit modeling to determine the weights for the variables selected.

**Step 2**

- Score each obligor using the model developed in step 1.
- Identify statistically significant ranges of scores (scores assigned to individual obligors might not be statistically different from each other) and assign PD to each significant range identified based on historical default rates.
- Or, as the number of statistically significant ranges of scores are typically less than what is required by Basel, we may want to have the same granularity as that of the master scale. Moreover, we want to determine our segments so that the historical default rate of each segment will match the master scale PD. That is, suppose we initially come up with three statistically different segments. We however need more granularity to match our master scale better. We therefore increase our granularity by creating subsegments.

An interesting issue is the risk rating philosophy for the retail models. Many FIs do not have a separate rating philosophy for retail models even though it could be quite different from that used for the wholesale portfolio. There are a few factors worth considering in determination of the appropriate risk rating philosophy.

- It is quite common that those variables (e.g., macroeconomic leading indicators) that are sensitive to the changes in credit cycle are missing in retail models; this deficiency hinders their ability to produce PIT PD measures.
- On the other hand, one-month (or two-month) delinquency rate is usually used as one of the explanatory variables in these retail models.[6] It improves the ability of the model in becoming more

sensitive to changes in credit cycle as delinquency rate increases during downturns. Delinquency rates are closely monitored and updated, and thus the changes in these rates are reflected in the PD output almost instantaneously via rating migration. The use of the delinquency rate as explanatory variable coupled with close monitoring of its changes over the cycle enhance the PIT-ness of the retail models. However, in these PD models, we do not capture how the obligors become delinquent in the first place; instead, they capture the increase in PD subsequent to more obligors becoming delinquent. If we were to model the probability of becoming delinquent, we would have used other independent explanatory variables. In practice, these independent explanatory variables are either ignored in the PD model or the weights assigned to them are insignificant given the overwhelming explanatory power of delinquency rates in explaining default over the subsequent period. In sum, these PD models will only react to a downturn after some accounts become delinquent, therefore PDs will not be truly PIT.

- An obligor's characteristics used as explanatory variables (e.g., annual income, address, marital status, etc.) do not necessarily change with credit cycles making the model nonreactive to changes in credit condition.

- When we assign historical PDs for each significant range identified, we use default rates time series. Therefore, PDs assigned most likely represent a longer risk horizon.

Considering all of the above, it is not obvious what the risk rating philosophy would be for the retail PD model described above. We can possibly say that the PDs become more PIT when we start observing an increase in delinquency rates, but not at any other times. As an alternative approach, we can directly use regression techniques similar to that used in building PD models for SME portfolios, so that each obligor would have its own unique (continuous) value of PD.

## THE USE OF LGD MODELS IN IRRS

The discussion above about the use of the PD models in IRRS also applies to LGD models, as expert judgment–based LGD models, quantitative LGD models, and hybrid LGD models can be used as the fundamental building blocks of IRRS. Expert judgment–based LGD templates are typically used for low-default portfolios, where LGD data are scarce. These templates, though calibrated to empirical results at a high level, use expert judgment to a large extent for more specific cases of LGD estimations. In other words, whereas high-level average LGDs are empirically estimated, the LGDs at the segment level are more or less judgment-based given that there is not enough empirical data. For example, Standard & Poor's Risk Solutions has commercially available LGD templates adopting the following high-level principles. The obligor's asset (enterprise) value is assumed to follow a normal distribution. The obligor is assumed to be in default when the enterprise value falls below a certain default point. The asset value distribution beyond the default point (i.e., the tail) is used in LGD estimation. Based on the priority structure of facilities (i.e., the amount of debts superior/inferior to each facility), the relevant area of the tail is integrated and averaged for specific mean LGD estimation. Expert judgment, along with available empirical data, is used to determine the appropriate asset value volatility and the types of the collaterals used. A list of potential inputs of the LGD template can be found in Figure 1.10.

For those sectors where LGD data are more readily available, quantitative models are commercially available. For example, the Moody's KMV LossCalc model is calibrated to historical market prices of defaulted instruments. Moody's KMV LossCalc calculates LGD for loans, bonds, and preferred stock based on the five major quantifiable drivers of LGD:

- Collateral
- Debt type and seniority class
- Borrower-specific information
- Industry-specific information
- Country and regional macroeconomic information

> - Economic Value of Collateral
> - Standard Deviation of Economic Value of Collateral
> - Haircut for Liquidation Value
> - Recovery Policy (Economic Value, Liquidity Value)
> - PD Rating of a Borrower
> - Total Debt
> - Facility Debt
> - Debt Cushion (%)
> - Debt Priority (%)
> - Recovery Costs (%)
> - Insolvency Regime
> - Recovery Enhancement

**Figure 1.10** Inputs to the LGD template.

The Standard & Poor's LGD model, LossStats Model, forecasts recovery either as the ultimate workout recovery value or the 30-day postdefault trading price.[7] LossStats Model is based on the maximum expected utility (MEU) approach. Rather than assuming a beta distribution of LGD, LossStats Model's calibration of the historical recovery and trading price data can be interpreted as applying the maximum likelihood estimation method over an exponential family of distributions.[8] The model forecasts the entire distribution of LGD values rather than a single point estimate. The model's advanced mathematical framework can capture any humps in the middle of the U-shaped distributions that might be observed in the historical data (Figure 1.11). It therefore outperforms simple and generalized beta distribution models, which cannot capture these humps (see the "Downturn LGD" section in Chapter 2 to read more about downturn LGD method 2).

Input variables to the LossStats Model include debt type, collateral type, and regional and industry default rates. The inclusion of regional and industry default rates is essential as it allows the model not only to effectively capture PD and LGD correlation but also to generate stressed LGD. We can enter stressed regional and industry default rates to generate stressed LGD. This feature of the model allows us to use it in downturn LGD estimation as well as in computing stressed LGD.

Hybrid LGD models, similar to hybrid PD models, consist of a core quantitative model together with a qualitative overlay. This type of model can be particularly attractive to those FIs that would like to use a quantitative model but at the same time also like to incorporate their internal experience and expert judgment. These FIs do not feel comfortable enough to

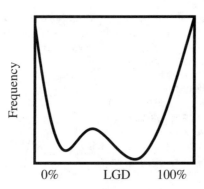

**Figure 1.11** A hump within the U-shape distribution of LGD.

rely solely on a quantitative model given the model's training data set may not be sufficiently representative of the FI's portfolios. The lack of representation leads to the validity of the absolute values of the LGD produced by the model becoming somewhat debatable. Nevertheless, the relative accuracy (i.e., the rank-ordering capability) of these models is much more comfortably accepted. In a hybrid framework, the quantitatively driven LGD outcome of the model is first converted into an LGD score that is, in turn, blended with qualitatively driven LGD scores to arrive at an overall LGD score and thus the corresponding LGD value. We therefore effectively preserve the rank ordering of the quantitative LGD model while allowing for the absolute level of LGD to be more closely calibrated to the FI's internal experience.

In general, as we move to mid-market/SME portfolios, where more internal data are available, it is more common to rely more on quantitative and automated LGD scoring models. It is however the opposite case when we are dealing with large corporate and/or specialized transactions (i.e., project finance).

When an FI chooses a quantitative LGD model to be used in its IRRS, it needs to make sure the training data set of the model, namely ultimate workout recoveries or market prices of defaulted instruments, are relevant to the FI's own collection practice. For example, the former training data set will be more relevant to those FIs for which the primary practice is to collect workout recoveries while only occasionally selling off their defaulted instruments.

## THE CHOICE OF LGD DISCOUNT RATE

When LGDs are estimated from historical data, the workout recoveries minus the direct and indirect expenses need to be discounted at the appropriate discount rate. Theoretically, the discount rate used in the estimation of LGD should reflect the (opportunity) costs of holding the defaulted asset over the workout period, including an appropriate risk premium required by the asset holders. This is also the typical interpretation adopted by the practitioners and Basel. The Basel document states that "when recovery streams are uncertain and involve risks that cannot be diversified away, net present value calculations must reflect the time value of money and a risk premium appropriate to the undiversifiable risk."[9]

The appropriate discount rate to be used to estimate the economic value of LGD at the time of default has been heavily debated in the industry. The higher the discount rate, the higher the LGD, and the higher the capital estimated. FIs, already concerned about the excessive conservatism perceived to be imposed by Basel II requirements (e.g., downturn LGD requirements), are sensitive to the topic of appropriate discount rates.

In practice, we observe a wide range of applications. Some FIs use default contractual rate as the discount rate (an argument that is theoretically difficult to justify as the pre-default, contractual rate has little, if anything, to do with explaining the postdefault LGD uncertainty that is commensurate with the LGD discount rate). Other FIs seem to use a discount rate within the range of 10% to 15% based on some educated guesses at best and peer comparisons. Other examples include the funding rate, the distress loan rate, the current comparable market rate, the opportunity cost of funds, the cost of capital, the accounting convention of discount rate, and the current risk-free rate. Maclachlan (2004) provides a survey of these different approaches.[10]

The issue had also been debated theoretically. When a firm defaults, creditors receive direct ownership in the firm's assets (or the collateral if the instruments are secured) and expect to generate a return on these assets. In the capital asset pricing model (CAPM) framework, adopted by Maclachlan (2004), the inherent risk premium $\delta_i$ (i.e., excess expected return over the risk-free rate) of a defaulted instrument $i$ is the product of the assets' beta $\beta_{i,m}$ and the market risk premium (MRP). Beta itself is a function of the correlation $\rho_{i,m}$ of the assets and a systematic market factor, the standard deviation $\sigma_m$ of the market factor, and the standard deviation $\sigma_i$ of the underlying assets. That is,

$$\delta_i = \beta_{i,m} \times \mathrm{MRP} = \frac{\sigma_i \times \rho_{i,m}}{\sigma_m} \times \mathrm{MRP}. \qquad \text{(Equation 1.1)}$$

Theoretically, those characteristics of the defaulted instruments and the prevailing economic environment that are related to $\sigma_i$, $\sigma_m$, $\rho_{i,m}$, and MRP should therefore govern the implicit discount rate. Specifically, we should expect an industry effect if different industry has different beta. Moreover, discount rate is expected to be time-varying if market risk premium varies with the business cycle. Furthermore, the uncertainty of the asset value may also affect the size of the risk premium through its role in determining the value of beta. Under reasonable assumptions of the sizes of market and asset volatility and MRP, Maclachlan (2004) demonstrates the use of this approach in computing the LGD risk premiums and in turn the corresponding discount rates. By either estimating the defaulted assets correlation empirically or by using the regulatory asset correlations of Basel II, LGD risk premiums of 200 basis points (bps) to more than 600 bps are obtained for different types of instruments according to the above CAPM formula.

Brady et al. (2007) approached the problem empirically. Rather than formally testing any theoretical pricing model, they conducted an empirical investigation. By matching the recovery cash flows received postdefault with the market prices of defaulted debts, they conducted an empirical analysis to study the determinants of the implicit risk premium.[11] They conducted the study using a comprehensive database (Standard & Poor's LossStats Database) comprising of the market prices and recoveries of both distressed bonds and loans. They find that investor uncertainty concerning the recovery value of defaulted debt is the primary driver of risk premiums. Risk premiums vary significantly by initial issuer ratings, whether or not the industry is in stress at the time of default, relative seniority to other debt, and instrument type. The risk premiums calculated both as point estimates and confidence interval around them provide another reference point for the practitioners in an environment where many ad hoc estimations are observed in practice. Their results also suggest a strong case for applying different risk premium to different defaulted instruments. A shortened version of their August 2007 paper follows.

## DISCOUNT RATE FOR WORKOUT RECOVERIES: AN EMPIRICAL STUDY*

Brooks Brady
Zions Bancorporation

Peter Chang
Standard & Poor's

*The views and opinions expressed here are those of the authors, not necessarily the views and opinions of the authors' employers, Standard & Poor's, the Federal Reserve Bank of Richmond, the Federal Reserve Board of Governors, or the Federal Reserve System. The authors would like to thank Michel Araten, Stuart Brannan, Christine Brown, Mark Carey, Michael Gordy, Andrea Resti, and Emilio Venezian for their valuable feedback.

Peter Miu[†]
McMaster University

Bogie Ozdemir
Standard & Poor's

David Schwartz
Federal Reserve Bank of Richmond

## Abstract

In order to comply with the Advanced Internal Rating-Based (IRB) approach of Basel II, financial institutions need to estimate the economic loss given default (LGD) of their instruments in order to compute the minimum regulatory capital requirement under Pillar I of the accord. One of the key parameters in the estimation of LGD is the appropriate discount rate (and thus risk premium) to be applied to the workout recovery values. By matching the recovery cash flows received postdefault with the market prices of defaulted debts, we conduct an empirical analysis to study the determinants of the implicit risk premium by using a comprehensive database comprising both distressed bonds and loans. We find that investor uncertainty concerning the recovery value of defaulted debt is the primary driver of risk premiums. Risk premiums vary significantly by initial issuer ratings, whether or not the industry is in stress at the time of default, relative seniority to other debt, and instrument type. The conclusions are found to be robust to potentially confounding determinants of required risk premium.

## Introduction

Implementation of the IRB approach under the Basel II minimum regulatory capital framework has been a major area of effort for many financial institutions. Among the issues debated in the industry is the appropriate discount rate to be used to estimate the economic value of LGD at the time of default.[12] Theoretically, the discount rate used in the estimation of LGD should be commensurate with the (opportunity) costs of holding the defaulted asset over the workout period, including an appropriate risk premium required by the asset holders.[13] This is also the typical interpretation adopted by the

[†]Correspondence should be addressed to Peter Miu, Associate Professor of Finance, DeGroote School of Business, McMaster University, 1280 Main Street West, Hamilton, Ontario L8S 4M4, Canada; Tel.: 1-905-525-9140, ext. 23981; Fax: 1-905-521-8995; E-mail: miupete@mcmaster.ca.

practitioners and Basel. For example, the Basel document states that "when recovery streams are uncertain and involve risks that cannot be diversified away, net present value calculations must reflect the time value of money and a risk premium appropriate to the undiversifiable risk."[14]

Given the scarcity of historical LGD data in general, it has been a very challenging task for the advanced IRB institutions to quantify and/or justify any LGD measures, including the LGD discount rate. Both practitioners and academicians approach the issue from a mostly theoretical standpoint, and several quite different arguments have been made. Our discussions with practitioners show that LGD discount rates used by the banks are typically the results of theoretical discussions, educated guesses, and peer comparisons. The discount rate used ranges from the funding rate, the distress loan rate, the contract rate, the current comparable market rate, the opportunity cost of funds, the cost of capital, the accounting convention of discount rate, and the current risk-free rate. Maclachlan (2004) provides a survey of these different approaches.[15] We hope to contribute to the discussion of this important issue by conducting an empirical study on the economic value of recovery cash flows.

Moreover, it is rarely the case that practitioners attempt to assign differentiated discount rates to different instruments according to the inherent degree of riskiness.[16] Without an appropriate risk adjustment, one could have consistently over- (under-) estimated the LGD of instruments with low (high) recovery risk. For an advanced IRB institution, it can translate into assigning disproportionately high (low) regulatory capital to instruments with low (high) recovery risk.

When a firm defaults, creditors receive direct ownership in the firm's assets (or the collateral if the instruments are secured) and expect to generate a return on these assets. In a CAPM framework, adopted by Maclachlan (2004), the inherent risk premium of a defaulted instrument is the product of the assets' beta and the market risk premium. Beta itself is a function of the correlation of the assets and a systematic market factor, the standard deviation of the market factor, and the standard deviation of the underlying assets. Theoretically, those characteristics of the defaulted instruments and the prevailing economic environment that are related to these determinants of the risk premium should govern the implicit discount rate. Specifically, we should expect an industry effect if different industry has different beta. Moreover, discount rate is expected to be time-varying if market risk premium varies with the business cycle. Furthermore, the uncertainty of the asset value may also affect the size of the risk premium through its role in determining the value of beta. In this paper, rather than formally testing any theoretical pricing model, we conduct an empirical investigation to study the determinants of the risk premium.

We attempt to shed some light on this issue by conducting a study using the Standard & Poor's LossStats Database, which is one of the largest databases commercially available capturing both workout recoveries and defaulted loan and bond prices. We examine the relation between the market prices and the actual workout recoveries of 1,139 defaulted loans and bonds from 1987 to 2005 issued by 439 defaulted obligors. We develop an estimation methodology and estimate the risk premiums, which are *most likely* used at the time of pricing by the market, reflecting the LGD uncertainty of the defaulted loans and bonds. Our choice of methodology is driven by our desire to be consistent with Basel II, which requires that for the estimation of LGD, realized recoveries be simply discounted by the appropriate discount rate.

We solve for the risk premium by interpreting it as the expected excess return (over the risk-free rate) of an investment in the defaulted instrument right after default has occurred. Such an investor pays for the instrument at the market price observed immediately after default in return for the future cash flows that could be realized during the workout process. In order to price the instrument appropriately, the investor needs to assess the expected future recoveries and the required risk premium, which is commensurate with the LGD uncertainty. In this study, we want to solve for the latter by estimating the former. Expected future recoveries are, however, not observable. Nevertheless, if the market is rational, the expected recovery should be identical to the average of the actual realized recoveries for a *reasonably* large and homogenous sample of default instruments in terms of their LGD uncertainty. Under this assumption, for each homogeneous segment of the data set, we solve for the risk premium that equates the discounted average realized recoveries to the market price, given the prevailing term structure of the U.S. Treasuries, which serves as the proxy of risk-free instruments.

We segment the data according to whether the instrument is secured or not, whether the instrument is rated speculative grade or not, the industry sector it belongs to, whether the instrument defaulted during the market-wide and industry-specific stress periods or not, the existence of *debt above* (DA) and *debt cushion* (DC) in the debt structure of the obligor, and its instrument types. Through the empirical analysis, we want to identify which are the important determinants of the estimated discount rates. We also provide theoretical explanations together with the related business intuitions for the empirical results.

We attempt to validate our results by also conducting the analysis at the subsegment level. We ask ourselves questions like: "If we only consider senior unsecured bonds, is the excess return of an instrument defaulted during an industry-specific stress period significantly different from that defaulted outside such period?" The subsegment level analysis allows us to control for the potentially confounding determinants of the discount rate. Furthermore, we confirm the robustness of our findings by conducting a multiple regression analysis, which caters for the interaction among all the significant determinants of discount rates.

For each segment, as data permit, we compute the point estimate of the risk premium together with the corresponding confidence interval around it. Estimating risk premium rather than the full discount rate allows us to control for the fact that risk-free rate varies considerably over our sample period. The risk premium results documented in this paper may therefore be readily used by practitioners in estimating LGD based on their internal workout recovery data and given the current interest rate environment. To obtain the appropriate LGD discount rate, they can simply add the current risk-free rate to the estimated risk premium documented here. For a quick reference, some of the most robust determinants together with the point estimates of risk premiums are presented in Table 1.1. More detailed information is provided in the subsequent sections regarding the definition of segments, the estimation methodology, and the interpretation of the results reported in Table 1.1.

The point estimates reported in Table 1.1 are subject to estimation errors. When we estimate the risk premium we also provide the confidence intervals around the above point estimates, so that probability statements may also be made about these estimates. For the case of senior subordinated bonds, of which the point estimate is −1.1%, the 90% confidence interval is in fact from −10.2% to +8.1%. We therefore cannot rule out the possibility that the true risk premium of this type of instrument may actually be positive. Our hope is that in an environment where we observe many ad hoc estimations in practice, our results provide another reference point for the practitioners. Our results also suggest a strong case for applying different risk premium to different defaulted instruments.

## TABLE 1.1

Point Estimate of Risk Premium

|  | Point Estimate of Risk Premium (%) |
|---|---|
| Investment grade (IG) | 17.7 |
| Noninvestment grade (NIG) | 0.0 |
| Industry in stress | 15.8 |
| Industry not in stress | 1.3 |
| Bank debts | 9.4 |
| Senior secured bonds | 4.1 |
| Senior unsecured bonds | 23.1 |
| Senior subordinated bonds | −1.1 |
| Subordinated bonds | 0.6 |

The following further summarizes the results:

1. Our results suggest that whether the instrument is investment grade (IG) or noninvestment grade (NIG), whether or not it defaults during an industry-specific stress period, and its instrument type are important determinants of recovery risk and thus the discount rate risk premium. Their statistical significances are confirmed in the subsequent subsegment-level analysis and the multiple regression analysis on the internal rate of returns of defaulted instruments.

2. Defaulted debts of an originally highly rated obligor (i.e., investment grade) tend to have higher recovery uncertainty and command higher risk premium. This seemingly counterintuitive finding is actually revealing an interesting phenomenon. It is useful to first emphasize that we attempt to measure recovery risk given default has occurred. High *default risk*, as measured by an instrument's credit rating prior to a default event, does not necessarily imply high *recovery risk* after a default event has been realized. For the investors of noninvestment grade bonds and loans, LGD is a real concern even though the obligor is still a going concern, and as such they require better mitigation of LGD risk via collaterals and guaranties, whereas this is less of a concern for the investors of investment-grade bonds and loans as the default probability is very remote. The lack of prior monitoring and risk mitigation therefore may lead to a higher level of recovery uncertainty and thus a higher discount rate risk premium if a default does occur for these instruments. This phenomenon is especially visible for the *fallen angels* (i.e., those rated as IG in their earliest ratings but subsequently becoming NIG one year before their defaults) as discussed in more detail later in the text.

3. During stress periods when default rates are high, not only expected recoveries can be lower but also the discount rate risk premium is larger, which results in an even larger economic LGD. This is the idea that, during the stress periods, not only the level of expected recovery decreases but also the recovery uncertainty increases. As a result, the correlation between default rates and economic LGD would be more pronounced when this increase in the discount rate is accounted for during downturns. Our results also suggest the industry-specific stress condition is more important than the market-wide stress condition in determining the appropriate discount rate risk premium.

4. The estimated risk premium of the *medium* seniority class (e.g., senior unsecured bonds) is much larger than those for the higher

and lower seniority classes (e.g., senior secured bonds and senior subordinated bonds, respectively). This may not be immediately intuitive as we expect the higher the seniority, the higher the level of expected recovery. Our focus here, however, is not in the estimation of the *level of expected recovery*, but rather the *uncertainty around the expected recovery* (i.e., recovery risk). Only the latter is measured by the discount rate risk premium. The fact that senior unsecured bonds have a higher risk premium than do senior subordinated bonds does not necessarily imply the LGD of the former is higher than that of the latter. The reverse is actually the norm, as the higher level of expected recovery of the former can more than offset the higher risk premium required by the asset holders, thus resulting in a lower LGD. Our results suggest that, disregarding the difference in the level of expected recovery across instruments of different seniority, the recovery risk of the medium seniority class is highest among all instrument types, thus investors demand the highest risk premium.

5. The subsegment results and the regression analysis do not support the secured versus unsecured differentiation. It is however likely to be due to data constraints.[17]

6. Realized recoveries have a very large dispersion. As a result, the mean LGD calculated from a small sample of workout recoveries is subject to a high level of error. When this is the case, market price appears to be a better alternative to the discounted workout recoveries in determining the economic LGD.

7. In general, investors demand a higher rate of return (i.e., discount rate of future cash flows) on defaulted instruments with higher recovery risk, providing empirical support for an appropriate risk-return trade-off. Serving as a proxy for recovery risk, the sum of square errors of the realized recoveries is found to be positively related to the required risk premium on the defaulted instruments.

In the rest of this paper, we first introduce the data set (see section *Data*) and the proposed segmentations together with their justifications (see section *Segmentation*). In the section *Estimation of Risk Premium – Methodology*, we first explain the estimation methodology in detail. We then report and interpret the empirical results in the section *Estimated Risk Premium* where relevant business intuitions are also discussed. In the section *Validation of Results*, we validate our results by conducting subsegment-level analysis. We further examine the robustness of our conclusions by performing multiple regression analysis in section *Regression Analysis*. In the section *A Note on Challenges in Practice and Areas for Future Research*, we touch on issues with respect to price formation in the defaulted debt markets, the valuation of ultimate recovery, controlling for the variation in time-to-recovery and our choice of pricing methodology. We also identify areas for future research. Finally, we conclude with a few remarks.

## Data

We extract the market prices and workout recoveries of the defaulted instruments from the LossStats Database. To estimate the excess returns, we construct daily risk-free term structures using market yields on constant maturity U.S. Treasury securities downloaded from the Federal Reserve Board Web site. Default rates data are from the CreditPro Database. The CreditPro Database and the LossStats Database are licensed by Standard & Poor's Risk Solutions.

### LGD Data

LossStats Database incorporates a comprehensive set of commercially assembled credit loss information on defaulted loans and bonds.[18] Public and private companies, both rated and nonrated, that have U.S.-issued bank loans and/or bonds of more than $50 million are analyzed and included in the database. Financial, real estate, and insurance companies are excluded. The companies must have fully completed their restructuring, and all recovery information must be available in order to be included in the LossStats Database. The database contains recovery information from 1987 through the second quarter of 2005. We choose the LossStats Database as a reliable source of data due to its unique feature in that it contains both the *30-day distressed debt trading prices* and the *ultimate recovery values* of the defaulted instruments, both of which are required in this study. The 30-day distressed debt trading price is the average trading price of the defaulted instrument over a 30-day window from day 15 to day 45 after the respective default event. In contrast, ultimate recovery is the value pre-petition creditors would have received had they held onto their position from the point of default through the emergence date of the restructuring event.[19]

A total of 1,139 defaulted instruments with both ultimate recovery values and 30-day distressed trading prices are included in the analysis.[20] These instruments are from 439 separate obligor default events from 1987 to 2005, and from a variety of industries. Table 1.2 reports the breakdown of the data set according to security, Standard & Poor's rating, and instrument type.

Although the LossStats Database contains recovery information on bankruptcies, distressed exchanges, and other reorganization events, we only take into account companies that had gone through a formal bankruptcy. This helps ensure the consistency between the 30-day distressed debt trading prices and the ultimate recovery values.[22]

**TABLE 1.2**

Composition of LGD Data (Number of Defaulted Instruments)

| Security | Secured | Unsecured | | | |
|---|---|---|---|---|---|
| | 323 | 816 | | | |
| **Standard & Poor's rating**[21] | Investment grade | Non-investment grade | Others | | |
| | 88 | 407 | 644 | | |
| **Type** | Bank debt | Senior secured bonds | Senior unsecured bonds | Senior subordinated bonds | Subordinated bonds | Junior subordinated bonds |
| | 227 | 103 | 396 | 241 | 161 | 11 |

## Risk-Free Yield Curve

To construct the risk-free yield curves, we obtain the daily time-series of market yields on constant maturity U.S. Treasury securities from the Federal Reserve Board Web site. We construct the yield curves by linear interpolation of the market yields of the 3-month, 6-month, 1-year, 2-year, 3-year, 5-year, 7-year, and 10-year U.S. Treasuries. For each defaulted instrument, a risk-free yield curve is computed to match the date on which the trading price is observed (i.e., 30 days after the respective default event).

## Default Rate Data

We use the commercially available CreditPro Database of ratings performance statistics to compile the aggregate default rates by industry. CreditPro, a subscription database of Standard & Poor's corporate rating histories, allows us to produce the time series of default rates for Global Industry Classification Standard (GICS) industry code classifications for Standard & Poor's–rated companies located in the United States.[23] This historical default rate information is used in the subsequent analysis in segmenting the LGD data according to market-wide and industry-specific stress condition, respectively.

## Segmentation

We consider several factors that may influence the appropriate risk premium to be applied to postdefault recoveries when estimating economic LGD. In this section, we describe the criteria we use to segment our data set.

**Secured/Unsecured** describes whether the instrument is secured by collateral or not.

**Standard & Poor's Ratings:** We segment our data based on whether the obligor is rated "BBB−" and above (IG) or "BB+" and below (NIG) by Standard & Poor's. We consider segmenting according to the earliest Standard & Poor's rating and the Standard & Poor's rating one year prior to default respectively. The Standard & Poor's obligor ratings indicate the amount of certainty that creditors have in their ability to receive all claims in full, meaning that companies with higher credit ratings would be less likely to default. Claims on issuers with higher ratings may lack provisions that would provide creditors with higher recovery rates; however, highly rated companies may also have more reliable business plans that would lead to a higher price on exit from default.

**GICS Industry Codes** describe the industry grouping to which each obligor belongs. Industry may affect expected recoveries because investors expect companies in certain industries to have a greater ability to deliver on a postdefault business plan, which may then result in superior recoveries to companies in other industries. The characteristics of the collaterals underlying the debts of different industries may also govern the recovery risks after defaults have occurred. In the subsequent analysis, we focus on the difference between the technology sector and nontechnology sector.

**Default in Market-wide Stress Period** describes whether the obligor defaults during a market-wide stress period or not. Using historical default rates extracted from the CreditPro Database, market-wide stress periods are defined as those years (1986, 1990–1992, and 1999–2003) where Standard & Poor's aggregate speculative-grade default rates are greater than its 25-year average of 4.7%. Market-wide stress periods may be filled with more uncertainty and pessimism, which would drive down the postdefault trading price as well as increase the risk premium for postdefault recoveries. It is also plausible that due to the correlation between probability of default (PD) and LGD, obligors' asset and collateral values are depressed during periods of high default rates.

**Default in Industry-Specific Stress Period** describes whether the obligor defaults during those periods where the obligor's industry (based on the GICS code) experiences a speculative-grade default rate of again more than the 25-year average aggregate speculative-grade default rate of 4.7%. In combining with the previous consideration of market-wide stress period, we can therefore examine whether it is industry-specific or marketwide downturn that drives the potentially higher risk premium of workout recovery.

**Debt Above (DA) and Debt Cushion (DC)** describe whether there is debt that is superior to or subordinated to each bond and bank loan for the given default event. DA is the sum of the amount of debt instruments that are contractually superior to the instrument that is being analyzed divided by total amount of debt. This is in contrast with DC, which is the sum of the amount of debt instruments that are contractually inferior to the instrument that is being analyzed divided by total amount of debt. Because of the variability of the debt structure of defaulted obligor, by defining according to its DA and DC, instruments can be more readily compared than by classifying according to the name of the instrument alone (e.g., senior secured bonds). In this study, we segment our sample into those with (1) no DA and some DC; (2) no DA and no DC; (3) no DC and some DA; and (4) some DA and some DC.

**Instrument Type** groupings are based on the legal description of the instrument. Instrument type is frequently used in practice in classifying instruments for LGD assessments. Similar to DA and DC, instrument type provides information about the seniority of the creditor within the list of claimants. However, the same instrument type can represent very different instruments when we compare obligors with very different debt structure. For example, a subordinated bond issued by an obligor having only a single class of debt may have a much lower recovery risk than is a subordinated bond issued by another obligor that also issued senior bonds. Classifying by DA and DC is considered to be a more appropriate way to control for any differences in debt structure across obligors. In this study, we consider the instrument types of (1) bank debt, (2) senior secured bonds, (3) senior unsecured bonds, (4) senior subordinated bonds, (5) subordinated bonds, and (6) junior subordinated bonds.

### Estimation of Risk Premium—Methodology

We estimate the risk premium for each segment by modeling it as the expected excess return (over the risk-free interest rate) on the investments in defaulted instruments belonging to that segment. We assume all instruments within a particular segment are identical in terms of their LGD risk and thus share the same expected excess return. The fact that the realized recovery turns out to be different from the expected recovery is solely because of LGD uncertainty during the recovery process. Unlike the proposed approach of Maclachlan (2004) of solving for the risk premium by postulating an asset pricing model, we directly solve for the risk premium by matching the ultimate recoveries with the market prices of the defaulted debts.[24] Specifically, consider an instrument $i$ defaults at time $t_i^D$, while a single recovery cash flow $R_i$ is realized at time $t_i^R$. We observe the market price ($P_i$) of this defaulted instrument at 30 days after it defaults. If we use $d$ to denote the expected return (i.e., the discount rate) on investing in this defaulted instrument, the price of the instrument is the expected recovery discounted at $d$:

$$P_i = \frac{E\left[R_i\right]}{\left(1+d\right)^{t_i^R - t_i^D - 30}}.$$                    (Equation 1.2)

Though being aware of other more theoretically appealing approaches such as the one suggested by Cangemi, Mason, and Pagano (2006), we have settled on the simple discounted present value pricing approach of Equation 1.2.[25] Our motivation is twofold. First, it allows for the risk premium to be estimated with relative ease in practice under the maximum likelihood estimation approach as described below. Second, and more importantly, it is consistent with the practice of economic LGD estimation for Basel II implementation. Currently, most banks estimate their economic LGD by discounting the workout recoveries ($R_i$) they experienced as per Equation 1.3,[26]

$$\text{LGD}_i = 1 - \frac{R_i}{(1+d)^{t_i^R - t_i^D}} \times \frac{1}{\text{EAD}_i}, \qquad \text{(Equation 1.3)}$$

where $\text{EAD}_i$ is the exposure-at-default of defaulted instrument $i$. As our purpose is to empirically solve for the risk premium of which practitioners can readily use within the Basel II framework, we use the pricing formula given in Equation 1.2, which is consistent with Equation 1.3.[27] Theoreticians will also notice that the uncertainty around the time-to-recovery ($t_i^R - t_i^D$) is ignored in the formulation of Equation 1.2. The exact length of the time required for a default event to be resolved is typically unknown at the time of default. In section *A Note on Challenges in Practice and Areas for Future Research*, we conduct robustness tests to ensure our findings are not affected by this assumption.

We are not interested in directly estimating the discount rate ($d$) implicit in Equation 1.3. Discount rate is the sum of two components: *risk-free yield* ($r_f$) and excess return ($r_x$). It is the latter, which measures the risk premium, that we are interested in estimating. Estimating excess return directly allows us to control for the variation in risk-free interest rate over our sample period. To use the results of this study in practice, the estimated risk premium can simply be added back to the risk-free yield that is found to be appropriate to the current interest rate environment, which might be quite different from what we have experienced in the past.

In using Equation 1.2 to estimate the risk premium, we need to match the observe market price ($P_i$) with the corresponding expected recovery ($E[R_i]$). Expected recovery $E[R_i]$ is, however, not observable. We can only observe the realized recovery $R_i$. Because of LGD uncertainty, we do not anticipate the expected and realized recovery to be identical unless by coincidence. However, if market is rational, the difference between the expected recovery and the *average* realized recovery should be small for a sufficiently large enough group of instruments that are homogeneous with respect to LGD risk. We can formalize this idea as below. Let $\varepsilon_i$ represent the difference between the expected and realized recovery, being normalized by the price of the instrument $P_i$:

$$\varepsilon_i = \frac{R_i - E[R_i]}{P_i}$$

$$\Leftrightarrow \varepsilon_i = \frac{R_i - P_i \times (1+d)^{t_i^R - t_i^D - 30}}{P_i}$$

$$\Leftrightarrow \varepsilon_i = \frac{R_i - P_i \times \left(1 + r_f + r_x\right)^{t_i^R - t_i^D - 30}}{P_i}. \qquad \text{(Equation 1.4)}$$

It can be interpreted as the *unexpected* return of the defaulted instrument $i$. It is, therefore, a *unit-free* measure of recovery uncertainty. Before we can solve for the excess return, we also need to model for the fact that recovery uncertainty can be a function of the time-to-recovery. As suggested by Miu and Ozdemir (2005), recovery uncertainty is likely to be an increasing function of the time-to-recovery as more and more information on LGD is revealed over time (i.e., less recovery uncertainty) as we approach the time when recovery is finally realized. In this study, we assume the standard deviation of $\varepsilon_i$ is proportional to the square root of time-to-recovery (i.e., $t_i^R - t_i^D - 30$ days). This assumption is consistent with an economy where information is revealed uniformly and independently through time.[28] With this assumption and if the market is rational, $\varepsilon_i / \sqrt{t_i^R - t_i^D - 30}$ days should be small on average across a homogenous group of defaulted instruments. By observing the market price ($P_i$), the realized recovery ($R_i$), and the risk-free yield ($r_f$), the *most-likely* excess return ($\hat{r}_x$) can therefore be obtained by minimizing the sum of the square of $\varepsilon_i / \sqrt{t_i^R - t_i^D - 30}$ days of all the defaulted instruments belonging to a certain segment. It serves as our point estimate of the risk premium for that particular segment. Formally,

$$\hat{r}_x = \arg\min \sum_{i=1}^{N} \left( \frac{\varepsilon_i}{\sqrt{t_i^R - t_i^D - 30 \text{ days}}} \right)^2, \qquad \text{(Equation 1.5)}$$

where $N$ is the number of defaulted instruments in that segment. A by-product of the above algorithm is the minimum sum of the squares of $\varepsilon_i$ (SSE) normalized by the square root of the time-to-recovery. It can be interpreted as a standardized measure of the recovery uncertainty (i.e., LGD risk) of that specific segment. An appropriate risk-return trade-off should therefore suggests that the larger the estimated excess return ($\hat{r}_x$), the larger the corresponding SSE.

The risk premium estimate obtained by solving Equation 1.5 is in fact the maximum likelihood estimate. That is,

$$\hat{r}_x = \arg\max L = \arg\max \sum_{i=1}^{N} \log\left[\phi\left(\frac{\varepsilon_i}{\sqrt{t_i^R - t_i^D - 30 \text{ days}}}\right)\right], \qquad \text{(Equation 1.6)}$$

where $L$ is the log-likelihood function and $\phi(\bullet)$ is the probability density of the standard normal distribution. We can also estimate the asymptotic standard deviation $\sigma_{\hat{r}_x}$ of $\hat{r}_x$ by evaluating the second derivative of $L$ with respect to $r_x$ at the point estimate $\hat{r}_x$,

$$\sigma_{\hat{r}_x} = \left(-\frac{d^2 L}{dr_x^2}\right)^{-0.5}_{r_x = \hat{r}_x}. \qquad \text{(Equation 1.7)}$$

We can therefore establish confidence interval around our point estimate of risk premium. For example, the confidence interval at the 90% confidence level is equal to[29]

$$\hat{r}_x \pm 1.6449 \times \sigma_{\hat{r}_x}. \qquad \text{(Equation 1.8)}$$

The above methodology can be readily extended to include default instruments with multiple recoveries.[30] Suppose there are a total of $m_i$ recovery cash flows ($R_{i,1}, R_{i,2}, \ldots, R_{i,j}, \ldots, R_{i,m_i}$), which are realized at times $t_{i,1}^R, t_{i,2}^R, \ldots, t_{i,j}^R$, $\ldots$ and $t_{i,m_i}^R$, respectively, for defaulted instrument $i$. The proportional difference between expected and realized recovery cash flow $j$ is therefore equal to[31]

$$\varepsilon_{i,j} = \frac{R_{i,j} - p_{i,j} \times \left(1 + r_{f,j} + r_x\right)^{t_{i,j}^R - t_i^D - 30}}{p_{i,j}}, \qquad \text{(Equation 1.9)}$$

where $P_i = \sum_{j=1}^{m_i} p_{i,j}$ and $r_{f,j}$ is the risk-free yield corresponding with the term of $t_{i,j}^R - t_i^D - 30$. The most-likely risk premium (i.e., our point estimate of the risk premium) can therefore be solved by

$$\hat{r}_x = \arg\min \sum_{i=1}^{N} \sum_{j=1}^{m_i} \left(\frac{\varepsilon_{i,j}}{\sqrt{t_{i,j}^R - t_i^D - 30 \text{ days}}}\right)^2, \qquad \text{(Equation 1.10)}$$

where the *outer* summation is across all $N$ defaulted instruments of the segment. The corresponding asymptotic standard deviation and confidence interval of the point estimate can also be computed in a similar fashion as outlined above.[32]

## Estimated Risk Premium

In this section, we report the risk premium estimated for each segment using the methodology outlined above. We also provide some interpretations on the results. It should be noted that the ultimate recoveries obtained from the LossStats Database are *gross* recoveries rather than *net* recoveries. That is, any direct and indirect collection costs such as legal fees, overheads, and other collection expenses typically encountered by a financial institution are not yet subtracted from the ultimate recoveries. For the purpose of measuring economic LGD, banks should apply the discount rate on their net recoveries rather than gross recoveries. By conducting our analysis using gross recoveries, we are therefore overestimating recoveries and thus the discount rate and risk premium to be used for the above purpose. As a result, if a financial institution applies the risk premiums estimated in this study to their net recoveries, the resulting LGD would be somewhat conservative.[33]

Before reporting the estimated risk premium, we present the histogram (Figure 1.12) of the excess returns of all individual instruments within our sample.

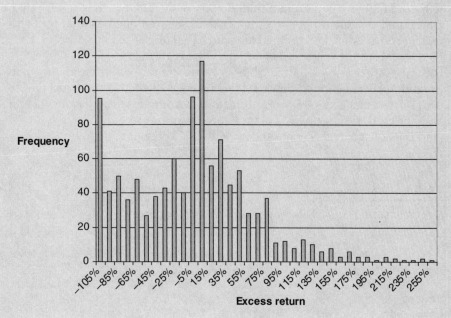

**Figure 1.12** Histogram of excess return of all instruments.

The negative rates presented in Figure 1.12 may appear to be counterintuitive, indication of "noneconomic behavior." This is not actually the case, as the negative excess return realized may simply be due to recovery uncertainty. In practice, we expect to observe negative excess return on some investments. A negative excess return does not necessarily suggest that the investor overestimated the value of the asset, but instead the investor may simply be unlucky. Investors price the defaulted instrument based on the expected value over a distribution of possible recovery cash flows. A negative excess return may then be realized if the actual cash flows turn out to be on the "loss" side of the distribution.

Excess returns have a large variation as observed from Figure 1.12. It is a bimodal distribution with a *thick* right-hand tail. The distribution is truncated at the left, and at the same time very large positive returns with low frequency are observed, suggesting an "option-like" behavior of the defaulted assets. If an investor purchases a defaulted instrument *randomly* immediately after default and holds it until it emerges, there is a 50% chance that the investment return is lower than the respective risk-free yield and a 5% chance that the investor cannot recover anything from the investment. The upside gain, however, can also be very substantial.

### Secured versus Unsecured

Judging from the point estimates reported in Table 1.3, unsecured debts tend to have a higher risk premium than do secured debts, which is as expected. Unsecured defaulted debts are riskier than secured ones, as creditors will only get what is left after secured are paid based on the absolute priority rule, therefore resulting in greater uncertainty to the recovery, and thus investors require a larger risk premium.[34] Not only are the recoveries more uncertain (total risks) for unsecured debts, but also there is likely to be a larger component of systematic risks. For example, the findings of Araten, Jacobs Jr., and Varshney (2004) suggest LGD of unsecured loans is more correlated with PD (and thus the general economy) than with LGD of secured loans.

**TABLE 1.3**

Risk Premium in Percent: Secured versus Unsecured Instruments

|  | Most Likely Estimate | Standard Deviation | 90% Confidence Interval | |
|---|---|---|---|---|
|  |  |  | Lower | Upper |
| **Secured** | 6.2 | 4.7 | −1.4 | 13.9 |
| **Unsecured** | 6.8 | 1.7 | 4.0 | 9.6 |

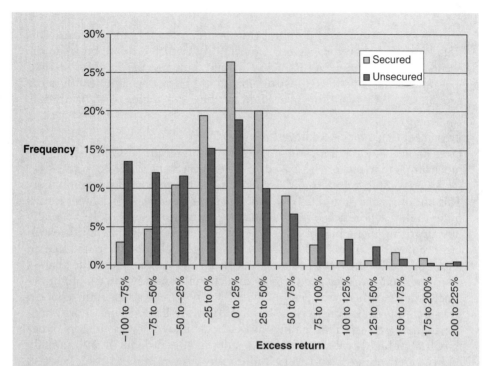

**Figure 1.13** Histogram of excess returns: secured vs. unsecured.

The idea of unsecured defaulted debts being riskier than secured debts is also supported by examining the distribution of the realized excess returns (i.e., internal rate of return in excess of risk-free yield) of individual instruments. The histogram reported in Figure 1.13 suggests it is more likely for the unsecured defaulted debts to generate significantly negative excess return (less than –25%) and significantly positive excess return (more than 75%) than the secured ones.

Despite the strong intuition and the evidence from the earlier studies, the wide and overlapping confidence intervals reported in Table 1.3 indicate that the results are not as strong as expected (refer to the section *Validation of Results* for further discussion). This is most likely due to the fact that the data do not allow us to distinguish the level of security but only the security type. That is, we could have two loans both classified as secured, but the first one may be 100% secured, whereas the second one may only be 5% secured. It might be one of the reasons why the standard deviation of the point estimate for the secured segment is much larger than that of the unsecured one as reported in Table 1.3.[35] It might therefore reflect the fact that the secured segment includes debts of varying degrees of security, whereas the unsecured segment is simply unsecured and thus is much more homogeneous. This data limitation therefore weakens our ability to differentiate between the secured and unsecured credits. The difference between the "highly" secured instruments and unsecured instruments might in fact be significantly more pronounced if we were able to account for the exact degree of securitization.

### Investment Grade versus Noninvestment Grade

From Table 1.4, the point estimate of the risk premium of IG instruments is much larger than that of NIG based on the earliest Standard & Poor's rating.[36] Nonoverlapping confidence intervals indicate the power of discrimination. This finding is also found to be robust when we consider subsegment results (refer to the section *Validation of Results* for further discussion). It is actually not surprising that a higher level of recovery risk is implicit in an IG instrument rather than in an NIG one.[37] Because it is highly unanticipated that an IG debt defaults, the fact that it defaults increases the riskiness of the distress instruments. Moreover, creditors of an originally highly rated obligor are much less concerned about its LGD when the obligor is still a going concern as its default risk is perceived to be slim. They are likely to pay more attention in monitoring and mitigating the LGD risk of lowly rated obligors rather than that of highly rated ones. As a result, defaulted debts of an originally highly rated obligor tend to be more risky and command a higher risk premium.

We also examine if the rating history has any bearing on the risk premium by segmenting the data jointly according to whether they are investment grade in the earliest Standard & Poor's ratings and in the Standard & Poor's ratings assigned one year before the respective default events. The results are reported in Table 1.5. The corresponding 90% confidence intervals are presented in brackets.

The *fallen angels* (i.e., those rated as IG in their earliest ratings but subsequently becoming NIG one year before their defaults) appear to have the highest uncertainty around their expected recoveries and thus require the highest risk premium. Fallen angels having higher recovery rates than

### TABLE 1.4

Risk Premium in Percent: IG versus NIG (Based on Earliest Standard & Poor's Rating)

|               | Most Likely Estimate | Standard Deviation | 90% Confidence Interval | |
|               |                      |                    | Lower | Upper |
|---------------|----------------------|--------------------|-------|-------|
| IG (earliest)  | 17.7                 | 5.0                | 9.5   | 25.9  |
| NIG (earliest) | 0.0                  | 3.4                | −5.6  | 5.6   |

**TABLE 1.5**

Risk Premium (in Percent) of Different Rating Histories

| | Most Likely Risk Premium (%) | |
| --- | --- | --- |
| | **IG (Earliest)** | **NIG (Earliest)** |
| **IG (1 year before)** | 10.3 (−1.0 to 21.6) | N/A |
| **NIG (1 year before)** | 28.0 (14.4 to 41.5) | −1.0 (−7.1 to 5.0) |

Note: Within our data set, there are only three observations that
are of NIG according to their earliest ratings and subsequently
become IG one year before the respective default events. Results
are therefore not reported for this case.

those debts which have always been rated speculative grade since origination
may be explained by the nature of the fallen angels. They are obligors that
used to have high credit quality before they defaulted. Some of those advan-
tageous qualities may carry over into the default work-out process. However,
when fallen angels default, market participants may be less likely to invest in
their defaulted debt due to the extreme change in the fortunes of the obligor,
thus demanding a larger risk premium than that for an otherwise identical
obligor that has always been rated as NIG. It is interesting that fallen angels
seem to have a combination of high risk premium and high recovery rate.

## Industry
Our intuition is that those industries with exposures typically collateralized
by tangible assets and real estate—of which values can readily be determined—would require a lower risk premium than do those with exposures
collateralized by assets of which values are more uncertain.

We study the industry effect by classifying the obligors in the data
set according to their GICS. We first compare technology-based against
non-technology-based industries.[38] We expect defaulted instruments issued
by the technology sector to have higher recovery uncertainty because they
are collateralized by typically intangible assets. An originally secured instrument can become essentially "unsecured" when the collateral loses its perceived value. As an example, the supposedly fully secured creditors involved
in the Winstar Communications, Inc. 2001 bankruptcy saw their positions
practically being wiped out. As the overcapacity in the telecom industry
leads to a large devaluation of the underlying collateral, the creditors saw
their collateral values decline along with that of the rest of the telecom
industry, essentially making the secured creditors into unsecured creditors.
The results reported in Table 1.6 substantiate the above hypothesis. Judging

**TABLE 1.6**

Risk Premium in Percent: Technology versus Nontechnology

|  | Most Likely Estimate | Standard Deviation | 90% Confidence Interval | |
|---|---|---|---|---|
|  |  |  | Lower | Upper |
| **Technology** | 20.3 | 5.8 | 10.8 | 29.9 |
| **Nontechnology** | 5.7 | 1.8 | 2.8 | 8.6 |

from the nonoverlapping confidence intervals, the estimated risk premium of defaulted instruments of the technology industries is significantly higher than those of the nontechnology industries.

The idea that defaulted instruments of technology-based industries should be riskier than those of nontechnology-based industries is also supported by examining the distribution of the excess returns of individual defaulted instruments. The histogram reported in Figure 1.14 suggests it is

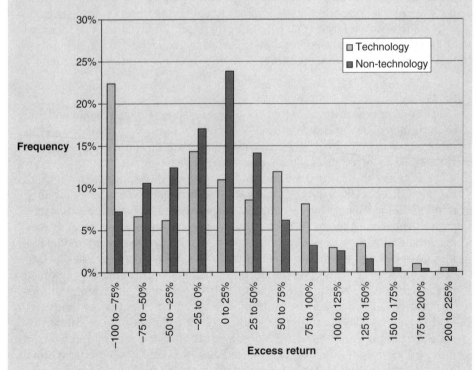

**Figure 1.14** Histogram of excess returns: technology vs. nontechnology.

more likely for the former to generate significantly negative excess return (less than −75%) and significantly positive excess return (more than 50%) than it is for the latter.

We further examine the industry effect by breaking down the non technology sector into further subsectors, namely energy & utilities, consumer staples/materials, but the results (not reported) are found to be inconclusive.

### Default During Market-wide Stress Period

In Table 1.7, we compare the estimated risk premium of those instruments defaulted during the market-wide stress periods with those defaulted outside those periods. Market-wide stress periods are defined as those years where Standard & Poor's aggregate speculative-grade default rates are greater than its 25-year average of 4.7%.

The finding that investors require a larger risk premium during a stress period is consistent with the fact that recovery risk is likely to be higher during the recessionary period. For example, the empirical studies of Araten, Jacobs Jr., and Varshney (2004) and Acharya, Bharath, and Srinivasan (2003) document larger LGD variation during stress periods. The higher risk can be due to the fact that uncertainly around the values of the collaterals and the defaulted companies' assets may increase during a marketwide stress period.

This finding also has interesting implications with respect to the correlation between default rate and LGD. A positive correlation between default rate and LGD is already documented by, for example, Araten, Jacobs Jr., and Varshney (2004) and Miu and Ozdemir (2006), which is primarily due to the fact that during the period of high defaults, recoveries tend to be low as assets and collateral values are depressed. These studies use a single discount rate to discount the workout recoveries for all defaulted instruments and thus the effect of market stress condition on risk premium studied here is not

**TABLE 1.7**

Risk Premium (in Percent): Marketwide Stress Condition

| | Most Likely Estimate | Standard Deviation | 90% Confidence Interval | |
| --- | --- | --- | --- | --- |
| | | | Lower | Upper |
| In marketwide stress period | 10.4 | 4.1 | 3.6 | 17.2 |
| Not in marketwide stress period | 6.1 | 1.8 | 3.2 | 9.1 |

accounted for. Unlike these studies, we can attribute the positive relation between default rate and LGD to the variation of risk premium across the different states of the economy. In other words, our results show that during recessionary periods when default rates are high, not only may expected recoveries be lower but also the discount rate is larger, which results in an even larger economic LGD.[39] This is the idea that, during the recessionary periods, not only does the expected recovery decrease but also the recovery uncertainly increases. As a result, the correlation between default rate and economic LGD would be more pronounced when the increase in risk premium documented in this study is accounted for during market downturns.

The higher discount rate during a stress period is also consistent with the theory of excess supply of defaulted debts during a marketwide stress period. Altman et al. (2005) suggests that the increase in LGD during recessionary periods is mainly due to an increase in the supply of defaulted instruments.

Judging from the overlapping confidence intervals reported in Table 1.7, the difference in risk premiums between the marketwide stress period and nonstress period is, however, not strong. Specifically, the effect is much weaker than that between the industry-specific stress period and nonstress period as reported subsequently. It, therefore, suggests the industry-specific effect is a more important determinant of the expected excess return than is the marketwide effect. This weaker marketwide effect is also documented in the section *Validation of Results* when we conduct the subsegment analysis.

### Default during Industry-Specific Stress Period

In Table 1.8, we compare the estimated risk premium of those instruments defaulted during the industry-specific stress periods with those defaulted outside those periods. Industry-specific stress periods are defined as those years when the industry to which the obligor belongs experiences a

**TABLE 1.8**

Risk Premium (in Percent): Industry-Specific Stress Condition

|  | Most Likely Estimate | Standard Deviation | 90% Confidence Interval | |
|---|---|---|---|---|
|  |  |  | Lower | Upper |
| In industry-specific stress period | 15.8 | 2.6 | 11.5 | 20.1 |
| Not in industry-specific stress period | 1.3 | 2.8 | −3.3 | 5.8 |

speculative-grade default rate of more than the 25-year average of 4.7%. The point estimate of risk premium during the industry-specific stress period is found to be much higher than that when otherwise. Judging from the nonoverlapping confidence intervals, the difference is highly statistically significant. The result is also found to be robust when we conduct the analysis at the subsegment level in the section *Validation of Results*.

The finding of defaulted instruments during an industry stress period being riskier than those not in a stress period is also supported by examining the distribution of the realized excess returns (over risk-free yield) of individual defaulted instruments. The histogram reported in Figure 1.15 suggests it is more likely for the former to generate significantly negative excess return (less than –50%) and significantly positive excess return (more than 25%) than it is for the latter.

Comparing the statistical significance of the results reported in Tables 1.7 and 1.8, we can conclude industry-specific stress condition is more important than marketwide stress condition in governing the expected excess return on

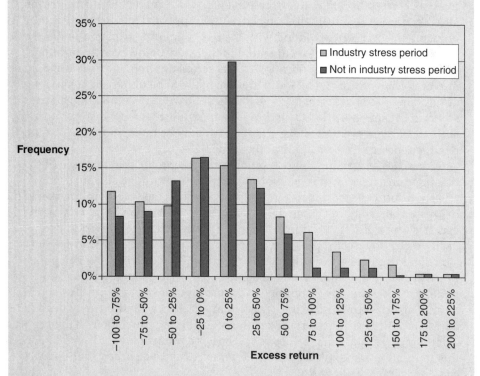

**Figure 1.15** Histogram of excess returns: industry-specific stress condition.

distress debt. This is consistent with the empirical findings of Acharya, Bharath, and Srinivasan (2003) and the theoretical model proposed by Shleifer and Vishny (1992). Shleifer and Vishny suggest financial distress is more costly to borrowers if they default when their competitors in the same industry are experiencing cash flow problems. It therefore supports the concept that there are cross-industry diversification effects in play, meaning that different industries have different LGD cycles.

Another plausible argument for industry undergoing stress situation leading to greater LGD risk is that the uncertainty around the values of the collaterals increases during an industry-specific stress period, assuming that collaterals are mostly industry specific, for instance, fiberoptic cable for the telecom sector.

The observation that industry-specific stress condition is more important than market-wide stress condition has an interesting implication on the computation of capital requirement. Under the Basel II Advanced IRB approach of regulatory capital calculation or under an economic capital framework, banks need to estimate LGD by discounting the workout recoveries at the appropriate discount rate. Capital is estimated at the extreme confidence interval, corresponding with extreme events, which is most likely to occur in stress periods. To fulfill this objective, the appropriate discount rate is arguably the one corresponding with the risk premium estimated under the marketwide stress period documented in this study. However, an argument can be made that the diversification effects across different industries should also be considered, as not all industries are likely to be under stress situation at the same time. Nevertheless, a capital event would be an extreme stress scenario causing a bank's capital to be wiped out by credit losses. During such an extreme event, it is likely that many, may be most, industries would be experiencing stress situation at the same time.

As we are extracting the risk premium by using the market price of the defaulted instrument, our estimated risk premium might also incorporate any short-term effects and risk measures specific to the secondary market of distressed instruments. Namely, as suggested by Altman et al. (2005), the excess supply of defaulted instruments during a distressed period can by itself exert a downward pressure on the market price and thus translate into a further increase in the implicit risk premium. For those banks with a policy to always work out their defaulted assets rather than selling them in the secondary market, they may not need to concern themselves with this short-term demand/supply issue in the secondary market and, thus, may need to adjust the risk premiums reported in this study before using them in their calculations of the economic values of LGDs. For a more detailed discussion on this interesting issue, please refer to section *A Note on Challenges in Practice and Areas for Future Research.*

## DA and DC

From Table 1.9, the priority of the instruments on the balance sheet as measured by DA and DC appears to be an important driving factor in determining the required risk premium. Specifically, judging from the point estimates and their confidence intervals, those instruments with some DC (whether with or without DA) have statistically significantly higher required risk premium than do those without DC (again, whether with or without DA). This effect of debt structure on recovery is consistent with the findings of Van de Castle (2000). This result is also found to be robust when we conduct the subsegment analysis in *Validation of Results* and when we control for other variables in the regression analysis in the section *Regression Analysis*.

The amount of debt cushion and collateral securing a position not only has an effect on the expected recovery rate. The results in Table 1.9 suggests that knowing the debt structure of the given obligor and the position of the instrument being analyzed in this structure may also shed some light on the amount of uncertainty surrounding the expected recoveries.

If a given instrument has no DA or DC, this would mean that there are no other bonds and loans with either higher or lower priority on the balance sheet. All creditors therefore share equally in the underlying assets securing the positions; resulting in a fairly predictable recovery rate. As expected, we observe the lowest required risk premium for instruments with no DA and no DC.[40]

Following the same argument, those instruments with some DA and some DC should have the largest uncertainty surrounding the expected recovery, as there are both senior and junior positions who will be vying for a portion of the defaulted obligors' assets. This is because the creditors do not know how much they need to pay the subordinated creditors in order to move the debt restructure plan forward, nor they know how much the senior creditors agree to pay them for the same reason. It is also consistent with the

**T A B L E  1.9**

Risk Premium (in Percent): DA versus DC

|  | Most Likely Estimate | Standard Deviation | 90% Confidence Interval | |
|---|---|---|---|---|
|  |  |  | Lower | Upper |
| **No DA, some DC** | 15.4 | 3.6 | 9.5 | 21.3 |
| **No DA and no DC** | −4.0 | 7.8 | −16.8 | 8.8 |
| **No DC, some DA** | 1.8 | 2.7 | −2.6 | 6.2 |
| **Some DA and some DC** | 22.3 | 3.9 | 15.8 | 28.8 |

idea suggested by Acharya, Bharath, and Srinivasan (2003) that more demanding coordination effort among creditors in the situation of larger "debt dispersion" leads to higher bankruptcy and liquidation costs, thus translating into a higher required rate of return. As expected, this effect is found to be even stronger if we confine ourselves to only unsecured instruments. The estimated risk premium of those unsecured instruments with some DA and some DC is found to be equal to 25.3% (refer to the subsegment results reported in Table 1.12).

For those instruments belonging to the categories of "No DA, some DC" and "No DC, some DA," the estimated risk premiums are in between those of the prior two categories discussed. From Table 1.9, instruments belonging to the category "No DC, some DA" have a lower estimated risk premium between the two. Because these instruments are at the bottom of the list of absolute priority, creditors expect not only a relatively low level of recovery rate but also a low variation around the expected value.[41] It therefore results in a lower recovery uncertainty and in turn a lower required risk premium. Finally, those instruments belonging to the category of "No DA, some DC" should have the highest expected recovery of all the four categories; however, there may still be a large level of uncertainty to the ultimate recovery. This uncertainty therefore leads to a high required risk premium.

### Instrument Type

From Table 1.10 and judging from the confidence intervals, we can conclude the estimated risk premium of senior unsecured instruments are statistically significantly higher than those of senior secured bonds, senior subordinated bonds, and subordinated bonds. Senior subordinated bonds have the lowest point estimate of risk premium among all the types. The differences in risk premiums should reflect the different degrees of uncertainty in the recovery

**TABLE 1.10**

Risk Premium (in Percent): Instrument Type

|  | Most Likely Estimate | Standard Deviation | 90% Confidence Interval | |
|---|---|---|---|---|
|  |  |  | Lower | Upper |
| **Bank debt** | 9.4 | 6.6 | −1.5 | 20.3 |
| **Senior secured bonds** | 4.1 | 6.7 | −6.9 | 15.0 |
| **Senior unsecured bonds** | 23.1 | 3.1 | 18.0 | 28.2 |
| **Senior subordinated bonds** | −1.1 | 5.6 | −10.2 | 8.1 |
| **Subordinated bonds** | 0.6 | 3.6 | −5.3 | 6.5 |

process for each instrument type. For example, the relatively higher (lower) risk premium for senior unsecured bonds (subordinated bonds) suggests a higher (lower) degree of recovery uncertainty. They are found to be consistent with a number of empirical studies (e.g., Altman and Arman [2002]), which suggest standard deviation of LGD is smaller for subordinated notes than for senior unsecured bonds. These results are also confirmed in our subsegment analysis conducted in the section *Validation of Results*.

### Risk-Return Trade-off

In this subsection, we would like to examine if there is an appropriate risk-return trade-off in the investment of defaulted instruments. Does a defaulted instrument of a higher recovery risk generate a higher excess return than does the one of lower recovery risk? We use the minimum sum of the square errors (SSE) $\varepsilon_i$ of realized recoveries (normalized by the square root of time-to-recovery) to proxy for the recovery risk for each segment. If recovery risk is a determinant of the required risk premium, SSE should be larger for those segments with higher risk premium. This is actually the case for most of the segmentations considered previously in this section. In Table 1.11, we report the SSEs of a number of segments.

Except for the segmentation between technology and nontechnology, the relative sizes of the SSEs are consistent with our expectation. Specifically, the unsecured, IG, market-wide stress, and industry-specific stress segments, which have higher risk premium, also have larger SSE than do the secured, NIG, marketwide nonstress, and industry-specific nonstress segments, respectively.

The positive relation between the estimated risk premium and SSE is also confirmed through a regression analysis. We regress the risk premium point estimates against the respective SSEs across all the segments examined in this section. The result is reported in Equation 1.11. The slope coefficient of 0.407 is weakly statistically significant with a *t*-statistic of 1.875:

$$\hat{r}_x = -0.484 + 0.407 \times SSE + e. \qquad \text{(Equation 1.11)}$$

### TABLE 1.11

Normalized Sum of Square Error of Realized Recovery

| | | | |
|---|---|---|---|
| Secured | 1.251 | Unsecured | 1.407 |
| IG | 1.453 | NIG | 1.406 |
| Technology | 1.358 | Nontechnology | 1.366 |
| Marketwide stress period | 1.429 | Not in marketwide stress period | 1.345 |
| Industry-specific stress period | 1.418 | Not in industry-specific stress period | 1.270 |

## Validation of Results: Subsegment Analysis

In this section, we examine the robustness of the differences in risk premiums across the segments by controlling for other ways to segment the data. For example, we would like to answer the following questions: Is the risk premium estimated during an industry-specific stress period still statistically significantly higher than that during a nonstress period if we only consider senior unsecured bonds? Is the estimated risk premium of those instruments with some DA and some DC still statistically significantly higher than those with no DA and no DC if we only consider facilities issued by the nontechnology sector?[42]

To answer these questions, we repeat the analysis at the subsegment level crossing all the segments we considered previously. For example, using the proposed methodology, we solve for the point estimate and the (asymptotic) confidence interval of the risk premium of the subsegment consisting of instruments issued by the nontechnology sector *and at the same time* with some DA and some DC. The point estimate is found to be equal to 26.1% and the corresponding 95% confidence interval is from 18.9% to 33.2%. We can then check if the estimated risk premium of this subsegment is statistically different from the corresponding estimated risk premiums at the segment level. Specifically, we want to check if respectively the risk premium obtained for all instruments in the nontechnology sector and the risk premium obtained for all instruments with some DA and some DC actually lie within the above interval. As reported in the previous section, the former is 5.7%, and the latter is 22.3%. Because the latter lies within the above confidence interval of the subsegment risk premium estimate, we cannot conclude that the nontechnology subsegment within the segment of some DA and some DC behaves differently from other subsegments. However, because the former lies outside the confidence interval, we can conclude that the subsegment of some DA and some DC is likely to have higher risk premium within the nontechnology sector.

We conduct the above analysis for each of the subsegments and the results are reported in Table 1.12. We only present the point estimates of the risk premiums of those subsegments that are statistically (at 95% confidence level) significantly different from that of the corresponding segment, which are presented in bold figures along the diagonal of Table 1.12.[43] Those risk premiums that are significantly higher (lower) than the corresponding segment risk premium are presented in round (square) brackets. We should interpret the risk premiums of the subsegments presented along *each row* and compare them with the value at the diagonal (i.e., the segment risk premium) when we look for statistically significant differences. Let us again use the nontechnology sector as an example. The segment risk premium is 5.7% (the value along the "nontechnology" row of Table 1.12 which is at the diagonal).

# TABLE 1.12

## Point Estimates of Risk Premium (in Percents) of Subsegments

| | Secured | Unsecured | IG (Earliest) | NIG (Earliest) | Technology | Non Technology | Market Stress Period | | Industry Stress Period | | DA & DC | | | | Instrument Type | | | | |
|---|---|---|---|---|---|---|---|---|---|---|---|---|---|---|---|---|---|---|---|
| | | | | | | | In Stress | Not in Stress | In Stress | Not in Stress | No DA Some DC | No DA and DC | No DC Some DA | Some DA and DC | Bank Debt | Senior Secured Bonds | Senior Unsecured Bonds | Senior Subordinated Bonds | Subordinated Bonds |
| Secured | **6.2** | | | | | | | | | | | | | | | | | | |
| Unsecured | | **6.8** | (18.5) | [-1.9] | (21.3) | | | (26.8) | (16.1) | | (26.8) | | | (25.3) | | | (23.0) | | |
| IG (earliest) | | | **17.7** | | | | | | | | | | | | | | | | |
| NIG (earliest) | | | | **0.0** | | | | | | | | | | | | | | | |
| Technology | | | | | **20.3** | | [-30.2] | (33.0) | | | (40.3) | | | [-52.2] | | | | | |
| Nontechnology | | | (16.8) | [-6.2] | | **5.7** | | | (15.0) | | [-11.8] | | | (26.1) | | | (21.6) | | |
| **Market stress period** | | | | | | | | | | | | | | | | | | | |
| In stress | | | | | | | **10.4** | | | | | | | | | | | | |
| Not in stress | | | | [-2.3] | | | | **6.1** | (18.9) | [-2.4] | (18.7) | | [-1.8] | (23.7) | | | (31.6) | [-14.0] | |
| **Industry stress period** | | | | | | | | | | | | | | | | | | | |
| In stress | | | | [4.4] | | | (15.8) | | **15.8** | | | | [5.4] | (29.1) | | | | [-0.3] | [-1.2] |
| Not in stress | | | | | | | | | | **1.3** | | | | | | | | | |
| **DA & DC** | | | | | | | | | | | | | | | | | | | |
| No DA, some DC | | | (26.8) | | | | | | (25.6) | | **15.4** | | | | | | (28.2) | | |
| No DA and DC | | | | | | | | | | | | **-4.0** | | | | | | | |
| No DC, some DA | | | (19.1) | | | | (12.3) | | | | | | **1.8** | | | | (12.2) | [-20.1] | |
| Some DA and DC | | | | | | | | | | | | | | **22.3** | | | (64.4) | | |
| **Instrument type** | | | | | | | | | | | | | | | | | | | |
| Bank debt | | | | | | | | | | | | | | | **9.4** | | | | |
| Senior secured bonds | | | | | | | | | | | | | | | | **4.1** | | | |
| Senior unsecured bonds | | | | [-2.0] | | | [7.1] | [4.3] | (41.6) | | | [-2.3] | [12.2] | | | | **23.1** | | |
| Senior subordinated bonds | | | | | | | (21.9) | | | | | | | | | | | **-1.1** | |
| Subordinated bonds | | | | | | | | | | | | | | | | | | | **0.6** |

Note: Those estimated subsegment risk premiums that are statistically significantly higher (lower) than the corresponding segment risk premium (at the diagonal) are presented in round (square) brackets.

Within this segment, the subsegment of "No DA and no DC" has an estimated risk premium of –11.8% which is significantly lower than 5.7%. On the other hand, the subsegments of "IG," "In industry-specific stress period," "Some DA and some DC" and "Senior unsecured bonds" have risk premiums of 16.8%, 15.0%, 26.1%, and 21.6%, respectively, which are all significantly higher than 5.7%. Because risk premiums are not reported for all the other subsegments, they are not found to be statistically different from 5.7%. The other rows can therefore be interpreted in the same fashion.

We can therefore examine the robustness of the results presented in the previous section by considering the results reported in Table 1.12. For example, except for within the segment "No DA, some DC," estimated risk premiums of secured and unsecured instruments are not significantly different from the corresponding segment risk premium.[44] Any difference between the secured and unsecured instruments in terms of risk premium is therefore not as strong as those obtained by segmenting the instruments in other ways discussed subsequently.

The difference in risk premiums between IG and NIG is found to be robust after controlling for a number of other variables. Within five segments (namely "Unsecured," "Technology," "Not in marketwide stress period," "In industry-specific stress period," and "Senior unsecured bonds"), the NIG subsegments have significantly lower risk premiums than the corresponding segment risk premiums. At the same time, the IG subsegments within the "Unsecured," "Nontechnology," and "No DC, some DA" segments have estimated risk premiums that are significantly higher than the respective segment values.

From Table 1.12, the robustness of the previous findings of the risk premium for the technology sector being higher than that of the nontechnology sector and the risk premium for instruments defaulted during the marketwide stress periods being higher than during the nonstress periods are however questionable. For example, if we only consider senior unsecured bonds, the estimated risk premium of those defaulted during the marketwide stress (nonstress) periods is actually significantly lower (higher) than the segment risk premium of 23.1%.

The difference between industry-specific stress period and nonstress period is found to be very robust. For all the cases, which are statistically significant, instruments defaulted during the industry-specific stress (nonstress) periods consistently have significantly higher (lower) risk premium after controlling for other variables.

The findings in the previous section regarding DA, DC, and instrument type are also confirmed by the results reported in Table 1.12. For example, "No DA, some DC" has significantly higher risk premium even if one confines herself to consider only unsecured instruments, within the technology sector, or during periods other than the marketwide stress periods. On the other hand, the risk premiums estimated for those "No DA and no DC" subsegments are lower than the corresponding segment risk premiums within the nontechnology and senior unsecured bonds. In terms of instrument type, senior unsecured bonds always have higher risk premium, whereas senior subordinated bonds have lower risk premium than the corresponding segment values.

The results reported in Table 1.12 also suggest that instrument type by itself cannot fully characterize the recovery risk (and thus the required risk premium) of the instrument. Controlling for instrument type, one can still observe a large variation of risk premiums across different DA and DC. Specifically, within the segment of senior unsecured bonds, those with some DA and some DC have significantly higher risk premium (64.4%), whereas those with no DA and no DC have significantly lower risk premium (–2.3%).

To summarize, the analysis conducted in this section confirm a number of our findings in the previous section. Specifically, (1) whether the instrument is rated IG or NIG; (2) whether it defaults during the industry-specific stress periods or not; (3) the existence of DA and/or DC; and (4) its instrument type are found to be important determinants of recovery risks. However, the results do not strongly support the secured versus unsecured differentiation, which is likely due to data constraints.[45] Moreover, the impact of industry characteristics (e.g., technology vs. nontechnology) and market-wide factors (e.g., stress vs. nonstress) is found to be inconclusive.

### Regression Analysis

In section *Validation of Results* we check for the robustness of our results obtained in *Estimated Risk Premium* section by considering the interactions of different ways to segment the data set in a *two-dimension* analysis. For example, we investigate the interaction between industry-specific stress period and instrument type and conclude that within the segment of senior unsecured bonds, the estimated risk premium during the industry-specific stress periods is still significantly higher than average. In this section, we would like to take one step further by conducting a multidimensional investigation through a pooled regression analysis. We want to study if the variation of the realized excess returns on individual defaulted instruments can be explained by the various characteristics of the instruments if we consider all the factors at the same time. We consider the same data set we use in obtaining the results in *Estimated Risk Premium* and *Validation of Results* sections. The dependent variable is the logarithmic of the annualized gross excess return (over the respective risk-free yield) on individual defaulted instrument, assuming the instrument is bought 30 days after default and is held until it emerges from bankruptcy.[46]

The explanatory variables considered here are those found out to be important determinants of recovery risk in *Estimated Risk Premium* and *Validation of Results* sections namely (1) whether the earliest Standard & Poor's rating is investment grade or not (IG vs. NIG); (2) whether the default event occurs during an industry-specific stress period; (3) the percentage amounts of DA and DC; (4) whether it is senior unsecured bonds or senior subordinated bonds (i.e., its instrument type).[47] In the regression analysis, we also control for the variation in the weighted average time-to-recoveries of the defaulted instruments.[48] We expect a positive relation between excess return and time-to-recovery, as recovery uncertainty is believed to be increasing with recovery horizon.

The most general version of the regression equation could be in the form of[49]

$$\log\left(1 + r_{x,i}\right) = c + a_1 \text{IG}_i + a_2 \text{IndS}_i + a_3 \text{DA}_i + a_4 \text{DC}_i +$$

$$a_5\left(\text{DA}_i \times \text{DC}_i\right) + a_6 \text{Ty}_{1,i} + a_7 \text{Ty}_{2,i} + a_8 \text{TTR}_i + \varepsilon_i, \quad \text{(Equation 1.12)}$$

where

- $r_{x,i}$ = annualized excess return on default instrument $i$;
- $\text{IG}_i$ = dummy variable: equal to "1" if instrument $i$'s earliest Standard & Poor's rating belongs to investment grade, "0" otherwise;
- $\text{IndS}_i$ = dummy variable: equal to "1" if instrument $i$ defaults during industry-specific stress period, "0" otherwise;
- $\text{DA}_i$ = amount of DA in percentage of total debt;
- $\text{DC}_i$ = amount of DC in percentage of total debt;
- $\text{DA}_i \times \text{DC}_i$ = product of DA and DC respectively in percentage of total debt;
- $\text{Ty}_{1,i}$ = dummy variable: equal to "1" if instrument $i$ is senior unsecured bond, "0" otherwise;
- $\text{Ty}_{2,i}$ = dummy variable: equal to "1" if instrument $i$ is senior subordinate bond, "0" otherwise;
- $\text{TTR}_i$ = the weighted average time-to-recovery of instrument $i$ (in years).

We include the product of DA and DC to study the effect of "debt dispersion" on excess return. We expect a positive relation between this product and the excess return if the more heterogeneity of the debt structure results in a larger required risk premium. The regression results are reported in Table 1.13. We present the estimated coefficients together with the corresponding $t$-statistics (in italic).

**TABLE 1.13**

Regression Analysis: Coefficients Together with the Corresponding *t*-Statistics (in Italic)

| | A | B | C | D | E | F | G | H | I | J |
|---|---|---|---|---|---|---|---|---|---|---|
| **Intercept** | -0.249** | -0.278* | -0.144** | -0.152** | -0.394** | -0.395** | -0.103 | -0.157** | -0.411** | -0.156** |
| | *-4.966* | *-4.143* | *-2.717* | *-2.865* | *-7.086* | *-7.084* | *-1.725* | *-2.968* | *-7.377* | *-3.006* |
| **IG (earliest Standard & Poor's rating)** | 0.282* | | | | | | | 0.323** | 0.359** | 0.217* |
| | *2.545* | | | | | | | *2.952* | *3.274* | *1.978* |
| **Industry-specific stress period** | | 0.048 | | | | | | | | |
| | | *0.772* | | | | | | | | |
| **DA and DC** | | | | | | | | | | |
| DA | | | -0.565** | -0.622** | | | | -0.636** | | |
| | | | *-5.326* | *-5.754* | | | | *-5.901* | | |
| DC | | | | | 0.774** | 0.770** | | | 0.813** | |
| | | | | | *5.891* | *5.724* | | | *6.045* | |
| DA × DC | | | | 2.501* | | 0.138 | | 2.726** | 0.292 | |
| | | | | *2.550* | | *0.141* | | *2.781* | *0.298* | |
| **Instrument type** | | | | | | | | | | |
| Senior unsecured bonds | | | | | | | -0.107 | | | |
| | | | | | | | *-1.618* | | | |
| Senior subordinated bonds | | | | | | | -0.476** | | | -0.413** |
| | | | | | | | *-6.086* | | | *-5.680* |
| **Weighted average time-to-recovery (year)** | 0.030 | 0.045 | 0.061* | 0.057* | 0.061* | 0.061* | 0.038 | 0.044 | 0.047 | 0.028 |
| | *1.091* | *1.649* | *2.273* | *2.148* | *2.299* | *2.270* | *1.437* | *1.632* | *1.732* | *1.056* |
| **R-square (adjusted)** | 0.008 | 0.002 | 0.028 | 0.033 | 0.034 | 0.033 | 0.035 | 0.040 | 0.042 | 0.037 |
| **p value of F test** | 0.012 | 0.230 | 0.000 | 0.000 | 0.000 | 0.000 | 0.000 | 0.000 | 0.000 | 0.000 |

Note: Coefficients significant at 5% and 1% level are marked with * and **, respectively. The p-value of *F*-test is for the hypothesis test where all coefficients are zero. Boldfaced coefficients are statistically significant.

Consistent with the findings in the previous sections, the single-variable regressions of Equations A, C, E, and G in Table 1.13 suggest:

- the realized excess return on a defaulted instrument is statistically significantly higher if its earliest Standard & Poor's rating is IG or if there is more DC;

- the realized excess return is however significantly lower if the defaulted instrument has more DA or if it is a senior subordinated bond. From Equation B of Table 1.13, the industry-specific stress condition seems to have a positive impact on excess return, however it is not statistically significant. Moreover, there is a positive relation between realized excess return and time-to-recovery, which is consistent with our expectation that the higher recovery uncertainty over longer recovery horizon results in a larger risk premium.

From Equation D of Table 1.13, the coefficient of the product term of DA and DC is positive and statistically significant after controlling for the level of DA. It therefore suggests that, for the same level of DA, the existence of an increasing amount of DC results in a higher excess return. This is consistent with our conclusion in *Estimated Risk Premium* section with respect to the positive effect of "debt dispersion" on the required risk premium. From Equation F of Table 1.13, this effect is however found to be much weaker once the level of DC is controlled for.

Equations H to J are regressions including multiple independent variables, which have been identified as statistically significant in Equations A to G.[50] All the respective coefficients are found to be of the expected sign and of the similar degree of statistical significant. The conclusions drawn above are therefore robust after controlling for other explanatory variables.

The estimated coefficients of the regression equations also allow us to quantify the impact of the various independent variables on the implicit excess return. For example, based on Equation H of Table 1.13, the size of the coefficient of the dummy variable of IG suggests that the gross excess return on an IG instrument is about 38% higher than that of an NIG instrument after controlling for other factors. In the same regression equation, the value of the coefficient of DA indicates that gross excess return reduces by about 0.63% if DA increases by 1% (of total debt value). Finally, from Equation J, based on the value of the coefficient of senior subordinated bonds, this type of defaulted debt generates a gross excess return that is about 34% lower than other types of defaulted debts.

## A Note on Challenges in Practice and Areas for Future Research

In this section, we would like to touch on issues with respect to price formation in the defaulted debt markets, the valuation of ultimate recovery, controlling for the variation in time-to-recovery and our choice of pricing methodology. We also identify areas for future research.

## Economic Value of LGD at the Time of Default

Given the high volatility of defaulted debt prices right after the default events, one might question the validity of the market prices used in this study. There are two reasons why we believe the volatility will not affect our analysis to a large extent. First, rather than relying on the price of a single trading day, Standard & Poor's LossStats Database follows the common practice in using the average market prices over a 30-day window from day 15 to day 45 after the respective default event.[51] The averaging should ensure the resulting market price is not distorted by a few abnormal price observations. Moreover, the large amount of volatility observed in the market prices right after the obligor defaults typically settles during the first 30 days of default and a robust market price emerges as the market absorbs the relevant information.[52] Second, in our analysis, we estimate the most-likely risk premiums for *groups of instruments*, which allows us to eliminate any noise inherent in the market prices of individual instruments.

Another point of discussion is the effect of institutional reasons in the formation of market prices of defaulted debts. Different banks may follow different philosophies in dealing with defaulted credits. Some banks may choose to sell out their holding of bonds and bank loans for institutional reasons once default is apparent or realized.[53] An argument can be made that the price impact due to these institutional reasons should not constitute an economic impact on other banks that commit to hold onto their defaulted instruments. This price effect should therefore be excluded or controlled for in the analysis. Suppose an institution sells a defaulted debt at 60 cents in the market due to some "institutional reasons" even though the expected ultimate recovery could be very high, eventually leading to a recovery cash flow of 130 cents. One might argue that it is a "noneconomical" action of a market player, and thus the implicit yield (and thus risk premium) obtained by comparing 60 cents with the ultimate recovery of 130 cents does not make economic sense. A counter argument, however, would be that the economic value is represented by the market price irrespective of whether it is driven by institutional reasons or not. Along this line of argument, from the perspective of the buyer of the above defaulted debt, the 60 cents represents the opportunity (economic) cost of holding this instrument until ultimate recovery. In an efficient market, any deviation from the equilibrium price resulting from the selling pressure (out of institutional reasons or not) of some market players should be arbitraged away.

A related point of discussion is the effect of the increased supply of defaulted instruments on the estimated risk premium during the stress periods (i.e., the results reported in the first rows of Tables 1.7 and 1.8). As discussed previously, because capital events represent extreme stress conditions, a discount rate incorporating the risk premium estimated during the stress periods is considered to be more appropriate than using that estimated outside those periods in the computation of economic LGD for the estimation of required capital. An argument can however be made that the excess supply of defaulted debts during the stress periods is likely to exert a downward pressure on the market prices and thus exaggerates the estimated risk premium during those periods. As a result, if a bank's collection practice is to work out recoveries rather than to sell the defaulted debts, the market prices and thus the estimated risk premium obtained over the stress periods should be irrelevant in its assessment of economic LGD. Any excess supply and the related price impact are believed to be temporary and should be relieved once the market condition improves.

Let us examine this argument by considering the possible causes of the increase in risk premium during stress condition. It is likely to be due to a combination of the following:

1. Depressed prices due to the short-term imbalance in supply and demand;

2. Increased recovery uncertainty (i.e., LGD risk) during market downturn; and

3. Investors demand a higher risk premium during a recession, which is unrelated to the short-term market imbalance.[54]

If the increase in risk premium during stress condition were solely due to no. 2 and no. 3 above, the estimated risk premium during the stress condition obtained in this study based on market prices could be used directly for capital calculation purposes even by those banks of which the collection policy is to hold onto the defaulted debts. However, if the increase were solely due to no. 1, arguably those banks that never sell their defaulted debts but always collect recoveries from them may want to ignore the stressed risk premium but to use the lower risk premium corresponding with the nonstress condition.

In reality, it is most likely that all the three factors together contribute to the higher risk premium during the stress periods. As a result, the appropriate risk premium for the above bank, which never sells defaulted debts, should reflect only no. 2 and no. 3 and thus should be smaller than the one reported in this study. Nevertheless, it is likely to be still larger than the estimated risk premium over the nonstress periods. Banks may therefore consider using a lower stress risk premium than that reported here, if they believe the short-term imbalance in supply and demand will be rectified over a short period of time. The partitioning of the contribution to a higher risk premium among the three factors would be an interesting subject for any future research.

Finally, even if the increase in the risk premium were solely due to no. 1, banks that never sell defaulted debts but always collect recoveries would need to demonstrate that they can maintain this practice even under extreme stress condition of a market downturn corresponding with a capital event.

### Economic Value of Ultimate Recovery

Ultimate recovery values of the defaulted debts are calculated in the LossStat Database by one of three methods:

1. *Emergence pricing*: trading price of the defaulted instrument at the point of emergence from default;
2. *Settlement pricing*: trading price at emergence of those instruments received in the workout process in exchange for the defaulted instrument; and/or
3. *Liquidity event pricing*: values of those instruments received in settlement at their respective liquidity events (e.g., suppose creditors receive newly issued bonds during the settlement process; liquidation event prices are the liquidation values of these bonds at their respective maturity dates).

When possible, all three methods are considered in the calculation of the recovery value of each instrument. Then, based on additional information, the method that is expected to be most representative of the recovery experience of the pre-petition creditors was used to arrive at the recovery value. Of all recovery values recorded in the data set, 29% are of emergence pricing, 61% of settlement pricing, and 10% are of liquidity event pricing.

Despite the potentially illiquid secondary market of default debts, we believe the recovery value obtained from the above pricing methodologies can still correctly reflect the true economic value of ultimate recovery. First, it should be noted that the lack of market liquidity does not affect the liquidity event pricing, which is not based on any market prices. Second, because the data set only includes typically large companies, which have greater than $50 million in outstanding bonds and loans at the point of default, the secondary markets of these instruments are considered to be liquid enough to ensure the true economic recovery values can be revealed under both emergence and settlement pricing methods.[55]

### Controlling for the Variation in Time-to-Recovery

Our data set covers default events from 1987 to 2005, which have also emerged before the end of 2005. We therefore exclude those defaults that occurred during this time period but have not yet been fully resolved by the end of 2005 (as the remaining cash flows are still unknown). However, otherwise similar defaulted instruments are included if they have much shorter resolution periods ending prior to the end of 2005.[56] If the length of the time-to-recovery is also a determinant of LGD risk premium, including instruments of short-lived resolutions but excluding those with longer resolutions may distort the results of our analysis.

We attempt to control for the variation in time-to-recovery by including it as an explanatory variable in our regression analysis in section *Regression*

*Analysis* (Table 1.13). The regression results show that realized excess return tends to be positively related to the time-to-recovery. The longer the time-to-recovery, the larger is the excess return on defaulted debts. The regression analysis also shows that the other determinants of risk premiums, namely initial issuer rating, whether or not the industry is in stress at the time of default, and relative seniority to other debts, remain robust after controlling for the variation in time-to-recovery.

An alternative way to mitigate the potential distortion caused by the variation in time-to-recovery is to impose a cut-off date of default, which is well before the end of the sample period in 2005. If we exclude all those LGD data recorded after end of 2002 (i.e., imposing a cut-off date that is 2.5 years prior to the end of our full sample), most of the instruments defaulted before this date should have already emerged before the end of the second quarter of 2005 and thus captured in our data set.[57,58] We will run into the risk of excluding vital information about the most recent market downturn of 2001–2002 if we impose a cutoff earlier than end of 2002.

We repeat the analysis and recompute the most-likely risk premiums of different segments considered previously by using the subsample obtained with the 2002 cut-off criteria. The results are reported in Table 1.14. For ease of comparison, the full-sample estimates (from Tables 1.3, 1.4, 1.6, 1.7, 1.8, 1.9, and 1.10) are also repeated in the last column of Table 1.14. Except for the technology sector, imposing the 2002 cut-off date does not economically alter the estimated risk premiums. The results reported in Table 1.14 confirmed most of our findings in *Estimated Risk Premium* section Namely, (i) IG instruments have significantly higher risk premium than do NIG instruments; (ii) instruments defaulted during industry-specific stress periods have significantly higher risk premium than do those defaulted outside those periods; and (iii) instruments with some DA and some DC have significantly higher risk premium than do those without DA and DC. Also consistent with *Estimated Risk Premium* section the effects of the degree of security and marketwide stress condition are weak. However, even though the technology sector still has a higher point estimate of risk premium than does the nontechnology sector, the difference is smaller than that obtained with the full sample. We cannot conclude the difference is statistically significant given the overlapping confidence intervals.

Finally, we further investigate the impact of ignoring the uncertainty of the time-to-recovery in our analysis by repeating the analysis on a subsample that is more homogenous in the time-to-recoveries than the full sample. We first present the distribution of the time-to-recoveries of the full sample in Figure 1.16. The mean and median time-to-recovery are 524 days (approximately 17 months) and 437 days (approximately 14 months), respectively. In this last analysis, we only consider those instruments with time-to-recoveries shorter than two years, which represents about 76% of the full data set.

**TABLE 1.14**

Most Likely Risk Premium (in %) of Different Segments after Imposing a Cut-Off Date of End of 2002

| | Subsample after Imposing Cut-Off Date | | | | Full Sample |
|---|---|---|---|---|---|
| | Most Likely Estimate | Standard Deviation | 90% Confidence Interval | | Most Likely Estimate |
| | | | Lower | Upper | |
| Secured | 5.3 | 4.9 | −2.7 | 13.3 | 6.2 |
| Unsecured | 6.4 | 1.8 | 3.5 | 9.3 | 6.8 |
| IG (earliest) | 17.6 | 5.0 | 9.3 | 25.8 | 17.7 |
| NIG (earliest) | −2.2 | 3.9 | −8.5 | 4.2 | 0.0 |
| Technology | 14.9 | 6.3 | 4.5 | 25.3 | 20.3 |
| Nontechnology | 5.7 | 1.8 | 2.7 | 8.6 | 5.7 |
| In marketwide stress period | 10.4 | 4.1 | 3.6 | 17.2 | 10.4 |
| Not in marketwide stress period | 5.5 | 1.9 | 2.4 | 8.6 | 6.1 |
| In industry-specific stress period | 14.6 | 2.7 | 10.1 | 19.1 | 15.8 |
| Not in industry-specific stress period | 1.2 | 2.8 | −3.4 | 5.8 | 1.3 |
| No DA, some DC | 15.1 | 3.7 | 9.1 | 21.1 | 15.4 |
| No DA and no DC | −4.3 | 7.9 | −17.4 | 8.7 | −4.0 |
| No DC, some DA | 0.7 | 2.9 | −4.1 | 5.5 | 1.8 |
| Some DA and some DC | 22.2 | 4.0 | 15.7 | 28.8 | 22.3 |
| Bank debt | 7.8 | 7.0 | −3.7 | 19.3 | 9.4 |
| Senior secured bonds | 4.2 | 6.7 | −6.9 | 15.2 | 4.1 |
| Senior unsecured bonds | 21.8 | 3.2 | 16.5 | 27.1 | 23.1 |
| Senior subordinated bonds | −0.8 | 5.7 | −10.1 | 8.5 | −1.1 |
| Subordinated bonds | 0.6 | 3.6 | −5.3 | 6.5 | 0.6 |

The results obtained with this subsample are found to be consistent with the findings reported in *Estimated Risk Premium* section, thus suggesting the modeling of the uncertainty in time-to-recovery is of secondary importance.[59]

## Choice of Pricing Methodology

As discussed in the section *Estimation of Risk Premium – Methodology*, though we settle for a straightforward pricing methodology (see Equation 1.2) due to our

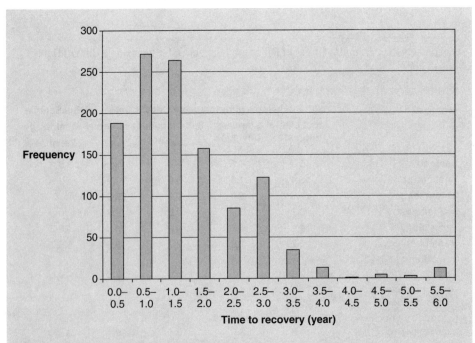

**Figure 1.16** Distribution of time-to-recovery.

desire to be consistent with Basel II, in terms of future research, we would like to examine alternative pricing methodologies. For example, an option-like approach of pricing defaulted debts may be theoretically quite attractive given its ability to capture any nonlinear payoff pattern and the pricing relation among defaulted debts of different seniority that are issued by the same obligor. However, one might need to overcome a number of practical obstacles when such an approach is implemented in practice. More importantly, we need to ensure the resultant pricing formula, from which the discount rate is solved, is consistent with that used for LGD estimation (i.e., Equation 1.3) in practice.

## Summary

In this study, we empirically solve for the risk premium required to estimate economic LGD from workout recoveries. We find that risk premiums vary according to the risk of return on defaulted debt as perceived by investors at the time of default. Risk premiums vary by the obligor's initial rating, whether or not the industry is in a stressed condition at the time of default, relative seniority to other debt, and instrument type. The subsegment level analysis and the multiple regression analysis conducted on the realized excess returns of defaulted instruments confirm the statistical significance of the results and the robustness of our conclusions.

Estimated risk premium of those instruments defaulted during the industry-specific stress periods is found to be much higher than that of those defaulted outside those periods. During the marketwide stress periods when default rates are, in general, higher, not only expected recoveries are lower, but also the recovery risk premium tends to be higher, which results in an even larger economic LGD and more pronounced PD and LGD correlations. Through this study, we provide a framework for financial institutions to determine the appropriate risk premium to be incorporated in their LGD estimation process in order to fulfill the requirement under both the advanced IRB approach of Basel II regulatory capital calculation and their internal economic capital measurement.

## REFERENCES

Acharya, V.V., S.T. Bharath, and A. Srinivasan, 2007, "Does Industry-Wide Distress Affect Defaulted Firms? Evidence from Creditor Recoveries." *Journal of Financial Economics*, vol. 85, pp. 787–821.

Altman, E.I., and P. Arman, 2002, "Defaults & Returns on High Yield Bonds: Analysis Through 2001." *Journal of Applied Finance*, vol. 12, no. 1, pp. 98–112.

Altman, E.I., B. Brady, A. Resti, and A. Sironi, 2005, "The Link between Default and Recovery Rates: Theory, Empirical Evidence, and Implications." *Journal of Business*, vol. 78, no. 6, pp. 2203–2227.

Araten, M., M. Jacobs Jr., and P. Varshney, 2004, "Measuring LGD on Commercial Loans: An 18-Year Internal Study." *RMA Journal*, vol. 86, no. 8, pp. 28–35.

Bos, Roger J. "Initial Trading Price: Poor Recovery Indicator for Defaulted Debt." New York: Standard & Poors Ratings Direct. January 14, 2003.

Cangemi, Jr., R.R., J.R. Mason, and M.S. Pagano, 2006, "How Much of a Haircut?" Working paper, Drexel University.

Davis, P.O., 2004, "Credit Risk Measurement: Avoiding Unintended Results: Part 3: Discount Rates and Loss Given Default." *RMA Journal*, vol. 86, no. 10, pp. 92–95.

Maclachlan, I., 2004, "Choosing the Discount Factor for Estimating Economic LGD." Working paper, Australia and New Zealand Banking Group Ltd.

Miu, P., and B. Ozdemir, 2005, "Practical and Theoretical Challenges in Validating Basel Parameters: Key Learnings from the Experience of a Canadian Bank." *Journal of Credit Risk*, vol. 1, no. 4, pp. 89–136.

Miu, P., and B. Ozdemir, 2006, "Basel Requirement of Downturn LGD: Modeling and Estimating PD & LGD Correlations." *Journal of Credit Risk*, vol. 2, no. 2, pp. 43–68.

Shleifer, A., and R.W. Vishny, 1992, "Liquidation Values and Debt Capacity: A Market Equilibrium Approach." *Journal of Finance*, vol. 47, no. 4, pp. 1343–1366.

Van de Castle, K., D. Keisman and R. Yang (2000), "Suddenly Structure Mattered: Insights into Recoveries of Defaulted Debt." S&P, May 2000.

## Appendix

We repeat the analysis conducted in *Estimated Risk Premium* section by directly using the *raw* unexpected recovery $\varepsilon_i$ rather than the *normalized* version of $\varepsilon_i / \sqrt{t_i^R - t_i^D - 30}$ days in Equations 1.5, 1.6, and 1.10. This alternative formulation is therefore consistent with an economy where the recovery uncertainty is assumed to be time homogenous. The results are reported in Table A.1.

**TABLE A.1**

Risk Premium (in %) of Different Segments (Time-Homogenous Uncertainty[60])

| | Most Likely Estimate | Standard Deviation | 90% Confidence Interval | |
| --- | --- | --- | --- | --- |
| | | | Lower | Upper |
| Secured | 2.9 | 3.0 | −2.1 | 7.9 |
| Unsecured | 2.8 | 0.9 | 1.4 | 4.2 |
| IG (earliest) | 14.7 | 3.2 | 9.4 | 19.9 |
| NIG (earliest) | −4.7 | 2.0 | −8.0 | 1.4 |
| Technology | 28.2 | 3.9 | 21.8 | 34.6 |
| Nontechnology | 1.9 | 0.9 | 0.5 | 3.4 |
| In marketwide stress period | 11.5 | 2.4 | 7.5 | 15.5 |
| Not in marketwide stress period | 1.9 | 0.9 | 0.4 | 3.4 |
| In industry-specific stress period | 15.0 | 1.5 | 12.5 | 17.5 |
| Not in industry-specific stress period | −1.5 | 1.4 | −3.7 | 0.8 |
| No DA, some DC | 9.9 | 2.4 | 6.0 | 13.8 |
| No DA and no DC | 0.0 | 4.9 | −8.0 | 8.3 |
| No DC, some DA | −1.0 | 1.3 | −3.1 | 1.1 |
| Some DA and some DC | 22.9 | 2.0 | 19.5 | 26.2 |
| Bank debt | 7.0 | 5.4 | −1.9 | 16.0 |
| Senior secured bonds | 1.7 | 3.7 | −4.4 | 7.7 |
| Senior unsecured bonds | 25.6 | 1.9 | 22.5 | 28.7 |
| Senior subordinated bonds | 3.8 | 3.4 | −1.7 | 9.4 |
| Subordinated bonds | −2.9 | 1.7 | −5.7 | −0.1 |

## CONCLUSIONS

In risk rating system design, FIs establish a process through which risk ratings or credit or facility scores are assigned to the obligors and the facilities. In this process, effectively obligors and facilities are first rank-ordered through risk ratings or credit or facility scores, and then the level of the risk corresponding to each rating is quantified. We can use expert judgment–based risk rating templates, quantitative models, or hybrid approaches for this purpose.

When sufficient historical default rate time-series data are not available, for example typically for low-default portfolios, expert judgment templates are commonly used. These templates provide an efficient, transparent, and replicable framework for capturing quantitative and qualitative credit risk factors in structured expert judgment system to assess obligor's default risk. Credit rating agencies are among the major providers of the templates. If an FI chooses to use the rating agency's standard methodology as is (or with minor modification), the rating agency's historical default rates can be used in assigning PDs to the internal risk ratings (or scores). Replacing the rating agency's standard methodology with existing (typically pre-Basel II) methodology may result in a shift in the FI's risk ratings. If this shift is not desired, templates can be calibrated to the current internal ratings (to minimize the shift in ratings). However if this is done, the link between the template methodologies and external default rates weakens.

When there are sufficient data available, quantitative models can be built and used in IRRS design for objective and consistent risk rating of obligors and facilities. A number of these models are commercially available producing continuous PDs and LGDs. These continuous PDs/LGDs can then be converted into PD and LGD scores or risk ratings. In a hybrid framework, the quantitative scores coming out of quantitative models are blended with qualitative scores obtained from assessing the qualitative factors to arrive at overall scores.

## REFERENCES

Brady, B., P. Chang, P. Miu, B. Ozdemir and D. Schwartz, 2007, "Discount Rate for Workout Recoveries: An Empirical Study." Working paper.

Friedman, C., and S. Sandow, 2003, "Ultimate Recoveries." RISK, pp. 69.

Standard & Poor's Credit Market Services, 2003, "LossStats Model – User Guide." Standard & Poor's.

## CHAPTER 2

# Risk Ratings System Quantification

## OVERVIEW

In risk ratings system quantification, each risk rating (design of which is discussed in Chapter 1) is assigned a unique PD, LGD, and EAD. With risk ratings system quantification, we therefore complete the risk rating assignment process, under which each obligor (and facility) is assigned a risk rating (RR) and through which is assigned corresponding PD, LGD, and EAD. Figure 2.1 illustrates the mapping we want to establish through risk rating quantification.

PDs assigned to the risk ratings reflect obligors' one-year real-life probability of default. Basel II requires that the risks beyond the first year be recognized in the quantification of PDs. This may seem confusing if this requirement is sometimes wrongly interpreted as the term of PDs are longer than one year. In fact, the requirement of capturing risks beyond one year does not contradict with PDs being one-year cumulative PDs. One-year cumulative PDs should capture all foreseeable risks. We can illustrate this point using the commonly used Merton framework. One-year cumulative PD can be assessed as the likelihood of assets values being less than the default point at the "one-year point" along the risk horizon. However, both the asset value and the default point encompass financial events that occur well beyond the one-year point. Default point, for example within the Moody's KMV framework, is defined as half of the short-term liabilities plus all of the long-term liabilities. Similarly, stock price, which is the primary determinant of the asset value, represents the free cash flows generated over the foreseeable future.

Basel II requires that the PDs assigned to the internal risk ratings reflect *long-run* default experience. These PDs are therefore frequently referred to as

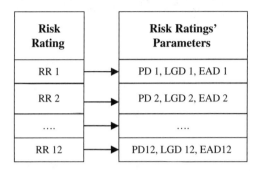

**Figure 2.1** Risk rating quantification.

*long-run PDs* (LRPDs), which can be estimated by observing historical default rates of the risk ratings. Attaining a credible measure of LRPD for low-PD risk ratings may easily become a formidable task as it is not uncommon to have very few or even no internal default data for low credit risk portfolio. Even if there are internal default data, the historical time series rarely covers a full credit cycle, not to mention reflecting a *long-run* situation. Besides, it is important to recognize the fact that LRPD is essentially the obligor's one-year *unconditional* default probability. An unconditional probability measure is required to ensure the consistency with the way value-at-risk (VaR) is formulated in the economic model underlying the Pillar I risk-weight function. Given that the observed default rate of a credit portfolio is a *conditional* probability measure, which incorporates both the unconditional PD and the inherent asset correlation within the portfolio, we need to control for the degree of asset correlation when we infer LRPD from the observed default rates. With a nonzero asset correlation, simple averaging of the observed annual default rates is unlikely to produce an appropriate LRPD measure. In the section *"Long-run PD,"* we consider a number of measures of LRPD that are consistent with the economic model of Basel II. We compare their performances with those of the alternatives in terms of their accuracies and the sizes of the potential errors in a number of validation tests.

LGDs and EADs assigned to the risk ratings represent the expected values of these values at the default point. There are, however, downturn LGD and EAD requirements for which we need to include markups to the expected values. The markups are required to compensate for the omission of the adverse relationship between default rate and LGD (and EAD) in formulating the Pillar I risk-weight function. This regulatory requirement will be discussed in the section *"Downturn LGD."* The term *LGD (EAD) risk rating* may be a bit confusing. Unlike in PD risk rating, an explicit LGD (EAD) risk rate mapping might not exist for some FIs. Many FIs use, for example, decision trees in quantifying the LGDs (EADs) of their facilities. Nevertheless, we can still categorize facilities into discrete LGD (EAD) risk ratings under these designs.

## RISK RATING PHILOSOPHY

### PD Philosophy

Basel II requires FIs to determine and disclose the risk rating philosophies adopted in their internal risk rating systems (IRRSs). Risk rating philosophy dictates the expected behavior of the IRRS with respect to credit cycle. Under a point-in-time (PIT) philosophy, we expect the assigned PDs of the obligors change with the credit cycle, namely they go up (down) during a recession (expansion). Assigned PDs are therefore risk sensitive and they reflect our best estimate of default probabilities over the next year. Conversely, under a through-the-cycle (TTC) philosophy, assigned PDs are not supposed to reflect our best estimate of default probabilities over the next year, but instead, they represent the average one-year default probabilities over the credit cycle (albeit credit cycle is not always well defined). Figure 2.2 illustrates the difference of the two philosophies in terms of assigned PD. Under a PIT IRRS, PDs of all obligors increase during a recession but decrease in a booming economy. The change in PD with respect to the state of the economy is however less pronounced under a TTC IRRS.

If an FI adopts a PIT risk rating philosophy, it needs to increase the obligors' PDs during a recession and to reduce them during an expansion. Within a typical IRRS design, where obligors are assigned to different risk ratings, risk ratings are in turn mapped to unique PDs via the master scale, but there are several ways to achieve the intended risk sensitivity:

1. We can keep the risk rating to PD mapping unchanged while we downgrade (upgrade) all obligors during a credit downturn (upturn) so that the downgraded (upgraded) obligors would be

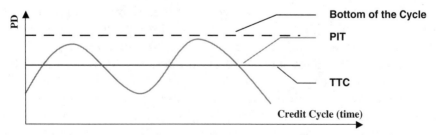

**Figure 2.2** Different risk rating philosophies.

assigned to the higher (lower) PDs corresponding with the new risk ratings to which the obligors are downgraded (upgraded). The onus of achieving a PIT philosophy is therefore on the continuous regrading of the obligors.

2. We do not downgrade (upgrade) the obligors during a downturn (upturn) but we assign higher (lower) PDs to the risk ratings so that the obligors' PDs would increase (decrease) during downturns (upturns). The onus of achieving a PIT philosophy in this approach is therefore on the continuous r-mapping of the PDs to the risk ratings.

3. A combination of both.

Here it is useful to reiterate the difference between PDs assigned to the risk ratings and the PDs assigned to the obligors. As discussed in the section *"Long-run PDs,"* PDs assigned to the risk ratings are intended to be unconditional long-run PDs. PDs assigned to the obligors can however be PIT (or TTC or a hybrid) via the above process. Risk rating philosophy refers to PDs assigned to the obligors.

In our experience, approach no. 1 is most commonly used, whereas approach no. 3 is usually kept as a last resort. Let us consider an FI whose risk rating philosophy is PIT via approach no. 1. We should expect that the migration rates under this PIT philosophy are significantly higher than those under a TTC philosophy. This implication allows us to assess the risk rating philosophy by quantifying the observed level of rating migrations through the mobility metric test (see section on "Backtesting" in Chapter 3). Let's also consider the process this FI needs to follow to maintain its intended PIT philosophy. At initiation (when a PD is first assigned to a new obligor), the assigned PD needs to be PIT reflecting the one-year forward-looking default probability. However, this is not sufficient, because as time passes and the inherent credit risk changes, we need to change the obligor's PD accordingly in order to remain the PIT-ness. This process therefore requires us to continuously monitor all information related to the obligor's default likelihood. We also need to act on this new information instantly and regrade the obligor accordingly. This is impossible for two reasons. First, not all information related to an obligor's default likelihood is observable. Second, it is unlikely we have a frictionless regrading system which allows us to act on the new information instantaneously without any delay. This is especially true for an SME portfolio where the obligors' files are reviewed at most on a semiannual frequency (annual reviews are in fact much more common). We can only act on the new information and regrade the obligors accordingly at the time of review. This example shows that a "pure" PIT IRRS is not achievable in practice even if it is the FI's intention to attain such a philosophy. It is in fact a hybrid of the two philosophies, somewhere in between "pure" PIT and "pure" TTC.

Let us now consider those IRRSs that are closer to the other extreme of the spectrum (i.e., TTC philosophy). For example, Standard & Poor's (S&P) risk rating philosophy is sometimes considered to be TTC. This is not true as it is likely to be a hybrid as well, only that it is considered to be closer to "pure" TTC than to "pure" PIT. Standard & Poor's does not rate companies based on one-year default probabilities but instead based on their relative rankings over a three- to five-year horizon.[1] Moreover, Standard & Poor's does not necessarily downgrade a company during a downturn despite the increase in its one-year PD, provided that the company's relative ranking does not change. These are clearly TTC attributes, but not enough to make the rating philosophy a "pure" TTC. If it were "pure" TTC, we would have observed no downgrades during a downturn due to systematic reasons, but only for idiosyncratic (i.e., company-specific) reasons. That is, if the downturn affects all companies systematically and their one-year PDs increase accordingly, as long as they preserve their relative ranking, none would have been downgraded. Only the ones whose relative rankings worsen due to company-specific reasons would have been downgraded. The downgrade actions of Standard & Poor's we observe in practice, however, suggest otherwise, indicating the presence of a (small) PIT element in the philosophy and making it in fact a hybrid philosophy. Figure 2.3 summarizes our discussions and defines the spectrum of risk rating philosophies. (For a discussion on risk rating philosophy for retail models, see the section on "The Use of Retail Models in IRRS" in Chapter 1.)

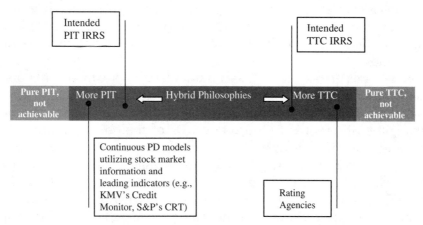

**Figure 2.3** Spectrum of risk rating philosophies.

It is necessary to distinguish the observed default rate of a portfolio from the PD of its constituents (i.e., obligors). The former is dictated not only by the PD but also by the level of the default correlation. This distinction is brought up here because risk rating philosophy has a role to play in determining the level of default correlation within each risk rating.[2] Let us consider two risk ratings in two IRRSs with the same assigned PD. For the first IRRS, the risk rating philosophy is fairly PIT, whereas it is rather TTC for the second. Suppose we have observed the default rates over a long period of time from these two risk ratings. How would we expect the distributions of these two default rate time series to differ due to the difference in the adopted risk rating philosophies? In the more PIT IRRS, the observed annual default rates should be fairly close to the PD assigned to that risk rating at any point in time. This is because, during a downturn and under the PIT philosophy, we would have already downgraded all obligors to the respective riskier risk ratings such that the actual PDs of the obligors within each risk rating will closely match the PD assigned to that risk rating. This will, however, not be the case for the more TTC IRRS. Under a TTC philosophy, reratings will not be conducted in a timely fashion resulting in the obligors' actual one-year forward-looking PDs not necessarily matching the assigned PD. For example, during a downturn, the risk rating under the TTC IRRS will contain some obligors (which would have been downgraded under the PIT IRRS) whose PDs are in fact higher than the PD assigned to that risk rating. The opposite would happen during an upturn. Because realized default rates are dictated by the actual PDs of the obligors rather than by the PDs assigned to the risk ratings, the distribution of the observed default rates from the risk rating under the TTC IRRS would be more disperse than the one from the PIT IRRS. This is consistent with Rösch (2004) who also show that default rates are more volatile under a TTC system than under a PIT system. Figure 2.4 depicts the distributions of default rates under the two different risk rating philosophies.

Now let us go back to the Basel framework where, for all obligors in a particular risk rating, we use the PD assigned to that risk rating regardless of the adopted risk rating philosophy. In this framework where we cannot cater for the differences in the actual PDs of the obligors, how can we account for the differences in the observed distributions of default rates illustrated above? The answer is in the appropriate choice of default correlation.[3] As formally illustrated in the subsequent section, default correlation under a TTC IRRS is larger than that under a PIT IRRS. This has profound implications in capital estimation and validation tests. For PIT (TTC) capital estimation, we need to use not only PIT (TTC) PDs but also PIT (TTC)

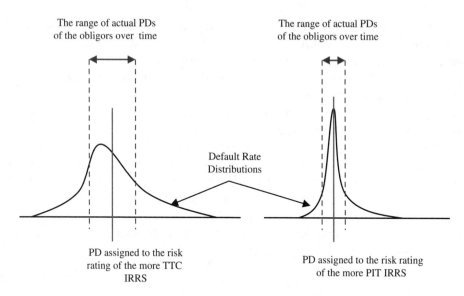

**Figure 2.4** Distributions of default rates under different risk rating philosophies.

default correlations. In validation tests (see Chapter 3), we need to incorporate a level of default correlation that is appropriate to the adopted risk rating philosophy, namely a higher default correlation in validating a TTC IRRS. PIT correlation can be interpreted as correlation conditional on all observable information, whereas TTC correlation is unconditional correlation. The subsequent section formally introduces this idea.

### Correlation Is Specific to Risk Rating Philosophy

In the literature, there have been lots of discussions on the relation between the level of PD and the rating philosophy. On the other hand, the relation between default correlation and rating philosophy has not been extensively studied. Banks need to estimate the correlation of PD (across obligors), which is also an important input of any internal credit risk model when they estimate economic capital. Miu and Ozdemir (2005) have shown that such a correlation parameter is rating philosophy specific. Given that a PIT rating is contingent on the current state of the economy whereas a TTC rating is not, the correlation in default risks under a PIT IRRS is lower than that of a TTC IRRS. Miu and Ozdemir (2005) interpret the former as a "conditional" correlation, while the latter is an "unconditional" correlation. The conditional correlation should be much smaller because a substantial component of the systematic movement in asset values is already in the information set by being able to observe the current state of the economy. Use of the relatively larger unconditional asset correlation can be interpreted as a way to "penalize" the TTC IRRS given the fact that we "pretend" the current state of the economy was not observed and thus we need to provide additional economic capital to cushion an uncertainty that has already been resolved.

The rest of this subsection is an excerpt of Miu and Ozdemir (2005) in which the idea is formally illustrated.[4] Let us consider the credit risks of two obligors under a simplified Merton model of which PD is solely governed by the stochastic variation of the asset value.[5] Suppose the change in asset value ($\Delta A_{i,t}$) of obligor $i$ from time $t - 1$ to $t$ is governed by both a systematic (i.e., economic-wide) component $S_t$ and an unsystematic (i.e., obligor-specific) component $U_{i,t}$:

$$\Delta A_{1,t} = \beta_1 \cdot S_t + U_{1,t}$$
$$\Delta A_{2,t} = \beta_2 \cdot S_t + U_{2,t}.$$

For ease of argument, let's assume the random variables $S_t$, $U_{1,t}$, and $U_{2,t}$ are independent and normally distributed with zero mean and unit variance. The constant $\beta_i$ therefore measures the sensitive of the obligor's asset value to the economic-wide systematic factor. Let $D_{i,t}$ be the *distance-to-default* of obligor $i$. That is, obligor $i$ defaults at time $t$ when $\Delta A_{i,t} < -D_{i,t}$. Without loss of generality, let's assume $\beta_1 = \beta_2 = 1$ and $D_{1,t} = D_{2,t} = D_t$.

At the beginning of the period, the probability of default of the obligors over the coming period can therefore be expressed as

$$\text{PD}_{i,t} = P\left(S_t + U_{i,t} < -D_t\right). \qquad \text{(Equation 2.1)}$$

Under a Merton's model like the Moody's KMV Credit Monitor, PD can be captured by the single measure of *standardized distance-to-default* (SDD), which is the ratio of distance-to-default to the respective standard deviation

$$\text{SDD}_{i,t} = \frac{D_t}{\left[\text{Var}\left(S_t + U_{i,t}\right)\right]^{0.5}} = \frac{D_t}{\sqrt{2}}. \qquad \text{(Equation 2.2)}$$

The joint default probability (JDP) can be expressed as

$$\text{JDP}_t = P\left(S_t + U_{1,t} < -D_t \cap S_t + U_{2,t} < -D_t\right). \qquad \text{(Equation 2.3)}$$

The corresponding asset correlation ($\rho$) can be computed as follows:

$$\rho = \frac{\text{Cov}(\Delta A_{1,t}, \Delta A_{2,t})}{\left[\text{Var}(\Delta A_{1,t}) \cdot \text{Var}(\Delta A_{1,t})\right]^{0.5}} = \frac{1}{2} = 0.5. \qquad \text{(Equation 2.4)}$$

Now suppose that right after the beginning of the period, the value of the systematic component $S_t$ is partly revealed (e.g., by observing the current state of the business cycle). And we can decompose the systematic component into its observable and unobservable parts

$$S_t = S_t^{\text{obs}} + S_t^{\text{unobs}}. \qquad \text{(Equation 2.5)}$$

Suppose the unobservable part $S_t^{\text{unobs}}$ is normally distributed with zero mean and a variance of 0.5. That is,

$$\text{Var}\left(S_t \mid S_t^{\text{obs}}\right) = \text{Var}\left(S_t^{\text{unobs}}\right) = 0.5. \qquad \text{(Equation 2.6)}$$

Now, consider the implications in using different risk rating philosophy. Under a PIT system, an obligor's risk rating might change based on this observation $S_t^{\text{obs}}$. For example, if $S_t^{\text{obs}}$ is sufficiently negative, both obligors will probably be reassigned to a lower risk rating. The revised PD of the obligors over the coming period can therefore be expressed as the following conditional probability:

$$\text{PD}_{i,t}^{\text{PIT}} = P\left(S_t^{\text{unobs}} + U_{i,t} < -D_t - S_t^{\text{obs}} \mid S_t^{\text{obs}}\right). \qquad \text{(Equation 2.7)}$$

The new SDD becomes

$$\text{SDD}_{i,t}^{\text{PIT}} = \frac{D_t + S_t^{\text{obs}}}{\left[\text{Var}\left(S_t^{\text{unobs}} + U_{i,t}\right)\right]^{0.5}} = \frac{D_t + S_t^{\text{obs}}}{\sqrt{1.5}}. \qquad \text{(Equation 2.8)}$$

And the new JDP can be expressed as the following conditional probability:

$$\begin{aligned} \text{JDP}_t^{\text{PIT}} = P(&S_t^{\text{unobs}} + U_{1,t} < -D_t - S_t^{\text{obs}} \cap S_t^{\text{unobs}} \\ &+ U_{2,t} < -D_t - S_t^{\text{obs}} \mid S_t^{\text{obs}}). \end{aligned} \qquad \text{(Equation 2.9)}$$

The corresponding conditional asset correlation ($\rho^{\text{PIT}}$) is as follows and is much smaller than its unconditional version (see Equation 2.4)[6]:

$$\rho^{\text{PIT}} = \frac{\text{Cov}\left(\Delta A_{1,t}, \Delta A_{2,t} \left| S_t^{\text{obs}}\right.\right)}{\left[\text{Var}\left(\Delta A_{1,t} \left| S_t^{\text{obs}}\right.\right) \cdot \text{Var}\left(\Delta A_{1,t} \left| S_t^{\text{obs}}\right.\right)\right]^{0.5}} = \frac{0.5}{1.5} = \frac{1}{3}. \qquad \text{(Equation 2.10)}$$

The situations are quite different under a TTC system. Here, after the information $S_t^{\text{obs}}$ is revealed, risk ratings of the obligors are unchanged if the information does not alter the credit risk outlook of these obligors at the trough of a business cycle. They will be assigned the same $\text{PD}^{\text{TTC}}$ (i.e., Equation 2.1) and having the same $\text{SDD}^{\text{TTC}}$ (i.e., Equation 2.2) as if the information is not revealed. The $\text{JDP}^{\text{TTC}}$ also remains the same as Equation 2.3 and asset correlation $\rho^{\text{TTC}}$ remains at 0.5 (see Equation 2.4).[7]

The following conclusions can be drawn by comparing the above findings regarding the two different rating philosophies:

- When the economy is in a booming state, using a TTC system will result in a smaller SDD and a larger unconditional asset correlation (and thus JPD) than will a PIT system. Credit capital requirement is therefore overstated.
- When the economy is in recession, it is also possible that a TTC system might still overstate capital requirement. It will be the case where, even though use of a TTC system results in a larger SDD, it is not sufficient to offset the effect due to the much larger unconditional asset correlation.

In the validation of default rate, it is therefore crucial that we are using consistent measures of PD and asset correlation. Specifically, if we are testing a TTC IRRS, we should be using $\text{PD}^{\text{TTC}}$ and unconditional asset correlation. On the other hand, if we are testing a PIT IRRS, we should be using $\text{PD}^{\text{PIT}}$ and the (smaller) conditional asset correlation. Using inconsistent measures could result in either wrongfully rejecting a true null or wrongfully accepting an alternative hypothesis. For example, in validating a PIT system, using the unconditional asset correlation may result in a confidence interval that is too wide and thus leading to the (wrong) endorsement of an observed default rate that is statistically unlikely given the assigned PD of the risk bucket (see also the section on "PD Backtesting" in Chapter 3).

The consistency between PD and asset correlation is also important when we develop a credit risk model. For example, if the model is measuring $\text{PD}^{\text{PIT}}$ (e.g., the Moody's KMV Expected Default Frequency [EDF]), portfolio value-at-risk should be calculated using asset correlation conditional on the current state of the economy.[8] If we however measure asset correlation unconditionally, which is typically the case in practice, economic capital requirement could be overstated. We do not believe this consistency requirement is fully addressed or well articulated in most of the proprietary credit risk models. Besides, the information about asset correlation can perhaps help us to validate the rating philosophy itself. We know we can never have either a "pure" TTC or a "pure" PIT system. We can examine the *ex post* (or implied) asset correlation to judge if the system is actually closer to a TTC or to a PIT system.

## LGD Philosophy

LGD philosophy, analogous to the risk rating philosophy for PD, defines the expected behavior of the assigned LGDs over a credit cycle.[9] Under a *cyclical* philosophy, LGD is intended to be synchronized with the cycle and thus changes with the cycle, whereas, under an *acyclical* philosophy, LGD remains constant over the cycle. Note that under the commonly used PIT philosophy, LGD is a cyclical measure reflecting the expected LGD over the coming, typically, 12 months. Conversely, under the TTC philosophy, LGD is acyclical and may define a *cycle-average* LGD, which is relatively constant over the cycle. Figure 2.5 illustrates a plot of the variation of assigned LGD (and thus the amount of capital assigned) over time for these two measures. Basel II requires bottom-of-the-cycle LGD, estimated over a "sufficiently" stressed period during which high default rates are observed. This is comparable with a PIT LGD during a market downturn (Figure 2.6).

Does the bottom-of-the-cycle LGD requirement necessitate the banks to adopt an acyclical LGD philosophy? It depends. If it is the motivation of Basel II to prevent cyclicality in the regulatory capital requirement, it warrants the adoption of an acyclical measure similar to the TTC philosophy.

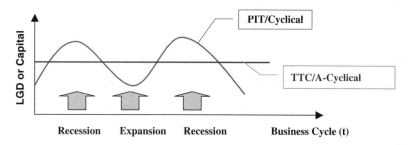

**Figure 2.5**  PIT versus TTC LGD.

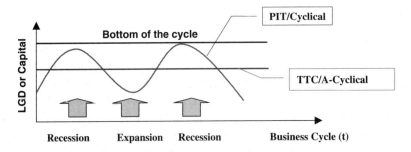

**Figure 2.6** Basel II requirement of bottom-of-the-cycle LGD.

However, if the requirement is solely for the compensation of the potential understatement of capital due to the lack of consideration of the correlation between PD and LGD in the Pillar I risk-weight function, we might as well fulfill this objective with a cyclical LGD philosophy. In this case, it becomes a calibration issue independent of the particular philosophy chosen. The question becomes: Given the adoption of a certain LGD philosophy, how should one assign a sufficiently conservative LGD value to achieve an appropriate capital number despite the fact that correlations are not captured? Figure 2.7 illustrates how conservatism can be incorporated under the TTC and PIT philosophy respectively. For example, under a cyclical LGD philosophy, we could consider increasing the PIT cycle-average LGD by a certain amount to cater for the lack of modeling of PD and LGD correlation (i.e., to the level of the dotted line labeled as "Conservative Cyclical" in Figure 2.7).[10] The resulting capital requirement, however, would still be cyclical. The amount of markup required can be ascertained by considering the impact of the correlations on the resulting capital requirement (e.g., via the stylized model as outlined in the section "Downturn LGD"). On the other hand, imposing a conservative acyclical LGD (i.e., the dotted line labeled as "Conservative A-Cyclical" in Figure 2.7) would result in a

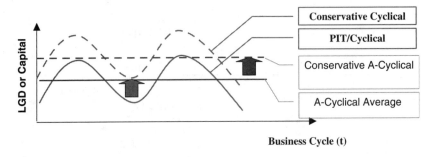

**Figure 2.7** Alternative conservative adjustments.

more stable but conservative capital requirement over the credit cycle. This issue is discussed in detail in Chapter 4.

The above theoretical argument makes a case for being able to use either the TTC or PIT philosophy while being conservative at the same time. However, our experience suggests most banks seem to adopt a fairly acyclical LGD philosophy where facility-level LGDs once set are not adjusted for any changes in the expectation of the LGD value over the next year. In most of the cases, LGDs are only adjusted for the changes in collaterals rather than for the changes in the outlook throughout the LGD cycle. In other words, most banks' philosophies seem to be closer to an acyclical measure within the spectrum of (cyclical vs. acyclical) LGD philosophies. Given that the adoption of a cyclical (acyclical) LGD philosophy will result in more (less) frequent changes in LGD ratings, we can check if the realized philosophy is consistent with the intended one by analyzing the observed LGD migration matrix (see the section "LGD Backtesting" in Chapter 3).

### EAD Philosophy

The above discussion about LGD philosophy also applies to EAD. Most banks seem to adopt an acyclical EAD philosophy where EAD once assigned to a particular facility is rarely reset according to the changing outlook throughout the credit cycle. Besides, similar to the downturn LGD requirement, there is a downturn EAD requirement. This is necessary to address the fact that the potential adverse relationship (i.e., positive correlation) between EAD and default rate is not captured in Pillar I risk-weight function (or most off-the-shelf economic capital models). There is empirical evidence suggesting that when PD increases, so does EAD. Omission of this adverse relationship would therefore result in the underestimation of capital requirement. To compensate for this underestimation, a markup should be applied to EAD. Primarily due to data constraints, downturn EAD has not been well studied, and most likely it is incorporated in the EAD estimation through an ad hoc conservative adjustment. Including this markup, EAD will likely to be adopted as a conservative acyclical measure, similar to LGD.

## LONG-RUN PD

### Introduction

As discussed earlier in this chapter, risk ratings are mapped to unique PDs so that all obligors in a certain risk rating would be assigned to the same PD

corresponding with that risk rating. Basel II requires that the PDs assigned
to the internal risk ratings reflect *long-run* default experience. These PDs are
therefore frequently referred to as *long-run PDs* (LRPDs), which can be
estimated by observing historical default rates of the risk ratings. There are
significant challenges in achieving a robust measure of LRPD. First, it is not
uncommon that there are very little or no internal default data, especially
for low PD risk ratings. Second, when there are internal default data, the
historical time series rarely covers a full credit cycle, not to mention reflecting a *long-run* situation. Moreover, the default rate time series naturally
covers the most recent years; how do we know the period we have data for
is "sufficiently stressed" relative to the long-run?

Many FIs estimate LRPDs by simply averaging the observed annual
internal default rates, if available. For low PD risk rating where there are no
internal data, the estimation of LRPD is frequently based on external
default data compiled by rating agencies. We need to be careful with both
approaches. First of all, the observed default rates are dictated by *both* PDs
and asset correlations (both serial and cross-sectional). When we infer
LRPDs from the observed default rates using internal data, we need to
account for the effect of correlations. We also need to quantify the average
stress level of the period, over which internal data are available, relative to
the long-run stress level. On the other hand, when external default rate
data are used for internal LRPD estimation, we need to adjust for the potential differences between the external and internal asset correlations. In the
rest of this section, we outline the main arguments and findings of Miu and
Ozdemir (2008a). The objectives of Miu and Ozdemir (2008a) are twofold.
They examine a number of efficient estimators of LRPD in utilizing the
historical default rates. To facilitate the validation of LRPD, the criteria for
optimal type I and II errors in a number of hypothesis tests are studied.
They show that LRPD is model-specific and propose an efficient LRPD estimator that is consistent with the underlying economic model of the Basel II
risk-weight function (i.e., a single-factor infinitely granular portfolio
model). The proposed estimator will therefore be appropriate for regulatory capital estimation under Basel II. Use of the simple average of historical default rates as an estimator is found to be prone to underestimation of
LRPD. They also show that information on cross-sectional and time-series
asset correlations can improve the efficiency of the proposed LRPD estimator. This is a considerable advantage as a number of previous studies do not
capture these cross-sectional and time dependencies in the estimation of
LRPD.[11] Moreover, the proposed approach enables the use of external
default rate data in supplementing the internal default rate data in attaining
more accurate estimates of LRPD.

Miu and Ozdemir (2008a) also examine alternative estimation methodologies of LRPD and their performances for finite number of borrowers (i.e., relaxing Basel's infinitely granular portfolio assumption). These LRPD estimators are considered to be more appropriate for the estimation of economic (credit) capital, where the advance simulation techniques are capable of modeling credit portfolios with specific number of borrowers. Simulation-based performance studies show that the performances of the proposed estimators are superior to that of their alternatives even under a number of small sample settings. Finally, Miu and Ozdemir (2008a) examine alternative ways of establishing confidence intervals (CIs) for the purpose of validating the *assigned* LRPD. In general, the CIs constructed based on the proposed maximum likelihood estimators result in fewer errors in the hypothesis tests.

### Estimation of LRPD for Basel II's Regulatory Capital Requirement

The meaning of LRPD and thus its estimation methodologies can be very different based on the economic model used in the formulation of the capital requirement. LRPDs obtained under an economic framework different from that of Basel II would not necessarily be suitable for the Basel II capital formula, even though the dependent structure of the default events is modeled appropriately. Consistency with the underlying economic model of Basel II ensures that the LRPDs estimated would be suitable for the capital requirement formula of Pillar I. We therefore need to formulate our LRPD estimation methodology consistently with the Basel II economic model, which is outlined below. Our purpose is to identify the parameter to be estimated as the appropriate LRPD input in computing the capital requirement consistent with the underlying assumptions.

Let us start with the single-factor model of the variations of asset values under Merton's structural model, which is also used by Vasicek (1987) in generating the loss distribution of a credit portfolio. This is the underlying economic model of Pillar I risk-weight function. We are interested in directly estimating LRPD and its statistical properties (e.g., confidence interval) given the observed default rates. We will, however, go one step further and incorporate a serially correlated systematic factor. Before we formally describe the model, let us examine some of the stylized characteristics through a couple of simulation exercises. In Figure 2.8, we plot the simulated default rates over a 25-year period by assuming an LRPD of 0.1%, while using different asset correlations (5% for Figure 2.8A and 25% for Figure 2.8B). Two observations are noteworthy. First of all, there is a higher (lower) chance of observing a default rate that is below

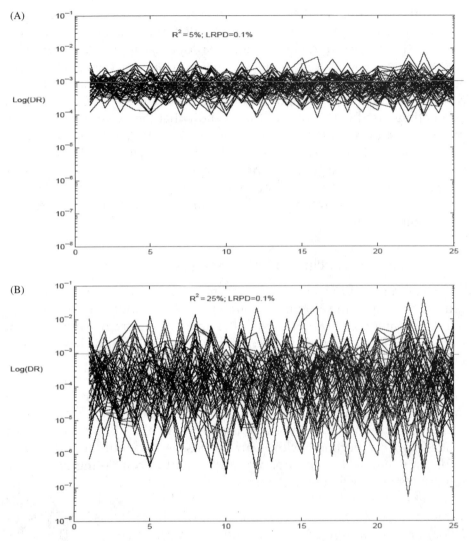

**Figure 2.8** Simulated default rates over a 25-year period by assuming an LRPD of 0.1%, while using different asset correlations (5% for Figure 2.8A and 25% for Figure 2.8B).

(above) the true LRPD of 0.1% (i.e., the level denoted by the horizontal lines in Figure 2.8). In other words, simple average of default rates over time tends to underestimate the true LRPD. Second, the likelihood of underestimation increases with the degree of asset correlation. An unbiased estimation of LRPD can only be attained by catering for the degree of asset correlation that is likely to be specific to an individual credit portfolio.

Let us consider Merton's (single-factor) structural model of credit risk, where $P_t$ is a normally distributed systematic risk factor and $R^2$ is the (cross-sectional) asset correlation[12]

$$p_t^i = R \times P_t + \sqrt{1 - R^2} \times e_t^i. \qquad \text{(Equation 2.11)}$$

Obligor $i$ defaults when $p^i$ becomes smaller than a threshold (i.e., default point, DP). Probability of default conditional on $P_t$ is therefore

$$\Pr\left[ p_t^i < \text{DP} \,|\, P_t \right] = \Phi\left( \frac{1}{\sqrt{1 - R^2}}(\text{DP} - R \cdot P_t) \right). \qquad \text{(Equation 2.12)}$$

*Unconditional* cumulative probability that number of defaults does not exceed $k_t$ (out of $n_t$ initial number of obligors) can be obtained by integrating over $P_t$,

$$F_{n_t}\left( \frac{k_t}{n_t} \right) = \sum_{j=0}^{k_t} \int_{-\infty}^{\infty} \Omega(j, n_t; P_t, R, \text{DP}) \, dP_t \qquad \text{(Equation 2.13)}$$

where

$$\Omega(k_t, n_t; P_t, R, \text{DP}) = \binom{n_t}{k_t} \times \left( \Phi\left( \frac{\text{DP} - R \cdot P_t}{\sqrt{1 - R^2}} \right) \right)^{k_t} \times \left( 1 - \Phi\left( \frac{\text{DP} - R \cdot P_t}{\sqrt{1 - R^2}} \right) \right)^{n_t - k_t}.$$

Limiting unconditional cumulative probability when $n_t$ approaches infinity (where $\theta_t = k_t / n_t$) is given by:

$$F_\infty(\theta_t) = \Phi\left( \frac{1}{R}\left( \sqrt{1 - R^2} \times \Phi^{-1}(\theta_t) - \text{DP} \right) \right). \qquad \text{(Equation 2.14)}$$

Reverting the last equation gives us the threshold default rate $\theta_{99.9\%}$, which will not be exceeded with a confidence level of 99.9%

$$\theta_{99.9\%} = \Phi\left( \frac{1}{\sqrt{1 - R^2}}\text{DP} + \frac{R}{\sqrt{1 - R^2}}\Phi^{-1}(0.999) \right). \qquad \text{(Equation 2.15)}$$

This is exactly the threshold default rate implicit in Pillar I risk-weight function (see BCBS [2004]). Moreover, to be consistent with the risk-weight function, the appropriate LRPD to be used as input should in fact be $\Phi(\text{DP})$, which is also the unconditional probability of default.

We can generalize the model, while staying within the Basel's economic model, to incorporate serial correlation of $P_t$.[13] For example, we can model $P_t$ such that it follows an autoregressive model of a single lag

$$P_t = \beta \times P_{t-1} + \sqrt{1 - \beta^2} \times \varepsilon_t \qquad \text{(Equation 2.16)}$$

where $\varepsilon_t$ is the i.i.d. normally distributed residuals, and $\beta$ is the lag-one serial correlation. Under this economic setup and assuming both $R^2$ and $\beta$ are known, the generalized least squares (GLS) estimator of $\Phi(DP)$ (i.e., LRPD) is in fact the maximum likelihood estimator (MLE).[14] It is asymptotically most efficient in the sense that it attains the *Cramér-Rao Lower Bound* as $T$ approaches infinity. The GLS estimator of LRPD is given by

$$\text{LRPD}_{\text{MLE}} = \Phi \left[ \frac{(1-\beta)\sqrt{1-R^2}}{(T-2)\beta^2 - 2(T-1)\beta + T} \right. \\ \left. \times \left( \Phi^{-1}(\theta_1) + \sum_{t=2}^{T-1} \Phi^{-1}(\theta_t) \cdot (1-\beta) + \Phi^{-1}(\theta_T) \right) \right]. \qquad \text{(Equation 2.17)}$$

A confidence interval for the LRPD may be constructed based on the sample variance of the GLS estimator

$$\text{CI}_{\text{MLE}} = \left[ L_{\text{MLE}}, U_{\text{MLE}} \right]$$

$$U_{\text{MLE}} = \Phi \left( \text{DP}_{\text{MLE}} + z_{\text{CL}} \times \frac{R \times \sqrt{1-\beta^2}}{\sqrt{(T-2)\beta^2 - 2(T-1)\beta + T}} \right) \qquad \text{(Equation 2.18)}$$

$$L_{\text{MLE}} = \Phi \left( \text{DP}_{\text{MLE}} - z_{\text{CL}} \times \frac{R \times \sqrt{1-\beta^2}}{\sqrt{(T-2)\beta^2 - 2(T-1)\beta + T}} \right)$$

where $z_{\text{CL}}$ is the critical value corresponding with the chosen confidence level under the standard normal distribution.

## Measuring the Performance of the Proposed LRPD Estimator

There is however no guarantee that the performance of the estimator is equally superior in a small sample setting (in terms of finite value of $T$).[15] In practice, we never have the luxury of observing an infinitely long historical default-rate time series. Banks rarely have internal historical default rates that go back more than 10 years.[16] In this section, through a number of simulation exercises, we investigate the performance of the MLE estimator of LRPD proposed by Miu and Ozdemir (2008a) under a few different scenarios of finite values of $T$ and compare the performance of the proposed estimator with those of the alternative estimators commonly used in practice. The estimators examined here are

1. **LRPD$_{ave}$**: Simple time-series average of observed default rates.
2. **LRPD$_{mod}$**: The LRPD resulting in the distribution of the average default rates attaining a mode that is equal to the simple average of the observed default rates. It was considered by the Canadian financial institutions regulator, the Office of the Superintendent of Financial Institutions (OSFI), to serve as a conservative estimator of LRPD. It incorporates the difference between the mean and mode of the distribution of the average default rates. For details, please refer to OSFI (2004).
3. **LRPD$_{MLE1}$**: MLE estimator proposed by Miu and Ozdemir (2008a).
4. **LRPD$_{MLE2}$**: MLE estimator proposed by Miu and Ozdemir (2008a), but assuming credit risk is time-independent (i.e., $\beta = 0$).

Steps of the performance test

1. We simulate time-series of default rates based on the infinitely granular single-factor model of the Basel II risk-weight formula by using the representative parametric values presented in Table 2.1. For each of the four cases, we simulate 5,000 time-paths of default rates. Each time-path represents a possible realization of default rates from which LRPD is estimated in practice.

**TABLE 2.1**

Parametric Values of Simulation Exercises

|                | Case 1 | Case 2 | Case 3 | Case 4 |
|----------------|--------|--------|--------|--------|
| True LRPD (%)  | 0.5    | 2.5    | 0.5    | 2.5    |
| $R^2$ (%)      | 20     | 20     | 20     | 20     |
| $\beta$ (%)    | 15     | 15     | 15     | 15     |
| $T$ (years)    | 12     | 12     | 20     | 20     |

2. We estimate the LRPDs using each realized time-path of the simulated default rates (i.e., one LRPD estimate per simulated path) and generate a distribution of these estimated LRPDs. We then compare the distributions of estimated LRPDs with the actual LRPD used in the simulation. The latter can therefore be interpreted as the *true* LRPD. This procedure is repeated using all the four LRPD estimators. An ideal estimator should be *unbiased* (i.e., the sample mean of the estimated LRPDs is equal to the true LRPD), while at the same time there are equal likelihoods of overestimating and underestimating the true LRPD (i.e., the sample median of the estimated LRPDs is equal to the true LRPD). Moreover, we are looking for the most efficient estimator (i.e., an estimator with the smallest sample standard deviation). We also seek for the smallest *type I error* in hypothesis tests (i.e., the probability of rejecting a true null).

Summary statistics of the sample distributions of the estimators across the 5,000 simulations are reported in Table 2.2.

The benefit of using the more efficient MLE estimators can be seen by comparing the sample standard deviations. Even in these small sample settings, the distributions of the MLE are much *tighter* than those of the other two estimators. For example, in Case 3, the standard deviation of $LRPD_{MLE1}$ is about 18% (22%) lower than that of $LRPD_{ave}$ ($LRPD_{mod}$). In other words, when $LRPD_{ave}$ and $LRPD_{mod}$ are used, there is a higher chance that the estimates are significantly different from the true LRPD. The use of the MLE estimators also allow for a more balanced chance of overestimation versus underestimation of the true LRPD. $LRPD_{ave}$ is not considered to be a conservative estimator, as the chances of underestimation are consistently higher than are those of overestimation. On the other hand, $LRPD_{mod}$ might be too conservative as the chances of underestimation are always less than 50%. In Figure 2.9, we plot the histograms of the LRPD estimates obtained from $LRPD_{ave}$ (Figure 2.9A) and $LRPD_{MLE1}$ (Figure 2.9B) via a simulation exercise where the true LRPD is 10 bps. The distribution of $LRPD_{MLE1}$ is tighter (i.e., more efficient) around the true LRPD of 10 bps (the vertical lines in Figure 2.9A and 2.9B) than that of $LRPD_{ave}$. Besides, the chance of $LRPD_{ave}$ underestimating the true LRPD is higher than that of overestimating. The chance of overestimation versus underestimation of the true LRPD is however more balanced when $LRPD_{MLE1}$ is used.

Figure 2.10 plots the ratio of the sample standard deviation of $LRPD_{MLE1}$ to that of $LRPD_{ave}$ against the length of the historical time-series (i.e., $T$). As expected, the benefit of using $LRPD_{MLE1}$ increases with $T$. Even

**T A B L E   2.2**

Summary Statistics of the Distribution of the Estimators of LRPD (in %)

| Case 1: True LRPD = 0.5%; $T$ = 12 years | | | | |
|---|---|---|---|---|
| | $LRPD_{ave}$ | $LRPD_{mod}$ | $LRPD^{17}_{MLE1}$ | $LRPD_{MLE2}$ |
| Mean | 0.508 | 0.673 | **0.550** | 0.550 |
| Median | 0.439 | 0.597 | **0.503** | 0.503 |
| Percent of times LRPD is underestimated (%) | 59 | 33 | **49** | 49 |
| Standard deviation | 0.287 | 0.320 | **0.239** | 0.240 |

| Case 2: True LRPD = 2.5%; $T$ = 12 years | | | | |
|---|---|---|---|---|
| | $LRPD_{ave}$ | $LRPD_{mod}$ | $LRPD_{MLE1}$ | $LRPD_{MLE2}$ |
| Mean | 2.533 | 2.900 | **2.658** | 2.658 |
| Median | 2.342 | 2.705 | **2.512** | 2.510 |
| Percent of times LRPD is underestimated (%) | 56 | 41 | **49** | 49 |
| Standard deviation | 1.024 | 1.080 | **0.922** | 0.923 |

| Case 3: True LRPD = 0.5%; $T$ = 20 years | | | | |
|---|---|---|---|---|
| | $LRPD_{ave}$ | $LRPD_{mod}$ | $LRPD_{MLE1}$ | $LRPD_{MLE2}$ |
| Mean | 0.504 | 0.618 | **0.528** | 0.528 |
| Median | 0.463 | 0.575 | **0.504** | 0.504 |
| Percent of times LRPD is underestimated (%) | 57 | 35 | **49** | 49 |
| Standard deviation | 0.218 | 0.228 | **0.178** | 0.178 |

| Case 4: True LRPD = 2.5%; $T$ = 20 years | | | | |
|---|---|---|---|---|
| | $LRPD_{ave}$ | $LRPD_{mod}$ | $LRPD_{MLE1}$ | $LRPD_{MLE2}$ |
| Mean | 2.515 | 2.692 | **2.587** | 2.587 |
| Median | 2.410 | 2.586 | **2.517** | 2.514 |
| Percent of times LRPD is underestimated (%) | 55 | 45 | **49** | 49 |
| Standard deviation | 0.782 | 0.796 | **0.700** | 0.701 |

when $T$ is short (e.g., less than 7 years), the variation of the estimator can still be materially reduced by using $LRPD_{MLE1}$.

In Figure 2.11, the same ratio of the sample standard deviations is now plotted against the true LRPD. The benefit of using $LRPD_{MLE1}$ is more significant in the estimation of the LRPD of borrowers of relatively high credit quality (i.e., low LRPD).

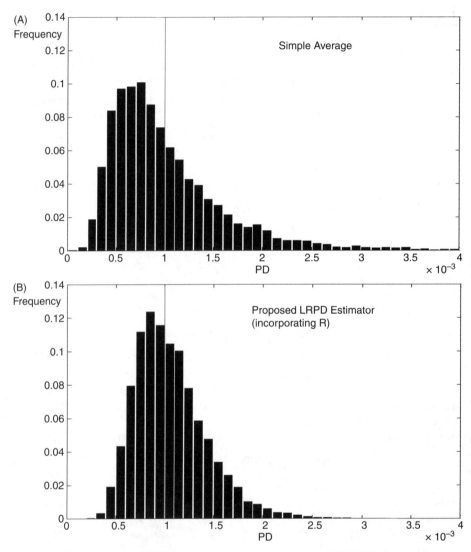

**Figure 2.9** Histograms of LRPD estimates obtained from (A) LRPD$_{ave}$ and (B) LRPD$_{MLE1}$ via a simulation exercise where true LRPD is 10 bps.

We summarize the observations as follows:

- There is a slight upward bias in terms of the sample means of the LRPD$_{MLE1}$ especially when historical data series is short.
- Based on the sample medians, there are always almost exactly equal chances that LRPD$_{MLE1}$ overestimates or underestimates the true LRPD.

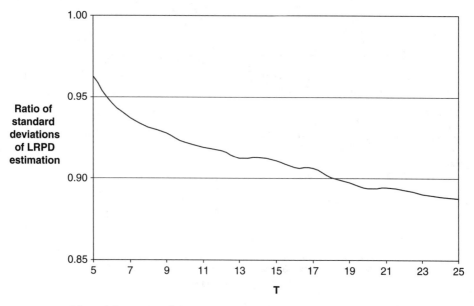

**Figure 2.10** Plot of the ratio of the sample standard deviation of $LRPD_{MLE1}$ to that of $LRPD_{ave}$ against $T$ (LRPD [i.e., $\Phi(DP)$], $R^2$, and $\beta$ are equal to 2.5%, 20%, and 15%, respectively).

- There is always a higher chance that $LRPD_{ave}$ will underestimate rather than overestimate the true LRPD, which therefore suggests simple average may not produce a conservative estimator of LRPD.
- On the other hand, the chance of overestimation is always higher than 50% for $LRPD_{mod}$. This is not surprising given that this estimator involves an upward adjustment from the mode to the mean of the positively skewed distribution of average default rates. $LRPD_{mod}$ may therefore be too conservative.
- The chance of underestimation (overestimation) of $LRPD_{ave}$ ($LRPD_{mod}$) is the highest when the true LRPD is low and the historical data series is short.
- Comparing the sample statistics of $LRPD_{MLE1}$ and $LRPD_{MLE2}$, the benefit of knowing and modeling for the serial correlation of the systematic factor is minimal when $T$ is large. There is, however, marginal improvement of efficiency in using $LRPD_{MLE1}$ rather than $LRPD_{MLE2}$ when $T$ is small.

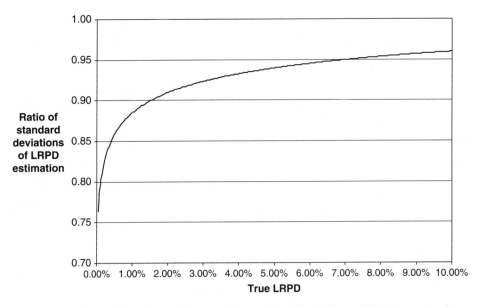

**Figure 2.11** Plot of the ratio of the sample standard deviation of $\mathrm{LRPD}_{\mathrm{MLE1}}$ to that of $\mathrm{LRPD}_{\mathrm{ave}}$ against the true LRPD ($T$ is equal to 12 years, and $R^2$ and $\beta$ are again equal to 20% and 15%, respectively).

## Validating Existing LRPDs

Many banks already assigned LRPDs to their IRRSs based on alternative methodologies and sometimes educated guesses in the absence of sufficient internal data. They will need to validate their LRPDs for Basel II compliance. In this section, we examine alternative ways of establishing the CIs in hypothesis testing of the current LRPDs. More specifically, we examine the validity of the proposed CIs given in Equation 2.18 for hypothesis tests on LRPD in small sample settings based on the following procedure:

1. Conduct the same simulation exercises described above to generate time-paths of default rates.
2. For each simulated time-path of default rates, construct the 95% CI (based on Equation 2.18) of a *two-tail* test of LRPD and check if the true null (i.e., LRPD of either 0.5% or 2.5%) lies outside of the interval and thus is rejected. We then count the percentage of simulations that lead to a rejection.

3. Measure the type I error of the *one-tail* test where the true null is higher than the upper bound of the CI, in which case the financial institutions may wrongfully reduce the assigned LRPD. We measure type I error of this one-tail test at the 97.5% confidence level.

We consider a total of four ways in establishing the CI:

1. CI ($CI_{MLE1}$) around $LRPD_{MLE1}$ based on Equation 2.18.
2. CI ($CI_{MLE2}$) around $LRPD_{MLE2}$ based on Equation 2.18 but assuming time-independent systematic factor (i.e., $\beta = 0$).
3. CI ($CI_{ave}$) around $LRPD_{ave}$ by assuming the standard deviation of the estimator being equal to the sample standard deviation of the observed default rates over the sample period divided by the square root of $T$. If the systematic factor is time-independent, *central limit theorem* ensures $CI_{ave}$ converges to the true CI as $T$ approaches infinity. It is likely to be too narrow if the systematic factor is in fact serially correlated and $T$ is finite.
4. CI ($CI_{mod}$) around $LRPD_{mod}$ by assuming a standard deviation of the estimator being equal to that of $LRPD_{ave}$ described above.

The simulated type I errors are given in Table 2.3.

**T A B L E  2.3**

Simulated Type I Errors

| Panel A: Two-tail Test at 95% Confidence Level | | | | |
|---|---|---|---|---|
| | $CI_{ave}$ (%) | $CI_{mod}$ (%) | $CI_{MLE1}^{17}$ (%) | $CI_{MLE2}$ (%) |
| Case 1: True LRPD = 0.5%; $T = 12$ | 23.7 | 16.8 | 4.8 | 9.0 |
| Case 2: True LRPD = 2.5%; $T = 12$ | 18.6 | 15.5 | 4.8 | 9.0 |
| Case 3: True LRPD = 0.5%; $T = 20$ | 19.4 | 11.4 | 5.3 | 9.0 |
| Case 4: True LRPD = 2.5%; $T = 20$ | 14.9 | 12.4 | 5.3 | 9.0 |

| Panel B: One-tail Test at 97.5% Confidence Level | | | | |
|---|---|---|---|---|
| | $CI_{ave}$ (%) | $CI_{mod}$ (%) | $CI_{MLE1}$ (%) | $CI_{MLE2}$ (%) |
| Case 1: True LRPD = 0.5%; $T = 12$ | 23.2 | 10.8 | 2.1 | 4.0 |
| Case 2: True LRPD = 2.5%; $T = 12$ | 17.3 | 11.3 | 2.1 | 4.0 |
| Case 3: True LRPD = 0.5%; $T = 20$ | 19.0 | 8.1 | 2.6 | 4.4 |
| Case 4: True LRPD = 2.5%; $T = 20$ | 13.8 | 10.2 | 2.6 | 4.4 |

Here are some observations: $CI_{MLE1}$ produces the smallest type I errors.[18] $CI_{ave}$ is too narrow, especially when LRPD is small and $T$ is short. Note that the majority of the rejection cases are those where the correct LRPD is wrongfully rejected believing it is statistically too high. This is a particular source of concern with the use of $CI_{ave}$. The performance of $CI_{mod}$ is better than that of $CI_{ave}$, even though the resulting type I errors are still material. $CI_{MLE2}$ where serial correlation is omitted results in materially larger errors, especially when $T$ is short.

### The Use of External Data together with Internal Data in Estimating LRPD: A Joint-Estimation Methodology

In this section, we examine the joint-estimation methodology proposed in Miu and Ozdemir (2008a). This methodology allows us to supplement the lack of internal default rate data (rarely covering a full credit cycle) with the more readily available external default rate data (covering multiple credit cycles) compiled by the rating agencies. The efficiency of the resulting LRPD estimator can be enhanced by conducting the estimation in a joint fashion together with the external data. Miu and Ozdemir (2008a) also use this approach to measure the *average stress level* over the period in which internal default rate data is available. It provides a tool for FIs to justify that the period over which the LRPDs are estimated is *sufficiently stressed* relative to the long-run.

Before we examine the joint-estimation methodology in detail, we need to be aware of the potential differences in the following characteristics between the bank's credit portfolio and those of the external data.

1. Regional/country composition;
2. Industry composition; and
3. Asset correlation (i.e., $R^2$) as a measure of the sensitivity to the systematic factor.

Any differences in regional/country and industry composition can be dealt with by matching the bank's portfolio composition, in terms of region and industry type, as closely as possible in the construction of the external default rate time series.[19] Any difference in asset correlations is explicitly catered for in the following joint-estimation methodology.

Miu and Ozdemir (2008a) consider borrowers within a certain *internal* risk rating having the same default risk and are related to the single *internal* systematic factor $P_t$ via Equation 2.19,

$$p_t^i = R \times P_t + \sqrt{1 - R^2} \times e_t^i.$$

(Equation 2.19)

Parameter $R^2$ is the *internal* pairwise correlation in asset values. The borrower defaults when $p_t$ is less than the default point (DP). They also consider the asset values $p_{x,t}$ of borrowers making up the *external* risk rating are related to an *external* systematic factor $P_{x,t}$ through Equation 2.20,

$$p_{x,t}^i = R_x \times P_{x,t} + \sqrt{1 - R_x^2} \times e_{x,t}^i. \qquad \text{(Equation 2.20)}$$

The idiosyncratic risks $e_t$ and $e_{x,t}$ are independent and follow the standard normal distribution, whereas the two systematic factors $P_t$ and $P_{x,t}$ are likely to be correlated with correlation coefficient, $\rho$. The borrower defaults when $p_{x,t}$ is less than the default point (DP$_x$) specific to this external portfolio. The external portfolio may also have a different pairwise correlation ($R_x^2$).

The joint model can be estimated by MLE using historical time-series of default rates $\theta_t$ and $\theta_{x,t}$ of the internal and external portfolios. We can simultaneously solve for the LRPDs of both portfolios; that is, $\Phi(DP)$ and $\Phi(DP_x)$. Miu and Ozdemir (2008a) show that the MLE estimators are respectively,[20],[21]

$$\text{LRPD}_{\text{MLE}} = \Phi\left( \frac{1}{T}\left( \sqrt{1 - R^2} \sum_{t=1}^{T} \Phi^{-1}(\theta_t) + \frac{R \cdot \rho}{R_x}\left( T \cdot \Phi^{-1}(\text{LRPD}_{\text{MLE},x}) \right.\right.\right.$$

$$\left.\left.\left. - \sqrt{1 - R_x^2} \sum_{t=1}^{T} \Phi^{-1}(\theta_{x,t}) \right) \right) \right). \qquad \text{(Equation 2.21)}$$

$$\text{LRPD}_{\text{MLE},x} = \Phi\left( \frac{\sqrt{1 - R_x^2}}{T_x}\left( \sum_{t=1}^{T_x} \Phi^{-1}(\theta_{x,t}) \right) \right). \qquad \text{(Equation 2.22)}$$

In this illustration, the internal and external samples are only partially overlapping. We only observe $\theta_{x,t}$ from $t = 1$ to $T_x - T$, whereas we observe both $\theta_t$ and $\theta_{x,t}$ from $t = T_x - T + 1$ to $T_x$.[22] Miu and Ozdemir (2008a) also derive the corresponding confidence intervals of the MLEs:

$$\text{CI}_{\text{MLE}} = \left[ L_{\text{MLE}}, U_{\text{MLE}} \right]$$

$$U_{\text{MLE}} = \Phi\left( DP_{\text{MLE}} + z_{\text{CL}} \times \frac{R\sqrt{1 - \rho^2}}{\sqrt{T}} \right) \qquad \text{(Equation 2.23)}$$

$$L_{\text{MLE}} = \Phi\left( DP_{\text{MLE}} - z_{\text{CL}} \times \frac{R\sqrt{1 - \rho^2}}{\sqrt{T}} \right)$$

$$CI_{MLE,x} = \left[ L_{MLE,x}, U_{MLE,x} \right]$$

$$U_{MLE,x} = \Phi\left( DP_{MLE,x} + z_{CL} \times \frac{R_x}{\sqrt{T_x + T\rho^2/(1-\rho^2)}} \right),$$

$$L_{MLE,x} = \Phi\left( DP_{MLE,x} - z_{CL} \times \frac{R_x}{\sqrt{T_x + T\rho^2/(1-\rho^2)}} \right)$$

(Equation 2.24)

where $z_{CL}$ is the critical value corresponding with a specific confidence level under the standard normal distribution. Statistically, the benefit of jointly estimating with the (partially) overlapping external default rate data is a more efficient LRPD estimator (Equation 2.21) and a tighter CI (Equation 2.23).

### Example
Suppose a bank only has six years of internal default rate data from 1999 to 2004 (see Table 2.4). Based on Equation 2.17, the LRPD estimate is 2.783%, which is obtained utilizing only these internal default rate data.[23] The bank can however improve its LRPD estimation by supplementing the internal data with a longer time-series of external default rate data and by adopting the joint-estimation method mentioned in this section. With the longer external default rate data, it can also measure the average stress level over the period 1999–2004 and compare it with the long-run average level. It can then see if the LRPD estimate obtained from the six-year period (which is unlikely to cover a full credit cycle) is in fact a prudent long-run credit risk measure. In achieving these objectives, the bank also collects Standard & Poor's speculative-grade default rates from 1981 to 2004, which serves as the long-run benchmark (also reported in Table 2.4).

For the purpose of illustration, we assume $R^2 = 0.20$, $R_x^2 = 0.10$, and $\rho = 0.50$ and compute the MLEs of the LRPDs and the corresponding CIs based on the above joint-estimation approach (i.e., using Equations 2.21 to 2.24). The results are reported in Table 2.5 together with those obtained *separately* (i.e., using Equations 2.17 and 2.18). Besides obtaining a more accurate point estimate of LRPD, joint estimation also allows for a more precise estimate (i.e., tighter CI) and thus enhances the power of the hypothesis tests conducted on the LRPD.

In Figure 2.12, we plot the *most-likely* systematic factor $P_t$ and $P_{x,t}$ over the sample period, which are estimated together with the LRPDs. Default rate is negatively related to these systematic factors. The higher the systematic (asset) value, the lower is the probability of default of the

**TABLE 2.4**

Internal and External Annual Default Rate Data

|      | Internal Risk Rating (%) | Standard & Poor's Speculative Grade (%) |
|------|--------------------------|------------------------------------------|
| 1981 | —     | 0.62  |
| 1982 | —     | 4.41  |
| 1983 | —     | 2.96  |
| 1984 | —     | 3.29  |
| 1985 | —     | 4.37  |
| 1986 | —     | 5.71  |
| 1987 | —     | 2.80  |
| 1988 | —     | 3.99  |
| 1989 | —     | 4.16  |
| 1990 | —     | 7.87  |
| 1991 | —     | 10.67 |
| 1992 | —     | 5.85  |
| 1993 | —     | 2.20  |
| 1994 | —     | 2.19  |
| 1995 | —     | 3.62  |
| 1996 | —     | 1.83  |
| 1997 | —     | 2.15  |
| 1998 | —     | 3.22  |
| 1999 | 1.15  | 5.16  |
| 2000 | 3.95  | 7.00  |
| 2001 | 4.36  | 10.51 |
| 2002 | 3.75  | 7.12  |
| 2003 | 1.30  | 5.55  |
| 2004 | 0.10  | 2.30  |

**TABLE 2.5**

Estimated LRPD of Internal and External Portfolio[24]

|                     | Bank's Internal Risk Rating | | Standard & Poor's Speculative Grade | |
|---------------------|---------|------------|---------|------------|
|                     | Jointly | Separately | Jointly | Separately |
| LRPD$_{MLE}$ (%)    | **2.086** | 2.783    | **4.827** | 4.827    |
| 95% CI              |         |            |         |            |
| Upper (%)           | **3.641** | 5.070    | **6.046** | 6.096    |
| Lower (%)           | **0.531** | 0.496    | **3.609** | 3.559    |

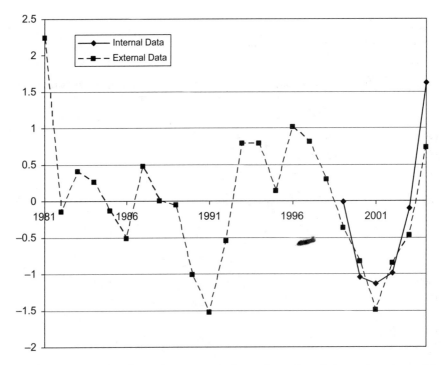

**Figure 2.12** Time-series plots of systematic factor based on joint estimation with both internal and external default rates.

borrowers under the single-factor models. The full sample period 1981–2004 serves as the benchmark long-run realizations of default rates over multiple credit cycles. The population mean of the systematic factor $P_{x,t}$ over this full sample period is zero, thus representing a *cycle-neutral* level of default risk. During the subsample of 1999 to 2004, the sample mean of the systematic factor $P_{x,t}$ is –0.548. We can therefore conclude that the average level of default risk over this six-year period was higher than the long-run average. This observation is consistent with the difference in the LRPD estimates of the bank's internal risk rating obtained in the "jointly" and "separately" estimation approaches (see Table 2.5). The lower LRPD estimate of the internal risk rating obtained in the joint estimation approach (i.e., 2.086%) is a more accurate representation of the cycle-neutral situation than that obtained when we ignore the external default data (i.e., 2.783%). We cater for the difference in the average systematic default risk between the subsample and the full sample in the estimation of the former but not in the latter.

### Estimating LRPDs for Finite Number of Initial Borrowers (for Uses Outside of Basel II Framework such as in the Computation of Economic Capital and Risk-Based Pricing)

Thus far, we have considered the most efficient estimator of LRPD and its CI within the economic model underlying the Basel II capital formula. Our purpose was to find the most appropriate parameters for the Basel II capital formula. Now we would like to consider situations where the infinite-granularity assumption is violated—like we see in practice. LRPD obtained from relaxing the *infinitely granular portfolio* assumption would arguably be more appropriate for the estimation of economic credit capital, where typically, the advance simulation techniques are capable of modeling credit portfolios of finite numbers of borrowers.

Miu and Ozdemir (2008a) consider *exact* MLE LRPD estimator under the assumption of finite number of initial obligors. It is essentially the *probit-normal Bernoulli mixture* model of Frey and McNeil (2003). Unlike in the case of infinite number of obligors, closed-form solution of the MLE estimator is unavailable, and one has to resort to numerical integrations in evaluating the point estimate and the corresponding confidence interval. Miu and Ozdemir (2008a) compare the efficiency of this exact but computationally intensive estimator with that of the previously derived closed-form LRPD estimator in recovering the *true* LRPD. The latter is now only an *approximate* estimator given the fact that the number of obligors is not infinite any more. It is therefore always inferior to the former. However, by what extent it is inferior will depend on the characteristics of the estimation problem on hand. Through a number of simulation exercises, Miu and Ozdemir (2008a) conclude that in the cases of relatively high LRPD (e.g., 2.0%) and large number of borrowers (e.g., equal to or more than 100), the marginal benefit of the former over the much more analytically tractable estimator of the latter might not be worthwhile for the effort of conducting the required computationally intensive analysis. Finally, Miu and Ozdemir (2008a) also examine and compare the potential errors in a number of validation tests when alternative methodologies are adopted in establishing the CIs of the estimated LPRD under finite number of initial obligors.

## Summary

In this section, we examined alternative methodologies in estimating LRPD from time-series of historical default rates. We considered efficient estimators of LRPD incorporating both the cross-sectional and serial asset correlation observed in practice and at the same time consistent with Basel's infinitely granular portfolio assumption. We compared the performances of the proposed estimators and demonstrate that the proposed estimators outperform the alternatives in most of the cases even in small sample settings. The results of the simulation exercises also suggest the simple averaging of the historical default rates as an estimator of LRPD is prone to the underestimation of the true LRPD. We also considered a methodology that enables us to supplement internal data with external data, which improves the accuracy of the LRPD estimate. Moreover, we examined alternative ways of establishing CIs for the validation of preassigned LRPDs. Finally, we summarized the findings of Miu and Ozdemir (2008a) in establishing efficient LRPD estimators when the infinite-granular assumption is violated. Such LRPD estimates are deemed to be more appropriate for the estimation of economic (credit) capital, where the advance simulation techniques typically encompass specific (i.e., finite) number of borrowers in their economic capital estimations.

## DOWNTURN LGD

### Introduction

High default rate periods tend to be accompanied by high LGD periods, intensifying the losses during these periods. During the estimation of portfolio losses for economic and regulatory capital requirement, this phenomenon can be accounted for by incorporating the correlations between PDs and LGDs. Basel II Pillar I risk-weight function (as well as most commercially available economic capital estimation models), however, assumes PD and LGD are independent, which may result in an underestimation of the capital requirement. One way to compensate for this while still utilizing the Pillar I risk-weight formula is to increase the LGD estimation, which serves as one of the inputs of the formula. Basel II adopts a principles-based approach in addressing the need of incorporating downturn LGD. Paragraph 468 of BCBS (2004) requires that downturn conditions and adverse dependencies between default rates and recovery rates, if any, be identified. This information should be incorporated in the estimation process so as to produce LGD parameter that is consistent with the identified downturn conditions. LGD estimation incorporating this adjustment is referred to as *downturn LGD*.

The downturn LGD requirement has been heavily debated in the industry. There is however little consensus with respect to the appropriate methods for incorporating the downturn conditions in the estimation of LGD. Some banks, concerned with excessive conservatism and implementation difficulties, take the view that default-weighted average LGD should be conservative enough. To our knowledge, this view has not been substantiated and accepted by the regulators. To shed some light on the issue, we approach the problem from three different angles.

1. Method 1: We can identify stressed periods from (internal or external) historical default rates; we then compute the default-weighted average LGD over these stressed periods and compare with that computed over all time periods.

2. Method 2: Using a *stressable* LGD model (e.g., Standard & Poor's LossStats), we can estimate the *stressed* LGD using default rate corresponding with the stressed periods identified as in Method 1. Default rates are an input to the LossStats Model in the estimation of LGDs. In this method, by inputting *stressed default rates* to the model, we generate stressed LGDs. (We can also stress LGDs based on macroeconomic factors; see the "Stress Testing" section for further discussion).

3. Method 3: We can explicitly incorporate PD and LGD correlation in a capital model and compute how much increase in mean LGD is required to make up for the lack of correlation in the Pillar I risk-weight function.

These three different approaches will provide three different answers, setting some boundaries for the problem at hand. We can also consider the U.S. Notice of Proposed Rulemaking (NPR) formula of 5% + 95% × Default-Weighted Average LGD for comparison purpose. By addressing the problem with different approaches, banks become well-prepared in justifying the selected downturn LGD to the regulators. Typically, the resulting markup of Method 3 is larger than that of Method 2, which is in turn larger than that of Method 1. These relative sizes of the markups are quite intuitive. In Method 1, because we have internal LGD data that typically span less than a single cycle, we quantify how much average LGD increases during a single downturn. In Method 2, we are able to look at multiple credit cycles (as default rate is available for multiple cycles unlike LGDs), and the LGD model allows us to quantify the effect on LGD. But only in Method 3 is the effect of correlations extrapolated into the extreme tail of the loss distribution where capital-at-risk is measured at. Therefore, the downturn LGD obtained from Method 3 is likely to be the most economically defendable, as it directly calibrates to the value-at-risk (VaR), which serves as the underlying risk measure in formulating Basel II regulatory capital requirement. Method 3 accounts for the lack of PD and LGD correlation in the Basel II formula, as well as in most of the off-the-shelf models for economic capital estimation. Method 3 is based on the research conducted by Miu and Özdemir (2006).

## Data Requirement

To accomplish the estimations of downturn LGD, both time-series and cross-sectional historical LGD (i.e., recovery rate) and default rate data are required for each segment of the credit portfolio under consideration.

## Definition of LGD

LGD is defined as one minus the ratio of the present value of workout recoveries to the book value at default

$$LGD = 1 - \frac{\sum_{i=1}^{n} \frac{CF_{t_i}}{(1+d)^{t_i}}}{\text{Book Value at Default}} \qquad \text{(Equation 2.25)}$$

where $CF_{t_i}$ is the net recovered cash flow at time $t_i$ after default; $d$ is the discount rate as described below; and $n$ is the total number of cash flows received during the whole recovery process.[25] Theoretically, LGD can also be estimated by using the price of the defaulted instrument observed in the secondary market immediately after default. An alternative definition of LGD is therefore

$$LGD = 1 - \frac{\text{Market Price after Default}}{\text{Book Value at Default}}. \qquad \text{(Equation 2.26)}$$

The latter is used in the absence of workout recoveries or when there is very limited recovery data within the particular segment.

The discount rate $d$ in Equation 2.25 should incorporate risk premium commensurate with the inherent recovery risk. The higher is the uncertainty of future recoveries, the larger should be the discount rate. Empirical studies (refer to Chapter 1, Section *"Discount Rate for Workout Recoveries: An Empirical Study"*) suggest higher discount rate for unsecured facilities, IT sector, and for defaults during recessionary periods.

## Method 1

We can estimate the downturn LGD by observing internal (or external) historical LGD data during periods of economic downturn. Downturn LGD is then the default-weighted average LGD (i.e., simple average) over these periods. There can be more than one way to define a marketwide economic downturn. For example, it can be defined as those periods (e.g., quarters) where the seasonally adjusted GDP growth rate is lower than the long-run average. Given that we are interested in measuring credit risk, historical default rate is a more direct measure of the credit risk cycle. Specifically, periods with relatively high default rates suggest credit risk downturn. In Method 1, downturn periods may be defined as those years where the default rates are greater than the long-term average default rate. In the identification of stress periods, either the banks' internal default rate data or external default rate data (e.g., extracted from Standard & Poor's CreditPro) may be used.

We prefer identifying the stress years based on the speculative-grade default rates for two reasons. First, default data are more readily available due to higher PD, and second, the speculative-grade default rates are more sensitive to changes in credit condition. Alternatively, we could also look at the downgrade ratios for the investment grade, but we would have to worry about the potential difference in risk rating philosophy between the external and internal default rates, as under a through-the-cycle philosophy, migration rates are less than those under a point-in-time philosophy.

Let us consider an example. Suppose we tabulate the internal historical LGD data from 1993 to 2002 for all defaulted instruments of a certain segment in Table 2.6, and Standard & Poor's speculative-grade default rates in 1993 and 1999–2002 are found to be higher than the long-term average default rate.[26] Downturn LGD can therefore be estimated by calculating the simple average of all the bold LGD numbers, which is found to be equal to 59%. That is,

$$\text{Downturn LGD} = \frac{\displaystyle\sum_{y=93,99-02} \sum_{i=1}^{8} \text{LGD}_{y,i}}{40} = 59\%. \qquad \text{(Equation 2.27)}$$

The above analysis can therefore be repeated using the historical LGD data of other segments to produce the respective downturn LGDs.

## Method 2

We demonstrate the use of Method 2 by using Standard & Poor's LossStats Model to generate conditional LGD, which corresponds with a level of

**TABLE 2.6**

Sample Historical LGD Data[27] (for Illustration Only)

| Year | LGD1 (%) | LGD2 (%) | LGD3 (%) | LGD4 (%) | LGD5 (%) | LGD6 (%) | LGD7 (%) | LGD8 (%) |
|------|----------|----------|----------|----------|----------|----------|----------|----------|
| 1993 | 91 | 92 | 97 | 83 | 74 | 15 | 15 | 64 |
| 1994 | 86 | 3  | 79 | 22 | 69 | 38 | 3  | 65 |
| 1995 | 67 | 65 | 71 | 69 | 72 | 22 | 23 | 45 |
| 1996 | 54 | 36 | 78 | 45 | 56 | 67 | 4  | 3  |
| 1997 | 34 | 56 | 34 | 89 | 99 | 23 | 3  | 6  |
| 1998 | 6  | 98 | 57 | 7  | 89 | 4  | 65 | 3  |
| 1999 | 77 | 98 | 79 | 89 | 61 | 54 | 61 | 24 |
| 2000 | 98 | 93 | 56 | 19 | 67 | 28 | 48 | 38 |
| 2001 | 18 | 6  | 71 | 79 | 74 | 98 | 15 | 8  |
| 2002 | 65 | 55 | 86 | 54 | 78 | 6  | 52 | 82 |

default rate (i.e., *regional default rate* in the terminology of LossStats Model) that is typically observed during an economic downturn. The LossStats Model is a Web-based application (http://www.lossstatsmodel.com) and applies an advanced mathematical framework to the largest commercially available database of ultimate recovery data and distressed debt trading price information on bonds and loans above $50 millions to forecast a distribution of LGD values. It is based on the maximum expected utility (MEU) approach. Rather than assuming a beta distribution of LGD, its calibration to the historical recovery and trading price data can be interpreted as applying the maximum likelihood estimation method over an exponential family of distributions.[28]

The LossStats Model determines the conditional probability density of LGD conditioned on the following input factors:

1. **Debt type** (e.g., senior secured bank debt, senior secured bond, senior unsecured bank debt, senior unsecured bond, subordinated bank debt, or subordinated bond).
2. **Debt above/below**: Debt above (below) is the percentage of debt on the obligor's balance sheet that is contractually superior (inferior) to the debt instrument being analyzed and is represented as a percentage number between 0 and 100.
3. **Collateral type** (e.g., all assets, cash, inventories/receivables, all non–current assets, PP&E, equipment, etc.): *collateral type is a required input only when user chooses to enter the debt above/below percentages.*

4. **Regional default rate** (i.e., market-wide default rate); and
5. **Industry factor** (e.g., utilities, telecommunications, etc.): industry factor is the industry default rate divided by the regional default rate; it is used to capture the industry-specific business cycles.

The estimation of conditional LGD can be conducted for individual loans or a portfolio of loans. The following steps are involved in the implementation of the LossStats Model.

### Step 1: Valuation Methodology

Users can choose to estimate LGD by using either (a) the discounted ultimate recovery cash flows or (b) the 30-day postdefault trading price of distressed instruments. The former therefore corresponds with Equation 2.25 and the latter with Equation 2.26.

### Step 2: Discounting Methodology

Users can define their own discount rate to be used in calculating the present value of future recovery cash flows by choosing "User Preferred Discount Rate and Expected Time Frame" option (Figure 2.13). Discount rate should incorporate risk premium commensurate with the inherent recovery risk. The discussions in Chapter 1, Section *"Discount Rate for Workout Recoveries: An Empirical Study"* provide the necessary references for the users to choose an appropriate discount rate.

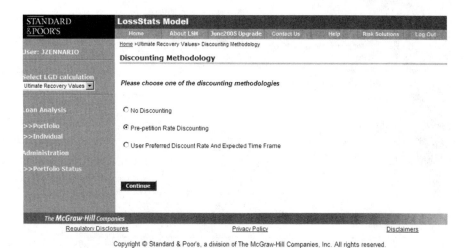

**Figure 2.13** Choice of discounting methodology in LossStats.

## Step 3: Input Parameters

For each facility in a segment, we either input its "debt type" or "the percentages of debt below/above"[29] (Figure 2.14). To simulate the economic downturn condition, we enter a "regional default rate" corresponding with the average default rate during the stress periods defined in Method 1 or the average PD estimated in Method 3 (see below) over the same stress periods. We enter an "industry factor," which corresponds with the historical average default rate of each industry again during the stress periods defined above. We then repeat the calculation by entering the long-run regional default rate and long-run industry-specific default rates over a full business cycle. The difference between the LGDs obtained in the two calculations therefore represents the required "markup" to satisfy the downturn LGD requirement.

We can simply enter 100% for the "probability of default" as we are interested in obtaining the LGD distribution rather than the actual loss distribution.[30] We can then enter an appropriate "discount rate" corresponding

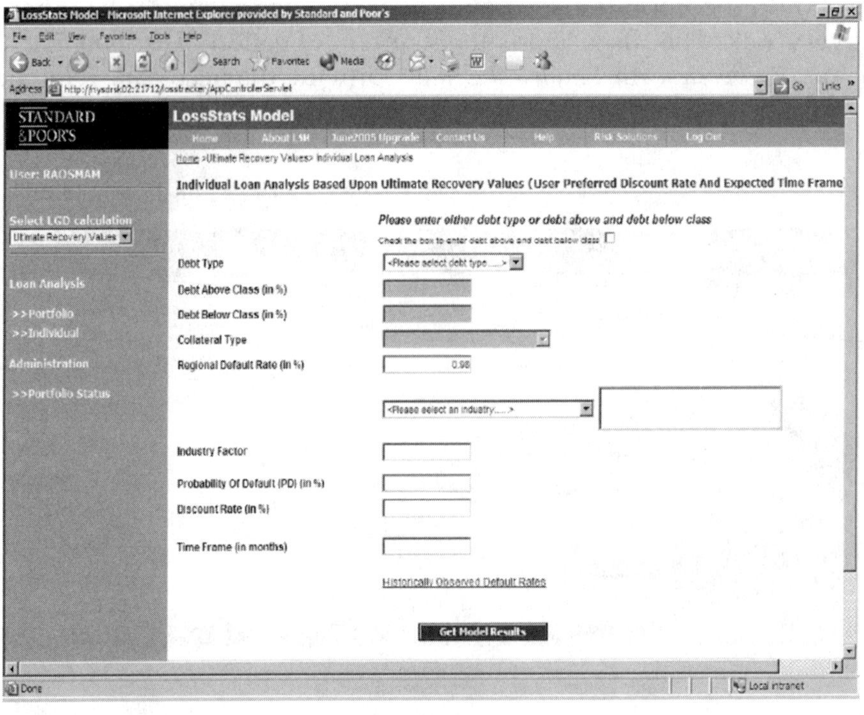

**Figure 2.14** Input parameters of LossStats.

with the particular segment. Finally, "time frame" will be our expected time to ultimate recovery (in months) of a defaulted instrument belonging to that particular segment. Refer to Figure 2.14 for the arrangement of the input parameters mentioned above in LossStats Model.

### Step 4: Outputs

For each facility, we then generate the estimated conditional probability distribution of LGD (Figure 2.15) and its summary statistics (Figure 2.16). Averaging the mean LGDs across all facilities within each segment therefore gives us the model-implied downturn LGD for that segment. Using a portfolio input file allows for the processing of multiple loans at the same time. Users need to organize the input parameters in the form of an Excel input template. The input file is then uploaded while LGDs are estimated for multiple loans at the same time. The outputs (Figure 2.17) are then organized in a form that can be downloaded into an Excel file.

### Method 3

The Pillar I risk-weight formula (as well as most of the off-the-shelf credit risk management systems) does not incorporate the correlations between

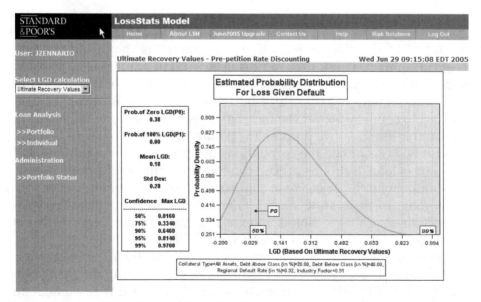

**Figure 2.15** Conditional probability distribution of LGD obtained from LossStats.

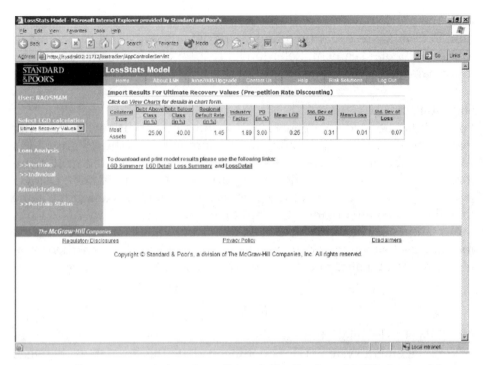

**Figure 2.16** Summary statistics of conditional distribution of LGD obtained from LossStats.

PD and LGD, therefore potentially underestimating the capital requirement. To compensate for this, some degree of conservatism is intended to be incorporated into the mean LGD. One way to estimate this downturn LGD requirement is to find out how much increase in mean LGD is required to compensate for the fact that correlations are not modeled. To address this question, we propose to (1) model PD and LGD correlation in its entirely; (2) estimate the correlations using historical default rate and LGD data of loan portfolios; and (3) conduct simulation of the portfolio loss distribution with the objective of comparing the capital requirements with and without incorporating specific components of PD and LGD correlations. The rest of this section is an excerpt of Miu and Ozdemir (2006) in which the analysis is formally illustrated.[31]

We start by describing the proposed stylized model of credit risk. Suppose there is a single systematic risk driver $X_t$ affecting the changes in both PD and LGD risks, which can be of different extent. We assume $X_t$ to be normally distributed with mean zero and unit standard deviation.

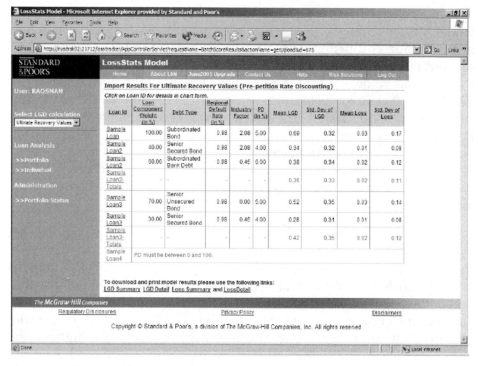

**Figure 2.17** Formatted output of multiple loans by using portfolio input file in LossStats.

Market-wide systematic PD and LGD risks at time $t$ ($P_t$ and $L_t$) are assumed to be driven by $X_t$ via the following equations:

$$P_t = \beta_{\mathrm{PD}} \times X_t + \varepsilon_{\mathrm{PD},t} \qquad \text{(Equation 2.28)}$$

$$L_t = \beta_{\mathrm{LGD}} \times X_t + \varepsilon_{\mathrm{LGD},t}. \qquad \text{(Equation 2.29)}$$

The coefficients $\beta_{\mathrm{PD}}$ and $\beta_{\mathrm{LGD}}$ therefore govern the degrees of impact of $X_t$ on $P_t$ and $L_t$. The residual changes ($\varepsilon_{\mathrm{PD},t}$ and $\varepsilon_{\mathrm{LGD},t}$) are independent of $X_t$ and are assumed to be mutually independent, normally distributed, and with standard deviations such that both $P_t$ and $L_t$ follow standard normal distribution.

In this economy, borrowers are uniform in terms of their credit risks. Their individual PD risk $p_t$ affected by both the systematic PD risk $P_t$ and the borrower-specific PD risk $e_{\mathrm{PD},t}$. For example, for borrower $i$,

$$p_t^i = R_{\mathrm{PD}} \times P_t + \sqrt{1 - R_{\mathrm{PD}}^2} \times e_{\mathrm{PD},t}^i. \qquad \text{(Equation 2.30)}$$

Individual PD risk $p_t$ therefore follows a standard normal distribution. Under Merton's framework, we can interpret $p_t$ as a latent variable, which is a normalized function of the borrower's asset value. The borrower defaults when $p_t$ becomes less than some constant default point (DP). Thus, the lower the value of $p_t$ (i.e., the closer to DP), the higher is the borrower's PD. The coefficient $R_{PD}$ is uniform across borrowers and measures the sensitivity of individual risks to the systematic PD risk. The square of this coefficient ($R_{PD}^2$) is therefore the pairwise correlation in PD risks among borrowers as a result of the systematic risk factor.

We have a similar setup for borrower's individual LGD risk $l_t$. Again, it can be partitioned into its systematic and idiosyncratic components. Thus, for borrower $i$,

$$l_t^i = R_{LGD} \times L_t + \sqrt{1 - R_{LGD}^2} \times e_{LGD,t}^i.$$

(Equation 2.31)

Individual LGD risk $l_t$ again is a latent variable and follows a standard normal distribution. We interpret $l_t$ as a normalized transformed distribution of the empirical distribution of LGD.[32] There is a one-to-one monotonic mapping between the value of $l_t$ and the LGD value, which is typically bounded between zero and one. The higher the value of $l_t$, the higher is the borrower's LGD. The coefficient $R_{LGD}$ is again uniform across borrowers and measures the sensitivity of individual risks to the systematic LGD risk. The parameter $R_{LGD}^2$ therefore becomes the pairwise correlation in LGD risks among borrowers as a result of the systematic risk factor.

It is interesting to note that Equations 2.30 and 2.31 together dictate the degree of correlation between PD and LGD of the same borrower via the systematic risk factors of $P_t$ and $L_t$. The correlation is

$$\text{Corr}(p_t^i, l_t^i) = \beta_{PD} \beta_{LGD} R_{PD} R_{LGD}.$$

(Equation 2.32)

However, correlation between PD and LGD of the same borrower does not only come from the systematic risk drivers. How about risk factors specific to the borrower under consideration? For example, if we are considering an unsecured loan made to a borrower, a borrower-specific credit event can cause an increase in both its PD and LGD. This event can have nothing to do with any market-wide systematic risk. In our model, such a characteristic can be modeled by ensuring the residuals $e_{PD,t}$ and $e_{LGD,t}$ in Equations 2.30 and 2.31 are not independent for the same borrower.[33] Let $x_t$ denote the borrower-specific credit risk factor, which is assumed to be normally distributed with zero mean and unit standard deviation. Then, for borrower $i$,

$$e_{PD,t}^i = \theta_{PD}^i \times x_t^i + \eta_{PD,t}^i$$

(Equation 2.33)

$$e^i_{\text{LGD},t} = \theta^i_{\text{LGD}} \times x^i_t + \eta^i_{\text{LGD},t}. \qquad \text{(Equation 2.34)}$$

The coefficients $\theta_{\text{PD}}$ and $\theta_{\text{LGD}}$ therefore govern the degrees of impact of $x_t$ on $e_{\text{PD},t}$ and $e_{\text{LGD},t}$. The residual changes ($\eta_{\text{PD},t}$ and $\eta_{\text{LGD},t}$) are independent of $x_t$ and are assumed to be mutually independent, normally distributed, and with standard deviations such that both $e_{\text{PD},t}$ and $e_{\text{LGD},t}$ follow standard normal distribution.

With the introduction of the borrower-specific risk factor, it can be shown that the correlation between PD and LGD risk drivers of the same borrower becomes

$$\text{Corr}(p^i_t, l^i_t) = \beta_{\text{PD}}\beta_{\text{LGD}}R_{\text{PD}}R_{\text{LGD}}$$
$$+ \theta^i_{\text{PD}}\theta^i_{\text{LGD}}\sqrt{1-R^2_{\text{PD}}}\sqrt{1-R^2_{\text{LGD}}}. \qquad \text{(Equation 2.35)}$$

The correlation is therefore made up of two parts. The first term (of Equation 2.35) represents the correlation due to systematic risk factors and the second term that of idiosyncratic (i.e., borrower-specific) risk factors. It is interesting to note that the larger the pairwise correlations of $R_{\text{PD}}$ and $R_{\text{LGD}}$, the larger (smaller) the impact of the systematic (idiosyncratic) factors. Moreover, no matter the values of $R_{\text{PD}}$ and $R_{\text{LGD}}$, we have zero correlation between PD and LGD for the same borrower if either one of the $\beta$s and either one of the $\theta$s are both equal to zero. It however does not imply there is zero LGD correlation among different borrowers, which is solely governed by $R_{\text{LGD}}$. The full correlation structure together with its relation with both the systematic and idiosyncratic factors is further illustrated in Figure 2.18.

Before we can conduct the simulation of portfolio credit loss, we need to estimate the correlation parameters governing our model using the available historical default rate and LGD data. We need to estimate these parameters for each LGD segment in order to assess their respective downturn LGD requirements. Among these correlation parameters, the pairwise PD correlation $R^2_{\text{PD}}$ is most studied and relatively well understood. Most banks have a very good idea of the PD correlation among borrowers of their loan portfolios. We would suggest that banks use the average pairwise PD correlations estimated as per Basel formula and/or estimated internally for economic capital requirement to conduct the simulations outlined below. In the subsequent illustration, we assume a pairwise PD correlation of 25%. The remaining parameters are however not as well documented. We start by describing a methodology to estimate pairwise LGD correlation $R^2_{\text{LGD}}$ by using historical LGD data. We then consider correlations of systematic PD and LGD risks (i.e., the parameters $\beta_{\text{PD}}$ and $\beta_{\text{LGD}}$).

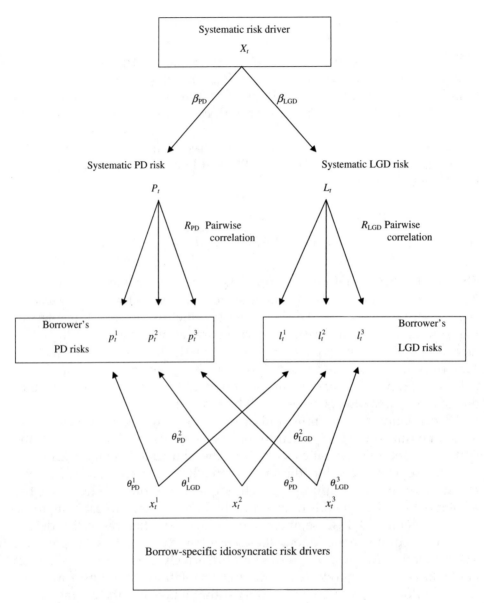

**Figure 2.18** Correlation structure showing relationship with the systematic and borrower-specific idiosyncratic risk factors.

To estimate the pairwise LGD correlation, we abstract from the full-fledged model of PD and LGD risks and focus on what's happening after the borrowers go into default. Essentially, we want to estimate Equation 2.31, which is restated here for easy reference:

$$l_t^i = R_{\text{LGD}} \times L_t + \sqrt{1 - R_{\text{LGD}}^2} \times e_{\text{LGD},t}^i.$$

In Equation 2.31, we partition a borrower's LGD risk $l_t$ into its systematic $(L_t)$ and idiosyncratic $(e_{\text{LGD},t})$ components. We assume individual's LGD risk $l_t$ follows a standard normal distribution, and we interpret $l_t$ as a normalized transformed distribution of the empirical distribution of LGD, which is assumed to follow a beta distribution.[34] There is a one-to-one monotonic mapping between the value of $l_t$ and the realized LGD value, which is bounded between zero and one under the beta distribution. The coefficient $R_{\text{LGD}}$ is assumed to be uniform across borrowers and measures the sensitivity of individual risks to the systematic LGD risk. It is therefore the pairwise correlation of LGD risks among borrowers as a result of the systematic risk factor.

In this setup, there are three parameters we need to estimate to fully define the LGD risks. Namely, the pairwise correlation $R_{\text{LGD}}^2$ of Equation 2.31 and the two parameters of the beta distribution (i.e., $a$ and $b$). For illustrative purpose, let's consider an example where we observe the historical LGDs of loans made to large corporate borrowers by a certain bank from 1993 to 2002. The number of defaults and their respective LGDs for each quarterly period were recorded during the sample period. The panel data comprises a total of 165 defaulted loans. Table 2.7 reports some summary statistics.

First of all, we estimate the parameters governing the beta distribution. From the properties of beta distribution, parameters $a$ and $b$ are related to the mean $(\mu)$ and variance $(Var)$ of the distribution according to the following equations:

$$\mu = \frac{a}{a+b} \qquad\qquad \text{(Equation 2.36)}$$

$$Var = \frac{ab}{(a+b+1)(a+b)^2}. \qquad\qquad \text{(Equation 2.37)}$$

Using the unconditional mean and variance (i.e., 39% and 0.0916) over the full sample period, we estimate $a = 0.630$ and $b = 0.975$. Given these parameter estimates, we can then obtain the normally distributed LGD risk factor $l_t$ by transforming each of the observed LGDs using the beta distribution

$$l_t^i = \Phi^{-1}\left(B\left(\text{LGD}_t^i; a, b\right)\right) \qquad\qquad \text{(Equation 2.38)}$$

**TABLE 2.7**

Summary Statistics of Historical LGD from 1993 to 2002 of Loans Made to Large Corporate
Borrowers by a Bank

|  | No. of Observations | Mean LGD (%) | Median LGD (%) | Standard Deviation of LGD (%) |
|---|---|---|---|---|
| 1993 | 48 | 35 | 26 | 32 |
| 1994 | 29 | 30 | 24 | 27 |
| 1995 | 18 | 29 | 30 | 17 |
| 1996 | 4 | 54 | 56 | 33 |
| 1997 | N/A | N/A | N/A | N/A |
| 1998 | 7 | 38 | 33 | 31 |
| 1999 | 7 | 26 | 25 | 16 |
| 2000 | 5 | 35 | 36 | 31 |
| 2001 | 16 | 55 | 64 | 34 |
| 2002 | 31 | 53 | 47 | 30 |
| All | 165 | 39 | 31 | 30 |

Note: Data are not available in 1997.

where $\text{LGD}_t^i$ denotes realized LGD of borrower $i$ at time $t$; $\Phi^{-1}(\bullet)$ denotes
the inverse of the cumulative standard normal distribution; and $B(\bullet; a,b)$
denotes the cumulative beta distribution with shape parameters $a$ and $b$.

From Equation 2.31, the standard deviation of $l_t^i$ at each time period $t$ is
always equal to $\sqrt{1 - R_{\text{LGD}}^2}$. Pairwise LGD correlation can therefore be estimated by calculating the following *pooled* estimate of standard deviation of $l_t^i$:

$$\sqrt{1 - \hat{R}_{\text{LGD}}^2} = \sqrt{\frac{\sum_{t=1}^{T}(n_t - 1)\hat{\sigma}_t^2}{\sum_{t=1}^{T} n_t - T}}, \qquad \text{(Equation 2.39)}$$

where $n_t$ and $\hat{\sigma}_t^2$ denote the number of LGD observations and the standard
deviation of $l_t^i$ in time period $t$, respectively. Using the historical LGD data
of which the summary statistics are reported in Table 2.7, $R_{\text{LGD}}^2$ is estimated
to be equal to 5.88% (5.20%) by grouping data within each quarter (year).
This is a fairly low level of correlation, which reflects the diversification
effect as the LGD data comes from different industries and countries. We
can also estimate the time-series of the market-wide systematic LGD risks
$(L_t)$, which is simply the mean values of $l_t^i$ within each time period divided
by the estimated value of $R_{\text{LGD}}$. These estimates are plotted in Figure 2.19

and will be used subsequently in the estimation of the correlation of systematic PD and LGD risks.

Previously, we estimate the pairwise LGD correlation ($R^2_{\text{LGD}}$) by using historical LGD data. Now, we focus on the correlation of systematic PD and LGD risk factors, which is governed by the parametric values of $\beta_{\text{PD}}$ and $\beta_{\text{LGD}}$ of our model. To estimate the correlation of systematic PD and LGD risk factors, we start by restating Equations 2.28 and 2.29, which describe the systematic credit risks:

$$P_t = \beta_{\text{PD}} \times X_t + \varepsilon_{\text{PD},t}$$
$$L_t = \beta_{\text{LGD}} \times X_t + \varepsilon_{\text{LGD},t}.$$

Market-wide systematic PD and LGD risks ($P_t$ and $L_t$, respectively) are assumed to be driven by a single systematic risk driver $X_t$, which is normally distributed with mean zero and unit variance. The coefficients $\beta_{\text{PD}}$ and $\beta_{\text{LGD}}$ therefore govern the degrees of impact of $X_t$ on $P_t$ and $L_t$. The residual changes ($\varepsilon_{\text{PD},t}$ and $\varepsilon_{\text{LGD},t}$) are assumed to be mutually independent and also independent of $X_t$. They are normally distributed with standard deviations such that both $P_t$ and $L_t$ follow standard normal distribution, again, with zero mean and unit variance. The correlation of $P_t$ and $L_t$ is therefore simply the product of the coefficients $\beta_{\text{PD}}$ and $\beta_{\text{LGD}}$. To facilitate subsequent discussions, let us denote this correlation between market-wide systematic PD and LGD risks as $R^2_M$. Our objective now is to estimate $R^2_M$ using historical default rate and LGD data.

As a by-product in the estimation of pairwise LGD correlation discussed above, we have already obtained the *most-likely* estimations of the systematic LGD risk factor $L_t$ over time. We can therefore calculate $R^2_M$ if we also have estimations of the systematic PD risk factor $P_t$ over the same sample period. Suppose, in each period $t$, we observe $k_t$ defaults in a uniform portfolio starting with $n_t$ borrowers. It can be shown in the Appendix that the probability of observing $k_t$ given the realization of $P_t$ is

$$\Omega\left(k_t, n_t; P_t, R_{PD}, \text{DP}\right) = \binom{n_t}{k_t} \times \left(\Phi\left(z(P_t, R_{PD}, \text{DP})\right)\right)^{k_t}$$
$$\times \left(1 - \Phi\left((z(P_t, R_{PD}, \text{DP}))\right)\right)^{n_t - k_t}. \qquad \text{(Equation 2.40)}$$

where DP is the constant default point; $\Phi(\bullet)$ is the cumulative normal distribution function; and[35]

$$z\left(P_t, R_{PD}, \text{DP}\right) = \frac{1}{\sqrt{1 - R^2_{PD}}}\left(\text{DP} - R_{PD}P_t\right).$$

The first step is to estimate DP by maximizing the time-series sum of the unconditional log likelihood of observing $k_t$ and $n_t$ from $t = 1$ to $T$.[36] Given that $P_t$ follows a standard normal distribution, the unconditional log likelihood function becomes

$$\log(L) = \sum_{t=1}^{T} \log \int_{-\infty}^{\infty} \Omega\left(k_t, n_t; u_t, \hat{R}_{PD}, DP\right) \cdot \phi(u_t) \cdot du_t \qquad \text{(Equation 2.41)}$$

where $\phi(\bullet)$ denotes the density function of the standard normal distribution. It can be shown in the Appendix that, as $n_t$ becomes large, the above function can be approximated by

$$\log(L) \cong \sum_{t=1}^{T} \left( \frac{1}{2}\log\left(\frac{1-\hat{R}_{PD}^2}{\hat{R}_{PD}^2}\right) + \frac{1}{2}\left(\Phi^{-1}\left(\frac{k_t}{n_t}\right)\right)^2 \right.$$
$$\left. - \frac{\left(\sqrt{1-\hat{R}_{PD}^2}\,\Phi^{-1}\left(k_t/n_t\right) - DP\right)^2}{2\hat{R}_{PD}^2} \right). \qquad \text{(Equation 2.42)}$$

For illustrative purpose, let's consider the historical default rates of a certain uniform midmarket loan portfolio from 1991 to 2000. The default rates are reported in Table 2.8. By maximizing the log likelihood function in Equation 2.42, the default point (DP) is estimated to be equal to $-1.8981$,

**TABLE 2.8**

Historical Default Rates (1991–2000) of a Uniform Portfolio of Midmarket Borrowers

|      | Starting Number of Borrowers ($n_t$) | Number of Defaulted Borrowers ($k_t$) |
|------|--------------------------------------|---------------------------------------|
| 1991 | 9,349                                | 183                                   |
| 1992 | 10,539                               | 135                                   |
| 1993 | 13,306                               | 218                                   |
| 1994 | 15,049                               | 196                                   |
| 1995 | 14,203                               | 138                                   |
| 1996 | 13,887                               | 228                                   |
| 1997 | 13,809                               | 205                                   |
| 1998 | 14,082                               | 198                                   |
| 1999 | 16,680                               | 186                                   |
| 2000 | 15,510                               | 253                                   |

which corresponds with a PD of 2.9%.[37] It therefore serves as an estimate of long-run PD of the obligors in this uniform portfolio of midmarket loans.

Moreover, the expected value of $P_t$ in each time period $t$ conditional on observing $k_t$ and $n_t$ can be shown in the Appendix to be equal to

$$E\left(P_t\middle|k_t,n_t;\ \text{DP},R_{\text{PD}}\right)=\frac{\text{DP}-\Phi^{-1}\left(k_t/n_t\right)\cdot\sqrt{1-R_{\text{PD}}^2}}{R_{\text{PD}}}.\qquad\text{(Equation 2.43)}$$

Given the estimated value of $-1.8981$ for DP and the assumed value of 0.25 for $R_{\text{PD}}^2$, we estimated the time-series of the systematic PD risks ($P_t$) using Equation 2.43 with the historical default rates reported in Table 2.8. In Figure 2.19, we plot the estimated $P_t$ along with the systematic LGD risk

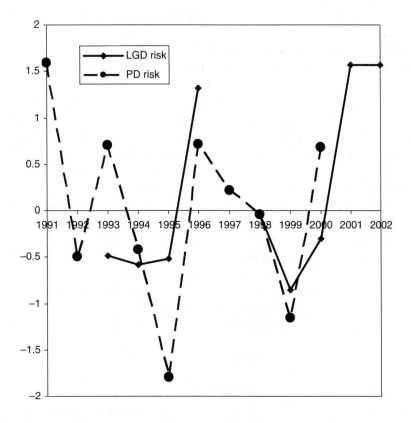

**Figure 2.19** Time-series plot of estimated systematic PD and LGD risks. They are the normalized time-series of $-P_t$ and $L_t$ estimated by MLE.

factor ($L_t$) obtained previously.[38] Systematic PD and LGD risks are found to be evolving in a synchronized fashion over the 1990s. Specifically, both PD and LGD risks are relatively high in 1996, 1997, and from 2000 onwards. On the other hand, both risks are relatively low in 1994, 1995, and 1999. Finally, $R_M^2$ is estimated to be equal to 0.53 by calculating the correlation between $P_t$ and $L_t$ over the years where we have data for both variables.[39]

With the correlation parameters estimated above, we can now conduct simulations of the portfolio credit risk by using our proposed model. For illustrative purposes, let's consider that a portfolio consists of a total of 2,000 loans made to 2,000 uniform borrowers within a certain segment. The promised repayment in one year is $1 each. The PD and LGD risk factors governing the credit risks are assumed to follow the descriptions of the proposed model. From the perspective of the bank, we are interested in measuring the economic capital requirement over a one-year risk horizon and at a confidence level of 99% and 99.9%, respectively.

The parametric and model assumptions adopted in the simulations are described below:

**PD risks:** The PD of each borrower is assumed to be 1%, which corresponds with the average PD of large corporate borrowers. We assume the PD risk of each borrower is governed by the random variable $p_t$ as defined in Equation 2.30. Specifically, we interpret $p_t$ as a normalized function of the borrower's asset value. Borrower defaults within the risk horizon when the realized borrower-specific $p_t$ becomes less than the constant default point of $-2.3263$, which is the inverse of the cumulative probability of 0.01 (i.e., PD = 1%).

**LGD risks:** If a borrower defaults, we assume the realized LGD follows a beta distribution with parametric values of $a = 0.630$ and $b = 0.975$. These parametric assumptions together imply a mean LGD of 39% and a LGD standard deviation of 30%, which are found to be consistent with that of large corporate loan portfolio. The LGD value realized is assumed to be governed by the random variable $l_t$ as defined in Equation 2.31. Variables $l_t$ follows a standard normal distribution and is a transformed distribution of the empirical beta distribution of LGD. That is, there is a one-to-one monotonic mapping between the realized value of $l_t$ and the realized LGD value

$$\text{LGD}_t^i = B^{-1}\left(\Phi\left(l_t^i\right), a, b\right).$$                    (Equation 2.44)

where $\text{LGD}_t^i$ denotes the realized LGD of borrower $i$ at time $t$, $B^{-1}(\bullet)$ denotes the inverse of the cumulative beta distribution with shape parameters $a$ and $b$, and $\Phi(\bullet)$ denotes the cumulative standard normal distribution, which transforms $l_t^i$ to a uniform distribution. Equation 2.44

therefore ensures we can transform normally distributed risk measures $l_t$ into LGD simulations that are bounded between zero and one and follow a beta distribution.

**Correlation parameters:** To fully define the model, we need to specify:

- The sensitivities ($\beta_{PD}$ and $\beta_{LGD}$) of the systematic PD and LGD risks ($P_t$ and $L_t$) to the single systematic risk driver $X_t$ as described in Equations 2.28 and 2.29: We assume $\beta_{PD} = \beta_{LGD} \equiv \beta$, and we consider the cases where $\beta^2$ is equal to 0.0, 0.2, 0.4, 0.6, and 0.8 (note that $\beta^2$ is previously estimated to be equal to 0.53).
- The pairwise PD correlation as defined in Equation 2.30: We consider different cases where the pairwise PD correlation ($R_{PD}^2$) takes on values ranging from 0.0 to 0.5.
- The pairwise LGD correlation as defined in Equation 2.31: We report the results where the pairwise LGD correlation is equal to 5.9% as estimated previously for large corporate borrowers. The corresponding $R_{LGD}$ is therefore equal to the square root of 0.059.
- The sensitivities ($\theta_{PD}$ and $\theta_{LGD}$) of the idiosyncratic PD and LGD risks ($e_{PD,t}$ and $e_{LGD,t}$) to the single borrower-specific credit risk factor $x_t$ as described in Equations 2.33 and 2.34: We assume $\theta_{PD} = \theta_{LGD} \equiv \theta$, and we consider the cases where $\theta^2$ is equal to 0.0, 0.2, 0.4, 0.6, and 0.8 respectively.

The portfolio value-at-risks (i.e., economic capital requirements) are defined as the differences between the mean year-end portfolio value and the year-end 99% and 99.9% critical portfolio values, respectively, at the loss tail. The distribution of portfolio values is obtained by simulating 20,000 credit scenarios each involving all the 2,000 uniform borrowers.

The followings outline the simulation process:

- **Step 1:** For each scenario, a single set of market-wide risk factors $X_t$, $\varepsilon_{PD,t}$, and $\varepsilon_{LGD,t}$ is first drawn from independent normal distributions. The systematic PD and LGD risk factors $P_t$ and $L_t$ are then computed via Equations 2.28 and 2.29.
- **Step 2:** A total of 2,000 sets of mutually independent borrower-specific credit risk drivers $x_t^i$, $\eta_{PD,t}^i$ and $\eta_{LGD,t}^i$ are then drawn from normal distributions. Borrower-specific idiosyncratic risks $e_{PD,t}^i$ and $e_{LGD,t}^i$ can then be constructed for each of the borrowers via Equations 2.33 and 2.34.
- **Step 3:** For each borrower, the borrower-specific PD and LGD risks ($p_t$ and $l_t$) can then be computed by combining the systematic

and idiosyncratic components obtained in step 1 and 2 and as defined by Equations 2.30 and 2.31.

- **Step 4:** We then check for each borrower if there is a default event (i.e., if $p_t < -2.3263$). If it defaults, ending value of the loan is equal to $1 minus the realized LGD, which is equal to the transformation of the borrower-specific $l_t$ under the above-mentioned beta distribution as per Equation 2.44. If it does not default, the loan value is simply equal to $1. The portfolio value is therefore the summation of all the loan values across the 2,000 borrowers.

- **Step 5:** Steps 1 to 4 are then repeated 20,000 times to obtain the distribution of year-end portfolio values for the calculations of economic capitals.

This simulation process is then repeated for each set of the correlation parametric values as described above. The objective is to measure the

**TABLE 2.9**

Simulated Economic Capitals (in $) at 99% and 99.9% for a Uniform Portfolio of 2,000 Loans (Each $1) under Different Scenarios of Systematic and Idiosyncratic Sensitivity Factors $\beta$ and $\theta$

| 99% | | | $\theta^2$ | | |
|---|---|---|---|---|---|
| $\beta^2$ | 0.00 | 0.20 | 0.40 | 0.60 | 0.80 |
| 0.00 | 61.98 | 77.55 | 93.13 | 111.49 | 128.19 |
| 0.20 | 66.80 | 83.53 | 100.39 | 115.76 | 132.80 |
| 0.40 | 74.89 | 89.62 | 104.85 | 121.47 | 133.40 |
| 0.60 | 82.16 | 96.01 | 111.81 | 126.56 | 139.31 |
| 0.80 | 86.35 | 102.19 | 117.90 | 132.59 | 144.33 |
| **99.9%** | | | $\theta^2$ | | |
| $\beta^2$ | 0.00 | 0.20 | 0.40 | 0.60 | 0.80 |
| 0.00 | 153.40 | 179.38 | 209.04 | 236.43 | 276.71 |
| 0.20 | 168.98 | 199.57 | 223.52 | 251.77 | 282.45 |
| 0.40 | 182.41 | 208.28 | 236.32 | 271.33 | 299.09 |
| 0.60 | 191.16 | 218.10 | 237.05 | 263.41 | 290.58 |
| 0.80 | 195.24 | 226.09 | 256.13 | 280.48 | 303.68 |

Note: Pairwise PD correlation is set at 0.25 (i.e., $R_{PD} = 0.5$). We use a pairwise LGD correlation of 0.059 (i.e., $R_{LGD} = 0.24$). Economic capital is defined as the difference between the mean portfolio value and the respective critical values at the loss tail at one-year risk horizon.

impact on the resulting economic capital. The results are reported in Table 2.9 and 2.11. In Table 2.9, we consider different scenarios of systematic and idiosyncratic sensitivity factors $\beta$ and $\theta$. Pairwise PD correlation is set at 0.25 (i.e., $R_{PD}$ equals 0.5). We use a pairwise LGD correlation of 0.059 (i.e., $R_{LGD}$ equals 0.24) from the previous estimation results. In Table 2.11, we consider different scenarios of the idiosyncratic sensitivity factor $\theta$ and the pairwise PD correlation $R^2_{PD}$. Same as Table 2.9, we use a pairwise LGD correlation of 0.059. However, the systematic sensitivity factor $\beta$ is set as the square root of 0.53, which corresponds with the correlation in systematic PD and LGD risks previously estimated.

Table 2.10 and 2.12 report the required percentage increase in the mean LGD (from 0.39) when correlations are set to zero. That is, we estimate the mean (*zero-correlation*) LGDs (by setting $\beta = \theta = R_{LGD} = 0$)

**TABLE 2.10**

Required Markup for LGD with Respect to Systematic ($\beta^2$) and Idiosyncratic Correlations ($\theta^2$)

| 99% | | | $\theta^2$ | | |
|---|---|---|---|---|---|
| $\beta^2$ | 0.00 | 0.20 | 0.40 | 0.60 | 0.80 |
| 0.00 | 3% | 28% | 52% | 83% | |
| 0.20 | 11% | 37% | 64% | 90% | |
| 0.40 | 23% | 47% | 72% | | 100+% |
| 0.60 | 35% | 57% | 84% | 100+% | |
| 0.80 | 42% | 67% | 94% | | |

| 99.9% | | | $\theta^2$ | | |
|---|---|---|---|---|---|
| $\beta^2$ | 0.00 | 0.20 | 0.40 | 0.60 | 0.80 |
| 0.00 | 0% | 16% | 35% | 52% | 78% |
| 0.20 | 10% | 29% | 44% | 62% | 82% |
| 0.40 | 18% | 35% | 52% | 75% | 92% |
| 0.60 | 24% | 41% | 53% | 70% | 87% |
| 0.80 | 26% | 46% | 65% | 80% | 95% |

Note: Percentage increases in LGD (from 39%) to match the corresponding economic capitals reported in Table 2.9. Simulations of economic capitals at 99% and 99.9% for a uniform portfolio of 2,000 loans are conducted by assuming $\beta = \theta = 0$, and zero pairwise LGD correlation $R_{LGD} = 0$. Same as Table 2.9, pairwise PD correlation is assumed to be equal to 0.25 (i.e., $R_{PD} = 0.5$). To produce the correct economic capital numbers, these percentages therefore represent the required "markup" in mean LGD in a model where LGD correlations are ignored.

**TABLE 2.11**

Simulated Economic Capitals (in $) at 99% and 99.9% for a Uniform Portfolio of 2,000 Loans (Each $1) under Different Scenarios of the Idiosyncratic Sensitivity Factor $\theta$ and the Pairwise PD Correlation $R_{PD}^2$

| 99% | $\theta^2$ | | | |
|---|---|---|---|---|
| $R_{PD}^2$ | 0.00 | 0.20 | 0.40 | 0.60 |
| 0.00 | 7.10 | 8.18 | 9.26 | 10.05 |
| 0.10 | 38.32 | 46.63 | 53.61 | 60.42 |
| 0.20 | 65.62 | 77.91 | 90.34 | 103.06 |
| 0.30 | 90.59 | 109.91 | 126.87 | 144.35 |
| 0.40 | 119.69 | 142.30 | 164.86 | 186.15 |
| 0.50 | 150.45 | 174.63 | 201.67 | 228.13 |
| 99.9% | $\theta^2$ | | | |
| $R_{PD}^2$ | 0.00 | 0.20 | 0.40 | 0.60 |
| 0.00 | 10.34 | 11.65 | 13.13 | 14.20 |
| 0.10 | 74.60 | 87.78 | 100.58 | 109.63 |
| 0.20 | 147.51 | 164.03 | 188.30 | 208.93 |
| 0.30 | 231.37 | 254.61 | 285.12 | 314.00 |
| 0.40 | 328.85 | 352.69 | 394.11 | 435.01 |
| 0.50 | 432.11 | 477.66 | 519.24 | 560.43 |

Note: As in Table 2.9, we use a pairwise LGD correlation of 0.059 (i.e., $R_{LGD} = 0.24$). The systematic sensitivity factor $\beta$ is set as the square root of 0.53, which corresponds with the value estimated above. Economic capital is again defined as the difference between the mean portfolio value and the respective critical values at the loss tail at one-year risk horizon.

required to arrive at the economic capitals reported in Table 2.9 and 2.11, respectively. The (percentage) difference between the *zero-correlation LGDs* and the original LGD of 39% represents the required "markup" in mean LGD (from an unbiased LGD estimate) in a model where LGD correlations are ignored or not explicitly modeled.[40]

From Table 2.10, even at a moderate level of $\theta$ (say $\theta^2 = 0.2$) and at a level of $\beta$ (say $\beta^2 = 0.5$) comparable with that estimated for large corporate borrowers, we need to increase the mean LGD by about 37% to achieve the correct economic capital under a model where LGD correlation is ignored.[41] This "markup" in mean LGD is therefore a measure of the appropriate conservatism required under the Basel II downturn LGD requirement.

**TABLE 2.12**

Required Markup for LGD with Respect to $R^2_{PD}$ and Idiosyncratic Correlations $(\theta^2)$

| 99% | | $\theta^2$ | | |
|---|---|---|---|---|
| $R^2_{PD}$ | 0.00 | 0.20 | 0.40 | 0.60 |
| 0.00 | 43% | 72% | 100% | |
| 0.10 | 32% | 60% | 85% | |
| 0.20 | 32% | 56% | 80% | 100+% |
| 0.30 | 26% | 54% | 77% | |
| 0.40 | 26% | 51% | 75% | 97% |
| 0.50 | 27% | 48% | 71% | 93% |

| 99.9% | | $\theta^2$ | | |
|---|---|---|---|---|
| $R^2_{PD}$ | 0.00 | 0.20 | 0.40 | 0.60 |
| 0.00 | 47% | 74% | 100+% | |
| 0.10 | 29% | 51% | 73% | 89% |
| 0.20 | 24% | 38% | 59% | 76% |
| 0.30 | 18% | 30% | 46% | 60% |
| 0.40 | 20% | 29% | 44% | 59% |
| 0.50 | 19% | 31% | 43% | 54% |

Note: Percentage increases in LGD (from 39%) to match the corresponding economic capitals reported in Table 2.11. Simulations of economic capitals at 99% and 99.9% for a uniform portfolio of 2,000 loans are conducted by assuming $\beta = \theta = 0$, and zero pairwise LGD correlation (i.e., $R_{LGD} = 0$). Pairwise PD correlation is assumed to be equal to the corresponding values of 0.0, 0.1, 0.2, 0.3, 0.4, and 0.5, respectively. To produce the correct economic capital numbers, these percentages therefore represent the required "markup" in mean LGD in a model where LGD correlations are ignored.

The results in Table 2.12 suggest the required "markup" in mean LGD is a decreasing function of pairwise PD correlation. As $R^2_{PD}$ increases, although the systematic component of the PD and LGD correlation of individual obligors increases (see Equation 2.35), the understatement of capital is relatively smaller because the portfolio credit risk becomes mainly governed by pairwise effects rather than PD and LGD correlation of individual obligors. Finally, the required "markup" becomes less sensitive to $\theta$ as $R^2_{PD}$ increases, as the systematic component of correlation together with the pairwise effects dominates the determination of the portfolio credit risk when $R^2_{PD}$ is large.

## Appendix

### To Prove Equation 2.40

The borrow-specific PD risk is represented by Equation 2.30:

$$p_t^i = R_{PD} \times P_t + \sqrt{1 - R_{PD}^2} \times e_{PD,t}^i.$$

The probability of default of borrower $i$ conditional on observing the systematic PD risk $P_t$ is therefore equal to

$$P\left[p_t^i < DP \mid P_t\right] = P\left[R_{PD} \times P_t + \sqrt{1 - R_{PD}^2} \times e_{PD,t}^i < DP \mid P_t\right]$$

$$= P\left[e_{PD,t}^i < \frac{DP - R_{PD} \times P_t}{\sqrt{1 - R_{PD}^2}} \mid P_t\right]$$

$$= \Phi\left(z\left(P_t, R_{PD}, DP\right)\right).$$

where DP is the constant default point, $\Phi(\bullet)$ is the cumulative normal distribution function, and

$$z(P_t, R_{PD}, DP) = \frac{1}{\sqrt{1 - R_{PD}^2}}(DP - R_{PD}P_t).$$

The probability of survival of borrower $i$ is therefore equal to

$$1 - \Phi\left(z\left(P_t, R_{PD}, DP\right)\right).$$

As $e_{PD,t}^i$ is independent of $e_{PD,t}^j$ for $i \neq j$, the probability of observing $k_t$ defaults out of $n_t$ borrowers given the realization of $P_t$ is therefore equal to

$$\Omega\left(k_t, n_t; P_t, R_{PD}, DP\right) = \binom{n_t}{k_t} \times \left(\Phi\left(z(P_t, R_{PD}, DP)\right)\right)^{k_t} \times \left(1 - \Phi\left((z(P_t, R_{PD}, DP))\right)\right)^{n_t - k_t}.$$

### To Prove Equation 2.42

From Equation 2.40, the cumulative probability that the number of defaults does not exceed $k_t$ is

$$F_{n_t}(k_t) = \sum_{j=0}^{k_t} \int_{-\infty}^{\infty} \Omega(j, n_t; P_t, R_{PD}, DP) dP_t$$

$$= \sum_{j=0}^{k_t} \binom{n_t}{j} \int_{-\infty}^{\infty} \left(\Phi(z(P_t, R_{PD}, DP))\right)^j \times \left(1 - \Phi\left((z(P_t, R_{PD}, DP))\right)\right)^{n_t - j_t} dP_t.$$

Let's consider the change of variable: $s = \Phi(z)$. Then,

$$F_{n_t}(k_t) = \sum_{j=0}^{k_t} \binom{n_t}{j} \int_0^1 s^j \times (1-s)^{n_t-j_t} \, dW(s)$$

where

$$W(s) = \Phi\left( \frac{\sqrt{1-R_{PD}^2} \times \Phi^{-1}(s) - DP}{R_{PD}} \right).$$

                                                                           (Equation 2.A1)

By the law of large numbers,

$$\lim_{n_t \to \infty} \sum_{j=0}^{k_t} \binom{n_t}{j} s^j \times (1-s)^{n_t-j} = 0 \quad \text{if} \quad \frac{k_t}{n_t} < s$$

$$= 1 \quad \text{if} \quad \frac{k_t}{n_t} > s,$$

and therefore the cumulative distribution function of the number of defaults on a very large portfolio is

$$F_\infty\left( \frac{k_t}{n_t} \right) = W\left( \frac{k_t}{n_t} \right).$$

The corresponding density function is therefore the derivative of Equation 2.A1:

$$f_\infty\left( \frac{k_t}{n_t} \right) = \frac{\sqrt{1-R_{PD}^2}}{R_{PD}} \times \exp\left( -\frac{1}{2R_{PD}^2}\left( \sqrt{1-R_{PD}^2} \times \Phi^{-1}\left(\frac{k_t}{n_t}\right) - DP \right)^2 \right.$$

$$\left. + \frac{1}{2}\left( \Phi^{-1}\left(\frac{k_t}{n_t}\right) \right)^2 \right).$$

The time-series sum of the unconditional log likelihood of observing $k_t$ and $n_t$ from $t = 1$ to $T$ is therefore

$$\sum_{t=1}^T \log\left( f_\infty\left( \frac{k_t}{n_t} \right) \right) = \sum_{t=1}^T \left( \frac{1}{2}\log\left( \frac{1-\hat{R}_{PD}^2}{\hat{R}_{PD}^2} \right) \right.$$

$$\left. + \frac{1}{2}\left( \Phi^{-1}\left(\frac{k_t}{n_t}\right) \right)^2 - \frac{\left( \sqrt{1-\hat{R}_{PD}^2}\,\Phi^{-1}(k_t/n_t) - DP \right)^2}{2\hat{R}_{PD}^2} \right).$$

**To Prove Equation 2.43**

From Equation 2.40, the probability of observing $k_t$ given the realization of $P_t$ is

$$\Omega\left(k_t, n_t; P_t, R_{PD}, DP\right) = \binom{n_t}{k_t} \times s^{k_t} \times (1-s)^{n_t - k_t}.$$

where

$$s = \Phi\left(\frac{1}{\sqrt{1 - R_{PD}^2}}(DP - R_{PD}P_t)\right).$$

The cumulative conditional probability that the number of defaults does not exceed $k_t$ is therefore

$$\sum_{j=0}^{k_t} \Omega\left(j, n_t; P_t, R_{PD}, DP\right) = \sum_{j=0}^{k_t} \binom{n_t}{j} \times s^j \times (1-s)^{n_t - j}.$$

Again, by the law of large numbers,

$$\lim_{n_t \to \infty} \sum_{j=0}^{k_t} \Omega\left(j, n_t; P_t, R_{PD}, DP\right) = \lim_{n_t \to \infty} \sum_{j=0}^{k_t} \binom{n_t}{j} \times s^j \times (1-s)^{n_t - j} = 0 \quad \text{if} \quad \frac{k_t}{n_t} < s$$

$$= 1 \quad \text{if} \quad \frac{k_t}{n_t} > s.$$

Given this step function, the expected value of $P_t$ in each time period $t$ conditional on observing $k_t$ and $n_t$ can therefore be solved by equating $k_t/n_t$ to $s$, that is,

$$\frac{k_t}{n_t} = \Phi\left(\frac{1}{\sqrt{1 - R_{PD}^2}}(DP - R_{PD}E(P_t))\right) \Rightarrow E(P_t) = \frac{DP - \Phi^{-1}\left(k_t/n_t\right) \cdot \sqrt{1 - R_{PD}^2}}{R_{PD}}.$$

## DOWNTURN EAD

What we have said about downturn LGD, in principle, also applies to downturn EAD. During credit downturns, the large number of defaults can be accompanied by above-average EADs, magnifying the portfolio losses. Many FIs recognize that an obligor's PD is among the risk drivers of EAD; the higher the PD, the higher the EAD in general. This can be accounted for by incorporating correlations between PDs and EADs in conducting simulations of portfolio losses. The Basel II risk-weight formula (as well as most of the commercially available economic capital estimation models), however, does not incorporate these correlations, which may therefore result in an underestimation of the capital requirement. One way to compensate for this within the constraints of the Basel II formula is to add a markup to the EAD estimation before using it in the estimation of capital requirement.

It can be argued that the simple average of historical EADs may have already incorporated a certain degree of downturn condition. After all, most of the historical EAD data are observed during economic downturns when default rates tend to be above average. However, first of all, the severity of the historical downturn periods we have experienced is unlikely to be comparable with that of the extreme capital event occurring at the very high confidence level (e.g., 99.9% in Basel II) that we are interested in the estimation of capital requirement. Second, we cannot be sure that we have fully compensated for the effect on the required capital given the fact that PD and EAD correlation is ignored. Therefore, similar to our estimation of downturn LGD under Method 3 described previously, the following steps may be taken to estimate downturn EAD:

1.  We first measure the relevant correlation parameters of PD and EAD using historical data.
2.  We then estimate the required capital through the simulations of portfolio losses with and without incorporating the estimated correlations.
3.  Taking the capital requirement under the full-correlation simulations as the target ("true") capital, we estimate how much we need to increase the EAD under the zero-correlation simulations in order to arrive at the target capital under the full-correlation simulations.

To our knowledge, this approach has not been adopted in the estimation of downturn EAD. It is likely that the lack of historical EAD data (which is even more common than is the lack of historical LGD data) has made the quantification of downturn EAD a formidable task. Some FIs have developed first-generation EAD stress-testing models, where EADs are stressed (extrapolated) with respect to default rates and macroeconomic factors. For example, we can estimate EADs under stress scenario, in which default rates and macroeconomic factors are assumed to attain levels that correspond with a specific number of standard deviations from the respective average levels (see the "Stress Testing" section for EAD stress testing).

In the absence of a fully correlated capital framework described above in the estimation of the required EAD markup, these EAD stress testing models can help us to gauge the downturn EAD requirements.

## DOWNTURN LGD: A CASE STUDY

The following case study is prepared to illustrate the three different methodologies described in the section *"Downturn LGD"* in the quantification of downturn LGD requirement. The LGD data sample we used can be categorized in three segments. *Borrower-level* LGD data is a subset of *facility-level* LGD data and are produced by grouping/consolidating facilities at the borrower level in cases where all facilities to a single borrower have the same collateral type. Borrowers with multiple collateral types are excluded. Subsequent analyses are conducted using both data sets. Time-series of annual default rate data are used in the analysis to define downturn period.

### Results and Discussion

#### Method 1

We identify the downturn periods using Standard & Poor's default rate data. The time-series of default rates are reported in Table 2.13. We use the time series of Standard & Poor's speculative-grade default rates and define the downturn periods as those years when the default rates are higher than the corresponding long-term (25-year) average default rate of 4.7%. The periods from 1990 to 1992 and then from 1999 to 2003 are therefore classified as downturn periods under this criterion.

In Table 2.14, we report the *time-weighted* average LGD of all those instruments defaulted during the downturn years and compare it with that over all the years (i.e., *cycle-average*) for each of the LGD segments. We conduct the analysis separately at both facility level and borrower level. To ensure our results will not be distorted by a few outliers, we ignore those segments where we have less than 30 and 60 observations for borrower-level and facility-level analysis, respectively.[42] We also ignore those segments in which there is no LGD observation in any of the years.

In Table 2.15, we report the *default-weighted* average LGD for each of the segments. To control for any credit risk–unrelated factors, which might result in changes in number of LGD observations over time, we compute the default-weighted average LGD by using Standard & Poor's speculative grade default rates. For example, the fact that our sample

**TABLE 2.13**

Historical Annual Default Rates

| Year | Standard & Poor's Speculative Grade (%) |
|------|------------------------------------------|
| 1990 | **7.872** |
| 1991 | **10.671** |
| 1992 | **5.848** |
| 1993 | 2.202 |
| 1994 | 2.190 |
| 1995 | 3.622 |
| 1996 | 1.834 |
| 1997 | 2.149 |
| 1998 | 3.223 |
| 1999 | **5.159** |
| 2000 | **7.000** |
| 2001 | **10.510** |
| 2002 | **7.118** |
| 2003 | **5.551** |
| 2004 | 2.305 |

data have more than three times the LGD observations in the last recession than in the second last recession might have nothing to do with the relative severity of the recession. It may simply be because of the increase in size of the loan portfolio. Using simple average will therefore result in inappropriately assigning too much weight to the last recession than to

**TABLE 2.14**

Time-Weighted Average LGD: Downturn versus Cycle-Average LGD Based on the Downturn Periods According to Standard & Poor's Speculative-Grade Default Rates

| Segment | Facility Level | | | Borrower Level | | |
|---------|----------------|---------------|----------------------|----------------|---------------|----------------------|
| | Downturn LGD | Cycle-Average LGD | Percent Increase (%) | Downturn LGD | Cycle-Average LGD | Percent Increase (%) |
| 1 | 0.4665 | 0.4210 | 10.81 | 0.4566 | 0.4203 | 8.65 |
| 2 | 0.4601 | 0.4071 | 13.01 | 0.4460 | 0.4126 | 8.08 |
| 3 | 0.4632 | 0.4096 | 13.09 | 0.4497 | 0.4116 | 9.23 |

**TABLE 2.15**

Default-Weighted Average LGD: Downturn versus Cycle-Average LGD Based on the
Downturn Periods According to Standard & Poor's Speculative-Grade Default Rates

| Segment | Facility Level | | | Borrower Level | | |
|---|---|---|---|---|---|---|
| | Downturn LGD | Cycle-Average LGD | Percent Increase (%) | Downturn LGD | Cycle-Average LGD | Percent Increase (%) |
| 1 | 0.4640 | 0.4437 | 4.59 | 0.4534 | 0.4379 | 3.55 |
| 2 | 0.4592 | 0.4356 | 5.41 | 0.4463 | 0.4321 | 3.28 |
| 3 | 0.4634 | 0.4386 | 5.65 | 0.4514 | 0.4350 | 3.77 |

the second-last recession. To avoid this distortion, we compute default-
weighted LGD as follows:

$$\text{Default-Weighted Average} = \frac{\sum_{y=1}^{T} \text{LGD}_y \cdot dr_y}{\sum_{y=1}^{T} dr_y},$$

where $\text{LGD}_y$ is the simple average of all LGD observations in year $y$, $dr_y$ is
the Standard & Poor's speculative-grade default rate in year $y$, and $T$ is the
total number of years in the sample.

## Method 2

In Method 2, we use Standard & Poor's LossStats Model to generate
facility-specific LGDs, which correspond with the market-wide and
industry-specific default rates that are typically observed during an economic downturn. To find out the percentage increase ("markup") in LGD,
we compare them with those LGDs obtained by using the *cycle-average*
versions of the default rate parameters. The analysis is conducted for each
of the three LGD segments considered above.

The LossStats Model determines the probability density of LGD conditioned on input factors like debt type, debt above/below, collateral type,
regional default rate, and industry factor. For more details, please refer to
Standard & Poor's Credit Market Services (2003).

In conducting the analysis using the LossStats Model, we adopt the
following user defined options/parameters:

- **Valuation method:** We choose to use the "Discounted Ultimate
  Recovery Cash Flows" option.

- **Discounting Methodology:** We choose to use the "User Preferred Discount Rate and Expected Time Frame" option. We use an expected time frame of 12 months and discount rates of 15.7% and 14.0%, respectively, for downturn and cycle-average analysis. The higher discount rate used in the downturn analysis is consistent with the higher perceived LGD risk (i.e., the degree of uncertainty of future recoveries) during an economic downturn. These discount rates are consistent with those documented in the section on "Discount Rate for Workout Recovery: An Empirical Study" in Chapter 1.
- **Debt Type:** We input the debt types for each of the facilities.[43]
- **Regional Default Rate** and **Industry Factor:** To simulate the economic downturn condition, we enter a "regional default rate" corresponding with the average historical default rate during the downturn periods from 1990 to 1992 and from 1999 to 2003, of which the Standard & Poor's speculative-grade default rates are higher than the corresponding long-term (25-year) average default rate of 4.7%. For each facility, we enter an "industry factor," which corresponds with the historical average default rate of that industry again during the downturn periods defined above.[44] To model the cycle-average condition, we repeat the calculations by entering the long-run regional default rate and long-run industry-specific default rates. The difference between the LGDs obtained in the two calculations therefore represents the required "markup" to satisfy the downturn LGD requirement.
- **Probability of Default:** We simply enter 100% for the "probability of default" because we are interested in obtaining the LGD distribution rather than the actual loss distribution.[45]

For each facility, we therefore generate the estimated probability distribution of LGD and its summary statistics. Averaging the mean (or median) of the LGDs across all facilities within each segment therefore gives us the model-implied downturn LGD for that segment. Same as for Method 1, we report (in Table 2.16) the results of the analyses conducted on both the borrower-level and facility-level LGD data.

The model-implied LGDs of Table 2.16 are found to be lower than those reported for Method 1 in Tables 2.14 and 2.15. It may be attributed to the fact that the time coverage of the historical data used in calibrating the LossStats Model can be quite different from that of the sample data considered here. Nevertheless, in measuring downturn LGD, we are more concerned about the relative difference between the downturn and cycle-average LGD rather their individual absolute values.

**TABLE 2.16**

Method 2: Downturn versus Cycle-Average LGD

Panel A: Downturn LGD according to the averaging of means

| Segment | Facility Level | | | Borrower Level | | |
|---|---|---|---|---|---|---|
| | Downturn LGD | Cycle-Average LGD | Percent Increase (%) | Downturn LGD | Cycle-Average LGD | Percent Increase (%) |
| 1 | 0.2889 | 0.2566 | 12.59 | 0.2896 | 0.2567 | 12.82 |
| 2 | 0.2725 | 0.2414 | 12.88 | 0.2718 | 0.2400 | 13.25 |
| 3 | 0.2727 | 0.2419 | 12.73 | 0.2721 | 0.2406 | 13.09 |

Panel B: Downturn LGD according to the averaging of medians

| Segment | Facility Level | | | Borrower Level | | |
|---|---|---|---|---|---|---|
| | Downturn LGD | Cycle-Average LGD | Percent Increase (%) | Downturn LGD | Cycle-Average LGD | Percent Increase (%) |
| 1 | 0.2554 | 0.2239 | 14.07 | 0.2560 | 0.2243 | 14.13 |
| 2 | 0.2389 | 0.2094 | 14.09 | 0.2382 | 0.2084 | 14.30 |
| 3 | 0.2391 | 0.2099 | 13.91 | 0.2384 | 0.2090 | 14.07 |

## Method 3

In Method 3, we measure the downturn LGD via computing by how much the mean LGD will be required to increase to compensate for the fact that correlations are not modeled. To address this question, we propose to (1) model PD and LGD correlation in its entirely; (2) estimate the correlations using historical default rate and LGD data of loan portfolios; and (3) conduct simulation of the portfolio loss distribution with the objective of comparing the capital requirements with and without incorporating specific components of PD and LGD correlations.[46]

Before we can conduct any simulation of portfolio credit loss, we need to estimate the correlation parameters governing our model using the available historical default rate and LGD data. We need to estimate these parameters for each LGD segment considered above to assess their respective downturn LGD requirements. Among these correlation parameters, the pairwise PD correlation $R^2_{PD}$ is most studied and relatively well understood. In the subsequent analysis, we use an average pairwise PD correlation of 0.22 as it is the average correlation for the portfolio under consideration.

The remaining parameters are, however, not as well documented. We start by estimating pairwise LGD correlation $R^2_{\text{LGD}}$ by using the sample LGD data. Similar to Methods 1 and 2, we conduct the analysis separately on the facility-level and borrower-level LGD data.

First of all, we estimate the parameters governing the beta distribution. From the properties of beta distribution, parameters $a$ and $b$ are related to the mean ($\mu$) and variance ($Var$) of the distribution according to the following equations:

$$\mu = \frac{a}{a+b} \qquad\qquad \text{(Equation 2.45)}$$

$$Var = \frac{ab}{(a+b+1)(a+b)^2}. \qquad\qquad \text{(Equation 2.46)}$$

We compute these parameters using the unconditional mean and variance of the LGD data of each segment. The results are reported in Table 2.17.

Given these parameter estimates, we can then obtain the normally distributed LGD risk factor $l_t$ by transforming each of the observed LGDs using the beta distribution[47]

$$l_t^i = \Phi^{-1}\left(B\left(\text{LGD}_t^i; a,b\right)\right), \qquad\qquad \text{(Equation 2.47)}$$

where $\text{LGD}_t^i$ denotes realized LGD of borrower $i$ at time $t$, $\Phi^{-1}(\bullet)$ denotes the inverse of the cumulative standard normal distribution, and $B(\bullet; a,b)$ denotes the cumulative beta distribution with shape parameters $a$ and $b$.

**T A B L E  2.17**

Beta Distribution Parameters $a$ and $b$

| Segment | Facility Level | | | | Borrower Level | | | |
| --- | --- | --- | --- | --- | --- | --- | --- | --- |
| | Mean | Variance | a | b | Mean | Variance | a | b |
| 1 | 0.4088 | 0.0878 | 0.7165 | 1.0363 | 0.4145 | 0.0835 | 0.7903 | 1.1162 |
| 2 | 0.3999 | 0.0815 | 0.7774 | 1.1665 | 0.4061 | 0.0761 | 0.8816 | 1.2895 |
| 3 | 0.3985 | 0.0835 | 0.7453 | 1.1249 | 0.3994 | 0.0773 | 0.8400 | 1.2631 |

Pairwise LGD correlation can therefore be estimated by calculating the following *pooled* estimate of standard deviation of $l_t^i$:

$$\sqrt{1 - \hat{R}_{\text{LGD}}^2} = \sqrt{\frac{\sum\limits_{t=1}^{T}(n_t - 1)\hat{\sigma}_t^2}{\sum\limits_{t=1}^{T} n_t - T}}, \qquad \text{(Equation 2.48)}$$

where $n_t$ and $\hat{\sigma}_t^2$ denote the number of LGD observations and the standard deviation of $l_t^i$ in time period $t$, respectively. The results are reported in Table 2.18.

We can also estimate the time-series of the market-wide systematic LGD risks ($L_t$), which are simply the mean values of $l_t^i$ within each time period divided by the estimated value of $R_{\text{LGD}}$.[48] The parameter $R_M^2$ can therefore be estimated by computing the time-series correlation between these segment-specific systematic LGD risks and the systematic PD risks ($P_t$) estimated below.

Because segment-specific default rates are not available, we conduct the analysis using Standard & Poor's speculative-grade default rates, which are reported in Table 2.13. Before we can extract the systematic PD risks, we estimate the corresponding default point (DP) by maximizing the log likelihood function in Equation 2.42. By setting $R_{\text{PD}}^2$ equal to the average pairwise PD correlation of 0.22, DP is estimated to be equal to −1.4971. The expected value of $P_t$ in each time period $t$ conditional on observing $k_t$ and $n_t$ is therefore equal to

$$E\left(P_t | k_t, n_t; \text{DP}, R_{\text{PD}}\right) = \frac{\text{DP} - \Phi^{-1}\left(k_t / n_t\right) \cdot \sqrt{1 - R_{\text{PD}}^2}}{R_{\text{PD}}}. \qquad \text{(Equation 2.49)}$$

**T A B L E  2.18**

Pairwise LGD Correlations

| Segment | Facility Level | Borrower Level |
|---------|---------------|----------------|
| 1       | 0.1017        | 0.1058         |
| 2       | 0.1167        | 0.1383         |
| 3       | 0.1145        | 0.1376         |

Finally, $R_M^2$ is estimated for each of the segments by calculating the time-series correlation between $L_t$ and $P_t$ obtained above. The results are reported in Table 2.19. Again, we present the results obtained by using both the facility-level and borrower-level LGD data.

With the correlation parameters estimated above, we can now conduct simulations of the portfolio credit risk by using our proposed model. We consider a portfolio consists of a total of 2,000 loans made to 2,000 uniform borrowers within a certain segment. The promised repayment in one year is $1 each. The PD and LGD risk factors governing the credit risks are assumed to follow the descriptions of the proposed model. From the perspective of the bank, we are interested to measure the economic capital requirement over a one-year risk horizon and at a confidence level of 99% and 99.9% respectively.

The parametric and model assumptions are described below.

**PD risks:** We assume the PD risk of each borrower is governed by the random variable $p_t$. Specifically, we interpret $p_t$ as a normalized function of the borrower's asset value. Borrower defaults within the risk horizon when the realized borrower-specific $p_t$ becomes less than the previously estimated default point of −1.4971.

**LGD risks:** If a borrower defaults, we assume the realized LGD follows a beta distribution with parametric values of $a$ and $b$ estimated previously and reported in Table 2.17. The LGD value realized is assumed to be governed by the random variable $l_t$, which follows a standard normal distribution and is a transformed distribution of the beta distribution of LGD,

$$\text{LGD}_t^i = B^{-1}\left(\Phi\left(l_t^i\right), a, b\right), \qquad \text{(Equation 2.50)}$$

where $\text{LGD}_t^i$ denotes the realized LGD of borrower $i$ at time $t$, $B^{-1}(\bullet)$ denotes the inverse of the cumulative beta distribution with shape parameters $a$ and $b$, and $\Phi(\bullet)$ denotes the cumulative standard normal distribution, which transforms $l_t^i$ to a uniform distribution.

**TABLE 2.19**

Correlation of Systematic PD and LGD Risks ($R_M^2$)

| Segment | Facility Level | Borrower Level |
|---------|----------------|----------------|
| 1       | 0.35           | 0.26           |
| 2       | 0.50           | 0.40           |
| 3       | 0.52           | 0.33           |

**Correlation parameters:**

- **Correlation of systematic PD and LGD risks ($R_M^2$):** We use the segment-specific values reported in Table 2.19.
- **Pairwise PD correlation ($R_{PD}^2$):** We use the average pairwise PD correlation of 0.22.
- **Pairwise LGD correlation ($R_{LGD}^2$):** We use the segment-specific values reported in Table 2.18.
- **Correlation of idiosyncratic PD and LGD risks ($R_S^2$):** We assume $R_S^2$ equals 0.2.

The portfolio VaRs (i.e., economic capital requirements) are defined as the differences between the mean year-end portfolio value and the year-end 99% and 99.9% critical portfolio values, respectively, at the loss tail. The distribution of portfolio values is obtained by simulating 20,000 credit scenarios each involving all the 2,000 uniform borrowers. Please refer to the section on "Downturn LGD" for further details regarding the simulations. The resulting economic capital requirements are reported in Table 2.20.

Finally, Table 2.21 reports the required percentage increase in the mean LGD when correlations are set to zero. That is, we estimate the mean (*zero-correlation*) LGDs (by setting $R_S = R_M = R_{LGD} = 0$) required to arrive at the economic capitals reported in Table 2.20.[49] We still assume $R_{PD}^2$ equals to the correlation of 0.22. The (percentage) difference between the zero-correlation LGDs and the original LGD represents the required markup in mean LGD in a model where LGD correlations are ignored or not explicitly modeled.[50]

Because borrower-level analysis is more consistent with the theoretical setup of the proposed model and the matching of 99.9% economic capital is more relevant under Basel II regulatory requirement, we focus on the LGD markups obtained under these situations. We have markups that

**T A B L E  2.20**

Simulated Economic Capital Requirement (in $) at 99% and 99.9% Confidence Levels

| Segment | Facility Level | | Borrower Level | |
|---|---|---|---|---|
| | 99% | 99.9% | 99% | 99.9% |
| 1 | 110.387 | 244.993 | 109.378 | 237.086 |
| 2 | 118.663 | 242.052 | 114.964 | 248.697 |
| 3 | 118.758 | 248.734 | 108.358 | 245.280 |

**TABLE 2.21**

Percentage Markup in Mean LGD to Match the Simulated Economic
Capital Requirement at 99% and 99.9% Confidence Level

| Segment | Facility Level | | Borrower Level | |
|---|---|---|---|---|
| | 99% | 99.9% | 99% | 99.9% |
| 1 | 43% | 37% | 40% | 31% |
| 2 | 57% | 38% | 50% | 40% |
| 3 | 58% | 43% | 44% | 40% |

range from 31% (for segment 1) to as high as 40% (for segment 2 and 3). The
relatively high markups for segment 2 and 3 are as expected given their
high pairwise LGD correlation and high correlation in systematic PD and
LGD risks as reported in Tables 2.18 and 2.19, respectively.

## Summary of Results

In Table 2.22 we summarize the most relevant markup LGDs obtained from
each method. Among the three methods, Method 3 is believed to be the
most "economically" relevant approach to measure the degree of conservatism required to compensate for the lack of modeling of the PD and LGD
correlation in the Basel II regulatory capital formula. Unlike the other two
methods, it directly calibrates against the economic capital of a credit portfolio. Moreover, it models extreme credit events, which are most relevant
for regulatory capital requirement. However, we approach the problem
from all three different angles to establish a framework and the terms of reference for assessing the markup factors under different methodologies to
meet the downturn LGD requirement.

**TABLE 2.22**

Summary of LGD Markups

| Segment | Method 1 (%) | Method 2 (%) | Method 3 (%) |
|---|---|---|---|
| 1 | 4–5 | 13–14 | 31 |
| 2 | 3–5 | 13–14 | 40 |
| 3 | 4–6 | 13–14 | 40 |

## ESTABLISHING A MASTER SCALE

Master scale maps risk ratings to ranges of values of PDs, LGDs, or EADs. It involves the assignment of the maximum, minimum, and midpoint values of these credit parameters for each risk rating. An example of a PD master scale is provided in Table 2.23 and Figure 2.20.

There are several uses of the master scales. The main use is to ensure consistency in the application of credit rating across the different lines of business within the organization. Many FIs are diversified across countries and in terms of business units. Within an FI, it is quite common that more than a single IRRS is being used at any point in time. For example, the IRRS used by the parent company might be different from those used by its subsidiaries. It is also not uncommon that different IRRSs are used in assessing the credit risk of commercial (midmarket) versus (large) corporate portfolios. These IRRSs differ not only in design (e.g., some utilize quantitative models, others expert judgment templates, etc.) but also in how the risk parameters are quantified (i.e., different PDs and LGDs might be assigned to the same risk rating; for example, a certain risk rating may be assigned a PD of 5% on the commercial side but a PD of 6% on the corporate side). There may be historical reasons for these differences, some justified and some not. With the implementation of Basel II, a broader degree of

**T A B L E  2.23**

An Example of a PD Master Scale

| Risk Rating | Minimum PD (%) | Midpoint PD (%) | Maximum PD (%) |
|---|---|---|---|
| 1 | 0 | 0.02 | 0.03 |
| 2 | 0.03 | 0.04 | 0.05 |
| 3 | 0.05 | 0.07 | 0.09 |
| 4 | 0.09 | 0.12 | 0.16 |
| 5 | 0.16 | 0.22 | 0.29 |
| 6 | 0.29 | 0.39 | 0.53 |
| 7 | 0.53 | 0.71 | 0.95 |
| 8 | 0.95 | 1.28 | 1.72 |
| 9 | 1.72 | 2.32 | 3.12 |
| 10 | 3.12 | 4.20 | 5.66 |
| 11 | 5.66 | 7.62 | 10.25 |
| 12 | 10.25 | 13.80 | 18.57 |
| 13 | 18.57 | 25.00 | 33.65 |

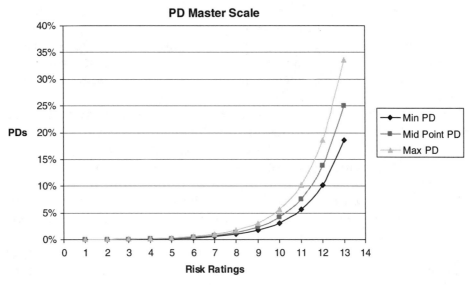

**Figure 2.20** An example of a PD master scale.

consistency at the "top-of-the-house" level is needed among the business units that have been historically fairly autonomous. The most basic criteria of consistency is to make sure the different IRRSs have the same number of risk ratings. Another step further will be to ensure the uniqueness of the PD assigned to each risk rating across the business units. This is however not easily achievable or sometimes even may not be desirable for several reasons. First of all, changing the assigned PD of any risk rating in an IRRS (for the sake of consistency) would result in the historical default rate data collected prior to the change being inappropriate to be used in the estimation of the default risk of the risk rating after the change. For example, suppose the assigned PD of a certain risk rating in a certain business unit of the bank has always been 6% and historical default rate data are available over the past five years based on this mapping. Suddenly changing the assigned PD to, say, 5% for the sake of consistency with those of other business units would make the historical data obsolete. Second, if we want to change the assigned PDs, we would also need to modify the underlying IRRS accordingly. Without having any relevant historical data for (re)calibration, this task would be difficult, requiring a number of years of data to be collected under the new IRRS in order to fulfill the validation requirements. Lastly, common to the implementations of any organizational changes, business units that have had enjoyed autonomy may be resistant to these changes to their PD mappings. For all these reasons, sometimes we may need to live with the second-best solution in achieving a consistent master scale. Slight differences in the assigned PDs are allowed, however all assigned PDs of the same risk rating have to be within the limits prespecified for that risk rating in the master scale. Specifically, business units with different IRRSs would be allowed to assign PDs that are lower (higher) than the maximum (minimum) values specified for each risk ratings. For example, for risk rating 10 of the master scale presented in Table 2.23, one business unit may choose an assigned PD of 4% whereas the other chooses 5%. Both are still within the prespecified range (maximum = 5.66%; minimum = 3.12%) of allowable values for this risk rating. However, no business units will be allowed to assign a PD that is lower (higher) than 3.12% (5.66%). This ensures some degree of consistency among different business units as any overlapping between adjacent risk ratings are ruled out.

The master scale is also used in the design of IRRSs. In the design of quantitative and hybrid models (as described in Chapter 1), we can use the master scale to convert continuous values of PDs and LGDs generated by quantitative models into scores or risk ratings. We also use the master scale in the validation process. For example, in the backtesting of LGD and EAD (as described in Chapter 3), use of the master scale enables the pooling of the individual realized LGDs and EADs in comparison with the respective predicted values.

### Construction of a Master Scale

Whereas there is no single way to construct the master scale, there are a number of principles we need to follow and characteristics we want to achieve. For example, we usually construct the master scale following the equal log-space principle. The master scale presented in Table 2.23 and Figure 2.20 is constructed this way. Table 2.24 reports the natural logarithms of the respective PD values presented in Table 2.23. From Figure 2.21, which presents the plots of the values reported in Table 2.24, it can be observed that PDs are linear on a log-scale and the log distances among the minimum, midpoint, and maximum PD values are equal. Whereas there is no particular theoretical reason why the master scale needs to be constructed this way, this method would produce a master scale that is fairly consistent with those of rating agencies, whose historical default rates are also more or less linear on a log-scale. We have noticed that a number of organizations uses this principle as a starting point and allow some variations based on historical experience and practices.

In terms of the desirable degree of granularity of the IRRS and thus the master scale, there are several considerations. Especially for

**TABLE 2.24**

Master Scale on Log Scale

| Risk Rating | Minimum Log (PD) | Midpoint Log (PD) | Maximum Log (PD) |
|---|---|---|---|
| 1 | | −8.517 | −8.220 |
| 2 | −8.220 | −7.923 | −7.626 |
| 3 | −7.626 | −7.329 | −7.032 |
| 4 | −7.032 | −6.734 | −6.437 |
| 5 | −6.437 | −6.140 | −5.843 |
| 6 | −5.843 | −5.546 | −5.249 |
| 7 | −5.249 | −4.952 | −4.655 |
| 8 | −4.655 | −4.358 | −4.060 |
| 9 | −4.060 | −3.763 | −3.466 |
| 10 | −3.466 | −3.169 | −2.872 |
| 11 | −2.872 | −2.575 | −2.278 |
| 12 | −2.278 | −1.981 | −1.683 |
| 13 | −1.683 | −1.386 | −1.089 |

the Basel-implementing FIs, a very important consideration is to satisfy the regulatory guidance and requirements. In Chapter 3, we show that the increased granularity requirement in the implementation of Basel II poses

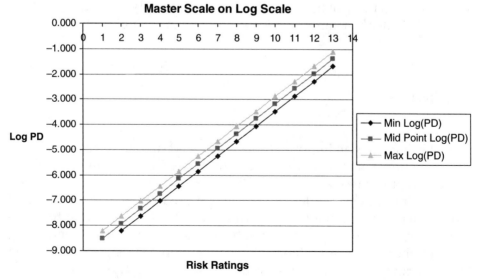

**Figure 2.21** Master scale on log scale.

challenges for FIs in validating especially low PD risk ratings. The other considerations are:

- *Stability versus granularity:* The degree of granularity should be commensurate with our ability to differentiate default risks among obligors. If our ability to differentiate cannot support the chosen degree of granularity, our risk rating system may be unstable over time. When this is the case, the observed default rates from especially adjacent risk ratings can easily violate the intended ranking and can overlap over time.

- *Differentiation of risk:* On the other hand, insufficient degree of granularly of IRRS will result in heterogeneity of the obligors assigned to the same risk rating in terms of their inherent default risks. This may be particularly a problem for the higher PD risk ratings as discussed in the section "PD Backtesting" in Chapter 3. Having a sufficient differentiation of risk is particularly important for high PD risk ratings from a sound risk management standpoint. The same amount of relative error in PD assignment will result in larger absolute error when PDs are higher. Stability versus homogeneity trade-off could be better balanced with not having excessive granularity for the low PD risk ratings (we most likely cannot differentiate very low PDs and validate them anyway). But we have sufficient granularity at the high PD risk ratings.

- *External benchmarking:* A close resemblance of an FI's master scale to those of Standard & Poor's and Moody's would allow for better benchmarking (see the "Benchmarking" section in Chapter 3).

## STRESS TESTING

### Overview

Stress testing plays an important role in risk and capital management. It is also a required component of Basel II implementation. Within the Pillar I framework, the parameters (PD, LGD, and EAD) need to be stressed, and within Pillar II, the stress testing results are used in the demonstration of capital adequacy. We first need to distinguish Basel stress testing from the more conventional stress testing the banks have already been conducting for a number of years. In Table 2.25, conventional stress testing is titled *Micro Level*, whereas Basel stress testing is titled *Macro Level*.

**T A B L E  2.25**

A Comparison of Micro Level and Macro Level Stress Testing

|  | Micro Level | Macro Level |
|---|---|---|
| Primary purpose | **Risk identification and mitigation** (Accuracy of quantification is of secondary importance) For example, as a value-add for an industry review, or when topical or the business line generates lots of questions or there are lots of exceptions in lending. | **Input into capital adequacy** Accuracy of quantification is important |
| Output | **Losses in general including foregone revenues** | **Stressed PDs, LGD, EADs, migration rates** |
| Coverage | **Any subportfolio can be targeted** When not enough data, expert judgment can be used | **Macro level by country, industry, etc.** Heavy dependency on data availability |
| Approach | **Expert judgment** Design a scenario and analyze the impact on capital and/or revenue and/or EL | **Quantitative methodologies** |
| Frequency | **As frequently as needed** | **Synchronized with capital planning** |
| Methodology | **Can be case-specific** Expert judgment and simpler quantitative approaches, like modeling the balance sheet or the income statement | **Needs to be standardized** |
| Examples | Bank's exposure to: 1. Real estate 2. Automotive 3. Hedge funds 4. Asset back commercial paper and impact on capital if brought into the bank's balance sheet | Global, industry-level, or regional downturns and recessions. Macro-level impact of historically observed or plausible hypothetical scenarios. |

The primary purpose of the micro-level stress testing is risk identification and mitigation. Although the stress testing results are quantifiable, the precision of this quantification is of secondary importance as the magnitude of the losses is classified, for instance, as large, medium, or small. Large potential stress testing losses identified should lead to senior management awareness and risk mitigation. In Basel stress testing, the quantification is much more important as the outcomes serve as important inputs to the regulatory capital adequacy framework. Consequentially, the methodologies adopted in Basel stress testing need to be standardized and performed as a part of the capital planning process. Micro-level stress testing, on the other hand, can be more case specific. We can use different methodologies and the results can be expressed in different risk measures including forgone revenues. The outputs of the Basel stress testing exercise are stressed PD, LGD, EAD, and migration rate. In this section, we will discuss stress testing with respect to Basel II requirements.

There are important questions to be answered with respect to both Pillar I and Pillar II implementations of stress testing:

1. With respect to Pillar I: We have already used long-run PDs, downturn LGDs and EADs, which incorporate conservatism. Why do we need to pursue "further" conservatism?

2. With respect to both Pillar I and Pillar II: How exactly do we use the resulting stressed parameters?

Pillar I implementation already incorporates long-run PDs, downturn LGDs and EADs, all of which are perceived as conservative adjustments. Although these requirements indeed result in increases in the values of these risk parameters, the reasons and rationale behind their usage are different from that of the stress testing requirement. As discussed in the section on "Long-Run PD" earlier in this chapter, long-run PD is just the unconditional estimation of the default likelihood, and a robust estimation of long-run PD may produce PD value higher than a simple arithmetic average of the default rates, especially when the default rate data are collected during the benign phase of the credit cycle. Downturn LGD and EAD requirements are for portfolio-level corrections due the fact that the adverse relationships between default rates and EADs and LGDs are not captured in Pillar I risk-weight function resulting in an underestimation of the regulatory capital requirements. Stress testing, on the other hand, attempts to measure the potential increase in credit risk and portfolio loss under plausible stress events. Stressed PD, LGD, and EAD are conditional parameters obtained under these prespecified stressed events.

How exactly do we use the resulting stressed parameters is an interesting question. Pillar I is accomplished with the estimation of the minimum regulatory capital requirement utilizing the estimated PDs, LGDs, and EADs in applying the risk-weight function. What role stress testing should play in Pillar I is perplexing, as only Pillar II extends to full capital adequacy framework where stress testing becomes an important ingredient. This lack of clarity for the role of stress testing in Pillar I is the likely explanation of the variety of regulatory interpretations of its usage we observed around the world. Whereas some regulators seem to overlook the stress testing requirement within Pillar I, others are seeking a meaningful interpretation, possibly because they still see the benefits of a "just-in-case" conservative adjustment. One regulatory interpretation we observed was as follows: *Calculate parameters corresponding with moderate stress events (a mild recession for example); estimate Pillar I regulatory capital using the resulting stressed parameters, and demonstrate that the resulting capital requirement is still less than the current capital level.* This interpretation sounds like a place holder until Pillar II is implemented.

Pillar II is about capital adequacy, and FIs will need to demonstrate that they have sufficient capital also to guard against the "stress losses." In using the stressed parameters in Pillar II's Capital Adequacy Assessment Framework, there appear to be two options:

1. We can calculate the stressed economic and regulatory capital requirements using the stressed parameters and demonstrate that the stressed capital requirements are less than the current capital level; or

2. We can estimate the marked-to-model (MTM) stress losses and demonstrate that the stress MTM losses are less than the current capital level.

This topic is discussed in detail in Chapter 4 together with some other issues of Pillar II implementation.

In the following sections, we will explain a number of pragmatic methodologies in producing stressed PDs, LGDs, and EADs. We adopt the generic approach depicted in Figure 2.22:

1. The first step is to express the selected historical and hypothetical stress scenarios in terms of selected observable variables (e.g., macroeconomic variables).

2. The second step is to model the time-series relations between default rates, LGDs and EADs, and these observable variables.

3. In the third step, we can compute the conditional PDs, migration rates, LGDs, and EADs by utilizing the model developed in the second step. The inputs to the model are the current (unconditional)

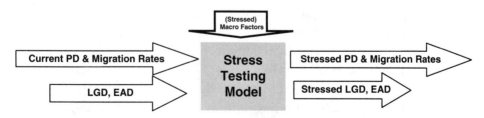

**Figure 2.22** Estimation of stressed parameters conditional upon explanatory factors.

PDs, LGDs, and EADs assigned to the risk ratings and the appropriate levels of the observable variables corresponding with the selected historical and hypothetical stress scenarios.

In the following subsections, we will consider methodologies in PD, migration rate, LGD, and EAD stress testing. Besides detailed illustrations of the proposed models, we also present two case studies in generating conditional PD and LGD under specific stress conditions. Finally, we will discuss the stressing of portfolio losses.

## PD Stress Testing Model

The proposed PD stress testing methodology described in detail subsequently entails a four-step process:

1. Extract the implicit PD from the observed external default rate data by catering for the level of asset correlation appropriate to the external data. It is essentially the same as decomposing an individual obligor's credit risk into its systematic and idiosyncratic components.
2. Model the systematic component of credit risk (which is now "free of any correlation effect" after the first step) obtained above by establishing the time-series relation with the observable variables (e.g., macroeconomic variables).
3. "Reconstruct" obligor-level PDs by incorporating the asset correlation specific to the bank's (internal) credit portfolio and bank's (internal) long-run PDs for each of the risk ratings.
4. Compute the conditional (internal) PDs contingent upon the stressed observed variables corresponding with the relevant historical or hypothetical stress scenarios to produce the stressed PD for each (internal) risk rating.

The approach presented above and described in detail subsequently has the following advantages:

1. It is entirely compatible with the IRRSs currently adopted by banks. The models are simple add-ons to FIs' current risk management processes making implementation and operations very time and cost effective.
2. Control for the effect of asset correlation; as a result:
   a. It leads to better (both conditional and unconditional) parameter estimations.

    *b.* It enables the use of external default rate data in calibrating
        the model, while we can still tailor for the LRPD and asset
        correlation specific to the bank's (internal) risk ratings.
3. It is fully consistent with the Basel II framework.
4. It enables industry-specific stress testing.

Now we can talk about the specifics of the methodology.

## Methodology [Please refer to Miu and Ozdemir (2008b) for further discussions.]

We again use the popular Merton structural framework where borrowers are
uniform in terms of their credit risks within a certain segment of the portfolio. Their individual PD risk $p_t$ at time $t$ is driven by both the systematic PD
risk $P_t$ and the borrower-specific PD risk $e_{PD,t}$. For example, for borrower $i$,

$$p_t^i = R_{PD} \times P_t + \sqrt{1 - R_{PD}^2} \times e_{PD,t}^i. \qquad \text{(Equation 2.51)}$$

Equation 2.51 is the single-factor model considered by Vasicek (1987) in
deriving the loss distribution of a credit portfolio. It is also the underlying
model implicit in the Basel risk-weight function. The idiosyncratic risk
factor $e_{PD,t}$ follows the standard normal distribution. Individual PD risk
factor $p_t$ can be interpreted as the borrower's asset value. That is, the
borrower defaults when $p_t$ becomes less than some constant default point
(DP). The coefficient $R_{PD}$ is uniform across borrowers and measures the
sensitivity of individual risks to the systematic PD risk. The parameter $R_{PD}^2$
is therefore the pairwise correlation in asset values among borrowers as
a result of the systematic risk factor.

    We would recall that LRPD ($p_{LR}$) is defined as the *unconditional* proba-
bility of $p_t$ being smaller than DP:

$$p_{LR} = \Pr\left[ p_t^i < DP \right]. \qquad \text{(Equation 2.52)}$$

LRPD is therefore a function of DP. This function is defined by the unconditional distribution of $p_t$, which is therefore governed by the unconditional
distribution of $P_t$ via Equation 2.51 above.

    We model the systematic PD risk $P_t$ as a function of $J$ explanatory vari-
ables, $X_t^1, X_t^2, \ldots, X_t^J$ as seen below:

$$P_t = f\left( X_t^1, X_t^2, \ldots, X_t^J, X_{t-1}^1, X_{t-1}^2, \ldots, X_{t-1}^J \right) + e_t. \qquad \text{(Equation 2.53)}$$

These explanatory variables could be macroeconomic variables, leading economic indicators, and/or industry-specific variables, which can explain the systematic PD risk of a particular sector. In Equation 2.53, besides the contemporaneous values of the explanatory variables, we can also include the lagged values of these variables as possible explanatory variables. The first term of Equation 2.53 (i.e., $f(\bullet)$) can be interpreted as the *explainable* component of $P_t$, whereas the second term $e_t$ is the *unexplainable* component. The residual $e_t$ is assumed to be normally distributed with zero mean and standard deviation equal to $\sigma_e$.

Under this framework, LRPD ($p_{LR}$), the parameters governing $f(\bullet)$ and the time-series of the expectation of $P_t$ conditional on $X_t^1$, $X_t^2$, ..., $X_t^J$ can be estimated by maximizing the log-likelihood of observing the time-series of historical default rates $\theta_t = k_t/n_t$ ($k_t$ is the number of defaults out of $n_t$ initial number of obligors during time period $t$). We may adopt different functional form for $f(\bullet)$, with the simplest versions being the linear and quadratic versions; for example,

$$f(\bullet) = \beta_{1,1} X_t^1 + \beta_{1,2} \left(X_t^1\right)^2 + \cdots + \beta_{J,1} X_t^J + \beta_{J,2} \left(X_t^J\right)^2. \qquad \text{(Equation 2.54)}$$

Empirical studies suggest it is quite likely that PD risk is serially correlated. Specifically, a higher than average default rate is more likely to be followed by a higher than average one than a lower than average one in the subsequent year. In the proposed model, part of this serial correlation in PD risk can be explained by the serial correlation inherent in the explanatory variables. Nevertheless, residual serial correlation effect might still remain after the explanatory variables are fully accounted for. We can cater for this residual effect by modeling $e_t$ itself as a time-series process. One of the simplest being an AR(1) process as depicted in Equation 2.55.

$$e_t = \rho \cdot e_{t-1} + u_t. \qquad \text{(Equation 2.55)}$$

The residuals $e_t$ therefore has a variance-covariance matrix of

$$\sigma_e^2 \Lambda_e = \sigma_e^2 \begin{bmatrix} 1 & \rho & \rho^2 & . & \rho^{T-1} \\ \rho & 1 & \rho & . & \rho^{T-2} \\ \rho^2 & \rho & 1 & . & \rho^{T-3} \\ . & . & . & . & . \\ \rho^{T-1} & \rho^{T-2} & \rho^{T-3} & . & 1 \end{bmatrix}, \qquad \text{(Equation 2.56)}$$

where $\rho$ is the serial correlation.

With the above specifications together with the assumption of infinitely granular portfolio composition, the joint likelihood of observing the historical time-series of default rates can be expressed as:

$$L = \frac{\exp\left[-\frac{1}{2}\left(\frac{DP - R_{PD}f(\bullet) - \sqrt{1 - R_{PD}^2}\,\Phi^{-1}(\theta)}{R_{PD}}\right)'\left(\sigma_e^2\Lambda_e\right)^{-1}\left(\frac{DP - R_{PD}f(\bullet) - \sqrt{1 - R_{PD}^2}\,\Phi^{-1}(\theta)}{R_{PD}}\right)\right]}{(2\pi)^{T/2}\left|\sigma_e^2\Lambda_e\right|^{1/2}},$$

(Equation 2.57)

where $\theta = [\theta_1\ \theta_2 \dots \theta_T]'$ is the vector of observed default rates. We can therefore obtain the MLE estimators of DP, $\beta$, $\sigma_e$, $R_{PD}^2$, and $\rho$ by maximizing $\log(L)$.[51] Once DP is estimated, we can then compute LRPD ($p_{LR}$) by numerically evaluating Equation 2.52 through the simulations of $p_t^i$. The individual PD risk $p_t^i$ is constructed by using Equations 2.51 and 2.53 through the simulations of the explanatory variables $X$ and thus the evaluation of $f(\bullet)$ via Equation 2.54 with the estimated parametric values of $\beta$. As a by-product of the estimation process, we can also retrieve the *explainable* (i.e., conditional on observing $X_t^1, X_t^2, \dots, X_t^J$) and the *unexplainable* component of $P_t$.

The proposed model allows us to calculate the conditional PDs under different stress scenarios. Given certain realizations of the explanatory variables (i.e., $X_t^1 = x_t^1, X_t^2 = x_t^2, \dots, X_t^J = x_t^J$), the conditional PD can be estimated by evaluating the conditional probability:

$$\Pr\left[p_t^i < DP \Big| X_t^1 = x_t^1, X_t^2 = x_t^2, \dots, X_t^J = x_t^J\right]$$

$$= \Pr\left[R_{PD} \times f\left(x_t^1, x_t^2, x_t^3\right) + R_{PD} \times e_t + \sqrt{1 - R_{PD}^2} \times e_{PD,t}^i < DP\right]$$

$$= \Phi\left[\frac{DP - R_{PD} \times f\left(x_t^1, x_t^2, x_t^3\right)}{\sqrt{1 - R_{PD}^2 + \sigma_e^2 R_{PD}^2}}\right].$$

(Equation 2.58)

### Model Development Process
*Segment Selection*   We usually develop a number of models. Some models are more broad-based such as "Overall U.S." or "Overall Canada," which helps FIs to quantify the impact of the stress events on the performance of the aggregate credit portfolio in a certain region/country. Other models are more industry specific, such as models specific to the oil and gas, real estate, or financial sectors. Through the uses of these industry-specific

models, FIs can achieve a more detailed understanding of the impact of the stress events on certain industries that are particularly important to them.

*Data Selection*   As the proposed methodology accounts for the potential differences in LRPD and asset correlations between the bank's (internal) credit portfolio and the (external) sample over which the rating agencies collect the default rate data, the model can be calibrated using the typically longer external default rate data, which enhances the accuracy of the estimations. There are a number of alternative external default data sets. For example, one may use the historical default rate data extracted from Standard & Poor's CreditPro. CreditPro allows users to specify the characteristics (i.e., its credit rating) of the portfolio over which default rate data are compiled. We recommend to focus on the historical default rates of speculative-grade issuers. The advantage of using speculative-grade issuers (rather than investment-grade or the overall portfolio) is that their default rate data tend to be less sparse and thus more informative and sensitive to the changing credit conditions. Arguably, we could have worked with migration rates of investment-grade obligors. But migration rates are philosophy specific. By focusing on only the default rates of speculative-grade borrowers, we do not need to concern ourselves with risk rating philosophy because default event is an objective event. We can also use overlapping data (e.g., quarterly-observed annual default rates) to enrich the data set and enhance the accuracy of the estimation, bearing in mind that any additional serial correlation generated with an overlapping data set will be picked up as a higher estimated value of the serial correlation coefficient $\rho$ of Equation 2.55.

*Selection of Explanatory Variables*   The following is a list of important criteria in selecting explanatory variables $X$:

- **Explanatory power:** Naturally we would like to use variables with the highest explanatory power in the modeling of the systematic credit risk.
- **Forecastability of the variables:** We need to make sure the variables selected can be forecasted by the FI (typically its economic department) under the specified stress events in a consistent fashion.
- **Stress testing models versus forecasting models:** If we would like to use these models also for forecasting of PD using the current values of the explanatory variables (rather than during the

stressed scenario), we need to consider the use of various *leading indicators* as explanatory variables (e.g., the national composite leading indicators).

- **Model coverage:** For broad-based ("general") models, such as an "Overall Canada" model, we need to use more generic macroeconomics factors (i.e., interest rate and GDP), whereas for industry-specific models we should consider industry-specific factors. See Figure 2.23 for a few examples.

- **Data availability:** Data availability is essential for modeling and forecasting. We need to be careful that even though historical

| **Canada General Model** |
| --- |
| • Real GDP |
| • Industrial production |
| • Unemployment |
| • Corporate profits |
| • Slope of the yield curve |
| • High-yield spreads |
| • Equity indices |
| • Composite index of leading indicators for Canada |
| • Consumer credit |
| • Delinquency rates (DR) |
| • Short-term interest rate |

**Real Estate Model**

| **General health of the economy:** |
| --- |
| • GDP |
| • Unemployment |
| • Interest rates |
| • Retail sales |
| • Composite Index of Leading Indicators |
| • Consumer Sentiment Index |
| • Durable goods |
| • S&P 500, TSE Composite Index |

| **Specific to the sector:** |
| --- |
| • S&P/TSX Capped Real Estate Index |
| • New building permits |
| • New housing starts (Leading Indicator - Stats Canada) |
| • Residential real estate (U.S.) |
| • House price appreciation |
| • Housing affordability index |
| • Commercial real estate (U.S.) |
|     • Vacancy rates |
|     • Rents per square foot |

**Figure 2.23**  Potential explanatory variables for Canada General Model and Real Estate Model.

time-series of some of the variables are available, the calculation methodology of the variables has been changed creating consistency problems.

- **Correlations among the variables:** We should not include highly correlated variables in the model to prevent multicollinearity and overfitting.
- **Representation and coverage:** We should try to include variables explaining the credit environment (e.g., ratio of downgrade to total rating actions, Standard & Poor's outlook distribution, etc.) as well as general economic and financial indicators.

### Modeling Procedure

*Step 1: Univariate Analysis*   We first examine all potential and available explanatory variables in a univariate setting. Essentially, we calibrate the proposed model repeatedly, every time using only a single but different explanatory variable in $f(\bullet)$ in Equation 2.53. The objective is to arrive at a "short list" of statistically significant variables. Besides judging by their statistical power, we also look for variables that are related to the observed default rates in an intuitive fashion. For example, we expect GDP growth rate to be negatively related to the change in default rates. Specifically, during a credit downturn, GDP growth rate decreases whereas default rates increase. This short list of variables will then be examined more closely in the subsequent multivariate analysis.

*Step 2: Multivariate Analysis*   In this step, we develop multivariate models using all possible combinations of the variables short-listed above following the protocols discussed below. We first check if the short-listed variables obtained in step 1 are highly correlated. Including highly correlated variables simultaneously in the multivariate analysis will generate spurious results and thus should be avoided. That is, any pair of variables with high pairwise correlation should not enter into the analysis simultaneously. Another criteria is the square of a variable is only included if its linear version is also included in the same model. We exhaust all possible combinations of variables satisfying these criteria and calibrate each of these models. For each model, we estimate the coefficients (i.e., $\beta$) of the explanatory variables and the corresponding $t$-statistics. We also consider an "intercept" model in which no variables are used. This is used as a benchmark model of which the estimated log-likelihood can be used in the subsequent likelihood ratio analysis to measure and compare the goodness-of-fit of each model. Besides looking for statistical significance, we also examine whether the models are intuitive and exclude those that are not. Specifically, a model is intuitive if the estimated coefficients are of the expected sign and the relative sizes of the estimated coefficients of the linear and quadratic terms make sense. We then select the best-fitted model based on the standards tests like log-likelihood ratio, McFadden's pseudo adjusted R-square (R-sq), Cox & Snell's pseudo R-sq, and the reduction in the Akaike Information Criterion (AIC) from the intercept model.

The McFadden's pseudo R-sq is equal to:

$$1 - \frac{\ln L_{\text{model}}}{\ln L_{\text{intercept}}}.$$

where $\ln L_{\text{model}}$ and $\ln L_{\text{intercept}}$ are the log-likelihoods of the specific model we want to appraise and that of the intercept model, respectively. The McFadden's pseudo adjusted R-sq penalizes models for including too many predictors. If the explanatory variables in the model are effective, then the penalty will be small relative to the added information of the variables. However, if a model contains predictors that do not add sufficiently to the model, then the penalty becomes significant and the adjusted R-sq can decrease with the addition of a variable. Selecting model based on the pseudo adjusted R-sq can therefore ensure the data are not overfitted. The McFadden's pseudo adjusted R-sq can be expressed as

$$1 - \frac{\ln L_{\text{model}} - J}{\ln L_{\text{intercept}}},$$

where $J$ is the number of explanatory variables in the model.

Cox & Snell's pseudo R-sq is expressed based on the likelihood ratio and thus invariant to any ignored constant term of the log-likelihood function:

$$1 - \left[ \frac{L_{\text{model}}}{L_{\text{intercept}}} \right]^{2/T},$$

where $T$ is the number of observation. Similar to McFadden's pseudo R-sq, there is no penalty to guard against overfitting.

Besides selecting model based on adjusted pseudo R-sq, we can also consider the AIC of the model

$$\text{AIC} = 2k - \ln L,$$

where $k$ is the number of parameters to be estimated in the model. The lower the AIC, the better is the goodness-of-fit (i.e., higher log-likelihood)

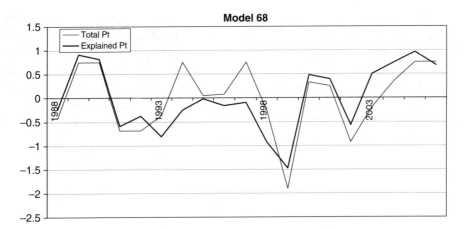

**Figure 2.24** Goodness of fit of estimated model: observed (total) Pt vs. explainable component of Pt.

and the more parsimonious (i.e., $k$ is small) the model. We rank all qualified models independently based on its McFadden's pseudo adjusted R-sq and the reduction in AIC from the intercept model and identify the model of the best in-sample goodness-of-fit.

Besides comparing the in-sample goodness-of-fit, we also conduct out-of-sample tests by exhausting all the different cases of holding out data points of the full sample. We estimate each model using the remaining data points and evaluate the root mean square errors (RMSE) of the hold-out sample (i.e., computing the mean of the square of the residual $u_t$ of Equation 2.55 at the hold-out sample points). We then rank the models from the smallest median RMSE to the largest. We then obtain a model with both high in-sample goodness-of-fit and out-of-sample performance. We also visually examine the goodness of fit by plotting the *observed* (total) $P_t$ against the *explainable component* of $P_t$ (i.e., $f(\bullet)$). An example is given in Figure 2.24.

## A Case Study: Generating PD under Stressed Condition

In this section, we demonstrate the use of a model calibrated against Standard & Poor's (external) default rate data under stressed conditions that can be expressed in terms of levels of the selected explanatory variables. Suppose we have developed this PD stress model for a specific industrial sector that attains the highest in-sample and out-of-sample performance rankings following the model-building procedure described above. The estimated parameters of this model (utilizing a total of three different explanatory variables) are summarized in Table 2.26.

Suppose the LRPD (i.e., unconditional PD) of an internal risk rating is 0.02%. The corresponding $DP$ is –3.38, which is obtained by simulating the explanatory variables. Further suppose the appropriate pairwise asset correlation for this risk rating is 0.25 and we are interested in a stress scenario that corresponds with a (minus) two standard deviation shock to all of the explanatory variables. We can evaluate the conditional PD of this risk rating under the stress scenario using Equation 2.58, that is,

$$\Phi\left[\frac{-3.38 - \sqrt{0.25} \times (0.218 + 0.224 + 0.371) \times (-2)}{\sqrt{1 - 0.25 + 0.227 \times 0.25}}\right] = \Phi[-2.8580] = 0.21\%.$$

The above evaluation can easily be repeated:

- for different levels of stress condition, by simply entering the corresponding number of standard deviations for each variable; and
- for other risk rating, by entering a DP corresponding with the LRPD of that risk rating.

**T A B L E  2.26**

Estimated Parameters for the PD Stress Model

|  | Point Estimate | t-Statistic |
|---|---|---|
| $\Phi(DP)$** | 0.031 | 7.000 |
| Estimated coefficient ($\beta$) |  |  |
| Variable 1 at $t-1$ | 0.218 | 1.966 |
| Variable 2 at $t-1$ | 0.224 | 2.167 |
| Variable 3 at $t$ | 0.371 | 3.517 |
| Variance of residual | 0.227 | — |
| Serial correlation $\rho$ | 0.272 | 1.205 |
| LRPD* | 2.4% | — |

*This is the LRPD estimate of the external default rate data and is a by-product of the estimation process. This estimate will not be used in the computation of the conditional PD of the bank's internal risk rating. In computing the conditional PD, we use the LRPD specific to the internal risk rating.

**$\Phi(\bullet)$ is the cumulative normal distribution function.

## Stressing Migration Rates

During stress periods and downturns, not only PDs increase but also the expected downgrade rates increase (whereas expected upgrade rates decrease). Similar to PD stress testing, we would like to model these changes with observable variables. Then, once we can express the historical and hypothetical scenario in terms of these explanatory variables, we can compute conditional migration rates under these stress conditions. Conditional migration rates can be used in assessing MTM loss, capital requirement, and risk rating composition of an FI's portfolio under the stress scenario.

Table 2.27 illustrates sample unconditional (i.e., long-run) and conditional transition matrices. If we look at risk rating 3 (in panel A) for

**T A B L E  2.27**

Unconditional and Conditional Transition Matrices[52]

Panel A: Unconditional (long-run) rating transition matrix

|  |  | Expected Transition Rates at the End of the Year | | | | | |
|---|---|---|---|---|---|---|---|
|  |  | Risk Rating 1 (%) | Risk Rating 2 (%) | Risk Rating 3 (%) | Risk Rating 4 (%) | Risk Rating 5 (%) | Unconditional PD (%) |
| Current Ratings | Risk rating 1 | 80 | 10 | 4 | 3 | 2 | 1 |
|  | Risk rating 2 | 2 | 65 | 15 | 10 | 4 | 4 |
|  | Risk rating 3 | 1 | 5 | 60 | 20 | 6 | 8 |
|  | Risk rating 4 | 0 | 2 | 3 | 50 | 30 | 15 |
|  | Risk rating 5 | 0 | 0 | 15 | 20 | 40 | 25 |

Panel B: Conditional rating transition matrix

|  |  | Expected Transition Rates at the End of the Year | | | | | |
|---|---|---|---|---|---|---|---|
|  |  | Risk Rating 1 (%) | Risk Rating 2 (%) | Risk Rating 3 (%) | Risk Rating 4 (%) | Risk Rating 5 (%) | Conditional PD (%) |
| Current Ratings | Risk rating 1 | 63 | 15 | 10 | 5 | 4 | 3 |
|  | Risk rating 2 | 0 | 42 | 25 | 15 | 10 | 8 |
|  | Risk rating 3 | 0 | 1 | 35 | 30 | 20 | 14 |
|  | Risk rating 4 | 0 | 0 | 0 | 30 | 40 | 30 |
|  | Risk rating 5 | 0 | 0 | 5 | 10 | 35 | 50 |

instance, long-run PD is 8%, expected downgrade probability to risk rating 4 is 20%, and expected upgrade probability to risk rating 2 is 5% over a one-year period. These are unconditional probabilities. During a stress period (panel B), for the same risk rating 3, the conditional PD increases to 14%. Moreover, expected conditional downgrade probability to risk rating 4 increases to 30%, whereas expected conditional upgrade probability to risk rating 2 reduces to 1%. By comparing the unconditional (long-run) and conditional transition matrices, similar effects can be observed for all other risk ratings.

Following the stress event, two kinds of portfolio deterioration are happening simultaneously:

1. PDs are increasing as seen above by comparing the unconditional PDs with their conditional counterparts; and
2. Expected downgrade (upgrade) probabilities are increasing (decreasing) relative to their unconditional counterparts.

The first effect above can lead to (immediate) downgrade actions of the obligors under a constant risk rating–PD mapping right after the stress event. The second effect, on the other hand, represents the expected deterioration of the portfolio in terms of increasing downgrade and decreasing upgrade probabilities within a year after the stress event. To quantify the total effect of the stress event, both effects are required to be modeled. We have seen that some FIs are only capturing the first effect by following the below process. They first estimate the conditional PDs (but not the expected conditional migration rates) as depicted in Table 2.28. Then, they downgrade their obligors according to their master scale (in Table 2.29).

**T A B L E   2.28**

Unconditional (LRPD) and Conditional PDs

|  | Unconditional PD (%) | Conditional PD (%) |
| --- | --- | --- |
| Risk rating 1 | 1 | 3 |
| Risk rating 2 | 4 | 8 |
| Risk rating 3 | 8 | 14 |
| Risk rating 4 | 15 | 30 |
| Risk rating 5 | 25 | 50 |

**TABLE 2.29**

Master Scale

|  | Master Scale | | |
| --- | --- | --- | --- |
|  | Minimum | Mid | Maximum |
| Risk rating 1 | 0 | 1 | 2.0 |
| Risk rating 2 | 2.0 | 4 | 6.0 |
| Risk rating 3 | 6.0 | 8 | 11.0 |
| Risk rating 4 | 11.0 | 15 | 20.0 |
| Risk rating 5 | 20.0 | 25 | 50.0 |

For example, PDs of the obligors in risk rating 1 will increase from 1% to 3% during the stress event, meaning that we need to downgrade all of them to risk rating 2 as per the master scale in Table 2.29. Similarly, PDs of the obligors in risk rating 2 will increase from 4% to 8%, thus they will be downgraded to risk rating 3 again as per the master scale ranges. Note that by doing so, we have only captured the downgrades right after the stress event but did not capture the expected increase in downgrades thereafter during the year following the stress event. This is because we never estimated the conditional expected rating transition rates, which are required in measuring the total effect of the stress event. In other words, we did not capture the longer-term effects of the stress event.[53]

What business questions we want to answer will dictate how we would like to calibrate our stress model. For example, if we calibrate our model by trying to relate the observed migration rate with lagging explanatory variables (e.g., the change in real GDP during the last 12 months), we will obtain the conditional transition matrix (TM), which covers the coming 12 months *after* observing the stressed explanatory variables as illustrated in Figure 2.25. The resulting conditional PD can be used to re-rate all obligors for possible (immediate) downgrades at time $T_{\text{Stress}}$. The resulting conditional TM can also be used to evaluate the MTM losses at time $T_{\text{Stress}}$. Alternatively, they can be used in the calculation of capital requirement over the next 12 months and in MTM calculation at the end of the next 12 months.

On the other hand, if we calibrate our model in a "contemporaneous" fashion (as illustrated in Figure 2.26), we will generate conditional TM over the last 12 months over which we also observe the changes in the explanatory variables. The resulting conditional TM would have already been realized when we observe the stressed explanatory variables at time $T_{\text{Stress}}$. In this case, we can use the conditional TM for MTM calculation as of $T_{\text{Stress}}$.

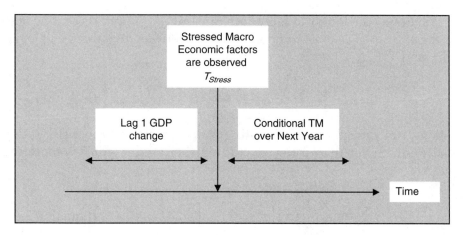

**Figure 2.25**  Calibration with lagging explanatory variables.

## Estimation of Conditional Transition Matrix

Similar to PD stress testing model, we model stress migration rates by assuming an obligor's asset value ($p_t$) is made up of a systematic component ($P_t$) and an idiosyncratic component ($e_{\mathrm{PD},t}$)

$$p_t^i = R_{\mathrm{PD}} \times P_t + \sqrt{1 - R_{\mathrm{PD}}^2} \times e_{\mathrm{PD},t}^i. \qquad \text{(Equation 2.59)}$$

where $P_t$ is related to the explanatory variables via function $f$

$$P_t = f\left(X_t^1, X_t^2, \ldots, X_t^J, X_{t-1}^1, X_{t-1}^2, \ldots, X_{t-1}^J\right) + e_t. \qquad \text{(Equation 2.60)}$$

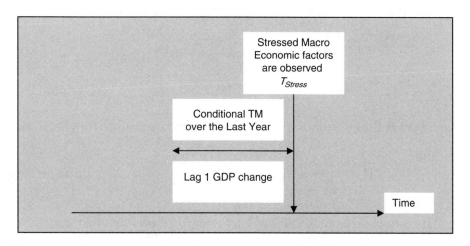

**Figure 2.26**  Calibration with contemporaneous explanatory variables.

We define the long-run migration rate ($\mathrm{mg}_{\mathrm{LR},m,n}$) from risk rating $m$ to $n$ as the *unconditional probability* of $p_t$ lying in between two threshold levels ($\mathrm{TH}_{m,n}$ and $\mathrm{TH}_{m,n+1}$), that is,

$$\mathrm{mg}_{\mathrm{LR},m,n} = \Pr\left[\mathrm{TH}_{m,n+1} < p_t^i < \mathrm{TH}_{m,n}\right]. \qquad \text{(Equation 2.61)}$$

The long-run probability of migrating from risk rating $m$ to a risk rating equal to or higher than $n$ (i.e., including the default state) is therefore equal to

$$\sum_{s=n}^{N} \mathrm{mg}_{\mathrm{LR},m,s} = \Pr\left[p_t^i < \mathrm{TH}_{m,n}\right]. \qquad \text{(Equation 2.62)}$$

Under this framework, the migration thresholds can be estimated by maximizing the log-likelihood of observing the time-series of historical migration rates $k_{m,n,t}/n_{m,t}$ (i.e., $k_{m,n,t}$ is the number of migrations from risk rating $m$ to risk ratings equal to or higher than $n$ at the end of time period $t$, and $n_{m,t}$ is the initial number of obligors of risk rating $m$ at the beginning of time period $t$) and by using the time-series values of $P_t$ estimated in the PD stress model of which the development is explained in the section on "PD Stress Testing Model" earlier in this chapter.

Let us start by examining the probability of migrating from risk rating $m$ to a risk rating equal to or higher than $n$ of borrower $i$ conditional on $P_t$

$$\Pr\left[p_t^i < \mathrm{TH}_{m,n}|P_t\right] = \Pr\left[R_{\mathrm{PD}} \times P_t + \sqrt{1-R_{\mathrm{PD}}^2} \times e_{\mathrm{PD},t}^i < \mathrm{DP}|P_t\right]$$

$$= \Pr\left[e_{\mathrm{PD},t}^i < \frac{\mathrm{TH}_{m,n} - R_{\mathrm{PD}} \times P_t}{\sqrt{1-R_{\mathrm{PD}}^2}}\middle|P_t\right]$$

$$= \Phi\left(z\left(R_{\mathrm{PD}}, \mathrm{TH}_{m,n}, P_t\right)\right), \qquad \text{(Equation 2.63)}$$

where $\Phi(\bullet)$ is the cumulative standard normal distribution function, and

$$z(\bullet) = \frac{1}{\sqrt{1-R_{\mathrm{PD}}^2}}\left(\mathrm{TH}_{m,n} - R_{\mathrm{PD}}P_t\right). \qquad \text{(Equation 2.64)}$$

The probability of survival of borrower $i$ is therefore equal to

$$1 - \Phi(z(\bullet)).$$

Because $e^i_{\text{PD},t}$ is independent of $e^j_{\text{PD},t}$ for $i \neq j$, the probability of observing $k_{m,n,t}$ migrations out of $n_{m,t}$ borrowers is therefore equal to

$$\Omega\left(k_{m,n,t}, n_{m,t}; R_{\text{PD}}, \text{TH}_{m,n}, P_t\right) = \binom{n_{m,t}}{k_{m,n,t}} \times (\Phi(z(\bullet))^{k_{m,n,t}}$$

$$\times (1 - \Phi((z(\bullet)))^{n_{m,t}-k_{m,n,t}}. \qquad \text{(Equation 2.65)}$$

The sum of the logarithmic of the joint likelihood of observing the time-series of $k_{m,n,1}, k_{m,n,2}, \ldots, k_{m,n,T}$ and $n_{m,1}, n_{m,2}, \ldots, n_{m,T}$ is therefore

$$\log L = \sum_{t=1}^{T} \log \Omega\left(k_{m,n,t}, n_{m,t}; R_{\text{PD}}, \text{TH}_{m,n}, P_t\right). \qquad \text{(Equation 2.66)}$$

By using the time-series of $P_t$ obtained in the PD stress model (of which the development is explained in the section on "PD Stress Testing Model"), we can estimate the migration threshold $\text{TH}_{m,n}$ by assuming a value for the pairwise asset correlation and by maximizing $\log L$ of Equation 2.66.

Once the thresholds are estimated, the conditional migration rate from risk rating $m$ to $n$ can be obtained by evaluating the conditional probability of the asset value falls in between the thresholds $\text{TH}_{m,n}$ and $\text{TH}_{m,n+1}$

$$\Pr\left[\text{TH}_{m,n+1} < p_t^i < \text{TH}_{m,n} \middle| X_t^1 = x_t^1, X_t^2 = x_t^2, \ldots, X_t^J = x_t^J\right]. \qquad \text{(Equation 2.67)}$$

Since it is most likely that we need to use transition matrices based on external data (due to the limited internal data) for the estimation of (unconditional) migration thresholds, there are a few things we need to be careful about. First, we need to "common size" the external and internal transition matrices. In most cases, we have to consolidate some of the external risk ratings (i.e., combining AAA+ and AAA) to match those of the internal ratings. Second, long-run default rates implied by the external data of the matching risk ratings are likely to be different from those implied by the internal risk ratings. To cater for this difference, we need to replace the external LRPD with the LRPD implicit in the internal default rates. Together with such changes, we also have to modify the external migration rates accordingly to make sure that the sum of default and migration probabilities still add up to unity for each risk rating. Third, we need to adjust for the difference in the external and internal risk rating philosophies. The chances are external ratings are more TTC than are internal ratings, resulting in lower migration rates than what would have observed internally, if we had had the data. We can account for this difference by using a (smaller) asset correlation (i.e., $R^2_{PD}$), which is appropriate for the bank's more PIT IRRS when we generate the conditional migration rates using Equation 2.67.

### Estimation of PDs in Developing Countries

Estimation of PDs in countries with structural changes is particularly challenging as the relevance of historical default rates is questionable. In some of these countries, due to their double-digit growth and the structural changes, it has been argued that the historical default rates are unlikely to be observed going forward and thus the long-run PDs estimated from the historical default rates would be overly conservative to serve as the current PD.

There is a pragmatic approach to deal with the issue using the methodology described above for stress testing PDs. We can estimate the long-run PDs using the historical data and condition these PDs on "favorable forecasted economic conditions." In effect, we are estimating PIT PDs that are less than the long-run PDs due to the favorable macroeconomic indicators (rather than stressed macroeconomic indicators corresponding with the stress events). Sometimes we observe that some FIs use, say, the arithmetic average of last couple of years' default rates as PIT PD citing that next year's economy is likely to be similar to that of the last two years. The approach of conditioning long-run PDs on the forecasted economic conditions while serving the same purpose of estimating PIT PDs provides an objective framework for it. Under this approach, we assume that the long-run PD did not change over time but instead we are at a good part of the cycle. If we would like to incorporate a structural change to our long-run PD estimation itself, this can be done as well.

### LGD Stress Testing Model

#### Overview [Please refer to Miu and Ozdemir (2008b) for further discussions]

In this section, we discuss how to estimate stressed LGDs conditional on selected explanatory variables. In this approach, as illustrated in Figure 2.27, the explanatory variables (e.g., macroeconomics factors) and the current unconditional LGDs serve as inputs of the stress model, whereas the conditional LGDs are the outputs. We may use two alternative methods. Under Method I, the systematic LGD risk factor will be modeled directly, whereas under Method II, the stress models for systematic PD risk factor (developed in the section "PD Stress Testing Model") will be utilized under specific assumptions. Although Method I is theoretically more appealing, it requires a long time-series of historical LGD data that might not be easily

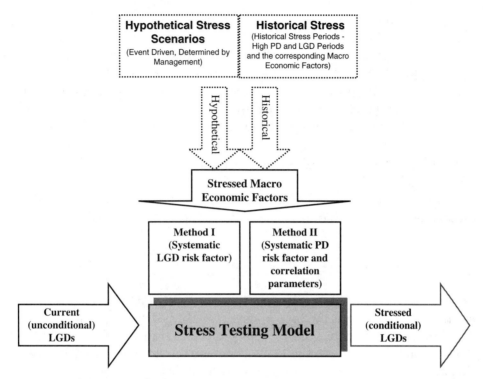

**Figure 2.27** Schematic of LGD stress testing.

available internally. Method II relies on historical default rate data, which is more readily available than is LGD data. It however also requires the estimation of the correlation parameters described in the section "Down-turn LGD" (method 3). Method II therefore allows us to leverage the PD stress models developed for PD stress testing. Both approaches allow us to generate conditional LGDs for different segments contingent upon the realizations of the explanatory variables that represent the historical and event-driven stress scenarios.

There have been a number of studies (e.g., Acharya et al., 2007; Schonbucher, 2003; Andersen and Sidenius, 2005; Varma and Cantor, 2005) proposing methodologies to estimate recovery rates (i.e., one minus LGD) using selected macroeconomic factors. Standard logit/probit models are commonly used to explain the level of LGD based on various explanatory factors. The approach presented below is uniquely different from these predecessors in the following ways:

1.  It incorporates the effect of correlations.
2.  It enables the use of external data in the calibration of the model.

3. It is consistent with the Basel II framework and allows for the estimation of conditional LGDs, which can in turn be used by banks in their existing models to simulate portfolio loss and capital requirement under different stress scenarios.

4. It lends itself for a convenient methodology, where stressed PDs and LGDs can be simulated in a correlated fashion to estimate portfolio losses under selected stress scenarios.

## Method I: Estimating Stressed LGDs Contingent upon Systematic LGD Risk Factor $L_t$

An individual facility's (or borrower's) LGD risk $l_{t,}$ is assumed to be a latent variable being made up of its systematic and idiosyncratic components as expressed in Equation 2.68.

$$l_t^i = R_{\text{LGD}} \times L_t + \sqrt{1 - R_{\text{LGD}}^2} \times e_{\text{LGD},t}^i. \qquad \text{(Equation 2.68)}$$

where $L_t$ represents the market-wide systematic LGD risk at time $t$. We assume the facility-specific (i.e., idiosyncratic) LGD risk $e_{\text{LGD},t}$ follows the standard normal distribution. We interpret $l_t$ as a transformed distribution of the empirical distribution of LGD. There is a one-to-one monotonic mapping between the value of $l_t$ and the realized LGD value, which is typically bounded between zero and one. The higher the value of $l_t$, the higher the facility's LGD. The coefficient $R_{\text{LGD}}$ is uniform across facilities and measures the sensitivity of the individual LGD risk to the systematic LGD risk factor $L_t$. The parameter $R_{\text{LGD}}^2$ therefore becomes the pairwise correlation in LGD risk among facilities as a result of the systematic risk factor.

LGD of facility $i$ can therefore be obtained by transforming $l_t$ via the following equation:

$$\text{LGD}_t^i = B^{-1}\left(\Phi\left(l_t^i\right), a, b\right) \qquad \text{(Equation 2.69)}$$

where $B^{-1}(\bullet)$ donates the inverse of the cumulative beta distribution with the shape parameters $a$ and $b$, and $\Phi(\bullet)$ donates the cumulative standard normal distribution, which transforms $l_t^i$ to a uniform distribution.

We model the systematic LGD risk $L_t$ as a function of $J$ explanatory variables, $X_t^1, X_t^2, \ldots, X_t^J$

$$L_t = f_L\left(X_t^1, X_t^2, \ldots, X_t^J\right) + \varepsilon_{\text{LGD},t}. \qquad \text{(Equation 2.70)}$$

These explanatory variables could be macroeconomic variables, leading economic indicators, and/or industry-specific variables, which are believed to govern the systematic LGD risk of a particular sector. Under this framework, the time-series of the expectation of $L_t$ conditional on $X_t^1$, $X_t^2, \ldots, X_t^J$ can be estimated from the time series of LGD observations, $\text{LGD}_t^i$.

*Estimation of Conditional LGDs under Stress Scenarios*   The proposed model allows us to calculate the conditional LGDs under different stress scenarios, once we have calibrated the relation between $L_t$ and the explanatory variables as expressed in Equation 2.70. Formally, given certain realizations of the explanatory variables (i.e., $X_t^1 = x_t^1$, $X_t^2 = x_t^2, \ldots, X_t^J = x_t^J$), the conditional distribution of LGD can be obtained by

$$\text{LGD}_t^i = B^{-1}\left(\Phi\left(l_t^i \middle| X_t^1 = x_t^1, X_t^2 = x_t^2, \ldots, X_t^J = x_t^J\right), a, b\right) \qquad \text{(Equation 2.71)}$$

which is equivalent to

$$\text{LGD}_t^i = B^{-1}\left(\Phi\left(R_{\text{LGD}} \times \left(f_L\left(X_t^1 = x_t^1, X_t^2 = x_t^2, \ldots, X_t^J = x_t^J\right)\right.\right.\right.$$
$$\left.\left.\left. + \varepsilon_{\text{LGD},t}\right) + \sqrt{1 - R_{\text{LGD}}^2} \times e_{\text{LGD},t}^i\right), a, b\right). \qquad \text{(Equation 2.72)}$$

We can then obtain the conditional mean and variance of LGD by simulating from the conditional distribution of Equation 2.72. The process can be summarized as follow:

1. Estimate the shape parameters $a$, and $b$, and $R_{\text{LGD}}^2$ using historical LGD data.
2. Estimate the function governing the relation between $L_t$ and the explanatory variables in Equation 2.70 using time-series of historical LGD data and explanatory variables; ideally, the function is formulated differently for different industry sectors and classes of facilities (e.g., secured vs. unsecured).
3. Hypothetical stress scenarios and/or historically observed stress events are expressed in terms of the selected explanatory variables taking on specific realized values (i.e., $X_t^1 = x_t^1$, $X_t^2 = x_t^2, \ldots, X_t^J = x_t^J$).
4. Simulate $e_{\text{LGD},t}^i$ and $\varepsilon_{\text{LGD},t}$, and construct

$$l_t^i = R_{\text{LGD}} \times \left(f_L\left(X_t^1 = x_t^1, X_t^2 = x_t^2, \ldots, X_t^J = x_t^J\right) + \varepsilon_{\text{LGD},t}\right) + \sqrt{1 - R_{\text{LGD}}^2} \times e_{\text{LGD},t}^i.$$

5. Construct the distribution of $\text{LGD}_t^i = B^{-1}(\Phi(l_t^i), a, b)$.
6. Numerically evaluate the conditional statistics of $E[\text{LGD}_t^i]$ and $\text{Var}(\text{LGD}_t^i)$.

The proposed methodology has the advantage of allowing for the use of external LGD data to supplement the lack of internal LGD data. Banks implementing stress-testing methodologies would need data for calibration. Internal LGD data are usually insufficient, as the time series is typically short not incorporating the historically observed major stress events. This creates a need to rely on external LGD data, for example Standard & Poor's LossStat Database, for calibration. The methodology presented above enables us to use the external LGD data as it strips out the portfolio-specific correlation effect. Because we can control for the potential difference in the degree of LGD correlation, we could estimate the time-series of $L_t$ from external LGD data, using the appropriate pairwise correlation, but can still use the estimated $L_t$ to conduct stress testing internally. We can also further enhance the analysis by establishing more correlation-homogeneous subsegments when we use the external data.

### Method II: Estimating Stressed LGDs Contingent upon Systematic PD Risk Factor $P_t$

Estimating stressed LGD contingent upon $L_t$ is a methodologically preferred method. We however may not always have sufficient LGD data from which we can robustly estimate $L_t$. In this section, we show that under some simplifying assumptions, we can also estimate stressed LGD contingent upon the default rate systematic factor $P_t$, which can be estimated from more readily available default data.[54] The other fundamental advantage of this alternative method is the utilization of the same default rate systematic factor, $P_t$, modeled for PD stress testing (see "PD Stress Testing Model" section).

More formally, our purpose is to estimate $E[\mathrm{LGD}_t^i \mid P_{t,\mathrm{Stress}}]$ per LGD segment for which $P_t$ is modeled as

$$P_t = f_P(X_t^1, X_t^2, \ldots, X_t^J) + \varepsilon_{\mathrm{PD},t}.$$

This can be done following the steps below.

1. Estimate time series of $P_t$ from the time series of default rate for the selected segment.
2. Model $P_t = f_P(X_t^1, X_t^2, \ldots, X_t^J) + \varepsilon_{\mathrm{PD},t}$.
3. Estimate $L_t$ contingent upon $P_t$.
4. Estimate the distribution of $l_t$ contingent upon $P_t$.
5. Transform the distribution of $l_t$ to distribution of LGD.

*Details*   The first two steps are described in detail in the "PD Stress Testing Model" section. Let's therefore start from the third step. We assume the distributions of $P_t$ and $L_t$ are bivariate normal with zero means, unit standard deviations, and correlation $R_M^2$. It can therefore be shown that the distribution of $L_t$ conditional on the realization of certain value of $P_t = P_s$ (i.e., stressed $P_t$ value) is also normal with mean equal to $R_M^2 P_s$ and standard deviation equal to $\sqrt{1 - R_M^4}$

$$L_t | P_t = P_s \sim \Phi\left(R_M^2 P_s, \sqrt{1 - R_M^4}\right). \qquad \text{(Equation 2.73)}$$

With Equation 2.73, we can therefore show that the conditional distribution of $l_t^i$ is also normal

$$l_t^i | P_t = P_s \sim \Phi\left(R_{\mathrm{LGD}} R_M^2 P_s, \sqrt{\left(1 - R_{\mathrm{LGD}}^2 R_M^4\right)}\right). \qquad \text{(Equation 2.74)}$$

With Equation 2.74, we can therefore obtain the conditional distribution of LGD of individual facility by

$$\mathrm{LGD}_t^i = B^{-1}\left(\Phi\left(l_t^i | P_t = P_s\right), a, b\right) \qquad \text{(Equation 2.75)}$$

where $B^{-1}(\bullet, a,b)$ denotes the inverse of the cumulative beta distribution with the shape parameters $a$ and $b$, and $\Phi(\bullet)$ denotes the cumulative standard normal distribution, which transforms $l_t^i$ to a uniform distribution.

Under this framework, we can calculate the conditional mean and variance of LGD as follows:

1. Given shape parameters $a$ and $b$, $R_{\mathrm{LGD}}^2$ and $R_M^2$.
2. Given stress scenario $X_t^1 = x_t^1, X_t^2 = x_t^2, \ldots, X_t^J = x_t^J$.
3. Obtain $P_t = f_P\left(X_t^1 = x_t^1, X_t^2 = x_t^2, \ldots, X_t^J = x_t^J\right)$. Rename this value as $P_s$.
4. Obtain the conditional distribution of $l_t^i$ using Equation 2.74.
5. Generate the conditional distribution of $\mathrm{LGD}_t^i$ using Equation 2.75.
6. Calculate $E[\mathrm{LGD}_t^i]$ and $\mathrm{Var}(\mathrm{LGD}_t^i)$ based on the conditional distribution of $\mathrm{LGD}_t^i$.

### A Case Study: Generating LGD under Stressed Condition

In this section, we demonstrate the use of the proposed methodologies to estimate LGD under stressed conditions, where stressed LGDs are estimated conditional upon selected explanatory variables.

## Numerical Example for Method I

*Historical LGD Data, Explanatory Variables, and Functional Forms* We develop a stress model to explain the observed LGD of the Industrials sector (GICS 20) of the United States from 1990:Q1 to 2006:Q3. LGD data are obtained from the Standard & Poor's LossStats Database. There are a total of 791 LGD observations for the Industrials sector over the sample period. The (unconditional) mean and (unconditional) standard deviation of LGD of the full sample set are equal to 51% and 37% respectively.

The LGD data are specified according to the respective bankruptcy date and instrument type. We group LGD data of which the bankruptcy dates fall on each quarterly period. We therefore construct an (unbalanced) panel data set of 67 groups of LGD data each over one quarterly period from 1990:Q1 to 2006:Q3. The size of each group $(N_t)$ is uneven over time. There is bound to be more LGD observations during a downturn period than over the booming state of the economic cycle.

We consider the following potential explanatory variables, of which we also collect their quarterly data over the same period of time[55]:

- **IP:** Four-Quarter Trailing Moving Average Industrial Production (Seasonally Adjusted)
- **VIX:** Quarterly Average CBOE Volatility Index
- **NRCC:** Four-Quarter Trailing Moving Average Change in Nonrevolving Consumer Credit (Seasonally Adjusted)
- **LRS:** Four-Quarter Moving Average Commercial Loan Rate Spread
- **TY:** Three-Month Treasuries Yield
- **DR:** Four-Quarter Trailing Moving Average Delinquency Rates
- **COR:** Four-Quarter Moving Average Charge-Off Rates
- **GDP:** Change in GDP

We consider the explanatory power of both the *levels* and *(quarterly) changes* (i.e., first difference) of these explanatory variables and the following (generic) quadratic functional form of $f_L(\bullet)$:

$$f_L(\bullet) = \alpha + \beta_1 \times X_t + \beta_2 \times X_t^2. \qquad \text{(Equation 2.76)}$$

where $X_t$ denotes the explanatory variable. Each time-series of explanatory variables are normalized (i.e., transformed to mean zero and unit standard deviation) prior to incorporating into function $f_L(\bullet)$. We also consider a linear version by restricting $\beta_2 = 0$. Besides considering single variable functions, we also consider functions that incorporate multiple explanatory variables. For example, below is a possible function incorporating both IP and VIX:

$$f_L(\bullet) = \alpha + \beta_1^{IP} \times IP_t + \beta_2^{IP} \times IP_t^2 + \beta_1^{VIX} \times VIX_t + \beta_2^{VIX} \times VIX_t^2. \quad \text{(Equation 2.77)}$$

*Estimation of Coefficients of Function $f_L(\bullet)$ and $R_{LGD}$*   We first estimate the shape parameters of beta distribution (i.e., $a$ and $b$) by using Equations 2.78 and 2.79 together with the unconditional means ($\mu$) and standard deviations ($\sigma$) estimated using all LGD observations. The estimated shape parameters are $\hat{a} = 0.411$ and $\hat{b} = 0.397$:

$$\hat{a} = \frac{\mu^2(1-\mu)}{\sigma^2} - \mu \quad\quad\quad \text{(Equation 2.78)}$$

$$\hat{b} = \frac{\hat{a}(1-\mu)}{\mu}. \quad\quad\quad \text{(Equation 2.79)}$$

From Equations 2.68 and 2.70, we have

$$l_t^i = R_{LGD} \times \left( f_L\left( X_t^1, X_t^2, \ldots, X_t^J \right) + \varepsilon_{LGD,t} \right) + \sqrt{1 - R_{LGD}^2} \times e_{LGD,t}^i \quad \text{(Equation 2.80)}$$

where $l_t^i = \Phi^{-1}(B(LGD_t^i), \hat{a}, \hat{b})$.

Let's first consider the realized (cross-sectional) LGD at time $t$. From Equation 2.80, the distribution of $l_t^i$ conditional on $f_L(\bullet)$ and $\varepsilon_{LGD,t}$ is normal with mean and standard deviation equal to $R_{LGD} \times (f_L(\bullet) + \varepsilon_{LGD,t})$ and $\sqrt{1 - R_{LGD}^2}$ respectively. That is,

$$l_i^t \sim \phi\left( R_{LGD} \times \left( f_L(\bullet) + \varepsilon_{LGD,t} \right), \sqrt{1 - R_{LGD}^2} \right). \quad \text{(Equation 2.81)}$$

Given that $\varepsilon_{LGD,t}$ is normally distributed with mean zero and standard deviation equal to $\sigma_\varepsilon$, the joint likelihood of observing $LGD_t^i$ (for $i = 1$ to $N_t$) at time period $t$ is therefore equal to

$$\Omega_t = \int_{-\infty}^{\infty} \left[ \prod_{i=1}^{N_t} \phi\left( l_i^t; R_{LGD}(f_L(\bullet) + \varepsilon_{LGD,t}), \sqrt{1 - R_{LGD}^2} \right) \right] \times \phi\left( \varepsilon_{LGD,t}; 0, \sigma_\varepsilon \right) d\varepsilon_{LGD,t}.$$

(Equation 2.82)

We can therefore jointly estimate pairwise LGD correlation $R_{LGD}^2$, coefficients of function $f_L$ (i.e., $\alpha$ and $\beta$) and standard deviation of $\varepsilon_{LGD,t}$ (i.e., $\sigma_\varepsilon$) by maximizing the summation of log-likelihood of observing the panel data of $LGD_t^i$ given the observed explanatory variables $X_t^1, X_t^2, \ldots, X_t^J$ over time (i.e., from $t = 1$ to $T$)

$$\underset{R_{LGD}, \alpha, \beta, \sigma_\varepsilon}{\arg\max} \sum_{t=1}^{T} \log(\Omega_t). \qquad \text{(Equation 2.83)}$$

*Estimation Result of Industrial Sector (GICS 20)*   We estimate the pairwise LGD correlation $R_{LGD}^2$, coefficients of function $f_L$ (i.e., $\alpha$ and $\beta$) and standard deviation of $\varepsilon_{LGD,t}$ (i.e., $\sigma_\varepsilon$) for the Industrial sector by maximizing Equation 2.83. We examined the *linear version* (i.e., restricting $\beta_2 = 0$) of the single-variable results, in which the explanatory variables enter into function $f_L (\bullet)$ as *levels* as well as *changes* (i.e., first difference). We also examined the quadratic versions of the results.

We then consider the use of multiple explanatory variables in explaining $L_t$. Based on the relative statistical significances of the single-variable results obtained and the examination of correlation among competing explanatory variables, we choose the following two right-hand-side variables[56]:

- The level of average CBOE volatility index (VIX)
- Quarterly change in three-month treasuries yield (TY)

The estimated model is presented in Equation 2.84.[57]

$$f_L(\bullet) = -0.3 + 0.15 \times VIX_t - 0.27 \times TY \qquad \text{(Equation 2.84)}$$

Using Equation 2.72, which is restated below,

$$LGD_t^i = B^{-1}\left( \Phi\left( R_{LGD} \times \left( f_L\left( X_t^1 = x_t^1, X_t^2 = x_t^2, \ldots, X_t^J = x_t^J \right) + \varepsilon_{LGD,t} \right) \right. \right.$$
$$\left. \left. + \sqrt{1 - R_{LGD}^2} \times e_{LGD,t}^i \right), a, b \right)$$

and the estimated model of Equation 2.84, we can compute the mean and standard deviation of LGD of the Industrial sector conditional on specific stress scenarios. Suppose we are interested in calculating the conditional LGD under the hypothetical scenario of having the following changes happening to the explanatory variables *simultaneously*:

- Realizing a level value of VIX equal to 35.682; and
- A quarterly decrease of three-month treasury yield of 85 bps.

Each of the above corresponds with a stress level that is equivalent to two standard deviations above the average level. The input parameters and the corresponding conditional mean and standard deviation of LGD of the Industrial sector are reported in Table 2.30.

**TABLE 2.30**

Unconditional and Conditional Mean and Standard Deviation of LGD of Industrial Sector (GICS 20) from 1995:Q2 to 2006:Q3 for Two Standard Deviation Shock

| Two Standard Deviation Stress Level VIX = 2, TY = −2; $f_L$ = 0.54 | Unconditional (%) | Conditional on Hypothetical Stress Scenario (%) |
|---|---|---|
| Mean LGD | 48 | 61 |
| Standard deviation of LGD | 37 | 35 |

The mean LGD conditional on the hypothetical stress condition is therefore about 27% (relatively) higher than the unconditional level. We have also estimated the conditional LGD for one standard deviation shock, resulting in a 10.4% increase in mean LGD (Table 2.31).

### Numerical Example for Method II

As discussed in detail in the section on *"PD Stress Testing Model,"* the systematic PD risk $P_t$ can be estimated based on selected explanatory variables. As an example, let us consider an example of a stress model to explain the systematic risk of the observed Standard & Poor's speculative-grade default rates of the Industrials sector (GICS 20) of the United States from 1990:Q1 to 2003:Q4. The selected model together with the estimated parameters are presented in Equation 2.85.

$$P_t = 0.305 \times IP_t - 0.288 \times NRCC_t - 0.443$$
$$\times NRCC_t^2 - 0.238 \times DR_t + \varepsilon_t \qquad \text{(Equation 2.85)}$$

where IP is quarterly change in industrial production; NRCC is quarterly change in nonrevolving consumer credit; and DR is quarterly change in delinquency rates.

**TABLE 2.31**

Unconditional and Conditional Mean and Standard Deviation of LGD of Industrial Sector (GICS 20) from 1995:Q2 to 2006:Q3 for One Standard Deviation Shock

| One Standard Deviation Stress Level VIX = 1, TY = −1; $f_L$ = 0.12 | Unconditional (%) | Conditional on Hypothetical Stress Scenario (%) |
|---|---|---|
| Mean LGD | 48 | 53 |
| Standard deviation of LGD | 37 | 36 |

Suppose we are interested in calculating the conditional LGD under the hypothetical scenario of having the following changes happening to the explanatory variables *simultaneously*:

- A quarterly *decrease* in industrial production (IP) of 2.886;
- A quarterly *increase* in nonrevolving consumer credit (NCRR) of 96,193; and
- A quarterly *increase* in delinquency rate (DR) of 0.250%.

Each of the above changes corresponds with a risk level that is equivalent to *two standard deviations* from the respective mean quarterly change. The corresponding stressed $P_t$ is therefore equal to –3.43 according to Equation 2.85. Stressed $P_t$ can be interpreted as stress level in systematic default risk in number of standard deviations. In the following illustration, besides computing the conditional LGD based on a 3.43 standard deviation change in $P_t$, we also compute those under a few other more moderate stress levels.

Besides selecting the stressed level of $P_t$, we also need to estimate a number of correlation parameters before we can compute the conditional distribution of LGD based on Equations 2.74 and 2.75 in the implementation of Method II. First of all, we need to estimate the correlation of the systematic PD and LGD risk ($R_M^2$). We also need to find out the pair-wise LGD correlation ($R_{LGD}^2$) among the facilities. The estimation of both correlation coefficients is discussed in the section on "Downturn LGD." From our experience, the commonly observed range of values of $R_M^2$ is 0–20% and 40–60% for commercial (midmarket) secured and large corporate unsecured loans respectively. The value of $R_{LGD}^2$ typically falls within the range of 5 to 25%.

Suppose we want to assess the stressed LGD based on the input parameters as presented in Table 2.32. We can then compute the conditional mean and standard deviation of LGD by simulating the conditional distribution of $LGD_t^i$ using Equations 2.74 and 2.75. Table 2.33 reports the

**T A B L E  2.32**

Input Parameters for Calculation of Stressed LGD based on Method II

| | |
|---|---|
| Unconditional mean of LGD | 50% |
| Unconditional standard deviation of LGD | 35% |
| $R_M^2$ | 50% |
| $R_{LGD}^2$ | 10% |

**T A B L E  2.33**

Conditional Mean and Standard Deviation of LGD under Different Stress Levels

| $P_t$: Stress Factor (No. of Standard Deviations) | Conditional Mean of LGD (%) | Conditional Standard Deviation of LGD (%) |
|:---:|:---:|:---:|
| 1 | 44 | 35 |
| 0 | 50 | 35 |
| −1 | 55 | 35 |
| −2 | 61 | 34 |
| −3 | 65 | 33 |
| −3.43 | 68 | 32 |

stressed LGD obtained under different stress levels of $P_t$. Excel spreadsheet "Stress Testing" (on the CD provided with the book) can be used to perform the computations outlined above.

It should be noted that $P_t = 1$ represents a "negative" stress event corresponding with a good part of the credit cycle when the systematic default risk is one standard deviation below average.

## EAD Stress Testing

Modeling EAD is particularly challenging as there is neither sufficient internal nor external EAD data. With the availability of only very short time-series of historical EAD data, it may not be worth directly modeling EAD as a function of explanatory variables (e.g., macroeconomic variables and leading indicators). Instead, sometimes it is modeled as a function of the observed default rates; that is, EAD = $f$(DR). Although the idea is intuitive, default rates are not ideal for the tasks as they are also governed by the level of asset correlation as well as other issues discussed in sections "Long-run PD" and "PD Stress Testing Model". A more ideal approach is to model EAD as a function of the systematic PD risk factor $P_t$; that is, EAD = $f(P_t)$. Its major advantage is in allowing for the stressed EAD being estimated using the same $P_t$ model (developed and estimated in section "*PD Stress Testing Model*") that is used in the generation of stressed PD and LGD. In other words, once the systematic $P_t$ risk factor is modeled in terms of the explanatory variables, the same $P_t$ function can be used for stressing EAD. We can therefore estimate stressed EAD based on specific realization of the explanatory variables corresponding with specific historically observed or hypothetical stress events.

## Stressing Portfolio Loss

The advantage of obtaining conditional PD, LGD, and EAD is that we can utilize our existing portfolio simulation tools to generate stressed portfolio losses. Most commercially available portfolio simulation engines do not incorporate PD and LGD correlations. If we are interested in incorporating the effect of correlations, the above stress testing framework also lends itself for a convenient methodology, where stressed PDs and LGDs can be simulated in a correlated fashion to estimate portfolio losses under selected stress scenarios. The simulation process is already outlined in the section *"Downturn LGD"* (method 3) in generating unconditional loss distribution. The distributions of the systematic LGD risk factor $L_{stressed}$ and systematic PD risk factor $P_{stressed}$ can be generated by sampling the residuals $\varepsilon_{PD,t}$ and $\varepsilon_{LGD,t}$ in Equations 2.86 and 2.87 once the stressed values of the explanatory variables are specified:

$$L_{stressed} = f_L(X_t^1 = x_{stressed}^1, X_t^2 = x_{stressed}^2, \ldots, X_t^J = x_{stressed}^J) + \varepsilon_{LGD,t} \quad \text{(Equation 2.86)}$$

$$P_{stressed} = f_P(X_t^1 = x_{stressed}^1, X_t^2 = x_{stressed}^2, \ldots, X_t^J = x_{stressed}^J) + \varepsilon_{PD,t}. \quad \text{(Equation 2.87)}$$

The simulation process is outlined below.

**Step 1:** We evaluate the explainable components of $L_{stressed}$ and $P_{stressed}$ (i.e., $f_L(\bullet)$ and $f_P(\bullet)$) according to the specific stressed values of the explanatory variables. We then simulate the normally distributed unexplainable components of $L_{stressed}$ and $P_{stressed}$ (i.e., $\varepsilon_{LGD,t}$ and $\varepsilon_{PD,t}$). The systematic LGD and PD risk factors $L_{stressed}$ and $P_{stressed}$ are then computed for each of the scenarios by adding up the two components.

**Steps 2 to 5** are exactly the same as the steps described in the section *"Downturn LGD"* (method 3).

## EAD ESTIMATION

This section is written by Stuart Brannan
of BMO Financial Group

Exposure at default (EAD) is one of the four risk parameters that can be set by banks that qualify for Advanced-IRB treatment under the Basel II framework. EAD simply refers to the amount that the defaulting borrower owes to the lender at the time of default. However, estimating EAD is not a simple exercise. There is uncertainty even in deciding which "amounts" ought to be included in the definition. Although funds that a bank has advanced to a borrower, and any interest owing on those advances, definitely need to be included, there are other forms of credit exposure that are less obvious. For example, at the time of default, the bank may have issued a letter of credit ("LC") on behalf of the borrower. LCs are a form of conditional payment obligation and, if the conditions associated with the LC are satisfied, then the bank is obliged to make a payment to the LC beneficiary, who is a party designated by the borrower, but is not the borrower. The terms of the LC, however, will call for the borrower to indemnify the bank for any amounts paid to the beneficiary. This creates EAD uncertaintly because, at the time of default, it may not known whether the LC conditions will be satisfied and so there is doubt as to whether the LC should be included in the EAD for the borrower.

The need to predict EAD only occurs when a lender establishes an arrangement that permits the borrower to make incremental borrowings within an approved credit limit. In some cases the lender will have made a formal commitment to the borrower to permit such borrowings, and so is legally obliged to permit its exposure to the borrower to increase, provided that the borrower is in compliance with all other aspects of the credit agreement. In other cases, the lender is not formally committed, but has advised the borrower that it will make further advances until such time as the lender decides to terminate the arrangement. These types of "soft-commitments" go by a variety of names in the banking industry: they are often knows as "demand" facilities, because the lender has the right to demand immediate repayment of all borrowings at any time, in other cases they are known as "advised" facilities, because the borrower has been advised of the availability of additional credit, and in other cases these are known as "uncommitted" facilities, to distinguish such lending arrangements from facilities where the lender has provided a legally enforceable commitment to lend a certain amount.

In other cases, the bank may not even have advised the borrower that it is prepared to permit additional advances, but may have established an internal limit that controls the amount that can be advanced to the borrower, if the borrower asks for a loan, without the loan officer needing to obtain specific credit authorization to make the advance. Although the borrower is not formally advised of the level at which this internal limit is set, or even of the existence of a limit, it would be naïve to think that there is no risk of incremental borrowings on such internal credit facilities. The borrower can become aware of the existence of these internal credit limits through a variety of means: in some cases loan officers may inadvertently or informally let the client know that such limits have been established, and more sophisticated borrowers can test for the existence of limits by shifting an increasing amount of their borrowing requests to the bank, and then observing the level at which the bank declines to make a voluntary loan. Although the bank would almost certainly refuse additional borrowing requests on such facilities once the bank recognizes that the borrower is in distress, when the borrower is aware of the existence of the bank's internal limit there is some risk that the borrower will request advances up to this limit *before* the bank recognizes that the borrower may be heading towards default. This is an unavoidable consequence of the fact that the borrower will always have more detailed knowledge of its financial condition than the bank, and will have economic incentives to take advantage of this information asymmetry.

Determining EAD in Basel II follows a process analogous to the "credit conversion factor," or CCF, that was used in Basel I. Under that approach, the CCF consisted of a series of factors that were applied to the undrawn amount to produce a drawn loan equivalent. This represents a crude form of risk-adjusting the undrawn portion of a facility to make it comparable to the drawn portion. For example, a CCF of 50% was applied to the undrawn portion of credit facilities that were originally committed for a period of 365-days or more. The regulatory capital requirement for an undrawn commitment of 365-days or more was therefore one-half of the requirement for a drawn loan to the same borrower. The CCF for facilities that were originally committed for a period less than 365 days was 0%. This naturally led to the explosive growth of loan agreements that included commitment periods of 364 days, which required no regulatory capital.

In Basel II, EAD refers to the total amount that may be owed to the lender at the time of default. This must be determined by adding a) the amounts outstanding at the time that the capital calculation is completed which, it is assumed, will remain outstanding on the day of default, and b) an estimate of the *incremental* borrowings that will occur between the capital calculation date and the date on which the borrower defaults. In effect, permits banks to estimate their own CCF for the undrawn portion of a facility, but imposes a CCF of 100% on drawn amounts, implicitly assuming that amounts drawn prior to default will remain drawn at default.

Examples:

$F_{BD}$ = The maximum authorized borrowings under facility F before default

$E_D$ = The *ex post* amount borrowed under the facility on the date of default (=EAD)

$E_{BD}$ = The *ex post* amount borrowed under the facility before default

Then $E_D$ can be estimated *ex ante* by:

$$E_D = E_{BD} + CCF * (F_{BD} - E_{BD})$$

We note that elsewhere CCF is referred to as the "Loan Equivalent Exposure," or LEQ, however we will use the same terminology as Basel II and use CCF to refer to the factor that is applied to a facility, or a portion of a facility, to determine the amount of exposure that is used to determine capital requirements.

Basel II is not prescriptive with respect to how the CCF is to be estimated, however the formula above suggests that the portion of credit facilities that were undrawn prior to default, but drawn by the time of default,

$$CCF = (E_D - E_{BD})/(F_{BD} - E_{BD})$$

could be calculated from default data in a bank's portfolio, or in a suitable reference data set, and that banks should seek to explain any variability in the observed usage by examining borrower and facility characteristics as possible CCF "drivers." One complicating factor is how to treat facilities that are established after the reference date, but prior to default. Strictly speaking there was no undrawn availability under these facilities on the reference date, and so any borrowings at default will result in an infinite CCF. In practice, the CCF for such facilities is usually determined using undrawn availability on the date on which the facility was established even though this was less than one year prior to default. To the extent that a bank is able to determine that time to default is a CCF driver, the bank could adjust the observed EAD to compensate for the fact that the bank was exposed to drawdown for an abbreviated period.

Using the above formula to estimate CCF immediately suggests some issues: namely, how to handle observations where $E_D < E_{BD}$, leading to a negative observed CCF, and observations where $(E_D - E_{BD}) > (F_{BD} - E_{BD})$, leading to CCF observations greater than 100%.

This approach necessitates the selection of a reference date "before default" at which point $F_{BD}$ and $E_{BD}$ will be measured. It is possible to justify a variety of dates as being plausible. Using a reference date one year prior to the date of default is consistent with the view that capital estimates should be based on a one year risk horizon. However, in practice this leads to an implicit assumption that, each time the Basel II capital is calculated, each entity in the portfolio is at least one year away from default. This is clearly not the case since defaults are not in any way related to a bank's capital calculation schedule. Accordingly, evaluating CCF using a one-year reference date may not produce accurate estimates of incremental borrowing patterns leading up to default. However, if the pattern of drawdown under a credit facility is such that borrowings increase as the period to default shortens, which is plausible since borrowers in distress often have ongoing needs to use borrowed funds to sustain their business when it is generating operating cash shortfalls, then using a reference date one year before default will produce conservative estimates of incremental borrowings, compared to any alternate, shorter reference date. If a bank is able to establish a relationship between incremental borrowings and time to default, then it may be able to use this to refine is estimate of CCF, and possibly achieve a lower capital requirement.

This uncertainty about something as fundamental as the time period over which borrowing behavior is to be evaluated illustrates a more general point: modeling EAD has not been extensively investigated. Neither academics, nor commercial interests (such as rating agencies) have been engaged in extensive conceptual, theoretical or empirical investigation into EAD behavior. As a result, EAD modeling has generally been treated as an afterthought by many practitioners and largely ignored by the academic community.

Two studies are generally recognized as being the basis for most practitioners understanding of EAD related issues: Asarnow and Marker (1995) examined the utilization of S&P rated borrowers during the period 1987 to 1993, and Araten and Jacobs (2001) examined internal results from JPMorganChase during six years ending December 2000. Interestingly, on a key point, the relationship between EAD and default risk, these studies had very different findings. While Araten and Jacobs found evidence that EAD decreases with perceived risk of default, Asarnow and Marker did not. The JPMorganChase study also revealed a strong relationship between EAD and loan tenor, but found no relationship with a range of other factors such as borrower size, facility size, nature of commitment, and industry. A weak relationship between EAD and facility utilization was found, however since borrowers with higher default risk also tend to have higher utilization, this relationship did not add significant predictive power.

Jiménez, Lopez and Saurina (2006) examined a very large database containing information on facilities provided to Spanish borrowers by banks operating in Spain from 1984 through 2005. They found a significant difference between facility utilization by borrowers that will ultimately default, compared to those with similar characteristics but which do not default. They also found evidence that EAD exhibits pro-cyclical behavior: i.e., facility utilization by defaulting borrowers is higher during periods of generally higher default rates than during more benign periods.

The general lack of enthusiasm for attempting to fully investigate usage patterns could be due to a variety of factors, which are discussed below.

It is likely that EAD is highly influenced by decisions made by management of a distressed borrower in the period immediately before default. As such the particular circumstances causing the borrower's distress, may induce different management behavior, and therefore could have a significant effect on the incremental borrowings. Estimating the probability of a borrower defaulting is, in itself, a challenging exercise but, while it is recognized that there are a wide variety of potential reasons that might lead to a borrower default, PD modeling does not normally attempt to identify the root cause of a default occurring, only its likelihood. If management's pre-default behavior is a dominant driver of EAD, then a modeling framework that does not predict the path to default for each borrower is likely to have significant variability in the accuracy of EAD estimates.

CCFs do not necessarily fall in the range of 0% to 100%. Despite the appeal of the hypothesis that distressed borrowers have strong incentives to draw down their bank facilities to obtain cash that can be used to sustain operations, both before and after default (if the borrower is able to obtain protection from creditors under bankruptcy of similar legislation) the fact is that borrowings under many facilities actually decline in the period leading to default, leading to a CCF of less than 0%. On the other hand, there are a variety of circumstances that can lead to borrowings exceeding the maximum permitted under a facility, leading to a CCF greater than 100%.

A reduction in borrowing prior to default could occur for a variety of reasons, including:

- Outstandings at the reference date are atypical; debt reduction after the reference date is a normal part of the borrower's business operations. For example, borrowings by seasonal businesses vary widely during the year. If the reference date for the EAD calculation occurred at a seasonal high point, then normal operations could cause a reduction in borrowings even if the business is on a path to failure.

- The loan agreement may include covenants that require repayment of outstanding loans if a covenant breach occurs. In other words, the reduction in borrowings may be the result of prudent loan structuring.
- The borrower may be concerned about a potential default on its obligations to its bank lenders and may have arranged, or be confident that it will be able to arrange, alternate sources of financing to replace bank borrowings. Even when a borrower is certain that it will default, it may be able to arrange "debtor-in-possession" financing that will permit it to continue to operate after default without the need to increase its usage of other facilities. Whatever its source, the availability of alternate financing would increase the likelihood that a borrower will not increase, and may in fact reduce, outstandings prior to default.

Observing CCF greater than 100% is possible for several reasons:

- The bank may have made an administrative error that allowed the borrower to exceed the limit.
- If the borrower is allowed to borrow in multiple currencies, there may have been a currency fluctuation between the reference date and the default date that led to borrowings exceeding the limit after conversion to a common currency. This is clearly more likely to be an issue for facilities with little undrawn availability on the reference date. The undrawn portion of multicurrency facilities effectively functions as a buffer to absorb exchange rate fluctuations on the drawn portion of the facility.
- The lender may have chosen to increase the facility limit that was in place on the reference date. Although it may appear perverse, there are situations where a bank could believe that allowing borrowings in excess of the limit would allow the borrower to avoid a default, perhaps by bridging a short-term liquidity shortfall. Alternatively, the incremental advances may be provided in exchange for concessions from the borrower, such as the provision of collateral or independent guarantees, which could enhance the bank's recovery on all borrowings, including those made before the borrower exceeded the limit. In this scenario, the bank would choose to allow a higher usage in exchange for a lower expected LGD.

In many of these cases, the observation of EAD greater than 100% represents a real increase in exposure to the borrower above the amount believed, on the reference date, to be the maximum. Accordingly these observations need to be included in the CCF estimate. However, there may be circumstances that lead to a different conclusion. For example, if a borrower consolidates multiple credit facilities after the reference date but prior to default, and transfers borrowings from one facility to another, it would not be appropriate to recognize only the increase in borrowings, and not the associated reductions on other facilities. However, this is exactly what would happen if the CCF for multiple facilities were evaluated independently. It is recognized that consolidation of borrowings is not a common practice, however as a practical matter, the occurrence of even a small number of unusual events can have a noticeable effect on CCF estimates. Remember that CCF estimation can only occur on those defaulted facilities that had an undrawn portion prior to default, and that defaults themselves are very rare for better rated borrowers.

Thus there are a variety of reasons that the CCF, observed in a bank's historical data, may be outside the 0% to 100% range.

There are a number of alternative approaches for the appropriate treatment of such observations, which we outline below:

*Treatment of observed CCF < 0%*

1.  The simplest approach to negative CCF observations is to treat them like any other observation and include them in any analysis without adjustment. This allows the negative CCF observations to offset the impact of positive CCF observations in the data, and will lower the average CCF for the entire dataset, and for any subset that includes negative CCF observations. This approach would likely not be acceptable for calibrating Basel II estimates because it effectively permits the borrower's pattern of repaying borrowings prior to default to be incorporated into the CCF. As noted earlier, Basel II imposes a 100% CCF factor on borrowings that are outstanding on the date of the capital calculation. As such it would be inconsistent to allow the pattern of repayment to be incorporated into the CCF for the undrawn portion of the facility, when incorporating it into the CCF for the drawn portion is not permitted.

2.  Another approach is to discard the negative CCF observations and exclude them from analysis. This approach is will lead to much higher average CCF observations than the first approach, and therefore possibly avoids CCF estimates that are overly optimistic. However, discarding negative CCF observations suffers from two weaknesses. First, as mentioned earlier, EAD

data are scarce, particularly in portfolios of borrowers that have low default probability. Every CCF observation contains important information about the behavior of a usage patterns on a real facility, and discarding data because it falls outside the range of expected behavior leads to greater reliance on a smaller dataset, reducing confidence that the results will be representative of CCF behavior for facilities not yet in default.

In addition, discarding negative CCFs creates a distinction between borrower behaviors that may, in fact, be closely related. Consider the management of two borrowers facing imminent default. Both borrowers have been experiencing deteriorating business conditions, and have drawn down their credit facilities nearly to their limit. The first borrower finds that its circumstances are such that it most recent cash collections from customers are not quite sufficient to pay amounts owing to employees for work they have completed. Although the borrower knows that default is inevitable, it believes that its workers should be paid for their work, and makes a drawing on its facility to pay workers before filing for bankruptcy. Since the facility was nearly fully drawn, this leads to the facility being fully drawn at default. The second borrower is in very similar circumstances, but finds that its most recent cash collections are slightly more than is needed to pay employees. The second borrower pays its workers from its own cash resources and applies the small surplus to reduce the balance on its revolving line of credit, and then files for bankruptcy. Although the difference between the two borrowers may have been a small difference in the timing of its employee's payroll schedule, the first borrower will appear as a positive CCF, while the second would have a negative CCF. Choosing to include the first data point, but exclude the second implies that the behaviors leading to the negative CCF have no information content that makes them relevant to constructing estimates of CCF. Clearly in our highly stylized example the behavior of the two borrowers was virtually identical and using only the first data point may not result in accurate CCF estimates.

3. The final approach is to include negative CCFs in the analysis, thereby taking advantage of scarce data, but to apply a 0% floor so that loan repayments prior to default do not have an effect on CCF estimates. This approach is a practical solution to the problems of the first and second approach, however if negative CCFs are common in the dataset, this could lead to a clustering of

observations at the 0% point, which may mask more important underlying distributions that go beyond the 0% boundary. This suggests that the complete data should be used to identify the relationship among CCF drivers, but that truncated data should be used to calibrate the CCF estimates.

## *Treatment of observed CCF > 100%*

As discussed above, CCF greater than 100% can occur due to administrative error, currency fluctuations, or through agreement by the lender to exceed the previously approved limit. Administrative error and currency fluctuations represent risks associated with structuring revolving credit facilities. Notwithstanding the fact that an upper limit on borrowings has been agreed with the borrower, the fact that borrowings exceeded this amount at default is an indication that the lender's control processes, or the structure of the loan facility itself, were prone to errors that led to higher than anticipated borrowings. Accordingly, it would be appropriate to include these observations in CCF analysis without adjustment or bounding.

The issue is less clear when the CCF is greater than 100% because of a lender's decision to increase the limit after the CCF reference date, but before default. On one hand, the decision to permit borrowings to exceed a previously established limit, particularly for high default risk borrowers, represents lender behavior that should be incorporated into CCF estimates. On the other hand, establishing a higher limit is tantamount to providing a new facility, and the CCF for this new facility should be measured in the same way as any other facility established between the reference date for CCF calculations and the default date. There is no clear best solution to this problem. The argument that these observations should be included in CCF estimates to fully reflect the effect of the lender's practices is sound, however it would be relatively easy to avoid the resulting increased CCFs by establishing a new credit facility rather than increasing the limit on an existing one. It would be preferable to avoid a CCF measurement approach that is overly sensitive to the form of the credit facility, rather than its substance.

Perhaps the practical solution is to adopt either of these approaches, but also conduct separate analysis on facilities that are newly established or increased in the period leading to default. This would provide opportunities for lenders to understand their own practices for lending to stressed borrowers, which would facilitate an informed decision about how best to incorporate this data into CCF estimates.

In fact, the distribution of CCFs may take on a barbell shape with significant mass at both ends. And although some of this is an artifact of the imposition of floors and ceilings on the empirical data, we speculate that this may also be related to the first point raised above, that EAD is highly influenced by the particular circumstances that have created financial distress for the borrower.

## REFERENCES

Acharya, V.V., S.T. Bharath, and A. Srinivasan, 2007, "Does Industry-Wide Distress Affect Defaulted Firms? Evidence from Creditor Recoveries." *Journal of Financial Economics*, vol. 85, pp. 787–821.

Andersen, L., and J. Sidenius, 2005, "Extensions to the Gaussian copula: random recovery and random factor loadings." *Journal of Credit Risk*, vol. 1, pp. 29–70.

Araten, M., and Jacobs, M. Jr., 2001, "Loan Equivalents for Revolving Credits and Advised Lines." *RMA Journal*, vol. 200, pp. 34–39.

Asarnow, Elliot, and James Marker. "Historical Performance of the U.S. Corporate Loan Market: 1988–1993," *The Journal of Commercial Lending*, vol. 10, no. 2, (Spring 1995), pp. 13–32 and private communication.

Basel Committee on Banking Supervision, 2004, "International Convergence of Capital Measurement and Capital Standards." *BIS*.

Blochwitz, S., S. Hohl, D. Tasche, and C.S. When, 2004, "Validating Default Probabilities on Short Time Series." Working paper, Deutsche Bundesbank.

Carling, K., T. Jacobson, J. Lindé, and K. Roszbach, 2007, "Corporate Credit Risk Modeling and the Macroeconomy." *Journal of Banking & Finance*, vol. 31, pp. 845–868.

Chava, S., C. Stefanescu, and S.M. Turnbull, 2006, "Modeling Expected Loss." Working paper.

Christensen, J.H.E., E. Hansen, and D. Lando, 2004, "Confidence Sets for Continuous-Time Rating Transition Probabilities." *Journal of Banking & Finance*, vol. 28, pp. 2575–2602.

Frey, R., and A.J. McNeil, 2003, "Dependent Defaults in Models of Portfolio Credit Risk." *Journal of Risk*, vol. 6, pp. 59–92.

Friedman, C. and S. Sandow, 2003, "Ultimate Recoveries." *RISK*, pp. 69.

Heitfield E., 2004, "Rating System Dynamics and Bank-Reported Default Probabilities under the New Basel Accord." Working paper, Board of Governors of the Federal Reserve System.

Hickman, A. and U. Koyluoglu, 1998, "Reconcilable Differences." Working paper, Mercer Oliver Wyman.

Jiménez, G., J.A. Lopez, and J. Saurina, 2006, What do one million credit line observations tell us about exposure at default? A study of credit line usage by Spanish firms.

Miu, P. and B. Ozdemir, 2005, "Practical and Theoretical Challenges in Validating Basel Parameters: Key Learnings from the Experience of a Canadian Bank." *Journal of Credit Risk*, vol. 1, no. 4, pp. 89–136.

Miu, P., and B. Ozdemir, 2006, "Basel Requirement of Downturn LGD: Modeling and Estimating PD & LGD Correlations." *Journal of Credit Risk*, vol. 2, no. 2, pp. 43–68.

Miu, P. and B. Ozdemir, 2008a, "Estimating and Validating Long-Run Probability of Default with Respect to Basel II Requirements." Forthcoming in the *Journal of Risk Model Validation*.

Miu, P. and B. Ozdemir, 2008b, "Conditional PDs and LGDs: Stress Testing with Macro Variables." Working paper.

Nickell, P., W. Perraudin, and S. Varotto, 2000, "Stability of Rating Transitions." *Journal of Banking & Finance,* vol. 24, pp. 203–227.

Office of the Superintendent of Financial Institutions (Canada), 2004, "Risk Quantification of IRB Systems at IRB Banks—Appendix: A Conservative Estimate of a Long-Term Average PD by a Hypothetical Bank."

Rösch, D., 2004, "An Empirical Comparison of Default Risk Forecasts from Alternative Credit Rating Philosophies." Working paper, University Regensburg.

Schonbucher, P.J., 2003, "Credit Derivatives Pricing Models." New Jersey: John Wiley & Sons Ltd.

Standard & Poor's Credit Market Services, 2003, "LossStats Model—User Guide." Standard & Poor's.

Varma, P. and R. Cantor, 2005, "Determinants of Recovery Rates on Defaulted Bonds and Loans for North American Corporate Issuers: 1983–2003." *Journal of Fixed Income,* vol. 14, pp. 29–44.

Vasicek, O., 1987, "Probability of Loss on Loan Portfolio." Working paper, Moody's KMV Corporation.

## CHAPTER 3

# Validation of Internal Risk Rating System

## OVERVIEW

Validation comprises all activities undertaken to analyze and verify the overall performance of the IRRS to ensure accuracy and consistency. In general, the validation entails activities along three different dimensions:

1. Confirmation of the conceptual soundness and initial risk quantification of the design of the IRRS.
   - Validation of concept, methodology, and assumptions.
2. Confirmation of the operations of the IRRS.
   - Verification of replicability and examination of override and exceptions monitoring, key performance indicators (KPIs), data integrity, and the use test.
3. Outcomes analysis: annual examination of the overall performance of the IRRS.
   - Backtesting, benchmarking, and annual health check.

We have frequently observed that the term *validation* is not well specified or narrowly defined. For example, *conceptual soundness, model validation,* and *backtesting* are often referred to as *validation* even though they are in fact components of validation, which is much more broadly defined under Basel II. All the three dimensions of validation stated above are important. In the first dimension, we start by examining the *blueprint* of the design of the IRRS to validate whether the risk rating system can be expected to do what it is intended to do. This is the validation of conceptual soundness. Does the conceptual design fulfill the intended objective of the IRRS? The

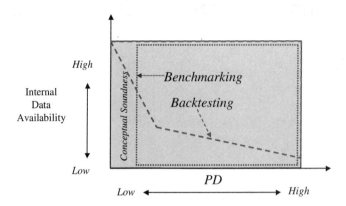

**Figure 3.1** Applicability of different validation dimensions.

second dimension is about the examination of the operation and implementation of the IRRS. The IRRS may have the best possible conceptual design, but it still needs to be correctly and effectively operated. In the last dimension, we need to conduct an outcomes analysis on an annual basis to examine the performance of the IRRS by comparing the expected and realized outcomes. All of these dimensions are discussed in detail in the following sections. It should be realized that there is no one magical validation test and that all these validation dimensions are critical as we look at a *mosaic of evidence*.

In Figure 3.1, we illustrate the applicability of the different validation dimensions in terms of two characteristics of the risk rating, namely the availability of internal default rate data and the level of PD. The assessment of conceptual soundness, though applicable to the whole spectrum (shaded area) of the two characteristics, is particularly important for those risk ratings with low PD and at the same time with limited default rate data. On the other hand, backtesting (the dashed-lined area) and benchmarking (the dotted-lined area) are especially useful for those risk ratings with higher PD where default rate data are more readily available for the required statistical analysis.

## CONFIRMATION OF THE CONCEPTUAL SOUNDNESS AND INITIAL RISK QUANTIFICATION OF THE DESIGN OF THE IRRS

This exercise is most closely related to *model vetting*. A validator (or model vetter) examines the *developmental evidence* including model methodology, fundamental assumptions, data utilizations, and all the rationale behind the model building. The validator, based on his or her expert opinion and by benchmarking the model methodology to those of comparable models, forms an independent opinion on the conceptual soundness of the model. All models have model risk. It is important that the model risk is identified, the impact of the model risk is quantified, and the applicable risk mitigation actions are put forward in the validation report. The theme of this component of the validation exercise is to form an expert opinion on the following question: *Given the developmental evidence, model methodology and its assumptions, can the model (IRRS) do what it is designed to do?* The actual validation practice, however, differs significantly among statistical quantitative models, expert judgment models, and hybrid models.

As discussed earlier, quantitative models are built based on statistical techniques using historical data. The emphasis of the vetter is therefore on the examination of the relevance of the statistical techniques, the validity of the methodology, and the soundness of the implementation. A sufficient level of model-building documentation and developmental evidence is essential to satisfy the vetting function. Ideally, the documentation should be comprehensive enough to allow for the replication of the model by an independent party. Unfortunately, from our experiences, comprehensive documentation is the exception rather than the norm. There is lots of room for improvement in terms of the quality of model documentation at many financial institutions. For internally developed models, comprehensive documentation is an excellent (if not the only) way of retaining organizational memory enabling ongoing model improvement and knowledge transfer. Although it may be seen as a costly requirement in the development stage, it is in fact of high value-added in the subsequent maintenance and improvement of the system. Different problem arises when external models are used. Vendors of many commercially available models do not provide full model methodologies arguing that they are proprietary and are considered to be vendors' intellectual properties. Consequently, many of these models are, if not *black*, at best *gray boxes*. How the regulators will accept these models for fulfilling Basel II requirements is still very much an open question. FIs naturally prefer that the vendors demonstrate the validity of their models directly to the regulators. Regulators, on the other hand, although interested in better understanding these models, make the point that the organizations that choose to use these models are ultimately responsible for the soundness of these models. Whereas this debate will be shaping up, the following could be a reasonable course of action:

1.  FIs examine and validate the model methodologies of the off-the-shelf commercial models as thoroughly as can be, given the available model documentation.

2. For those "tailor-made" models developed by external parties
   using an FI's own data, the FI should negotiate for full disclosure
   of the model methodologies, thus enabling a comprehensive
   validation of their conceptual soundness.
3. All models should be backtested and benchmarked.

Validating the conceptual soundness of the quantitative models requires
advanced knowledge of probability theory and statistics as well as model-
building experience. Expert judgment templates on the other hand are
based on fundamental credit knowledge, and thus validating them
requires skills similar to those mastered by the credit analysts of the rating
agencies. As discussed in Chapter 1, these models (also named risk rating
templates, risk rating matrices, or credit score cards) are built based on
expert judgment utilizing both financial and business risk drivers.
Quantitative risk drivers, usually financial ratios, are complemented by
qualitative risk drivers in arriving at a risk rating for the obligor. The validator of these models needs to convince himself or herself that:

1. The proper risk drivers are captured. The validator has to ask
   questions like: Why are some of the financial ratios omitted?
   Are those financial ratios included representative?
2. The *weight* (i.e., relative importance) assigned to each risk driver
   is appropriate. The validator has to ask questions like: Is it
   appropriate to assign a larger weight to the leverage ratios
   rather than to the profitability ratios?

The validator of these models needs to possess credible fundamental credit
risk knowledge. Even then, validating these models is very challenging as
these models are typically used for low-default portfolios, which do not
allow for the effective backtesting of the IRRS. There are, however, three
things that can be done to facilitate the validation process:

1. Seeking the opinion of an independent expert on the
   appropriateness of the models, the risk drivers used, and
   their weights.
2. Benchmarking (see the section on Benchmarking later in this
   chapter) of the internal ratings to those of available external
   ratings and independent credit estimates.[1]
3. Benchmarking of the model methodologies to those of external
   rating agencies. We are not suggesting that the methodologies
   adopted by the rating agencies are the ideal methodologies for
   the FIs in developing their own IRRSs. Given the track records of
   the rating agencies and the wealth of their historical data, such

benchmarking would naturally provide the necessary degree of comfort.

Hybrid models utilize statistical and quantitative models as the core models with the necessary qualitative overlay. The validation of this type of model therefore involves both quantitative and qualitative validation elements discussed above.

In terms of conceptual soundness, the mapping between the internal ratings and external ratings deserves a special attention. As discussed in Chapter 1, almost all FIs use some kind of mapping between their internal risk ratings and the external ratings. These mappings are used for assigning PDs to internal ratings, establishment of master scales, and also in validation (especially in benchmarking). The validation of these mappings is critical. From our experience, it is quite common that these mappings are somewhat ad hoc, not well justified, and represent "intended" mappings rather than ones that are backed by sound methodological considerations. Correctly mapping the internal risk ratings to the external ones is critical not only in the validation exercises (e.g., backtesting and benchmarking) but also in assigning the correct PDs to the risk ratings, such as in long-run PD estimation. If there are considerable differences between the internal and external rating methodologies, establishment of this mapping becomes even more challenging. It is therefore our opinion that these mappings should be validated before any external data, which are organized based on these mappings, should be used in the long-run PD estimation and the subsequent validation exercises.

Conceptual soundness needs to be confirmed when the model is first initiated and at every time when it is modified. The next two sections of the chapter ("Validation of the Conceptual Soundness of EAD" and "Validation of the Conceptual Soundness of the Effective Term-to-Maturity"), which represent an excerpt of Miu and Ozdemir (2005), summarize our experiences in validating the conceptual soundness of EAD and effective term-to-maturity (ETTM).[2] Both of these risk parameters are less studied than PD and LGD.

## Validation of the Conceptual Soundness of EAD

In the evaluation of developmental evidence, we examine the appropriateness of the EAD methodology and the risk drivers used in a particular FI. In this regard, we look at the formulation of EAD, segmentation, and the implications to regulatory credit capital estimation in accordance with Basel II and the bank's internal economic capital estimation.

EAD is an estimate of the exposure of a facility if it happens to go into default at the risk horizon.[3] It is modeled by estimating the appropriate EAD factor, which is defined as a fraction of the current drawn and undrawn amounts of the total commitment. For bonds, the EAD factor is therefore equal to one. However, for other lending products, the EAD factor is expected to be a number between zero and one, because prior to default, the borrower may have only drawn a portion of the total committed amount.

The facility-specific EAD factors are estimated from the historical experience on how credit is drawn by different borrowers. In practice, it is quite common to use the historical outstanding amounts at two points in time: at default and at one year prior to default (given that the risk horizon is one year).

Suppose an FI adopts the EAD formulation of Equation 3.1 in computing the exposure of a facility at the time of default while considering the facility position and authorization amount at one-year prior to default. It is proposed to express the dollar amount of EAD as a linear function of the current drawn and undrawn amounts of the specific facilities

$$\$EAD = DrawnAmount \times EAD(Drawn)$$
$$+ UndrawnAmount \times EAD(Undrawn) \quad \text{(Equation 3.1)}$$

where EAD(Drawn) and EAD(Undrawn) are the respective EAD factors. It is proposed to estimate these two factors by observing the historical drawn and undrawn amounts at default and at one year prior to default, respectively; that is, evaluating the historical average of Equations 3.2 and 3.3

$$EAD(Drawn) = \frac{Min(Drawn_{@dft}, Drawn_{@dft-1yr})}{Drawn_{@dft-1yr}} \quad \text{(Equation 3.2)}$$

$$EAD(Undrawn) = Min\left[\left(\frac{Max(Drawn_{@dft} - Drawn_{@dft-1yr}, 0)}{Undrawn_{@dft-1yr}}\right), 1\right]$$

$$\text{(Equation 3.3)}$$

where $Drawn_{@Dft}$ represents the amount drawn on the facility at time of default, $Drawn_{@Dft-1yr}$ represents the amount drawn on the facility at time one year prior to default, and $Undrawn_{@Dft-1yr}$ represents the amount not drawn on the facility at time one year prior to default.

The validity of Equations 3.2 and 3.3 and the appropriateness of the proposed EAD formulation can be verified under different scenarios of exposures. Given the estimation process is accurate, Equation 3.1 should result in a dollar amount EAD equal to $\text{Drawn}_{@Dft}$ when we substitute $\text{Drawn}_{@Dft-1yr}$ and $\text{Undrawn}_{@Dft-1yr}$ as DrawnAmount and UndrawnAmount, respectively.

There are two cases: either the drawn amount increases or decreases as default approaches.

### Case 1: Drawn Amount Increasing

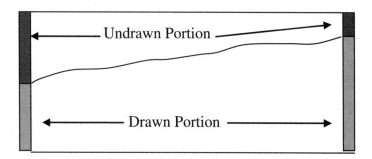

In the case that the drawn amount increases as default approaches, $\text{Drawn}_{@dft} > \text{Drawn}_{@dft-1yr}$, and the authorization limit is constant (i.e., $\text{Drawn}_{@dft} - \text{Drawn}_{@dft-1yr} \leq \text{Undrawn}_{@dft-1yr}$),

$$\$EAD = \text{Drawn}_{@dft-1yr} \times \frac{\text{Min}(\text{Drawn}_{@dft}, \text{Drawn}_{@dft-1yr})}{\text{Drawn}_{@dft-1yr}} + \text{Undrawn}_{@dft-1yr}$$

$$\times \text{Min}\left[\left(\frac{\text{Max}(\text{Drawn}_{@dft} - \text{Drawn}_{@dft-1yr}, 0)}{\text{Undrawn}_{@dft-1yr}}\right), 1\right]$$

$$= \text{Min}(\text{Drawn}_{@dft}, \text{Drawn}_{@dft-1yr})$$

$$+ \text{Min}((\text{Max}(\text{Drawn}_{@dft} - \text{Drawn}_{@dft-1yr}, 0), \text{Undrawn}_{@dft-1yr})$$

$$= \text{Drawn}_{@dft-1yr} + \text{Min}(\text{Drawn}_{@dft} - \text{Drawn}_{@dft-1yr}, \text{Undrawn}_{@dft-1yr})$$

$$= \text{Drawn}_{@dft-1yr} + \text{Drawn}_{@dft} - \text{Drawn}_{@dft-1yr}$$

$$= \text{Drawn}_{@dft}.$$

## Case 2: Drawn Amount Decreasing

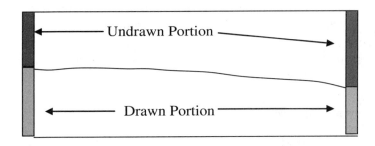

In the case that the drawn amount decreases as default approaches, $\text{Drawn}_{@dft} < \text{Drawn}_{@dft\text{-}1yr}$,

$$\$EAD = \text{Drawn}_{@dft\text{-}1yr} \times \frac{\text{Min}(\text{Drawn}_{@dft}, \text{Drawn}_{@dft\text{-}1yr})}{\text{Drawn}_{@dft\text{-}1yr}} + \text{Undrawn}_{@dft\text{-}1yr}$$

$$\times \text{Min}\left[\left(\frac{\text{Max}(\text{Drawn}_{@dft} - \text{Drawn}_{@dft\text{-}1yr}, 0)}{\text{Undrawn}_{@dft\text{-}1yr}}\right), 1\right]$$

$$= \text{Min}(\text{Drawn}_{@dft}, \text{Drawn}_{@dft\text{-}1yr})$$

$$+ \text{Min}((\text{Max}(\text{Drawn}_{@dft} - \text{Drawn}_{@dft\text{-}1yr}, 0), \text{Undrawn}_{@dft\text{-}1yr})$$

$$= \text{Drawn}_{@dft} + \text{Min}(0, \text{Undrawn}_{@dft\text{-}1yr})$$

$$= \text{Drawn}_{@dft} + 0$$

$$= \text{Drawn}_{@dft}.$$

Thus, the formulation (i.e., Equations 3.2 and 3.3) used in estimating the EAD(Drawn) and EAD(Undrawn) factor is consistent with identifying the exposure of a facility at default under both situations.

The above EAD factors are estimated for different types of credit facilities; for example, Uncommitted, Demand, Committed Revolver, and the Commercial Paper (CP) Backup. Further segmentation can be considered for Demand loans (by facility size), Committed Revolvers (by maturity), and CP Backup (by type).

Based on our experience, some of the other major issues are

- The estimation of the EAD factors relies heavily on business judgment due to data limitations. It is difficult to validate the proposed EAD factors and the appropriateness of the segmentation until sufficient data become available.
- The U-shaped empirical distributions observed may lead to distortions in expected loss (EL), credit spread, and pricing calculations.
- One of the assumptions in the above estimation method for EAD factors is that the authorization is constant over the risk horizon, which might not be valid in practice. Moreover, the behavior of exposure with respect to time is not fully captured in the above EAD formulation.[4] It can be shown that any violation of the assumed time variation in exposure may lead to either underestimation or overestimation of the total exposure at default, the EL, and the capital requirement.
- In most credit risk models (whether internally developed or commercially available), the relationship between EAD and PD is not modeled, resulting in a potential underestimation of the capital requirement (see the "Downturn EAD" section of Chapter 2).

The following subsections further elaborate on these issues in more detail.

### EAD Segmentation: Empirical Analysis and Data Limitation

Some banks conduct empirical analysis, as outlined above, to estimate the EAD factors for demand loans and committed revolvers. Example factors are reported in Table 3.1.

**TABLE 3.1**

Example EAD Factors Estimated for Different Loan Types

| Facility Type | EAD Factor (%) | Remarks |
|---|---|---|
| Uncommitted | 0–20 | Expert judgment |
| Demand Loan | 40–50 | Empirical support |
| Committed Revolver | 40–65 | Empirical support |
| CP Backup | 5–100 | Expert judgment |

We have also investigated the relationship between the EAD factors and alternative facility-specific information (i.e., risk drivers), namely *industry, risk rating, commercial paper (CP) backup, margin requirement, geographical region,* and *facility size.* Whereas the historical data was not sufficient to draw any statistically significant conclusions, some findings are summarized as follows.

### Industry
The data shows possibly distinct EAD factors for different industry. The analysis supports the notion that financial companies have higher EAD.

### Risk ratings
There is anecdotal evidence that a relationship between PD and EAD exists. Some banks actually incorporate PD as a potential driver of EAD. Economic intuition tells us that as financial distress worsens, a borrower will typically draw down as much as possible on existing unutilized facilities in order to avoid default.[5] Besides, anecdotal evidence also suggests that better-quality borrowers would draw more heavily before default than would the lower-quality borrowers; these obligors therefore need to be monitored more closely and tighter covenant structures impeding their ability to draw as risk rating deteriorates should be imposed. Specifically, deterioration of PDs can be flagged and the increase in borrowing has to be closely watched. The empirical analysis on historical data on revolvers made to large corporate entities also suggests a negative relation between EAD and PD.

### Facility size
A negative relationship between facility size and EAD is evidenced. Facilities of smaller size are found having a larger EAD than bigger-size facilities. This finding is consistent with the information asymmetry theory for the smaller firms.

### U-shaped Distribution of EAD and Its Implications

U-shaped empirical distributions of EAD factors are observed in all segments. Truncation is not the cause of the U-shaped distribution.[6] The distribution is still U-shaped (but with much longer tails) even when we remove the constraint that EAD has to lie between zero and one.

Using the mean of the U-shaped empirical distribution as the EAD factor for the segment can be a concern in the expected loss (EL) calculations for pricing. It is especially troubling for small and heterogeneous (in terms of notional size) portfolios. The U-shape indicates that EAD is correct on average in the portfolio sense, but not so for individual loans. In other words, the EADs for the loans are either underestimated or overestimated individually but correct on average. Let us consider the case of pricing a portfolio consisting of facilities of significantly different size, say $100,000 loans and $10,000,000 loans. In using the mean EAD, the bank runs into the risk of underestimating the EAD and thus EL for the $10,000,000 loans, which cannot be offset by an overestimation of the EAD and thus EL for the $100,000 ones. The more heterogeneous the portfolios, the more significant could be the problem of mispricing.

The U-shaped distribution could also be an indication of inappropriate segmentation as a result of not being able to capture all appropriate risk drivers of EAD. It is, therefore, important that as data become available, more empirical analysis has to be conducted to investigate the significance of the risk drivers identified above and to consider alternative ways of segmentation.

### Time Variation of Exposure

Better understanding of the behavior of the authorization with respect to time, especially during the year before default, is important in order to verify the critical assumption in EAD formulation, namely that authorization remains constant during this period. This assumption appears appropriate if changes in authorizations are independent of credit decisions. At least on average, the increases in authorizations of some facilities are balanced out by the decreases in authorizations in others over the risk horizon. If the authorization amount in fact tends to be increasing throughout the risk horizon, the above EAD formula will underestimate the total exposure at default.

In the above estimation of EAD factors, the outstanding amount is captured only at two points in time: at default and one year before default. The behavior of exposure in terms of the outstanding amount and the authorization with respect to time is not fully characterized. If this behavior actually suggests an observable pattern for increasing draws and authorizations before default, it is possible to obtain some useful insights for loss prevention.

Understanding this behavior is also important for EL and economic capital estimation. For example, if there is a tendency for borrowers to draw on their credit limits prior to one year, the EAD amounts based on a one-year window will be understated, and so would economic capital and EL. If these patterns are better understood, necessary adjustments in economic capital and EL estimations can be made to better accommodate the behavior of exposure with respect to time within a one-year risk horizon.[7]

Let us consider an example in which exposure at risk might be underestimated. Suppose the historically EAD behavior is as follows: For an authorization limit of $100, at 13 months prior to default, the drawn

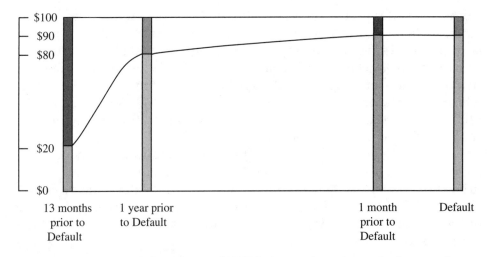

**Figure 3.2** A numerical illustration of EAD being underestimated when we do not have complete information about the changes in EAD over the life span of a loan.

amount is $20. At one year prior to default, the drawn amount increases to $80 and increases to $90 one month prior to default and remains at that level until default occurs (Figure 3.2).

Thus at the horizon of one month prior to default and at default, the exposure of the facility is the same. However, using the EAD estimation at one year prior to default will not accordingly capture the exposure profile in the capital calculations prior to default. Between one month prior to default and time of default, the portfolio exposure does not change yet the capital requirements over the risk horizon do change between the as-of dates 13 months and 1 year prior to default due to the change in the exposure amount.

Historically, estimated EAD gives an Undrawn EAD factor of 50%:

$$\text{Undrawn(EAD)} = \text{Min}\left(\frac{\text{Max}(\text{Drawn}_{\text{Dft}} - \text{Drawn}_{\text{Dft-1yr}}, 0)}{\text{Undrawn}_{\text{Dft-1yr}}}, 1\right)$$

$$= \text{Min}\left(\frac{\text{Max}(\$90 - \$80, 0)}{\$20}, 1\right)$$

$$= 50\%.$$

Thus the EAD factor for a facility to be input into the credit VaR model is

$$\text{EAD} = 100\% \times \text{Drawn} + 50\% \times \text{Undrawn}.$$

## Case 1: The Window is from 13 Months Prior to Default to 1 Month Prior to Default: The Risk is Underestimated

At the point 13 months prior to default, the EAD factor that will be input into an internal credit VaR model is $60:

$$\begin{aligned} EAD_{Dft\text{-}13mths} &= 100\% \times Drawn + 50\% \times Undrawn \\ &= \$20 + 50\% \times \$80 \\ &= \$60. \end{aligned}$$

Thus in estimating the facility value at the risk horizon (one month prior to default), the maximum exposure of the facility is only $60. However, based on the behavior of the facility, at the risk horizon one month prior to default, the exposure is in fact $90. Thus the exposure at risk is underestimated at the risk horizon. This underestimation will lead to a lower capital and EL. (Note that the opposite would be true if the drawn amount decreases between 13 and 12 months prior to default.)

## Case 2: The Window is 12 Months Prior to Default: The Risk is Correctly Captured

At the point one year prior to default, the EAD factor input into an internal credit VaR model is $90:

$$\begin{aligned} EAD_{Dft\text{-}1yr} &= 100\% \times Drawn + 50\% \times Undrawn \\ &= \$80 + 50\% \times \$20 \\ &= \$90. \end{aligned}$$

At the risk horizon, when the facility goes into default, the exposure will therefore be correctly captured.

### Potential Relationship between EAD and PD

Investigating the relationship between the change in PD and EAD in a one-year window prior to default is important in understanding the limitation of any credit risk models (whether internally developed or commercially available) where EAD is assumed to remain constant (i.e., independent of PD) during the risk horizon. In practice, there are economic reasons to suggest EAD may vary with credit migration. The following are possible scenarios under upgrades and downgrades:

- Rating downgrade → EAD amount increases as obligor draws down its loan → credit loss underestimated → capital underestimated.
- Rating upgrade → EAD amount decreases because of refinancing → credit gain overestimated.

During the rating downgrade, the obligor may become more difficult to borrow new money and thus may rely heavily on the line of credit. In this case, the usage amount (or EAD factor) of the given commitment will increase. Anecdotally, the higher the credit quality of the obligor, the higher its tendency to increase the usage when its credit quality deteriorates. The credit risk of these obligors may therefore be understated. These obligors draw very little at origination but later rely quite heavily on the credit lines when their financial situation deteriorates. On the other hand, when the obligor's credit quality improves, EAD can decrease as the obligor tries to refinance the loans at a cheaper cost. In this case, any credit gain from the improvement of credit quality will be overestimated if this systematic decrease in EAD is not captured.

For obligors with low credit quality, usage may not fluctuate as much, as their credit qualities are monitored more closely than are those of better quality obligors. These obligors draw heavily at origination and thus have less undrawn amount left for the future.

### Validation of the Conceptual Soundness of the Effective Term-to-Maturity

Besides PD, LGD, and EAD, the effective term-to-maturity (ETTM) of the credit instrument is also an important determinant of the portfolio credit risk. Using too long (short) an ETTM will result in an inappropriately high (low) credit capital estimate. In this section, we study the effects of the embedded (both implicitly and explicitly) options and grid pricing in distorting the loss distributions when internal models are used.

Unlike bonds, anecdotal evidence shows that ETTM of a commercial loan is typically less than its contractual term to maturity due to refinancing and repayment. Capital will thus be overestimated if the contractual maturity is used without any adjustment. It is however difficult to satisfactorily characterize the prepayment process given that the mechanism is not at all explicit. Typically, prepayment is an outcome of the strategic interaction and negotiation between the bank and its client. There are many factors that drive the needs of prepayment. For example, an obligor may want to prepay because of mergers and acquisitions (M&A) activity or it may want to refinance because its credit rating has improved. Some other possible conditions governing the refinancing decision are listed below:

- Companies whose risk increases continue to refinance their bank loans when there is a change in their borrowing needs that cannot be accommodated within existing facilities (e.g., acquisition or new capital expenditure).

- Many term loans have mandatory amortization payments that reduce authorized and outstanding amounts prior to final maturity.

- Many term loans give the borrower the right to request that the final maturity date be extended to restore the facility to its original term. These early renewal dates generally occur 364 days after the origination date. The bank is under no obligation to extend the maturity, and if it does not, the original maturity date remains. However, if one or a few banks in a syndicate decline(s) to extend the final maturity date, but most others agree to the extension, then the borrower often chooses to replace the declining banks rather than have multiple maturity dates within the same facility. The net effect is that the bank has the opportunity to exit a facility in the face of declining creditworthiness.

- Many companies whose risk improves actually increase their debt levels to maintain a target capital structure. In many cases, the proceeds are used for share repurchase programs. In other words, improved credit risk is sometimes transitory and companies actually react to improving risk by taking on more leverage rather than refinancing to take advantage of lower pricing that might be available to them.

- Most term loans contain financial covenants that permit repricing or renegotiation prior to maturity if the borrower's risk increases. Most commonly, it results in a reduction in credit availability (which should lower capital) or an enhancement to the security offered to the lender (which would lower capital) or better pricing (which would improve risk adjusted return on capital (RAROC)). The covenants in a bank loan agreement are generally much stronger than those in other financial instruments (e.g., bonds) so they are tripped earlier and are intended to give the bank as many options to control potential losses as possible.

- Companies generally want to refinance at least 12 months prior to final maturity to avoid a large increase in short-term debt on their financials. With the rating agencies' current focus on liquidity management, it is expected that companies are to be more diligent in this regard than may have been the case in the past.

- There are also situations where the bank participates in refinancings for both improving and deteriorating credits beyond the final maturity date even though it would prefer to exit.

Ideally, we would have collected as much historical data on refinancing as possible to try to characterize the circumstances surrounding the refinancing events. The ultimate goal is to recover the structural relation between the distribution of the term to refinancing and the particulars of the loan contract and its obligor. For instance, small firms (less bargaining power) in mature industry (less M&A activities) may have an expected term to refinancing closer to the contractual maturity.[8] Validation of ETTM will therefore involve the investigation of whether the structural relation identified is supported by empirical data consistently over time.

Even if we could accurately estimate the expected term to refinancing and make the adjustment to the contractual maturity accordingly, we still cannot guarantee that credit capital can be correctly estimated using an internal model if the refinancing event is not independent of the credit migration or default event of the obligor (i.e., when PD and ETTM are correlated).[9] The problem can be illustrated by considering two common features of a commercial loan contract; namely, (1) the borrower having either explicit or implicit option to refinance and (2) grid pricing arrangement.

### The Asymmetric Decision to Refinance

It is expected that borrowers are more likely to refinance when they experience an upgrade rather than a downgrade. In other words, the loan tends to behave as if it is a callable loan. Using the expected term to maturity could actually underestimate the expected loss and credit capital. For example, when the credit rating of the borrower improves, the borrower would like to prepay the current loan and refinance at a lower interest rate. On the other hand, the borrower would do nothing if its credit rating deteriorates.[10] Under this scenario, the *correct* term to be used is conditional on whether an upgrade or downgrade occurs. Conditional on a downgrade at horizon, we should use the contractual term. However, the correct term is expected to be much shorter than the contractual term if there is an upgrade. The unconditional expected term to maturity, which should be in between the two extremes, could be irrelevant in the determination of credit capital requirement.

It can be shown that using the unconditional expected term can result in distortions to the resulting portfolio loss distribution and the underestimation of capital requirement. At the *loss tail* of the distribution, of which most of the facilities involve a downgrade, the borrowers are less likely to refinance and thus the unconditional expected maturity underestimates the actual maturity. Credit loss is therefore underestimated. On the other hand, at the *profit tail* of the distribution, the creditworthiness of most of the facilities has improved, and thus many borrowers would like to prepay and

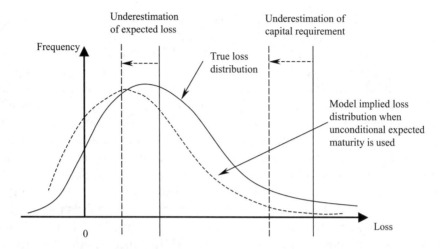

**Figure 3.3** The impact on ETTM of the decision to refinance being asymmetric to the change in the underlying credit risk. Specifically, the effective term to maturity is likely to be shorter when the borrower is upgraded rather than downgraded. This figure illustrates the underestimation of capital requirement when the unconditional expected maturity is used, which ignores this asymmetric effect.

refinance at a lower interest rate. The unconditional expected maturity is therefore likely to overestimate the actual maturity resulting in overestimation of the bank's profit from a general improvement in credit risk. Figure 3.3 presents a graphical illustration of the impact.

### Grid Pricing Arrangement

Grid pricing is a related issue that may also affect the credit capital requirement of the bank's loans. Under a grid pricing arrangement, the loan in a way behaves like a loan with floating credit spread. The credit spread chargeable on a loan is adjusted in accordance with the prevailing credit risk measures (e.g., financial ratios and external credit ratings) of the borrowers.

For such a loan, the change in value due to migration risk is small regardless of the term to maturity. Under the ideal situation where the measures chosen can accurately capture the creditworthiness of the borrower in a timely fashion and the corresponding adjustment in the credit spread can correctly incorporate the required risk premium, grid pricing can eliminate all the credit migration risk. ETTM should therefore be close to the risk horizon regardless of the remaining contractual maturity.[11] Using the unconditional expected term to maturity is therefore likely to overstate the capital requirement for a loan portfolio with a grid pricing arrangement.

In practice, there is no such timely credit risk measure that can be observed, and thus not all the credit migration risk can be eliminated. In that case, the grid pricing agreement can be catered for by again using some sort of effective term to maturity. Suppose the credit risk measure used in grid pricing (can be financial ratios or external ratings) can correctly capture the creditworthiness of the borrower. Then, the only reason why the bank is still exposed to loss due to credit migration risk is the existence of a time lag between the change in the actual creditworthiness and the time when the measure is reviewed or updated. For example, if the measure is an external credit rating, the rating will not change unless there is a significant improvement or degeneration of the borrower's creditworthiness and the rating is being reviewed by the rating agency. Conceptually, we can thus model grid pricing by using an effective term that matches this time lag for those loans with grid pricing agreement. The term should therefore be adjusted differently from those contracts without a grid pricing agreement.

## CONFIRMATION OF RISK RATING SYSTEM OPERATIONS

### Verification of Replicability

Basel II requires that internal risk rating assessment process be replicable and auditable. The motivation for this requirement is quite understandable. Especially in the pro-Basel days, the rating process had been heavily dependent upon the expert judgment of the analyst. Although expert judgment has been recognized as valuable, the process itself needed to be more transparent. In a way, the thought process of the analyst needed to be codified to make it more transparent and audible. One way to ensure transparency and audibility of the process is to conduct replicability testing. Initially, this requirement is interpreted as the following: an independent party should be able to arrive at the original rating using the original inputs and risk rating assessment process followed by the risk analyst who rated the obligor or the facility. The difficulty, however, is that the analyst still uses her or his judgment while using a transparent process and at times overrides the model results. The independent party conducting the replication may disagree with these judgment calls (e.g., she or he may think the management quality is quite different than what was assigned). These disagreements could make exact replication very difficult, if not impossible. A newer and more sensible interpretation of the replication test is as follows: it is okay to have different opinions on the subjective elements of the rating process and the overrides. However, there needs to be sufficient documentation provided by the analyst to explain his or her rationale in arriving at these (subjective) conclusions and overrides. If the independent party conducting replication can follow the analyst's rationale, even if he or she disagrees with it, the replication is still achieved.

### Examination of Override and Exceptions Monitoring

Especially in the early years of a new model's use in an IRRS, a large number of overrides and exceptions are expected. Models, especially expert judgment–based templates, will be quite frequently overridden as the model result may differ from what was thought by the analyst, who was accustomed to arrive at her or his rating after a lot less formal thought process. As discussed, the models are supposed to a great extent codify this thought process to make it transparent and replicable. In other words, in many cases, the analyst used to start with a rating for the company (at least with a ballpark figure) and then rationalize his or her opinion by looking at the components of risk rating, following in a way a deductive reasoning process. With the use of the models, this process is reversed to an inductive reasoning process. Therefore, especially in the earlier days of model use, the analyst inclined to override the model result arrived at using the new process with his or her result arrived at using the old (deductive reasoning) process. This is not necessarily an undesired outcome but only a natural progress. The important thing is to keep an electronic record of all exceptions and overrides and analyze them at least annually. If the analysis shows systematic overrides, the models need to be modified accordingly. It should be expected that with these annual modifications, the number of overrides should go down over time. A common question we are asked is what percent of overrides is acceptable. In our experience, there is no magic answer to this question. Naturally, the override ratio should be reasonable. However, a more important question, as explained, is to identify the systematic reasons of overrides and modify the models accordingly.

### Risk Rating System KPIs

Most validation activities are done periodically but not very frequently, therefore there is also a need for *continuous* monitoring. Although we used the term *continuous*, it is not truly continuous but a lot more frequent than other validation activities (continuous may mean, for example, weekly or monthly). Complete backtesting and benchmarking activities, for instance, are very informative but cannot be done very frequently as it requires (historical) data collection over a period of time, and it takes time to conduct the tests. Therefore, it is useful to identify some KPIs of the risk rating system (such as most recent default and migration rates, realized LGDs, etc.) and monitor them frequently. Organizations need to define their own KPIs that they can monitor and for which they can establish tolerance limits. When KPIs exceed the tolerance levels, higher levels of management need to be informed and more comprehensive validation activities should be triggered in order to better understand the reasons for the KPI results.

## Data Integrity

Validation of data integrity is one of the most challenging components of the validation where, in our experience, many FIs are facing difficulties. The reasons for the challenges are quite understandable. First of all, not all data (typically LGD and EAD data) was kept electronically. Many organizations had to go through paper files to capture the data electronically. This data-entry process may be prone to errors in terms of both data representativeness and potential human errors. Many regulators are questioning the presence of proper quality control and quality assurance for these data-entry processes.

Another common observation is that many organizations, within their organization, have different and sometimes aging IT systems that do not communicate to each other well.

Data integrity is very important considering the role data plays. Historical data are used in model building. If the data used are not reliable, neither are the models built on them. The risk rating assignment process is also data intensive, considering all inputs used in risk rating, overrides, and resulting rating outputs need to be stored and maintained under some form of data system. Lastly, during the validation process especially back-testing and benchmarking, integrity of the historical data is again critical to arrive at accurate results.

In our experience, validation of data integrity is one of the least advanced areas of overall validation with only a few organizations implementing some cross-querying and sample testing methodologies to confirm data integrity.

## The Use Test

Basel II requires that Basel parameters (e.g., PDs, LGDs, EADs, etc.) be used within daily decision-making processes. The requirement is known as the *use test*. The motivation for the use test is straightforward; the regulators desire that implementation of Basel II goes beyond regulatory compliance and that the benefits of having more robust and risk reliable parameters are fully extended into better risk-management and decision-making practices.

The pricing for retail and small SME portfolios surfaced as the first contravention to the use test, as many FIs argued they are simply price takers in these markets, and thus, they cannot use Basel parameters for pricing. Even though these institutions may well be price takers, they can still use the Basel parameters to analyze their profitability and comparative advantage in these markets and make strategic decisions accordingly. This valuable analysis goes with the spirit of use test requirement and its demonstration should satisfy the use test requirement.

Some banks have argued that PDs used for regulatory capital estimation need to be more TTC than those used for economic capital and pricing, and similarly PDs used for pricing and RAROC calculations need to be more PIT than those used for economic and regulatory capital estimation. Similarly, downturn LGDs include markups to compensate for the omission of correlations between PDs and LGDs in capital estimations (refer the "Downturn LGD" section of Chapter 2). Naturally, this markup is a portfolio-level correction (specifically for capital estimation) and thus is not appropriate at the deal level for pricing and RAROC estimation. The same argument applies to downturn EAD. These are some reasons for using different sets of parameters for different purposes, which appears to violate the use test requirement. However, the use test requirement should not be interpreted as strict requirement to use the same risk parameters for all purposes but instead as a requirement to explain and document the rationale for using different parameters for different purposes when there are justifiable reasons to do so. An institution's risk appetite is an ideal place to capture and rationalize those differences and preferences.

## ANNUAL EXAMINATION OF THE OVERALL PERFORMANCE OF THE RISK RATING SYSTEM

At a minimum, benchmarking, backtesting, and "annual health check" must be undertaken annually.

### Benchmarking

Benchmarking is the examination of the performance of a risk rating system relative to the comparable risk rating systems. We can conduct benchmarking for both performing and defaulted instruments.

### Benchmarking of the Performing Instruments

As a first exercise, we can benchmark internal ratings against the external ratings. External ratings are available for the obligors rated by the rating agencies. For the nonrated obligors, for example, Standard & Poor's Credit Estimates or CreditModel can be used. Standard & Poor's Credit Estimates are the nonpublic external ratings obtained from Standard & Poor's. CreditModel produces Standard & Poor's letter-grade rating symbols, in lowercase, reflecting quantifiable rating methodologies but not the qualitative and confidential information that are also used in public ratings. A typical benchmarking exercise is provided in Figure 3.4.

For the performing loans, we can also utilize PD/LGD models for benchmarking by comparing the internal PD (LGD) risk ratings with the implied PD (LGD) risk ratings from independent PD (LGD) models. We calculate PDs (LGDs) for the obligors (facilities) using an independent PD (LGD) model and establish PD (LGD) bands for the model-implied risk ratings. We then assign the obligors to the respective model-implied risk ratings based on which PD [LGD] intervals the obligors' model-implied PDs [LGDs] fall into. We can then compare model-implied risk ratings with the internal risk ratings. PD/LGD models used in benchmarking must be

| Internal scale | # of credits | D | SD | CC | CCC- | CCC | CCC+ | B- | B | B+ | BB- | BB | BB+ | BBB- | BBB | BBB+ | A- | A | A+ | AA- | AA | AA+ | AAA |
|---|---|---|---|---|---|---|---|---|---|---|---|---|---|---|---|---|---|---|---|---|---|---|---|
| | | | | | | | | | | | | | | | | | | | | | | | Standard & Poor's rating → |
| 1 | 5 | | | | | | | | | | | | | | | | | | | | | | 5 |
| 2 | 0 | | | | | | | | | | | | | | | | | | | | | | |
| 3 | 3 | | | | | | | | | | | | | | | | | | | | 3 | | |
| 4 | 11 | | | | | | | | | | | | | | | | | | 1 | 4 | 4 | | 2 |
| 5 | 10 | | | | | | | | | | | | | | | | 1 | 1 | 6 | 2 | | | |
| 6 | 22 | | | | | | | | | | | | | | | 1 | 1 | 17 | 3 | | | | |
| 7 | 18 | | | | | | | | | | | | | | | 3 | 9 | 6 | | | | | |
| 8 | 21 | | | | | | | | | | | | | | 2 | 13 | 6 | | | | | | |
| 9 | 39 | | | | | | | | | | | | | 1 | 30 | 6 | 1 | | | | 1 | | |
| 10 | 27 | | | | | | | | | | | | 1 | 20 | 5 | 1 | | | | | | | |
| 11 | 13 | | | | | | | | | | | | 1 | 6 | 3 | 2 | 1 | | | | | | |
| 12 | 11 | | | | | | | | | | 3 | 1 | 4 | 1 | | | 1 | 1 | | | | | |
| 13 | 5 | | | | | | | | | 2 | 2 | 1 | | | | | | | | | | | |
| 14 | 4 | | | | | | | | | | 1 | 2 | 1 | | | | | | | | | | |
| 15 | 6 | | | | | | | | 1 | | | 2 | | 2 | 1 | | | | | | | | |
| 16 | 1 | | | | | | | 1 | | | | | | | | | | | | | | | |
| 17 | 0 | | | | | | | | | | | | | | | | | | | | | | |
| 18 | 2 | | | | | | | | 2 | | | | | | | | | | | | | | |
| 19 | 1 | | | | | | | | 1 | | | | | | | | | | | | | | |
| 20 | 1 | | | | | | | 1 | | | | | | | | | | | | | | | |
| Totals | 200 | 0 | 0 | 0 | 0 | 0 | 0 | 1 | 2 | 2 | 8 | 8 | 12 | 27 | 40 | 25 | 19 | 25 | 10 | 6 | 8 | 0 | 7 |

**Figure 3.4** Benchmarking of internal ratings against the external ratings. The numbers in cells represent the number of obligors rated under the internal scale and by Standard & Poor's (external rating) respectively.

independent from the ones used in internal risk rating assignment. For example, if Moody's KMV PD or LGD models are used, even partially in the internal risk rating assignment, we can use Standard & Poor's Credit Risk Tracker (for PDs) and LossStats (for LGDs) models to benchmark against. An example is provided in Figure 3.5.

In both figures, the obligors (facilities) on the diagonal are the ones where the internal ratings are in agreement with the independent ratings, whereas the ones on the off-diagonals are less in agreement. In general, we expect a heavier concentration on the diagonal elements. This, however, does not mean that we should expect a perfect agreement between IRRS and the benchmark ratings. It means that any disagreement needs to be investigated, understood, and justified. For example, in Figure 3.5, a number of obligors (shown in red) are rated much more conservatively by the independent benchmark model. There may be legitimate reasons for these obligors being rated more optimistically by the rating analyst that is paid to provide his or her expert opinion. What is useful, however, is that these differences are noticed, justified, and monitored.

There may be a number of reasons for divergences in ratings. For Standard & Poor's–rated obligors, for instance, different opinions on the subjective elements of the rating process and the differences in rating philosophies are common ones. A very important aspect of the benchmarking exercise is to monitor the stability of mapping between internal and external ratings over time using the techniques described in the section

| Internal Scale | PD impled Risk Ratings (from an independent PD Model) | | | | | | | | | | | | | | | #of Credits |
|---|---|---|---|---|---|---|---|---|---|---|---|---|---|---|---|---|
| | 1 | 2 | 3 | 4 | 5 | 6 | 7 | 8 | 9 | 10 | 11 | 12 | 13 | 14 | 15 | |
| 1 | 3 | 2 | | | | | | | | | | | | | | 5 |
| 2 | 2 | 8 | | | | | | | | | | | | | | 10 |
| 3 | 5 | 5 | 15 | | | | | | | | | | | | | 25 |
| 4 | 5 | 10 | 15 | 15 | 3 | | | | 1 | 1 | | | | | | 50 |
| 5 | | 5 | 5 | 5 | 30 | 1 | 2 | 2 | | | | | | | | 50 |
| 6 | | 1 | 2 | 2 | 5 | 35 | 1 | 2 | 2 | | | | | | | 50 |
| 7 | | | 1 | 2 | 2 | 5 | 70 | 5 | 5 | 5 | 5 | | | | | 100 |
| 8 | | | | | 5 | 5 | 5 | 60 | | | | | | | | 75 |
| 9 | | | | | | 5 | 5 | 10 | 30 | 10 | | | | | | 60 |
| 10 | | | | | | 1 | 1 | 1 | 1 | 1 | 15 | 2 | 1 | 1 | 1 | 25 |
| 11 | | | | | | | | 1 | 2 | 3 | 15 | 1 | 2 | 1 | | 25 |
| 12 | | | | | | | | | | 1 | 2 | 5 | 2 | | | 10 |
| 13 | | | | | | | | | 1 | 1 | 1 | 5 | 1 | 1 | | 10 |
| 14 | | | | | | | | | | 1 | | 1 | 3 | | | 5 |
| 15 | | | | | | | | | | | | 1 | 1 | 1 | 2 | 5 |

**Figure 3.5** Benchmarking of internal ratings against the external PD implied ratings. The numbers in cell represent the number of obligors rated under the internal scale and the model-implied rating respectively.

of Validation of Mappings between Internal and External Risk Rating Systems later in this chapter. These techniques will help identify systematic trends and change in trends. For example, it is desired that in the mapping tables, the majority of the obligors are on the diagonal, which shows agreement between the risk rating systems. It is possible that over time, this may change. Several examples are given below.

**Example:** Mapping between Internal and External Ratings

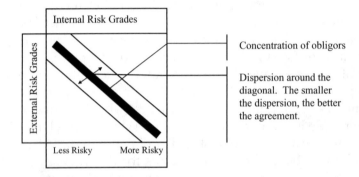

**Trend 1**  Increase in dispersion: The agreement decreases

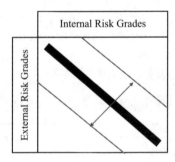

**Trend 2**  Parallel shift in diagonal: IRRS is becoming less conservative

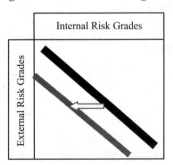

**Trend 3** Parallel shift in diagonal: IRRS is becoming more conservative

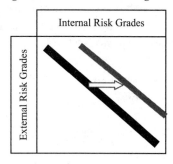

**Trend 4** Nonparallel shift in diagonal: IRRS is becoming less conservative for the low-risk grades and more conservative for the high-risk grades

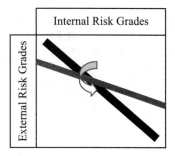

**Trend 5** Nonparallel shift in diagonal: IRRS is becoming more conservative for the low-risk grades and less conservative for the high-risk grades

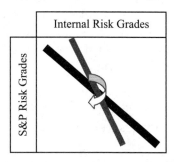

A common exercise for the regulators is to obtain PDs, LGDs, and EADs from different banks for the commonly rated obligors and facilities and compare them among the banks. If a bank is systematically optimistic in its ratings, it may be subject to regulatory scrutiny.

### Benchmarking Defaulted Loans

We also need to examine if realized default and migration rates, LGD, and EADs are consistent with the relevant industry experience. For example, we can use the Standard & Poor's database CreditPro, which provides default rates, rating migrations, and default correlation statistics customized by industry, geographic region, and time period based on Standard & Poor's rating universe and default data.

## Backtesting

Backtesting is the examination of the performance of the risk rating system based on its historical data comparing realized and predicted outcomes. Backtesting applies to PDs, LGDs, and EADs in Pillar I context. In all cases, we compare the outcomes predicted a year before default with the realized outcomes at default, consistent with the one-year risk horizon for capital estimation. As discussed, the risk rating process is composed of two distinct steps: first pooling the obligors into risk-homogeneous risk ratings that rank order (via risk rating assignment) and then assigning risk measures to those risk ratings (via calibration between the risk ratings and the corresponding risk parameters). We need to backtest both steps as discussed below.

## PD Backtesting

### Overview

Backtesting is the comparison of realized and predicted outcomes. Backtesting of a risk rating system against the observed default rates needs to consider multiple dimensions. Whereas each dimension is important by itself, all are needed to obtain a complete picture of the performance of the risk rating system. These dimensions are

1. Testing the discriminatory power of the risk rating system: How good is the system in distinguishing default risk? To test this dimension, standard tests such as *Gini* or *accuracy ratio* can be used.
2. Testing the calibration of the risk rating system: Are the values of the PDs assigned accurate given the observed default rates? To test this dimension, a *Monte Carlo simulation tool* and *geometric mean probability* can be used.
3. Testing the realization of the risk rating philosophy: Given the observed default rates and realized LGDs, are our risk rating

philosophies what we believe it they are? To test this dimension, *mobility metric and ROC term profile* can be used.

4. Testing the homogeneity of the risk ratings: All obligors in the same risk rating are supposed to have the same PDs irregardless of the geography and industry they are in. This needs to be confirmed via *subportfolio-level validation*.

### Testing the Discriminatory Power of the Risk Rating System

The first test is an empirical measurement of the discriminatory power of the risk rating system. The purpose is to validate the correctness of the ordinal ranking of the obligors by riskiness. Standard well-known tests such as Gini are the natural candidates for the task. It is important to remember that Gini is more useful in measuring the relative rather than the absolute discriminatory power of the risk rating system. The reason is that Gini is designed for a two-state, "good" vs. "bad," world. Under Gini, a perfect discriminatory power can only be achieved when we have only two risk ratings. The higher risk rating is for "good" obligors and assigned with a PD of 0%, whereas the lower risk rating is for the "bad" obligors with a PD of 100%. A perfect score can then be achieved if none of the obligors in the former rating default before those in the latter rating. Given that the test is typically applied under situations which are very different from this perfect two-state setup, it is not the absolute Gini score but rather the relative Gini score that is informative. For example, we may compare (1) the Gini scores obtained from alternative ways of risk rating, both internal and external (such as external models and agency ratings); (2) the Gini scores obtained over time from the same risk rating system; or (3) the Gini scores when applying to different credit portfolios (e.g., corporate vs. commercial). Alternatively, we can look at the cumulative accuracy profile (CAP) which is similar to the Gini curve and is also a commonly used measure in the industry. The CAPs of a large corporate loan portfolio over two consecutive years are presented in Figure 3.6.

It should be noted that portfolio composition matters when the Gini test is conducted. Controlling for all other factors, the accuracy ratio tends to increase when the portfolio is made up of more firms with low credit ratings. It can have nothing to do with the discriminatory power of the rating system. We therefore need to be very careful when we compare the Gini scores across portfolios of very different credit compositions. For example, assume that a certain midmarket portfolio was found to have an accuracy ratio of 60%. It will be unfair to compare this ratio with the ratio (85%) of the large corporate portfolio and conclude that the discriminatory power of the rating system for the midmarket portfolio is inferior. The difference can

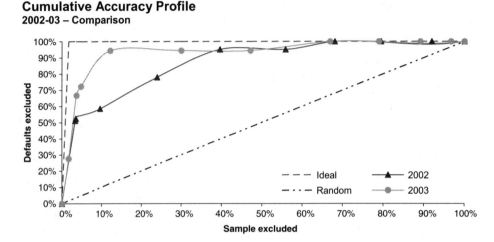

**Figure 3.6** Cumulative accuracy profile of an example of corporate loan portfolio.

also be attributed to the fact that the large corporate portfolio is made up of more firms with low PD. To resolve these potentially confounding issues, we need to recompute the accuracy ratio of a *normalized* midmarket portfolio, which was ensured to have the same percentage of firms in each risk rating as did the large corporate portfolio. Assume this accuracy ratio was found to be equal to 75%. Now, we can attribute the difference between 85% and 75% to the higher discriminatory power of the large corporate rating system and the difference between 60% and 75% to the difference in portfolio composition between the two portfolios.

Gini is also used for performance benchmarking. We measure and compare the Gini score relative to the alternative ways of risk rating the obligors. For instance, is the Gini score higher if the obligors are risk ranked based on CRT, CreditModel, and so forth? We first identify the available alternative risk rating systems which may serve as appropriate benchmarks for our internal rating system. We then calculate the Gini scores of the same portfolio but now rated by these alternative systems. It is desired that the Gini score of our internal risk rating system is still higher than those obtained using the benchmarks. Again, the benchmarking should be performed against an alternative system (model) that is not used in the internal risk rating process.

### Testing the Calibration of the Risk Rating System

The Gini score and other rank-ordering tests do not validate the absolute level of PDs assigned to the risk ratings. In other words, they tell us how good a job our risk rating system does in separating good credits from the bad ones but do not tell us if the level of PDs assigned to the credits are correct in relation to the observed default experience. Even though the assigned PDs might be systematically too high or too low, the ordinal ranking of the obligors by riskiness, as validated above, would still be preserved. Consequently, a quantitative test of consistency between the PD assigned and the actual observed number of defaults is needed. This is commonly called the *calibration test*.

The section below describes a Monte Carlo simulation test used for this purpose.

*A Monte Carlo Simulation–Based Calibration Test*   A Monte Carlo simulation is used to validate the assigned PDs of the risk ratings. The proposed simulation approach is considered to be a more desirable solution than are alternative analytical approaches, which are commonly used in the practice (e.g., Tasche, 2003). Specifically, it is not subject to the modeling error in the distribution assumption of the observed default rate. Moreover, the proposed method is not vulnerable to any bias due to small sample size. The model is consistent with the approach suggested by Vasicek (1987). It, however, is general enough to accommodate different correlation parameters for the individual obligors rather than a single pairwise correlation. Moreover, the framework can handle nonuniform correlation structure.

The validation of the calibration of the risk rating scale involves the investigation of the appropriateness of the number and dispersion of the risk buckets used. Designing an appropriate risk rating scale involves a trade-off between having a granular risk rating scale and being (statistically) confident enough that the correct PD is assigned to each risk rating. Ideally, we would like to pinpoint the PD of each individual obligor by having lots of risk buckets. However, as we have more and more risk buckets relative to the number of obligors, the probability of assigning an obligor to a wrong risk bucket increases. The validations of the PD for each risk rating are therefore not conducted in isolation but rather in a joint fashion (across all risk ratings).

To investigate the consistency of the predicted default probability with the actual default rates, we collect historical default data of the bank's portfolio and compare them with the assigned PDs. For example, Figure 3.7 presents example historical default rates vs. assigned PDs.

Notice that the assigned PDs are quite different from the observed historical default rates for a number of risk ratings, namely no. 5, no. 10, and no. 11. Before we can conclude these assigned PDs are inappropriate, we need to check if these observations are statistically plausible or not. We

| | | Default Rate | Assigned PD |
|---|---|---|---|
| | 1 | 0.05% | 0.03% |
| | 2 | 0.02% | 0.05% |
| | 3 | 0.09% | 0.10% |
| | 4 | 0.13% | 0.20% |
| | 5 | 0.44% | 0.30% |
| Risk Rating | 6 | 0.41% | 0.45% |
| | 7 | 0.96% | 1.00% |
| | 8 | 1.80% | 2.00% |
| | 9 | 7.90% | 8.00% |
| | 10 | 23.5% | 13.50% |
| | 11 | 41.4% | 25.00% |
| | Default | 99.29% | |

**Figure 3.7** Example historical default rates and assigned PDs.

therefore conducted hypothesis tests via Monte Carlo simulations of the distributions of default frequency. The null hypothesis was that the PD assigned to the risk rating was in fact correct. Using normal copulas to model default correlations, a distribution of possible default rates under different scenarios was generated.[12] For each of the risk ratings, we can then construct confidence intervals by assuming the PDs assigned were correct (Figure 3.8).

In the above example, it can be shown that the null hypothesis of the assigned PDs being correct for risk ratings no. 10 and no. 11 can be rejected at high level of confidence. That is, the observed default rates were outside the confidence intervals.

Distribution of the number of defaults per risk rating segment is constructed by way of a Monte Carlo simulation. Default correlations are taken into account via the use of normal copula. The number of defaults corresponding with a given confidence level can then be determined. For example, the median number of defaults corresponds with a 50% chance of exceeding.

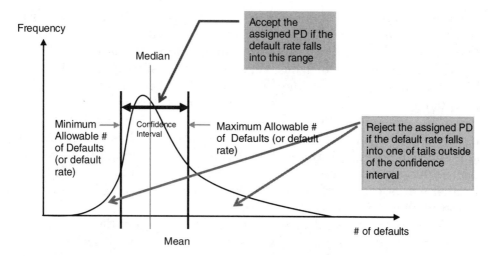

**Figure 3.8** Distribution and confidence intervals for probability of default constructed by Monte Carlo simulation. The null hypothesis is that the assigned PD is the correct PD of the borrowers within the risk rating.

The simulation procedure consists of generating a large number of scenarios. For each scenario:

- A correlated asset return for each obligor is generated and whether the obligor has defaulted or not is determined.
- The number of obligors that defaulted for the scenario is recorded.

The inputs are the probability of default, pairwise asset correlation, number of obligors in the segment, and the predefined confidence level. The outputs include the median number of defaults for the segment as well as the threshold number of defaults (i.e., confidence interval) around the median for a given confidence level. In its simplest setting, it is assumed that each risk rating segment is homogeneous with respect to the probability of default and the pairwise asset correlation. That is,

- Each obligor is assumed to have the same probability of default.
- The pairwise asset correlation between all obligors is assumed to be identical for all obligors within the segment.

*Choosing an Appropriate Confidence Level*   Choosing an appropriate confidence level can be tricky in practice. On the one hand, we would like to set a high confidence level (i.e., wide confidence interval) to ensure the probability of wrongfully rejecting a true null hypothesis is small (i.e., *type I error*).

On the other hand, we do not want to have too wide a confidence interval, which might lead to wrongfully accepting the alternative hypothesis (i.e., *type II error*). We do not want to wrongfully endorse the assigned PD of a risk bucket, which in fact has very different historical default rates. Moreover, too wide a confidence interval would result in overlapping acceptance intervals between adjacent risk ratings (Figure 3.9).

If the observed default rate of a risk bucket falls in the overlapping region, it can be considered to be *equally consistent* with either of the two adjacent risk ratings. To rule out or minimize such ambiguity, the confidence intervals should be chosen so that there is none or little overlapping. In other words, each interval cannot be too wide, that is, type I error cannot be too small.

Given a certain confidence level, the width of the confidence interval is mainly governed by the value of the assigned PD, the asset correlation, and the number of obligors in the risk bucket. For example, the widths of the intervals are found to be increasing with the pairwise asset correlation. As correlation increases and borrowers are more likely to default at the same time, it becomes less unlikely to find the observed default rate being very different from the assigned PD even under the null hypothesis. We can illustrate this point by constructing confidence intervals for an example

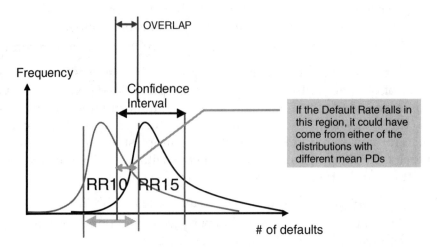

**Figure 3.9** Distribution and confidence intervals for probability of default of two adjacent risk ratings (RR10 and RR15) constructed by Monte Carlo simulation. The respective null hypothesis is that the assigned PD is the correct PD of the borrowers within each risk rating. The overlapping region represents the cases where the observed default rate is (statistically) consistent with both risk ratings.

portfolio under different assumptions of asset correlation. With the objective of attaining minimal overlapping, the confidence level can be improved from about 40% to 50% when the asset correlation decreases from 10% to 5%. Figures 3.10 and 3.11 present the resulting confidence intervals of the risk ratings under these two different assumptions of asset correlation.

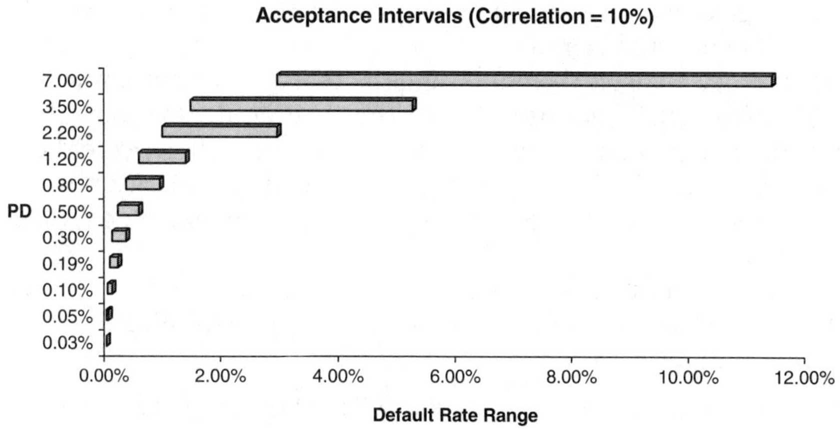

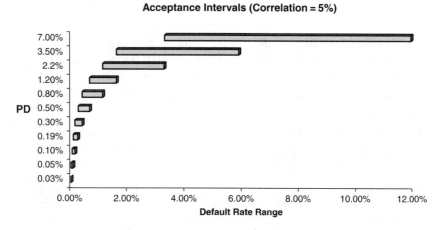

**Figure 3.10** Confidence interval constructed for each risk rating by Monte Carlo simulation with specific confidence level. Asset correlation is assumed to be equal to 10%.

**Figure 3.11** Confidence interval constructed for each risk rating by Monte Carlo simulation with specific confidence level. Asset correlation is assumed to be equal to 5%.

Moreover, given a certain confidence level, the widths of the confidence intervals are found to decrease when the number of obligors increases. Thus, with the objective to minimize the overlapping in acceptance intervals, both type I and II errors can be reduced when we have more obligors in each risk bucket. In other words, to achieve the same discrimination power in PD validation, we would expect the risk rating system for a retail lending portfolio can afford to be more granular than that for a portfolio of large corporation lending simply because of the relatively larger number of obligors to be rated.

The above analysis therefore suggests that a rating system with more than 10 different risk buckets is likely to be too granular to ensure there are both minimal type I and II errors and high discrimination power between adjacent risk buckets. The choice of the degree of granularity, however, is not up to the bank's own decision but is, to a certain extent, governed by the regulators.

Given the above observations, we recommend a target confidence level of 51% in the validation of the risk rating system illustrated above. The underlying principals are

1. The possibility of rejecting the *right* PD (i.e., type I error) is not more than 50%; and

2. Given (1), the probability of accepting the *wrong* PD (i.e., type II error) is minimized.

*Mechanics of Running the Test*

1. For each obligor rating, calculate the realized annual default rate.

2. By assuming the assigned PDs being correct, generate the distribution of the number of defaults for each risk rating by Monte Carlo simulation. The major inputs are the assigned PDs, the pair-wise asset correlation, and the numbers of obligors of the risk ratings.

3. Determine the acceptable minimum and maximum number of defaults (i.e., confidence interval) for each risk rating given a pre-defined confidence level.

4. Compare the realized number of defaults with the minimum and maximum predicted number of defaults derived above to check if they lie within or outside the confidence intervals. One will then accept the null hypothesis (i.e., the assigned PDs being correct) if it is the former, whereas reject it if it is the latter.

*Choosing the Correlations*   In an earlier section (see the section of Correlation is Specific to Risk Rating Philosophy in Chapter 2), we showed that correlations are risk rating specific; under a TTC system, the correlations are unconditional, whereas under a PIT system, the correlations are conditional (on observable information). We have also showed that unconditional correlations are materially larger than their conditional counterparts. When we conduct the calibration test:

1.  For a TTC system, we need to enter TTC PDs and the corresponding unconditional correlations.
2.  For a PIT system, we need to enter PIT PDs and the corresponding conditional correlations.

Suppose we are conducting calibration tests for TTC and PIT systems with identical PDs. As seen in the diagram below, the distribution of the realized default rate for the TTC system would be more dispersed and skewed than that for the PIT counterpart due to the larger correlations. This, all else being the same, would make it more difficult to pass the calibration test (i.e., accepting the null hypothesis) under a PIT system than under a TTC system. For example, given the realized default rate "X" in Figure 3.12, we would have to reject the assigned PIT PD where we cannot reject the the assigned TTC PD under the same confidence level.

This is actually quite intuitive if we think about it. As discussed in the section of PD Philosophy in Chapter 2, PIT PD is more aligned with the

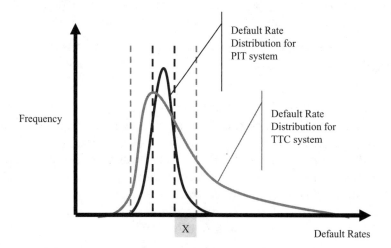

**Figure 3.12** Confidence intervals of calibration tests in PIT and TTC rating systems.

default rates resulting in a tighter default rate distribution. Therefore, if our intended philosophy is PIT, we are subject to a tougher calibration test as our intended PIT philosophy requires synchronization with (the cycle of) one-year forward-looking probability of defaults. More generally, the more PIT the intended philosophy, the smaller the correlations, and thus the tougher the calibration test.

In practice, whereas some FIs are aware of the issue of correlations being risk rating specific, the majority currently use the same set of correlation parameters regardless of the differences in their risk rating philosophies.[13] Therefore, even when their intended PD philosophy is PIT, with the use of unconditional correlations, their capital estimation is not PIT, but a conservative version of it. This issue is also discussed in Chapter 4.

A practical question is what correlations to use in the calibration test when correlations are not estimated specific to the intended risk rating philosophy. There are two readily available candidates: Basel II correlations and the correlations used for economic capital estimations. There are issues with both. First, neither is risk rating philosophy–specific as discussed above. Moreover, Basel II correlations are known to have issues as they are a function of PDs rather than company size and industry type, which are recognized as the better determinants of correlations. The use of Basel II and/or economic capital correlations might be justified, however, considering the calibration test's being consistent with capital estimation process and the practical issue of not having philosophy-specific correlations.[14] We would like to highlight, however, that when we use the unconditional correlations in the calibration test, we introduce a bias in favor of validation of PIT systems, as we are easing up the acceptance requirements for them.

*Supplementary Analysis*   To complement the tests discussed above, two additional tests can be conducted per risk rating in each year's annual health check:

1. A cross-sectional regression analysis can be conducted by regressing the realized default rates of the risk ratings against the respective assigned PDs. It gives us a full picture of the calibration of the whole IRRS incorporating information on all the risk ratings in their entirety. A more theoretically correct way would be to regress the realized default rates against the medium default rates (rather than the assigned PD) obtained from the Monte Carlo simulation tool discussed above.

2. Once a sufficiently long default rate time series is obtained for each of the risk ratings over time, the corresponding long-run PD can be estimated and compared with the PD assigned to each risk

rating. Details of how long-run PDs can be estimated can be found in the section on Long-Run PD in Chapter 2.

*Geometric Mean Probability*   Another test for calibration is geometric mean probability–log-likelihood (see Friedman and Sven 2006). Gini only tells us whether the model assigns higher PDs to defaulters than to nondefaulters. It does not tell us whether the model estimates the magnitude of the PDs correctly. *Geometric mean probability* measure overcomes this deficiency by assessing the ability of the IRRS in estimating the magnitude of the PDs correctly, not just their rank. Geometric mean probability tells us if the rating system is getting the probabilities (of default) right. It is given by the equation

$$\log(\text{likelihood}) = \sum_{i=1}^{N} \log\left[ y_i p(x_i) + (1 - y_i)(1 - p(x_i)) \right], \quad \text{(Equation 3.4)}$$

where $y_i$ is 1 or 0 (default or no default) and $p(x_i)$ is the probability of default assigned to obligor $i$ (in a portfolio of $N$ obligors).

Intuitively, if $y_i$ is equal to 1 (i.e., obligor $i$ defaults), then the terms in brackets reduce to $p(x_i)$ (as the second term becomes a 0). This is the likelihood of observing obligor $i$ defaults. Similarly, if $y_i$ is equal to 0 (i.e., obligor $i$ survives), then the terms in brackets reduce to $[1 - p(x_i)]$. In this case, $[1 - p(x_i)]$, or (1 – the probability of observing obligor $i$ defaults), is the likelihood of observing obligor $i$ survives. The logs of these probabilities are therefore the log-likelihood of a single observation. When one performs these calculations and sums up over $N$ observations (obligors), the result is the log-likelihood measure for the whole portfolio (or risk rating).

The log-likelihood described above is a negative number that is between $-\infty$ and 0, with 0 indicating perfect performance. Because the resulting scale is difficult to interpret, we suggest using the following measure of model validity: the geometric mean probability of the observed outcomes:

$$\text{GMP} = e^{\frac{1}{N}(\log\_\text{likelihood})}, \quad \text{(Equation 3.5)}$$

which lies in the interval [0, 1]. As described above, the log-likelihood measure is the sum of $N$ individual log-likelihoods. Dividing the log-likelihood by $N$ results in an average or mean log-likelihood. Because we are exponentiating, we have a geometric mean likelihood, or geometric mean probability.

When we implement the measure on our most recent portfolio (time $t$), we use prior year's (time $t - 1$) PDs for the survived obligors, whereas the

PDs a year before the time of default (time $t_{\text{default}} - 1$) for the defaulted obligors.

*Performance Benchmarking*  A perfect model would have estimated $p(x_i) = 1$ (i.e., assign a PD of 1) for all defaulted obligors ($y_i = 1$) and $p(x_i) = 0$ (i.e., assign a PD of 0) for all survived ones ($y_i = 0$) and any deviation from it would be a mistake. In this case, there is no error and Equation 3.4 gives us zero (since $\log(1) = 0$), and thus GMP = 1. Now assume we randomly assign PD = 0.5 for all obligors, and some default, some survive. In this case, GMP equals 0.5. We can draw a conclusion from this that GMP < 0.5 should definitely be unacceptable.

However, a typical performance comparison would be against a "naïve" model. A typical naïve model can be the following: a model that correctly predicts the average default rate for the portfolio as a whole but is unable to distinguish among the obligors. For instance, assume we have observed a 1% default rate for a portfolio (note we are ignoring default correlations). Our naïve model predicts one year before default (time $t - 1$) that all obligors have a PD = 1% and 1% of the obligors will default at time $t$. We should expect that our model outperforms this naïve model in terms of GMP. In our experience, $\text{GMP}_{\text{OurModel}} - \text{GMP}_{\text{Naive}}$ should be at least 50 to 100 bps. The larger the difference, the better the performance.

We need to be careful about one potential bias. Our formula makes no distinction between the errors on the survival side ($1 - y_i$) $\times$ ($1 - p(x_i)$) and the default side $y_i \times p(x_i)$. If the portfolio default rate is very low, the naïve model will assign a very low PD to all obligors and fail very substantially for all of the defaulted obligors. However, as the number of defaults is so low, the overall performance would still look good despite the large error made for the defaulted obligors.

## Testing the Realization of the Risk Rating Philosophy

The next and a critical dimension is the validation of the risk rating philosophy. We need to confirm that the risk rating philosophy is what we believe it is given the observed default and migration rates. The philosophy can be point-in-time (PIT), through-the-cycle (TTC), or a hybrid of the two. For a PIT system, PDs are intended to be our best estimates of the obligors' default likelihood over (usually) the next 12 months. These PDs are estimated taking all available cyclical, noncyclical, systematic, and obligor-specific information into account. TTC PDs, on the other hand, are the estimates of the obligors' default likelihood over a credit cycle and they are calculated based on noncyclical information. Therefore, PIT PDs should be validated against the 12-month default rates and TTC PDs against some kind of cycle average default rates.

Before embarking on any validation exercise, we might want to consider how easily one can adopt a PIT system and have it effectively maintained. Adopting a pure PIT PD is likely to be an ambitious endeavor, if not an unattainable one, for the commercial loans portfolio and loans to private companies considering that there is a general lack of *forward-looking* market information (e.g., stock price) to conduct a timely assessment of the likelihood of default in the coming 12 months for a specific obligor. At most, some forward-looking macroeconomic information might be available together with industry-specific leading indicators, which can be utilized to increase the *forward-lookingness* and thus the predictive power of the PDs in order to be more PIT.

Maintaining an effective PIT rating system is also a nontrivial task given the *friction* inherent in the risk rating regrading process. Suppose it is our intention to keep the mapping of risk rating to PD relatively constant over time while actively rerating the obligors to capture the changes in their PDs due to all relevant factors including cyclical ones. In other words, obligors' PDs will be updated via changing their risk ratings. In this approach, the onus is on the effectiveness of the re-rating process to achieve PIT PD. If the obligors are not re-rated frequently enough, obligors' PDs will not reflect the current expectation of the default likelihood and thus will not be PIT. The 12-month credit outlook of each obligor therefore needs to be monitored continuously. The obligor is regraded corresponding with the new PD assessment once its credit worthiness has changed.

This is usually done via a regular and/or triggered regrading process based on some *early warning triggers.* It is essential that these triggers are also forward looking (e.g., leading indicators, stock market performance of the relevant industry sector). Over time, it needs to be determined if the obligors' risk ratings are being upgraded or downgraded effectively enough to capture their PIT PDs. Validation of the rating system can help the bank to assess the *degree of PIT-ness* of the rating systems of different credit portfolios, which can have implications in the allocation of economic capital to different portfolios.

To summarize, the plausible sources of friction in the regrading process are

- There may be resistance from the account managers to downgrade certain obligors as they may lose control over the accounts or be biased due to their relationship with the owners/managers.
- The regrading process may not be frequent enough.
- The regrading triggers may not be sufficiently forward looking.

Whatever the reason, if there is too much friction in the regrading process, PIT PDs cannot be achieved and, consequently, the obligor regrading process would need to be supplemented with a remapping process, with the PDs corresponding with the risk ratings adjusted following the credit cycles.

Then, how can we validate our intended risk rating philosophy given the observed default and migration rates? One way is to examine the risk rating migration rates. The more PIT the PDs, the more migrations should be observed especially during the changes in business cycle. Constructing a risk rating migration matrix helps monitor this. For example, Table 3.2 reports the migration matrix of an example portfolio.

As a standard measure of migration, various migration or mobility metrics have been suggested. One measure of ratings mobility is the *Euclidean distance* between the observed transition matrix and the stable ratings case (i.e., the identity matrix). Jafry and Schuermann (2003) demonstrate a method to rescale the Euclidean distance to measure the mobility in a transition matrix. Conceptually, the smaller the friction, the larger will be the probability of transitioning to a different rating, and the *less concentrated* will be the transition matrix along its diagonal. The degree of concentration of the transition matrix along its diagonal can therefore serve as a measure

**T A B L E  3.2**

An Example Migration Matrix

| | | Risk Rating | | | | | | | | | | | |
|---|---|---|---|---|---|---|---|---|---|---|---|---|---|
| | | 1 | 2 | 3 | 4 | 5 | 6 | 7 | 8 | 9 | 10 | 11 | Default Rate |
| Risk Rating | 1 | 82.5% | 2.91% | 2.41% | 3.03% | 3.21% | 2.22% | 1.84% | 1.14% | 0.33% | 0.34% | 0.00% | 0.05% |
| | 2 | 0.52% | 72.3% | 10.9% | 6.43% | 5.99% | 2.05% | 1.18% | 0.52% | 0.03% | 0.02% | 0.00% | 0.02% |
| | 3 | 0.32% | 3.35% | 69.5% | 10.7% | 8.45% | 4.10% | 2.37% | 0.92% | 0.14% | 0.09% | 0.00% | 0.09% |
| | 4 | 0.12% | 1.22% | 5.64% | 66.0% | 14% | 7.16% | 3.25% | 1.91% | 0.21% | 0.15% | 0.00% | 0.13% |
| | 5 | 0.09% | 0.31% | 2.12% | 5.66% | 67% | 13% | 7.29% | 3.24% | 0.48% | 0.36% | 0.00% | 0.44% |
| | 6 | 0.07% | 0.14% | 0.75% | 2.26% | 10.3% | 64.9% | 13.2% | 6.33% | 1.02% | 0.64% | 0.00% | 0.41% |
| | 7 | 0.09% | 0.06% | 0.35% | 0.82% | 5.12% | 12.3% | 65.0% | 12.4% | 1.66% | 1.29% | 0.00% | 0.96% |
| | 8 | 0.03% | 0.06% | 0.25% | 0.69% | 2.86% | 7.40% | 14.6% | 67.1% | 3.39% | 1.79% | 0.00% | 1.80% |
| | 9 | 0.12% | 0.01% | 0.16% | 0.33% | 1.45% | 3.38% | 9.46% | 18.1% | 52.5% | 6.61% | 0.00% | 7.90% |
| | 10 | 0.00% | 0.00% | 0.01% | 0.02% | 0.11% | 0.48% | 2.54% | 4.70% | 3.57% | 65.1% | 0.00% | 23.5% |
| | 11 | 0.00% | 0.00% | 0.00% | 0.00% | 0.00% | 0.00% | 0.00% | 0.00% | 0.06% | 0.03% | 58.5% | 41.4% |
| Default | | 0.00% | 0.00% | 0.00% | 0.00% | 0.00% | 0.00% | 0.02% | 0.04% | 0.42% | 0.23% | 0.00% | 99.29% |

of the friction. A higher mobility metric suggests a lower friction in the risk rating system. By computing this single number, we can therefore:

- Compare the degree of friction of the bank's internal rating system against those of external benchmarks, such as that of Standard & Poor's transition matrix.
- Compare the degree of friction of the internal rating systems across the different risk rating processes used in the bank.
- Track the change of the degree of friction of the same internal rating system over time.

Suppose we want to calculate the *mobility metric* (proposed by Jafry and Schuermann) for both a bank's historical transition matrix and the Standard & Poor's "comparable" transition matrix. Standard & Poor's risk ratings are determined using a longer risk horizon (usually three or five years) than 12 months, and thus, Standard & Poor's rating philosophy is fairly TTC. If the bank's risk rating philosophy is more PIT than that of Standard & Poor's, we expect that the mobility metric for the bank's historical transition matrix is larger than that of Standard & Poor's or vice versa.

To obtain a fair comparison, we need to replicate the bank's portfolio composition in terms of industries as closely as possible when we construct a comparable Standard & Poor's transition matrix. We also need to *common-size* the matrices that are to be compared. When the banks' internal rating systems are more granular than that of Standard & Poor's, the higher value of the mobility metric may as well be due to the higher granularity. To control for this potentially confounding factor, we need to convert the internal ratings, and thus the corresponding transition matrix, to those of Standard & Poor's before the metric can be compared. We need to *aggregate* some of the bank's risk ratings such that the resulting transition matrix has the same number of risk buckets as that of Standard & Poor's, thus we *common-sized* the transition matrices. In this process, a bank's current mapping between Standard & Poor's ratings and internal risk ratings is used.

As it is stated, in the short-run, the purpose is not to interpret the absolute value of the mobility metric to determine if the rating system is sufficiently point-in-time, but to look at it over time and relative to the other risk rating systems.

*Benchmarking the Mobility Metric*   Based on our experience, we provide the following guidance on benchmarking the mobility metric: The full spectrum of mobility metric ranges between .1 (for full TTC) and .6 (full PIT).[15] Realistically, most risk rating systems are some sort of a hybrid and lie in between the two extremes of this spectrum. The mobility metrics of

Standard & Poor's matrices are usuallyaround the .25–.35 range. Banks with more PIT philosophies score higher than that of Standard & Poor's, but in practice, we have never seen any bank scoring higher than .4 despite its clearly stated PIT philosophy. On the other hand, seldom have we seen any banks scoring less than those of Standard & Poor's despite their clearly stated TTC philosophies. It should however be noted that all else being the same, the less granular the transition matrix, the lower the mobility metric.

*Supplementary Analysis*    Another test is the *receiver operating characteristics* (ROC) accuracy ratio, which measures the *early warning* capability of PDs (for details regarding the implementation of ROC test, refer to Van Deventer and Wang, 2003). Formally, the ROC accuracy ratio can be defined as the average percentile ranking of the defaulting obligors in the universe of nondefaulting observations. To compute the ROC accuracy ratio, defaulted and nondefaulted obligors are randomly paired up and their assigned PDs are compared at different periods prior to the period or year of default. It is expected that the PDs of the defaulted obligors will be higher than those of the undefaulted ones at all times. We then measure the percentage of the time this is in fact the case at different periods before the period or year of default. Validation should be conducted over a, say, one-month time interval, when sufficient data become available to analyze a time series of changes in the ROC over time preceding an obligor's default. For a reasonably predictive model, the ratio would normally be expected to increase progressively over time as the obligor approaches the time of default. This is because the risk rating system should be able to discriminate the high-risk obligors, which have ultimately defaulted, and more so, as approaching default via downgrades. A high score closer to 1.0 would indicate that the rating model is reasonably accurate in differentiating higher risk obligors from lower risk obligors. A perfect score of 1.0 implies 100% accuracy in ranking all of the defaulted obligors in the pair as higher risk; versus a 50% score would imply that the validity of the model is questionable, as this is equivalent to flipping a coin. Figure 3.13 presents the ROC profiles of an IRRS and a random model.

The more PIT the PDs are, the more forward looking and thus predictive they would be. Thus, an assessment of the early warning capability of PDs can be used to measure and determine how PIT the PDs are.

We need to be cautious in interpreting the results given that a great majority of the defaults of the portfolio under review may have come from the "problem account ratings." As these accounts had very high PDs to begin with, it is only expected that their PDs would be higher than those

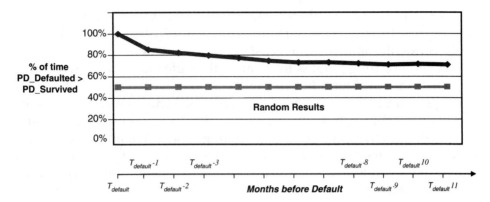

**Figure 3.13**  An example ROC profile.

from other ratings at any time, which results in an overall high level of ROC accuracy ratio. Therefore, the results explain not only the forward-looking nature of the PDs but also the discriminatory power of the risk rating system. The increase in ROC ratio as approaching default (in Figure 3.13) should be interpreted as the predictive power or the forward-looking nature of the PDs. Thus, besides examining the level of the ROC ratio, we should also document the pattern of the ROC term profile.

### Homogeneity Testing: Subportfolio-Level Validation

*Overview*    The underlying principle in any validation exercise is that the results should be actionable. Banks should be able to learn from their validation exercise and act on it for continuous improvement. This requires that we pinpoint what exactly went wrong, if anything, in the risk rating system. It is therefore necessary to conduct subportfolio-level validation. The more we mix up portfolios with different characteristics, the more difficult to identify the problem, as the performance of the risk rating system with regard to the subportfolios will be masked.

Then, the practical question is how to classify obligors and facilities into subportfolios in PD validation. The objective is to maintain the homogeneity of the subportfolios as much as possible. The more granular, and thus the more risk-homogeneous, the subportfolios are, the easier the diagnosing of the problems is. Homogeneous subportfolios can also ensure that credit characteristics inherent in certain subsegments of a targeted subportfolio are not masked or negated by the behavior of a larger subsegment or by otherwise distinctly differing behavior of two or more other subsegments. However, achieving homogeneity needs to be balanced with considerations for materiality, feasibility, practicality (e.g., data limitations, statistical significance, etc.), and cost of implementation.

A good starting point is to examine the differences in the risk rating procedures adopted for different facilities within the bank. The differences in the risk rating systems include the input risk factors used as well as the process determining how the individual risk factors are considered and weighted in arriving at a certain risk rating. The differences in portfolios include commercial (midmarket) versus public (large corporation) as well as the industry differences. It is plausible that a risk rating system performs well for certain portfolios or for certain industries, whereas poorly for others. Another very critical dimension is the exposure size. In the validation, we should be more interested in ensuring the rating system performs reasonably well for the *large* exposures than for the *small* exposures. In other words, default on a large exposure should carry a heavier weight than does default on a small exposure.

To summarize, the major criteria that are recommended for consideration in the subportfolio classification for PD validation may include the following:

*Size*   Exposure Size: The potential of PD being influenced by the size of the exposure or authorized amount. We want to avoid as much as possible mixing up large and small exposures. The current Basel framework does not make a distinction between a $10,000 and a $10,000,000 loan (a default is a default), which is dangerous from the risk management perspective. For instance, to properly manage the bank's earnings volatility, it is more important that the rating system be working properly for large corporate portfolios and that its performance not be masked by the behavior of the midmarket portfolio.

Company Size: Obligors falling within a similar size range, as measured by assets or sales, and operating within the same industry or asset class are generally assumed to exhibit similar default behavior.

*Industry*   The uniqueness of each industry with respect to legal, regulatory, and operating environments may impact the choice of risk drivers and/or their calibration, which in turn will impact probability of default.

*Risk Rating Process*   Methodology: The same risk rating process and methodology, from a materiality and practicality perspective, should be applied to all obligors aggregated into a subportfolio. The same risk rating process should be employed for all loans in the subportfolio. For instance, if some of the risk ratings assigned were regression based whereas the others judgment based, we would not know at the end of the validation tests which process failed and which one passed.

Geography: Geographic differences that can encompass different regulatory, legal, or operating environments can result in material differences in the specific risk drivers, or their calibration, that can lead to material differences in PD.

Notwithstanding the above, under certain circumstances, such as in cases where data limitations exist, the determination of the subportfolios will have to be done based on expert judgment. However, it is critical that the rationale is well thought through and documented.

Finally, do we need both subportfolio-level validation and validation at aggregate level (or one bank-wide level)? Is subportfolio-level validation by itself sufficient to justify the soundness of the risk rating system? Subject to business and data/sample size constraints, validation should be performed at the lowest possible subportfolio/subsegment level. If all of the subportfolios underneath a level-up larger portfolio are validated, the level-up portfolio does not need to be validated on a consolidated basis unless it is required by the regulators and/or other external parties, because each of the subportfolios are more risk-homogenous than is the consolidated portfolio. In other words, if the validation results are satisfactory at the subportfolio level(s), the level-up portfolio will, by construct, be satisfactorily validated. On the other hand, if the validation of at least one of the subportfolio is not satisfactory, the aggregate portfolio validation can still be satisfactory. In other words, validation at the aggregate levels is usually not value-adding and thus should not be required unless data limitation significantly compromises the quality of subportfolio-level validation.

*Operational Principles*   When operationalizing the subportfolio-level validation, the above-mentioned principle should be evaluated within a cost-benefit framework. Ideally, the tests mentioned above in this Section on "Backtesting" should be repeated for all subportfolios identified. This, however, is time consuming and expensive. One way to tackle the issue could be the following:

1.   The entire validation exercise (all tests mentioned above in this Section on "Backtesting") is conducted for only the large subportfolios identified. These subportfolios can be identified based on geography (e.g., United States vs. Canada), and portfolio characteristics (corporate vs. midmarket). This large

subportfolio selection needs to be justified by the sizes of the subportfolios. The bank therefore repeats the entire validation exercise for only a few large subportfolios identified.

2.  If any of the validation tests indicates potential problems, the subject test and potentially other tests are then conducted at the more granular subportfolios to determine the source of the problem.

3.  Even when the subportfolios identified at the high level produce satisfactory validation results, the PD homogeneity of each of the risk ratings for each of the high-level subportfolios is confirmed via significance testing described below, where the default rates of the more granular subportfolios per risk rating are compared.

4.  When the significance testing results are not satisfactory, indicating the obligors in the risk ratings may not be PD homogeneous as they are supposed to be, further tests mentioned previously in this Section on "Backtesting" are then conducted to determine the source of the problem.

*Significance Testing*    In this test, we examine each of the risk ratings for each of the high-level subportfolios identified. The underlying assumption is that all obligors in a certain risk rating have the same PD regardless of geography, industry, size of the exposure, risk rating template used, and so forth.

There are two ways to tackle the homogeneity question. One way to test this is the following. Suppose we want to confirm the PD homogeneity of risk rating 5 (RR5), which has an assigned PD of, say, 3.5%. We identify a few dimensions that may influence the PD of the obligors. Assume these are geography, size, industry, and government guaranteed loans. We then divide the obligors in RR5, based on one of the dimensions chosen at a time, and compare the realized defaults rates and see if they are significantly different. For example, we are examining the government guaranteed loans of RR5 and find out the default rate for these loans is 5%, whereas it is only 2% for the rest of the population in RR5. Using the Monte Carlo calibration test mentioned previously, we can test if the observed default rates of 5% and 2% for government guaranteed and nonguaranteed RR5 loans are significantly different from the assigned PD of 3.5%. By assuming a certain pairwise asset correlation, we can generate the distribution of the default rate given the null hypothesis of PD equals 3.5% (Figure 3.8) for the two subportfolios individually. By setting a certain confidence level, we can then check if the 5% and 2% default rates lie within the confidence interval. We can reject the PD homogeneity of RR5 if either one of these two default rates is found to lie outside the confidence interval.

The second way would be to compare the realized default rates of the two subportfolios (e.g., government guaranteed vs. nonguaranteed RR5 loans) using the following (pooled) $t$-test. Here, we assume default events are independent.

$$t = \frac{p_1 - p_2}{s_p \sqrt{\dfrac{1}{n_1} + \dfrac{1}{n_2}}} \qquad \text{(Equation 3.6)}$$

where

$$s_p^2 = \frac{(n_1 - 1)p_1(1 - p_1) + (n_2 - 1)p_2(1 - p_2)}{n_1 + n_2 - 2}. \qquad \text{(Equation 3.7)}$$

$p_1$ and $p_2$ are the default rates of subportfolio 1 and 2 respectively, whereas $n_1$ and $n_2$ are the respective numbers of obligors in subportfolio 1 and 2. For $n_1 > 30$ and $n_2 > 30$, we can test for the statistical significance of the difference by comparing the $t$-statistic with the $t$-distribution with a degree of freedom equal to $n_1 + n_2 - 2$. For example, if $p_1 = 3\%$, $p_2 = 1\%$, $n_1 = 200$, and $n_2 = 150$, the $t$-statistic is 1.281 according to Equation 3.6. This $t$-statistic corresponds with a confidence level of 79.9% (in a two-tail test) under the $t$-distribution with a degree of freedom equal to 348 ($= 200 + 150 - 2$). We can therefore only reject the hypothesis that subportfolio 1 and 2 belonging to the same population with 79.9% confidence level.

*Supplementary Analysis*   The above analysis assumes that defaults are independent, which we know is not true. We therefore developed a Monte Carlo simulation approach where correlations are taken into account. The fundamentals of the simulations are similar to those outlined in calibration testing mentioned previously except that instead of obtaining a distribution of possible default rates for a PD-homogenous segment, we generate the distribution of the differences of the defaults rates of two subportfolios with the same assigned PD.[16] Suppose we have a certain risk rating (say RR5) with an assigned PD of 2%. We would like to see if this portfolio is homogenous with respect to the geographical locations (Canada vs. United States) of the obligors. Further suppose that the realized default rate of the obligors in RR5 in Canada is 3%, whereas it is only 1% for those in the

United States in the same risk rating. We want to find out if the obligors in RR5 are PD-homogenous between the United States and Canada.[17] We run the Monte Carlo simulations and generate the distribution of the differences of default rates under the assumption that they are in fact homogenous with a true PD equal to 2% (see Figure 3.14). If the 2% difference (3% − 1%) is within, say, the 95% confidence interval, we do not reject the hypothesis that both U.S. and Canadian obligors in RR5 have PD of 2%.[18]

The simulation is similar to that described in the Section of "A Monte Carlo Simulation–Based Calibration Test" earlier in this chapter. In each scenario, we first sample a systematic risk factor. Then, under this systematic risk factor, the specific risk factor for each obligor is generated. We then combine the systematic and specific risk factors and determine, under a given systematic risk factor, which obligors are in default, and thus what the default rate is under that scenario (represented by the systematic risk factor). When we determine the default rates for the second subportfolio (e.g., U.S. obligors in RR5), we keep the same systematic factor as in the first subportfolio (e.g., Canadian obligors in RR5) and sample the specific risk factors for each obligor in the second subportfolio. When we construct the total risk factor for the obligors, we use the asset return correlation specific to the particular subportfolio to which the obligors belong.

### Common Observations on PD Backtesting

We have frequently observed that especially high PD risk ratings fail the calibration test in a way that the realized default rates suggest significantly higher PDs than those assigned for these risk ratings. That is, we would have to reject the assigned PDs given the realized default rates being statistically too high. Like all validation tests, this is only a symptom, which should trigger

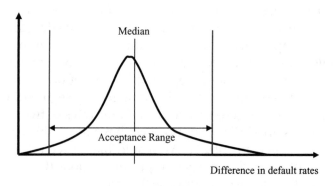

**Figure 3.14** Distribution of the different in default rates of two subportfolios generated by Monte Carlo.

a thorough analysis to diagnose the problem and have it corrected. In our experience, the following are the common reasons for this phenomenon:

1. Credit policies of banks do not allow initiation of new loans below a certain risk rating. Originators with aggressive targets initiate high-PD loans anyway, but these loans are superficially assigned lower PD risk ratings to comply with the credit policy. The high PDs of these loans results in default rates higher than those suggested by the PD of the assigned risk ratings.

2. There is organizational friction to downgrade the obligors below certain risk ratings (usually the lowest performing risk rating). Typically, the account manager would have to pass the account onto a different group (e.g., the *special accounts management unit*; SAMU), which may explain the hesitation to downgrade these accounts.

3. Especially for commercial portfolios, account reviews are quite infrequent resulting in delays in downgrades (or upgrades).

There are different ways of dealing with the issues above. The first issue can be dealt with by better aligning the organization's risk appetite (as expressed in the credit policy in this example) with the business objectives. The second issue can be dealt with by more frequent review of the obligors in the riskier risk ratings by independent parties (other than the account managers). The last issue is more difficult to tackle as increasing the review frequency for a large number of the SME obligors can be costly for an organization. One possible solution is to monitor some industry-specific leading indicators and macroeconomic indicators. When these indicators point to a credit downturn, it can trigger a review of the obligors accordingly. Some FIs also realize that the riskier part of the risk ratings is not granular enough. As a result, the obligors in these risk ratings are not risk-homogeneous as high-PD obligors are combined with lower ones in the same risk ratings. Because of the existence of those obligors with high PD, the realized default rates of these risk ratings are more likely to be higher than the assigned PD. The best way to mitigate this problem is to separate the ratings into two risk ratings so that the obligors can be categorized into these two new risk ratings now with different and appropriately assigned PD.

### Case Study: PD Backtesting

#### Sample Panel Data
This case study summarizes the results of PD backtesting performed using sample data for 2000 and 2001 presented in Table 3.3 to 3.5.

**TABLE 3.3**

Sample Default Rates of Year 2000 and 2001

| Starting Risk Rating | Assigned PDs (%) | Average $R^2$ | Year 2000 | | Year 2001 | |
|---|---|---|---|---|---|---|
| | | | Number of Obligors | Number of Defaults | Number of Obligors | Number of Defaults |
| 1 | 0.02 | 0.15 | 35 | 0 | 30 | 0 |
| 2 | 0.05 | 0.22 | 400 | 2 | 460 | 4 |
| 3 | 0.10 | 0.45 | 700 | 0 | 528 | 0 |
| 4 | 0.30 | 0.33 | 1300 | 2 | 1300 | 8 |
| 5 | 1.00 | 0.20 | 2567 | 20 | 2780 | 22 |
| 6 | 3.00 | 0.17 | 1802 | 51 | 1109 | 35 |
| 7 | 8.00 | 0.22 | 149 | 15 | 225 | 35 |
| 8 | 25.00 | 0.16 | 88 | 42 | 119 | 29 |
| 9 | 35.00 | 0.16 | 50 | 18 | 73 | 30 |

**TABLE 3.4**

Sample Transition Rates in Year 2000

| | Year 2000 Transition Rates | | | | | | | | | |
|---|---|---|---|---|---|---|---|---|---|---|
| | 1 | 2 | 3 | 4 | 5 | 6 | 7 | 8 | 9 | Default |
| 1 | 92.9% | 0.5% | 3.3% | 1.4% | 1.4% | 0.5% | 0.0% | 0.0% | 0.0% | 0.0% |
| 2 | 0.7% | 89.8% | 3.2% | 2.1% | 3.8% | 0.0% | 0.0% | 0.0% | 0.0% | 0.5% |
| 3 | 3.7% | 0.0% | 86.6% | 6.6% | 2.6% | 0.5% | 0.0% | 0.0% | 0.0% | 0.0% |
| 4 | 0.6% | 0.0% | 1.8% | 80.3% | 16.2% | 0.4% | 0.0% | 0.0% | 0.6% | 0.2% |
| 5 | 0.4% | 0.0% | 0.4% | 2.7% | 87.5% | 6.5% | 0.0% | 0.0% | 1.7% | 0.8% |
| 6 | 2.6% | 0.0% | 0.1% | 0.2% | 21.7% | 58.8% | 0.0% | 0.0% | 13.7% | 2.8% |
| 7 | 0.0% | 0.0% | 0.0% | 0.0% | 2.9% | 5.0% | 56.0% | 15.0% | 11.0% | 10.1% |
| 8 | 0.0% | 0.0% | 0.0% | 0.0% | 0.0% | 0.0% | 1.0% | 50.1% | 1.2% | 47.7% |
| 9 | 1.7% | 0.0% | 0.4% | 0.0% | 0.4% | 6.3% | 0.0% | 0.0% | 55.2% | 36.0% |
| Default | 0.0% | 0.0% | 0.0% | 0.0% | 0.0% | 0.0% | 0.0% | 0.0% | 0.0% | 100.0% |

## Testing the Discriminatory Power of the Risk Rating System

The empirical measurement of the discriminatory power of the risk rating system is presented in Table 3.6 for the two years we have sample data for.[19] (See the Excel spreadsheet "PD Backtesting" provided on the CD which comes with the book.)

**TABLE 3.5**

Sample Transition Rates in Year 2001

| | 1 | 2 | 3 | 4 | 5 | 6 | 7 | 8 | 9 | Default |
|---|---|---|---|---|---|---|---|---|---|---|
| | | | | **Year 2001 Transition Rates** | | | | | | |
| 1 | 90.9% | 2.1% | 2.3% | 2.4% | 1.5% | 0.5% | 0.3% | 0.0% | 0.0% | 0.0% |
| 2 | 0.8% | 88.8% | 3.0% | 2.2% | 3.0% | 1.4% | 0.0% | 0.0% | 0.0% | 0.9% |
| 3 | 1.5% | 1.0% | 82.2% | 13.3% | 2.1% | 0.0% | 0.0% | 0.0% | 0.0% | 0.0% |
| 4 | 0.6% | 0.2% | 1.4% | 83.8% | 12.6% | 0.3% | 0.0% | 0.0% | 0.6% | 0.6% |
| 5 | 0.4% | 1.1% | 0.3% | 2.8% | 86.4% | 6.5% | 0.0% | 0.0% | 1.7% | 0.8% |
| 6 | 1.2% | 0.0% | 0.3% | 0.3% | 22.5% | 61.8% | 1.9% | 0.0% | 9.0% | 3.2% |
| 7 | 0.0% | 0.0% | 0.0% | 0.4% | 3.0% | 3.0% | 55.0% | 13.0% | 10.0% | 15.6% |
| 8 | 0.0% | 0.0% | 0.0% | 0.0% | 0.5% | 0.0% | 1.0% | 58.1% | 16.0% | 24.4% |
| 9 | 0.9% | 0.0% | 0.4% | 0.0% | 0.3% | 2.3% | 0.0% | 1.8% | 53.2% | 41.1% |
| **Default** | 0.0% | 0.0% | 0.0% | 0.0% | 0.0% | 0.0% | 0.0% | 0.0% | 0.0% | 100.0% |

Hosmer and Lemeshow (2000, p. 162) provided the following guidelines for performance benchmarking for accuracy ratio: 70% to 80% is acceptable, 80% to 90% is considered excellent, and more than 90% is outstanding discrimination. According to this performance benchmarking, the results presented above are excellent.

When the performances of the different portfolios are compared, the portfolio compositions need to be controlled for to ensure a fair comparison. In Table 3.7, we compare the Gini and accuracy ratios for the commercial and corporate portfolios using the sample data for 2000.

In our experience, the performance of the commercial (i.e., mid-market) portfolios could be inferior to that of corporate portfolios due to the lack of forward-looking surveillance tools and less frequent reviews for the commercial portfolios. This appears to be the case as well for this

**TABLE 3.6**

Gini Scores and Accuracy Ratios of Sample Data

| | 2000 | 2001 |
|---|---|---|
| Accuracy ratio | 85.0% | 83.4% |
| Gini | 69.9% | 66.9% |
| Default rate | 2.1% | 2.5% |

**TABLE 3.7**

Gini Scores and Accuracy Ratios of Corporate vs. Commercial Portfolios

|  | Corporate | Commercial |
|---|---|---|
| Accuracy ratio | 95.8% | 84.0% |
| Gini | 91.6% | 68.0% |
|  | **Corporate** | **Commercial (Adjusted to Match Composition of Corporate)** |
| Accuracy ratio | 95.8% | 84.1% |
| Gini | 91.6% | 68.1% |
|  | **Corporate (Adjusted to Match Composition of Commercial)** | **Commercial** |
| Accuracy ratio | 83.9% | 84.0% |
| Gini | 67.8% | 68.0% |

sample data, as the performance of the corporate portfolio, as seen in the first box above, is better than that of the commercial. In the second and third boxes, we investigate how much of this superior performance is due to the differences in portfolio composition. In the second box, we adjust the commercial portfolio to match the composition of the corporate portfolio, and the other way around in the third box. The last box indicates that the corporate portfolio's performance would be very similar to that of the commercial portfolio if the corporate portfolio had the composition of the commercial portfolio. This exercise allows us to compare the performances of different portfolios while controlling for the composition effect. (See worksheet "Gini-Corporate vs. Commercial" in the Excel spreadsheet "PD Backtesting" provided on the CD which comes with the book.)

Another approach for achieving an apples-to-apples comparison is the following. We can assume that each rating has the same number of initial obligors (i.e., $1/9$ of the total number of obligors in each of the risk ratings) while we calculate Gini scores by preserving the observed default rates. For this sample data, we would therefore consider the adjusted portfolios and numbers of defaults presented in Table 3.8.

### Testing the Calibration of the Risk Rating System

The results of the Monte Carlo simulation-based calibration (i.e., level) tests suggest that the number of defaults is within the bounds of the 51% confidence interval for most of the RRs over the sample period (see in Table 3.9).[20]

**TABLE 3.8**

Adjusted Portfolios with Equal Number of Obligors in Each Risk Rating

| Risk Rating | Number of Obligors: Year 2000 | | | |
| --- | --- | --- | --- | --- |
| | Corporate (Initial Number of Obligors) | Commercial (Initial Number of Obligors) | Corporate (No. of Defaults) | Commercial (No. of Defaults) |
| 1 | 787.9 | 787.9 | 0.0 | 0.0 |
| 2 | 787.9 | 787.9 | 0.0 | 5.2 |
| 3 | 787.9 | 787.9 | 0.0 | 0.0 |
| 4 | 787.9 | 787.9 | 0.0 | 1.3 |
| 5 | 787.9 | 787.9 | 9.8 | 6.0 |
| 6 | 787.9 | 787.9 | 78.8 | 21.3 |
| 7 | 787.9 | 787.9 | 157.6 | 73.7 |
| 8 | 787.9 | 787.9 | 393.9 | 375.6 |
| 9 | 787.9 | 787.9 | 393.9 | 279.0 |

There are, however, a few exceptions, which are listed in Table 3.10 with the violations of the respective bounds shaded. In all these violations, the observed default rates are higher than the maximum number of defaults allowed at the 51% confidence level. These results possibly suggest that there may be some friction in the regrading process. Specifically, some of the obligors in these risk ratings should have been downgraded before they ultimately defaulted.

**TABLE 3.9**

Monte Carlo Simulation-Based Calibration Test Results

| | Year 2000 | | | Level Test | |
| --- | --- | --- | --- | --- | --- |
| Starting Risk Rating | Average $R^2$ | Number of Obligors | Number of Defaults | Minimum Allowed Number of Defaults | Maximum Allowed Number of Defaults |
| 1 | 0.15 | 35 | 0 | 0 | 0 |
| 2 | 0.22 | 400 | 2 | 0 | 0 |
| 3 | 0.45 | 700 | 0 | 0 | 0 |
| 4 | 0.33 | 1300 | 2 | 0 | 2 |
| 5 | 0.20 | 2567 | 20 | 4 | 30 |
| 6 | 0.17 | 1802 | 51 | 17 | 73 |
| 7 | 0.22 | 149 | 15 | 4 | 16 |
| 8 | 0.16 | 88 | 42 | 13 | 30 |
| 9 | 0.16 | 50 | 18 | 11 | 23 |

(Continued)

**T A B L E  3.9**

Monte Carlo Simulation-Based Calibration Test Results (*Continued*)

| | Year 2001 | | | Level Test | |
|---|---|---|---|---|---|
| Starting Risk Rating | Average $R^2$ | Number of Obligors | Number of Defaults | Minimum Allowed Number of Defaults | Maximum Allowed Number of Defaults |
| 1 | 0.15 | 30 | 0 | 0 | 0 |
| 2 | 0.22 | 460 | 4 | 0 | 0 |
| 3 | 0.45 | 528 | 0 | 0 | 0 |
| 4 | 0.33 | 1300 | 8 | 0 | 3 |
| 5 | 0.20 | 2780 | 22 | 4 | 32 |
| 6 | 0.17 | 1109 | 35 | 9 | 45 |
| 7 | 0.22 | 225 | 35 | 5 | 25 |
| 8 | 0.16 | 119 | 29 | 17 | 40 |
| 9 | 0.16 | 73 | 30 | 17 | 33 |

## Supplementary Analysis

### Geometric Mean Probability

Geometric mean probability–log-likelihood results are given below for 2000 and 2001 in Table 3.11. They are calculated in worksheet "GMP 2000" and "GMP 2001" in Excel spreadsheet "PD Backtesting" on the CD which comes with the book.

Here the performance of our model (IRRS) is compared against that of a "naïve" model: a model that correctly predicted the average default rates of 2.12% and 2.46% for 2000 and 2001, respectively, but was unable to distinguish the default risks among the obligors. That is, for example for year 2000, our naïve model predicted one year before default (time $t-1$) that all obligors

**T A B L E  3.10**

Violations in Calibration Tests Conducted on the Sample Data

| Year | Risk Rating | Number of Defaults | Minimum Allowed Number of Defaults | Maximum Allowed Number of Defaults |
|---|---|---|---|---|
| 2001 | 2 | 4 | 0 | 0 |
| | 4 | 8 | 0 | 0 |
| | 7 | 35 | 5 | 25 |
| 2000 | 2 | 2 | 0 | 0 |
| | 8 | 42 | 13 | 30 |

**TABLE 3.11**

Geometric Mean Probabilities in Year 2000 and 2001

|  | Year 2000 | |
|---|---|---|
|  | **Our Model** | **Naïve Model** |
| Log-likelihood | − 534.70 | − 726.79 |
| Average log-likelihood | − 0.08 | − 0.10 |
| GMP | 0.93 | 0.90 |
| Pick up over naïve model | 271 basis points | |
|  | Year 2001 | |
|  | **Our Model** | **Naïve Model** |
| Log-likelihood | − 586.35 | − 764.84 |
| Average log-likelihood | − 0.09 | − 0.12 |
| GMP | 0.92 | 0.89 |
| Pick up over naïve model | 269 basis points | |

have a PD = 2.12%, whereas exactly 2.12% of the obligors defaulted at time *t*. We would expect our model outperforms this naïve model, which it did. In our experience, a "pick up" over the naïve model in the range of 50 to 100 basis points (bps) should be considered as good performance. Of course, the larger the pick-up, the better the performance. In Table 3.11, the pick-up rate is above 200 bps, thus indicating a very good performance. We, however, need to be careful about one thing: the pick-up rate over the naïve model depends on the portfolio default rate. For low-default portfolios (less than 1% overall default rate), the naïve model performs respectably even though it fails to distinguish the default risks among the obligors. The naïve model assigns the same PD for all of the obligors, thus fails for all defaulted ones. However, since there are only a very small number of realized defaults, this mistake will be averaged out over the entire portfolio and the performance in terms of GMP will still look good. Thus, a pick-up rate of 50–100 bps should be considered as good performance only if the GMP test is conducted on a low-default portfolio. We should be expecting a pick-up rate well above the range of 50–100 bps for those portfolios with high default rates.

### Testing the Realization of the Risk Rating Philosophy

The next and a critical dimension is the validation of the risk rating philosophy. We need to confirm the risk rating philosophy is what we believe it is given the observed default and migration rates.[21] We calculated the *mobility metric* proposed by Jafry and Schuermann (2003) for both our sample historical transition matrices and Standard & Poor's "comparable" transition matrices.

*Mobility Metrics of Year 2000 and 2001*    The mobility metrics calculated from the historical transition matrices of our sample data are reported in Table 3.12. The calculations are also presented in worksheets "Mobility 2000 – 9 Grades" and "Mobility 2001 – 9 Grades" in Excel spreadsheet "PD Backtesting" provided on the CD which comes with the book. It is difficult to assess the PIT-ness of these matrices without comparing the mobility metrics with that of a benchmark transition matrix (e.g., Standard & Poor's transition matrix). Such benchmarking will be performed subsequently. However, we can still judge the performance based on our experience: When transition matrices with dimensions of equal to or higher than $10 \times 10$ are used, the full spectrum of mobility metric ranges between 0.1 (for full TTC) and 0.6 (full PIT).[15] According to our experience, the mobility metrics of our sample data reported in Table 3.12 seem to be close to what we would have expected Standard & Poor's transition matrices to score. It therefore resembles more of a TTC philosophy than a PIT philosophy. The next analysis providing a formal comparison with Standard & Poor's matrices should provide further information.

*Direct Comparison with Mobility Metrics of Standard & Poor's Transition Matrices*    To obtain a fair comparison, we construct comparable Standard & Poor's transition matrices by replicating the portfolio composition (both in terms of industries and risk ratings) of the sample data. Besides, to ensure any difference in the mobility metrics is not the result of the difference in granularity between the internal rating system and Standard & Poor's ratings, we common-sized the matrices by aggregating some of the internal and Standard & Poor's risk ratings such that the resulting transition matrices have the same dimension of $7 \times 7$ (including the default state).[22] The common-size mapping is presented in Table 3.13.

**TABLE 3.12**

Mobility Metrics of Year 2000 and 2001

| Year | Dimensions of Matrix (Excluding Default Column/Row) | Mobility Metric |
|------|-----------------------------------------------------|-----------------|
| 2000 | $9 \times 9$ | 0.29 |
| 2001 | $9 \times 9$ | 0.28 |

**TABLE 3.13**

Common-Size Mapping

| Standard & Poor's Risk Rating | Internal Risk Rating (Our Model) |
|---|:---:|
| AAA/AA+ | 1 + 2 |
| AA/AA–/A+ | 3 |
| A/A–/BBB+ | 4 |
| BBB/BBB–/BB+ | 5 |
| BB/BB–/B+ | 6 |
| CCC | 7 + 8 + 9 |
| Default | Default |

The resulting mobility metrics are reported in Table 3.14. The computations are also presented in Excel spreadsheet of "PD Backtesting" on the CD which comes with the book.

As seen in Table 3.14 and as expected, our sample risk rating system shows more mobility than does that of Standard & Poor's in both 2000 and 2001. We can therefore conclude our risk rating philosophy is more PIT than that of Standard & Poor's.

In the above analysis, we document the "realized" risk rating philosophy of the internal risk rating system by computing the mobility metrics of historical transition matrices. For our sample data, it turns out that the realized philosophy is more PIT than that of Standard & Poor's, though it is likely to be far away from a perfectly PIT system. This "realized" philosophy should be compared with the "stated" risk rating philosophy of the bank. Any inconsistencies between the "realized" and "stated" philosophy need to be rectified.[23]

### Homogeneity Testing: Subportfolio-Level Validation

The importance of subportfolio-level validation is emphasized in the PD backtesting guidelines. Banks need to determine at what aggregate levels

**TABLE 3.14**

Mobility Metrics of Common-Sized Transition Matrices of Dimension of 7 × 7 (Including Default State)

| Year | 2000 | 2001 |
|---|:---:|:---:|
| Our model | 0.21 | 0.22 |
| Standard & Poor's | 0.13 | 0.15 |

the validation exercise will be repeated. In our experience, global banks repeat the entire validation exercise at least for two or three of their major divisions usually categorized by geographic regions and portfolio types.

Then, the practical question is how to select the subportfolios in PD validation. The objective is to maintain the homogeneity of the subportfolios as much as possible. The more granular the subportfolios, then the more risk homogeneous the subportfolios are, and the easier the diagnosing of the problems is. However, this needs to be balanced with considerations for materiality, feasibility, practicality (e.g., data limitations, statistical significance, etc.), and cost consideration. For further discussion, refer to the "PD Backtesting" section earlier in this chapter.

*Significance Testing*   In this test, we examine each of the risk ratings for each of the high-level subportfolios identified. The underlying assumption is that all obligors in a certain risk rating have the same PD regardless of geography, industry, size of the exposure, risk rating template used, and so forth. Below is an example of how this can be done. Using a different sample data, we record the number of obligors and number of defaults in two subportfolios (corporate vs. commercial) of each of the internal risk ratings observed over a certain year. They are reported in Table 3.15.[24]

A visual examination shows some discrepancies in the observed default rates between the two subportfolios for risk ratings 11 and below. By using the pooled $t$-test (Equations 3.6 and 3.7), we can assess the significances of these differences. For example, for risk rating 12, $p_1$ = 4.3% (default rate of commercial subportfolio), $p_2$ = 2.4% (default rate of corporate subportfolio), $n_1$ = 46 (number of obligors in commercial subportfolio), and $n_2$ = 82 (number of obligors in corporate subportfolio). Using Equations 3.6 and 3.7, we obtain a $t$-statistic of 0.597, which corresponds with a (two) tail probability of 55.2% under the $t$-distribution with a degree of freedom equal to 126 (= 46 + 82 − 2). We can therefore only reject the hypothesis that the two subportfolios belong to the same population at 44.8% confidence level. Results for the other risk ratings are presented in Table 3.16.

According to the test results reported in Table 3.16, we can only reject the hypothesis that the two subportfolios belonging to the same population at relatively low confidence level for RR12 and RR13. However, the hypothesis of identical default rates between the two subportfolios for RR14-16 may be readily rejected at high confidence level. Nevertheless, given that this test is only valid when the number of obligors is sufficiently large (e.g., $n_1 + n_2 > 40$), we need to be careful in drawing any conclusion obtained for RR15 (marginally valid since $n_1 + n_2 = 38$) and RR16 solely based on these test results.

**TABLE 3.15**

Number of Obligors and Number of Defaults of a Sample Risk Rating System

| RR | Commercial | | | Corporate | | | Assigned PD (%) |
|---|---|---|---|---|---|---|---|
| | Number of Obligors | Number of Defaults | Default Rate (%) | Number of Obligors | Number of Defaults | Default Rate (%) | |
| 1 | 10 | 0 | 0.00 | 30 | 0 | 0.00 | 0.02 |
| 2 | 121 | 0 | 0.00 | 400 | 0 | 0.00 | 0.05 |
| 3 | 101 | 0 | 0.00 | 450 | 0 | 0.00 | 0.08 |
| 4 | 133 | 0 | 0.00 | 720 | 0 | 0.00 | 0.10 |
| 5 | 23 | 0 | 0.00 | 201 | 0 | 0.00 | 0.15 |
| 6 | 502 | 0 | 0.00 | 600 | 0 | 0.00 | 0.20 |
| 7 | 550 | 0 | 0.00 | 301 | 0 | 0.00 | 0.30 |
| 8 | 1,400 | 1 | 0.07 | 365 | 0 | 0.00 | 0.40 |
| 9 | 120 | 0 | 0.00 | 149 | 0 | 0.00 | 0.80 |
| 10 | 300 | 1 | 0.33 | 201 | 0 | 0.00 | 1.00 |
| 11 | 10 | 0 | **0.00** | 63 | 1 | **1.60** | 1.60 |
| 12 | 46 | 2 | **4.30** | 82 | 2 | **2.40** | 3.30 |
| 13 | 29 | 1 | **3.40** | 44 | 3 | **6.80** | 13.00 |
| 14 | 24 | 4 | **16.70** | 33 | 1 | **3.00** | 25.60 |
| 15 | 8 | 7 | **87.50** | 30 | 7 | **23.30** | 35.50 |
| 16 | 6 | 5 | **83.30** | 19 | 6 | **31.60** | 59.60 |

**TABLE 3.16**

Pooled $t$-test on Difference in Default Rate between Commercial and Corporate Subportfolios

| RR | $s_p$ (%) | $t$ | Two-Tail Probability (%) | CL at which the Null Hypothesis Can Be Rejected (%) |
|---|---|---|---|---|
| 12 | 17.4 | 0.597 | 55.2 | 44.8 |
| 13 | 22.7 | −0.620 | 53.7 | 46.3 |
| 14 | 27.4 | 1.854 | 6.9 | **93.1** |
| 15 | 40.7 | 3.965 | 0.0 | **100.0** |
| 16 | 44.6 | 2.476 | 2.1 | **97.9** |

*Supplementary Analysis*   The above analysis assumes that defaults are independent, which we know is not true. We therefore also consider a Monte Carlo simulation approach where correlations are taken into

**TABLE 3.17**

Monte Carlo Simulation Approach of Homogeneity Test

| RR | Commercial | | | Corporate | | | Assigned PD (%) | $DR_1 - DR_2$ (%) | Minimum Difference $(DR_1 - DR_2)$ (%) | Maximum Difference $(DR_1 - DR_2)$ (%) |
|----|------------|--------|----------------------------|------------|--------|----------------------------|------|-------|-------|-------|
| | Number of Obligors $(n_1)$ | $R^2$ (%) | Default Rate $(DR_1)$ (%) | Number of Obligors $(n_2)$ | $R^2$ (%) | Default Rate $(DR_2)$ (%) | | | | |
| 11 | 10 | 13.70 | 0.00  | 63 | 21.30 | 1.60  | 1.60  | −1.60 | −7.90  | 10    |
| 12 | 46 | 12.80 | 4.30  | 82 | 28.10 | 2.40  | 3.30  | 1.90  | −9.10  | 6.50  |
| 13 | 29 | 13.60 | 3.40  | 44 | 21.60 | 6.80  | 13.00 | −3.40 | −18.90 | 15.10 |
| 14 | 24 | 12.80 | 16.70 | 33 | 16.50 | 3.00  | 25.60 | 13.60 | −23.50 | 22.30 |
| 15 | 8  | 13.30 | 87.50 | 30 | 23.30 | 23.30 | 35.50 | **64.20** | −37.50 | 36.70 |
| 16 | 6  | 13.10 | 83.30 | 19 | 12.30 | 31.60 | 59.60 | **51.80** | −45.60 | 41.20 |

account. The inputs and results are presented in Table 3.17 at the 95% confidence level.

For RR11-14, we cannot reject the hypothesis that default rates of commercial and corporate subportfolios are generated from the same PD (assigned to the respective risk rating) at the 95% confidence level (CL), as the difference in default rates falls within the confidence interval generated by the simulations. This is, however, not true for RR15 and RR16 where we have to reject the hypothesis at the 95% CL. For these two RRs, the commercial subportfolio has a significantly higher default rate than that of the corporate subportfolio. Note that the results are consistent between the pooled *t*-test and the Monte Carlo simulation test. For example, we can only reject the null hypothesis for RR 14 at the 93.1% CL according to the pooled *t*-test (i.e., we cannot reject it at the 95% CL). It is therefore not surprising to find out that we also cannot reject the null hypothesis at the 95% CL when we conduct the simulation test on RR14.

## LGD Backtesting

### Overview and Practical Issues

There are two fundamental differences between PD and LGD backtesting:

1. PDs are backtested against default rates, which are defined for a group of obligors. For example, two defaults out of 100 obligors result in a 2% default rate, which represent a group of (100) obligors. On the other hand, expected LGDs are backtested against individually realized LGDs.

2. Default vs. no default is a two-state outcome, whereas LGD outcomes are continuous as realized LGD can take on any value between 0% and 100%.[25]

These two differences dictate the different approaches in conducting PD and LGD LGD backtesting. Nevertheless, the dimensions we need to test remain the same in a complete backtesting exercise. Specifically, we need to test:

1. Discriminatory power of the LGD risk rating system: cumulative LGD accuracy ratio (CLAR) as a *modified accuracy ratio*.

2. The calibration of the LGD risk rating system: *various analyses at individual facility level and aggregated level*.

3. Realization of the LGD risk rating philosophy: *mobility metric*.

4. Homogeneity of the LGD risk ratings: *subportfolio-level validation and significance tests*.

The realized LGDs should be compared with the expected LGDs one year prior to default to test the accuracy of the rating system. The reference point for LGD ratings, one year before the default event, is consistent with the economic capital risk horizon and is used throughout as the de facto reference point for all LGD rating analysis/tests involving comparison with realized LGD rates.

Unlike the observed default rates, we do not know the realized LGDs at the time of default. It typically takes a couple of (or more) years to realize the workout recoveries, unless it is the practice of the FIe to sell the defaulted loans soon after the default events. LGD backtestings are therefore usually conducted with a time delay. If we determine that, say, 90% of the recoveries are usually collected during the first 18 months, an assumption can be made for the amount of the "yet-to-be-collected" recoveries after that. This assumption would need to be verified and monitored as an on-going process.

Another fundamental challenge with LGD backtesting is the lack of relevant historical data. The annual number of defaults is limited to achieve statistically significant backtesting results. Some FIs conduct the backtesting using the aggregated data rather than annual data to better deal with this challenge. The drawback of this approach is we sacrifice the ability to recover any recent trends (or any time-series pattern) once we pool the LGD data realized over different periods of time. As a result, if an FI is conducting LGD backtesting on the aggregated data, it needs to be complemented with at least some basic analyses using the most recent data.

Interpretation of the LGD backtesting results is also difficult due to lack of performance benchmarking. In PD backtesting, for example, Gini coefficient has been used for many years, thus, it is easier to benchmark the performance results. LGD backtesting is much newer with some of the tests still evolving. We do not yet have the same level of experience that we have in PD backtesting for performance benchmarking.

LGD modeling is relatively new and still evolving. It is not yet clear that all LGD risk drivers have been captured in the LGD models.[26] Backtesting exercise can be used to test and identify new LGD risk drivers. LGD observations, besides being used in the backtesting of LGD risk ratings, are often segmented by potential LGD risk drivers to better understand the characteristics of the LGD data and improve the LGD models accordingly.

## Testing the Discriminatory Power of the Risk Rating System

Limited data and large standard deviations associated with the U-shaped distributions of LGD may create significant noise in conducting any statistical tests in an exposure-by-exposure analysis. Grouping the LGD observations into prespecified ranges (i.e., in segments or bands) can help reduce this statistical noise and thus allowing for a more accurate view of the expected value of LGD. The LGD ranges should be used to compare LGD ratings to realized LGDs in the discriminatory test described below. A natural candidate for the LGD bands is the bank's LGD risk rating system. A sample of such is presented in Table 3.18.

The purpose of the discriminatory test is to validate the correctness of the ordinal ranking of the facilities by LGD risk. If a LGD risk rating system can effectively discriminate LGD risks, we expect that most of the high realized LGDs come from high-predicted LGD buckets. In other words, an important aspect of a LGD risk rating system is its ability to correctly rank-order LGD risk. Discriminatory power analysis assesses how well a model or rating system discriminates between different rating grades and tests for the ordinal ranking of the LGD ratings. The cumulative LGD accuracy ratio (CLAR) serves as a measure of this rank-ordering ability.

The first step is to determine the number of facilities being assigned the LGD rating (predicted LGD) in each LGD band as defined in previous section. These LGD bands are termed *predicted LGD bands*. The realized LGDs are then sorted in descending order and grouped such that the number of realized LGDs in each of the bands is equal to the number of facilities being assigned the LGD rating in each of the predicted LGD bands. For example, assume the worst predicted LGD band has 10 facilities; the 10 worst (i.e., highest) realized LGDs are thus assigned to the equivalent *realized LGD band*. Next, we record how many of the observations in the realized LGD bands in fact originated from the corresponding predicted LGD band. It is repeated on a cumulative basis, each time including

**TABLE 3.18**

Sample LGD Bands Constructed based on LGD Risk Rating System

| RR | Minimum (%) | Mid (%) | Maximum (%) |
|----|-------------|---------|-------------|
| 1  | 0           | 5       | 10          |
| 2  | 10          | 15      | 20          |
| 3  | 20          | 25      | 30          |
| 4  | 30          | 35      | 40          |
| 5  | 40          | 45      | 50          |
| 6  | 50          | 55      | 60          |
| 7  | 60          | 80      | 100         |

one more band with better (i.e., lower) predicted and realized LGD. For example, we next count how many of the observations in the two worst realized LGD bands in fact originated from the corresponding two worst predicted LGD bands. After that, we repeat the counting with three worst combined ratings, and so on.

The CLAR coefficient, which is similar to the Gini score, can then be calculated by completing the counting process described above. We may also plot the CLAR curve, which is similar to the CAP profile in a Gini test. The y-axis of the CLAR curve is the cumulative percentage of correctly assigned realized LGD, whereas the x-axis keeps track of the cumulated percentage of observations in the predicted LGD bands. If rank ordering is perfect, the observations in the realized and predicted bands exactly match each other, and on a cumulative basis the CLAR curve would fall on the 45-degree line. In reality, there will be some deviation between realized and predicted LGD observations and therefore the CLAR curve will lie below the 45-degree line indicating a less than perfect rank ordering. The CLAR coefficient can be defined as 2× the area under the CLAR curve. The CLAR coefficient ranges from 0 to 1, where 1 represents perfect discriminatory power. The higher the CLAR score, the better the discriminatory power of the LGD risk rating system. Like other discriminatory tests, the analysis is generally more valuable when used in comparative terms (e.g., benchmarking the performance of the bank's rating model against other predictive LGD models). The plotting of the CLAR curve could provide for additional information on the distribution of the realized LGD that may not be apparent from the CLAR coefficient itself.

### Mechanics of the Discriminatory Test

As a first step, we need to bucket the predicted LGDs in order to establish a discrete LGD risk rating system. Table 3.19 presents an example where five predicted LGD bands are used.

The next step is to segment the "realized LGD" based on their ordinal ranking. The following is an example where we have 50 LGD observations. Let's assume there are exactly ten LGD observations in each band. We rank-ordered these observations from the worst (say 100%) to the best (say 1%) and determine the minimum and maximum LGD for each realized LGD band. That is, the maximum for band 1 is the worst observation (100%) and the minimum for band 1 is the tenth worst observation (say 40%). The maximum for band 2 is therefore the eleventh worst observation (say 40%) and the minimum for band 2 is the twentieth worst observation (say 20%). The maximum for band 3 is the twenty-first worst observation (say 20%), and the minimum for band 3 is therefore the thirtieth worst observation (say

**TABLE 3.19**

Sample Prediced LGD Bands

| Band | Predicted LGD | | |
|------|------------------|--------------|------------------|
|      | Minimum LGD (%) | Mid LGD (%) | Maximum LGD (%) |
| 1 | 80 | 90 | 100 |
| 2 | 60 | 70 | 80 |
| 3 | 40 | 50 | 60 |
| 4 | 20 | 30 | 40 |
| 5 | 0 | 10 | 20 |

5%), and so on for band 4 and 5. The five realized LGD bands constructed above is reported in Table 3.20.

Putting Tables 3.19 and 3.20 side-by-side, we have in Table 3.21 the completed comparison table with both the predicted and realized bands as constructed above.

Now, for facilityin our sample data, we determine which predicted and realized LGD band should this obligor be assigned to respectively. For example, suppose an obligor was originally predicted a LGD value of 95%, whereas when it eventually defaults, the realized LGD is only 45%.[27] Based on the LGD bands established in Table 3.21, the 95% predicted LGD would put this obligor to the predicted band 1, whereas the 45% realized LGD would also put this obligor to the realized band 1. Suppose another obligor had 35% predicted LGD and 55% realized LGD. The 35% predicted LGD would put this obligor to the predicted band 4, whereas the 55% realized LGD would put this obligor to the realized band 1. After identifying the

**TABLE 3.20**

Sample Realized LGD Bands

| Band | Realized LGD | | No. of Observations |
|------|--------------------|--------------------|---------------------|
|      | Minimum LGD (%) | Maximum LGD (%) | |
| 1 | 40 | 100 | 10 |
| 2 | 20 | 40 | 10 |
| 3 | 5 | 20 | 10 |
| 4 | 3 | 5 | 10 |
| 5 | 1 | 3 | 10 |

**TABLE 3.21**

Sample Prediced and Realized LGD Bands

| Band | Prediced LGD | | | Realized LGD | | No. of Observations |
|------|-----------------------|-----------------|----------------------|-----------------------|----------------------|-----|
| | Minimum LGD (%) | Mid LGD (%) | Maximum LGD (%) | Minimum LGD (%) | Maximum LGD (%) | |
| 1 | 80 | 90 | 100 | 40 | 100 | 10 |
| 2 | 60 | 70 | 80 | 20 | 40 | 10 |
| 3 | 40 | 50 | 60 | 5 | 20 | 10 |
| 4 | 20 | 30 | 40 | 3 | 5 | 10 |
| 5 | 0 | 10 | 20 | 1 | 3 | 10 |

predicted and realized band for each obligor in our sample portfolio, we are ready to run the discrimination test. We start with band 1. The first point $(x_1, y_1)$ on the CLAR curve is defined by:

- Cumulative predicted LGD observations $(x_1)$: the cumulative percentage of the obligors in predicted band 1 (it is 20% from Table 3.21); and
- Cumulative correctly assigned realized LGD $(y_1)$: among the obligors in predicted band 1, the percentage of the obligors that actually belong to realized band 1. Suppose it is 6%, i.e., out of all the obligors in predicted band 1, the obligors eventually falling into realized band 1 represent 6% of the total number of obligors.

We then consider and combine both bands 1 and 2. The second point on the CLAR curve $(x_2, y_2)$ is:

- Cumulative predicted LGD observations $(x_2)$: the cumulative percentage of the obligors in predicted band 1 and band 2 (it is 40% from Table 3.21); and
- Cumulative correctly assigned realized LGD $(y_2)$: among the obligors in predicted band 1 and band 2, the percentage of the obligors actually belong to either realized band 1 or band 2. Suppose it is 20%, i.e., out of all the obligors in predicted band 1 and band 2, the obligors eventually falling into either realized band 1 or band 2 represent 20% of the total number of obligors.

We then consider and combine bands 1, 2, and 3. The third point on the CLAR curve $(x_3, y_3)$ is:

- Cumulative predicted LGD observations $(x_3)$: the cumulative percentage of the obligors in predicted bands 1, 2, and 3 (it is 60% from Table 3.12); and
- Cumulative correctly assigned realized LGD $(y_3)$: among the obligors in predicted bands 1, 2, and 3, the percentage of the obligors actually belong to either realized band 1, 2, or 3. Suppose it is 44%, i.e., out of all the obligors in predicted bands 1, 2, and 3, the obligors eventually falling into either realized band 1, 2, or 3 represent 44% of the total number of obligors.

And so on. The data points defining the CLAR curve obtained above are presented in Table 3.22. From these data points, we can then plot the CLAR curve in Figure 3.15. In Figure 3.15, the pink 45-degree line represents the case of perfect discrimination. The area under the blue line measures the discriminatory power of the LGD risk rating system. CLAR coefficient is defined as two times this area, which is found to be equal to 0.77 in this example. In this framework, the maximum CLAR coefficient is 1.0 (i.e., perfect discrimination).

## Testing the Calibration

A number of tests can be performed to compare the level of predicted and realized LGD at individual facility level and at aggregated level. Given the scarcity of data and high volatility around historical LGD estimates, as witnessed in both internal and external LGD data, the results of these accuracy

**TABLE 3.22**

Data Points Defining the CLAR Curve

|  | Cumulative Predicted LGD Observation | Cumulative Correctly Assigned Realized LGD (%) |
| --- | --- | --- |
| $(x_0, y_0)$ | 0 | 0 |
| $(x_1, y_1)$ | 20 | 6 |
| $(x_2, y_2)$ | 40 | 20 |
| $(x_3, y_3)$ | 60 | 44 |
| $(x_4, y_4)$ | 80 | 72 |
| $(x_5, y_5)$ | 100 | 100 |

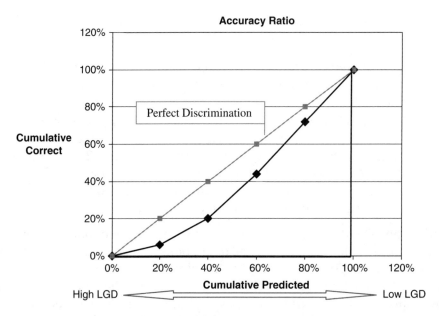

**Figure 3.15**  CLAR curve of sample data.

tests need to be carefully considered prior to drawing any definitive con-clusions. In particular, the results of any one test or ratio should not be viewed in isolation but rather combined with the results of the overall set of accuracy tests to follow.

*Tests at the Individual Facility Level*    At the individual facility level, there are a number of standard tests to be conducted.

1.  A simple scatterplot, with predicted LGDs of the facilities on the horizontal axis and the corresponding realized LGDs on the vertical axis, should be used to visually investigate the overall relationship and highlight any bias in the overall LGD rating process.

2.  In addition, a mean square error estimate can be calculated as below:

$$\text{MSE} = \text{Sum(Realized LGD} - \text{Predicted LGD)}^2/$$
$$\text{Number of observations.}$$

3.  A cross-sectional regression analysis between the predicted LGDs (dependent variable) and the realized LGDs (explanatory variable) should be performed and the results should be examined. For example, $R^2$ of the regression is a measure of the

explanatory power (the square root of which is the correlation between predicted and realized LGDs).

## Tests at the Aggregated Level

### Accuracy Ratio

One test we can run at the aggregate level is similar to the CLAR test described above. The only difference is that we do not construct a separate set of realized bands, but instead also using the predicted bands in categorizing the realized LGDs. That is, realized bands are now the same as predicted bands. Please see the below example. Assume we have the same predicted LGD bands as before (presented again as Table 3.23).

We then use the bands defined in Table 3.23 to categorize each of the observations (i.e., obligors or facilities) in terms of their predicted and realized LGD values. The categorizations of the first eleven observations of our sample data are reported in Table 3.24.

The expectation is that predicted and realized LGDs fall into the same LGD band (i.e., for each obligor, its predicted band is equal to its realized band). The rest of the test is the same as the CLAR test discussed above.

*Confidence Interval Approach*   Another test we can run is the hypothesis test based on *confidence intervals*, where we compare the realized mean LGDs with the predicted ones for each of the LGD bands. Given the difference in statistical properties, the exact form of tests to be conducted is dictated by the richness of the LGD data set available to the risk manager.

1. *When we have more than 30 data points (realized LGD) in the LGD band*: We can perform hypothesis tests by established confidence interval (CI) around the sample mean according to the $t$-distribution. This

**T A B L E   3.23**

Sample Predicted and Realized LGD Bands

| Band | Prediced and Realized LGD | | |
|------|-----------------|--------------|----------------|
|      | Minimum LGD (%) | Mid LGD (%)  | Maximum LGD (%) |
| 1    | 80              | 90           | 100            |
| 2    | 60              | 70           | 80             |
| 3    | 40              | 50           | 60             |
| 4    | 20              | 30           | 40             |
| 5    | 0               | 10           | 20             |

**T A B L E  3.24**

Categorization of the First 11 LGD Observations by LGD Bands

| Obligor | Predicted LGD (%) | Predicted Band Assigned | Realized LGD (%) | Realized Band Assigned |
|---------|-------------------|-------------------------|------------------|------------------------|
| 1 | 90 | 1 | 65 | 2 |
| 2 | 90 | 1 | 100 | 1 |
| 3 | 70 | 2 | 75 | 2 |
| 4 | 70 | 2 | 45 | 3 |
| 5 | 50 | 3 | 5 | 5 |
| 6 | 50 | 3 | 100 | 1 |
| 7 | 30 | 4 | 3 | 5 |
| 8 | 30 | 4 | 90 | 1 |
| 9 | 10 | 5 | 5 | 5 |
| 10 | 10 | 5 | 5 | 5 |
| 11 | 10 | 5 | 75 | 2 |

CI is found to be reliable for sample data that contains more than 30 data points. Specifically, the CI is:

$$\bar{y} \pm t \times s / \sqrt{n}, \qquad \text{(Equation 3.8)}$$

where $\bar{y}$ = sample mean (i.e., the average of realized LGDs in the band); $t$ = critical value under the $t$-distribution (with a degree of freedom equal to $n - 1$) corresponding with the desired confidence level; $s$ = sample standard deviation (i.e., standard deviation of realized LGDs in the band); and $n$ = number of data points in the sample set (i.e., the number of realized LGDs in the band).

We suggest to use a confidence level materially larger than 50%. If we use 50%, effectively we will wrongfully reject a true predicted mean LGD in half of the situations. That is, type I error is large. Unlike the PD validation, there is not a clear trade-off with a type II error if there is no obvious alternative hypothesis.

For example, for a 80% confidence level and $n = 30$, $t = 1.311$ from the $t$-distribution with a degree of freedom equal to 29.[28] Multiplying this $t$ value by $s/\sqrt{n}$ will give us the acceptable difference in value between the observed sample mean LGD and predicted LGD. If the actual difference is larger than the acceptable value computed above, we can reject the hypothesis that the predicted LGD is in fact the mean of the sample at the 80% confidence level.

2. *When we have less than 30 data points (realized LGD) in the LGD band*: Given the fact that the distribution of individual realized LGD is typically far from a normal distribution, *t*-distribution becomes a poor approximation of the distribution of its sample mean when sample size is small (less than 30). When this is the case, we suggest using the results obtained from the Hoeffding inequality to derive limit for the confidence level in our hypothesis test (see Hoeffding, 1963).[29] The Hoeffding inequality only provides the bound of the tail probability, thus resulting in a wider confidence interval and reducing the power of the hypothesis test. The upper bound of the (tail) probability that the difference between the realized sample mean and the predicted value being larger than a certain critical value "*a*" is given in Equation 3.9.

$$\Pr\left[\,\overline{y} - E\left(\overline{y}\right) \geq a\,\right] \leq e^{-2 \times n \times a^{2}}, \qquad \text{(Equation 3.9)}$$

where $\overline{y}$ = sample mean (i.e., the average of realized LGDs in the band), $E[\overline{y}]$= predicted LGD value (i.e., the mean predicted LGD for the band under investigation), and $n$ = number of observations.

Let's consider an example. Suppose we have an LGD band with a predicted LGD of 40% and we have a total of 35 observations of realized LGDs with a sample mean of 25.39% (thus $\overline{y} - E(\overline{y}) = -14.61\%$).[30] A one-tail probability of 25% (i.e., confidence level of 50%) corresponds with an "*a*" value of 14% (= $[\ln(0.25)/(-2 \times 35)]^{0.5}$). In other words, the probability that $\overline{y} - E(\overline{y})$ will be larger than 14% (or $\overline{y} - E(\overline{y})$ will be smaller than $-14\%$) will not be larger than 25%. Thus, we can safely reject the predicted LGD at 50% confidence level.

*Using the Two Approaches Jointly*   A recommended approach for using the two approaches jointly is shown in the graphs of Figure 3.16, where:

1. When $n > 30$, we use the confidence interval constructed with the *t*-distribution.
2. When $10 > n > 30$, we use the Hoeffding inequality as the primary tool but also consider the *t*-distribution in a conservative manner as suggested below:
   a. If the realized mean LGD falls outside the CI established with the Hoeffding inequality, reject the predicted LGD.

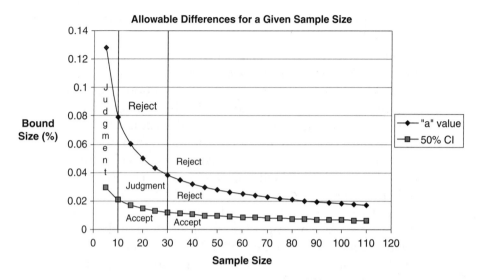

**Figure 3.16**   Joint approach in hypothesis test on sample mean of LGD.

     b. If the realized mean LGD falls inside the CI under the
          $t$-distribution (and thus also within the CI of the Hoeffding
          inequality), accept the predicted LGD.
     c. If the realized mean LGD falls inside the CI of the
          Hoeffding inequality but outside of that of the
          $t$-distribution, exercise judgment in accepting or
          rejecting the predicted LGD.
   **3.** When $n < 10$, we exercise judgment in accepting or rejecting the
      predicted LGD.

### Testing the Realization of the Risk Rating Philosophy

As discussed previously (in the section on "LGD Philosophy" in Chapter 2),
LGD philosophy, analogous to the risk rating philosophy for PD, defines an
assigned LGD's expected[31] behavior over a business/economic cycle.[32]
Under a *cyclical* philosophy, assigned LGD is intended to be synchronized
with the cycle and thus changes with the cycle, whereas under an *acyclical*
philosophy, assigned LGD remains (almost) constant over the cycle. Most
banks seem to adopt a fairly acyclical LGD philosophy where facility LGDs
once set are not adjusted for the expectations over the next year. The
assigned LGDs are only adjusted for the change in collaterals (rather than
the change in LGD cycles). In other words, within the spectrum of cyclical

and acyclical LGD philosophies, the philosophy of most banks seems to be closer to an acyclical measure. Similar to the checking of PD philosophy, we can analyze the LGD migration matrix to check if the realized philosophy is in fact consistent with the intended one.

Unlike the other tests, the data set for the philosophy analysis consists of all performing exposures at a specific point in time. For each exposure, the current assigned LGD value and the assigned LGD value in existence one year earlier must be captured. We then map the assigned LGD values (both current and one year earlier) to their respective LGD band (i.e., categorizing the exposures into different LGD risk ratings) introduced in the previous section and create an annual LGD migration matrix. We expect to observe a "concentrated" diagonal with large probabilities (e.g., 90% and above) for acyclical philosophy but a less concentrated one (i.e., there are considerable amount of transitions to other bands) for a cyclical philosophy especially during LGD cycle changes. Furthermore, a mobility metric, similar to the one calculated in checking PD philosophy, can be computed based on the LGD migration matrix. The expectation for acyclical philosophy is a low mobility score and vice versa for cyclical one.

If the results are not as expected, investigation using applicable subsegments (i.e., collateral type, sector, country, etc.) must be undertaken to determine the cause of the higher than expected migration mobility. Particular action must be taken to ensure definitive conclusion is not made without identifying the source of the higher than expected migration mobility. From a philosophy perspective, we are only concerned with migration occurring due to cyclical factors rather than, say, the changes in the characteristics of the underlying collaterals.

In each successive validation study, the analysis should be extended to time periods greater than one year. This will ensure LGD philosophy is consistent regardless of the time period chosen in the analysis.

## Homogeneity Testing: Subportfolio-Level Validation

Similar to PD backtesting, subportfolio-level validation is useful for LGD backtesting to provide further insight into the performance of the LGD rating system. Which of the above-mentioned backtesting tests and analysis will be repeated at the subportfolio level should be decided within a cost-benefit framework, especially considering data availability. As we are already working with small samples even in aggregate, the loss of statistical power in dividing the data into subsegments may outweigh any benefits derived from additional testing. However, when feasible, the subset-level analysis provides an indication of whether the homogeneity assumptions of the various identified LGD risk factors are valid. The dimensions to be considered include, but are not limited to, the following:

| | |
|---|---|
| Facility characteristics | • Collateral |
| | • Margin/borrow base arrangements |
| | • Covenant package (bank loan vs. bond) |
| | • Contractual and structural seniority and subordination |
| Entity characteristics | • Asset class (corporate, bank, sovereign, securitization) |
| | • Industry |
| | • Geography |

*Significance Tests*  For a given LGD rating, we can compare the sample means (assuming that realized LGDs are independent) of two potentially different subportfolios and test if they are in fact statistically different. Because there is no reason why the population standard deviations of the two subportfolios would be different, the pooled test would be more appropriate:

$$t = \frac{\bar{y}_1 - \bar{y}_2}{s_p \sqrt{\dfrac{1}{n_1} + \dfrac{1}{n_2}}} \qquad \text{(Equation 3.10)}$$

where

$$s_p^2 = \frac{(n_1 - 1)s_1^2 + (n_2 - 1)s_2^2}{n_1 + n_2 - 2}, \qquad \text{(Equation 3.11)}$$

$\bar{y}_1$ and $\bar{y}_2$ are the means of the realized LGDs of subportfolio 1 and 2; $s_1^2$ and $s_2^2$ are the variances of the realized LGD of subportfolio 1 and 2; whereas $n_1$ and $n_2$ are numbers of LGD observations in subportfolio 1 and 2 respectively. For $n_1 > 30$ and $n_2 > 30$, the *t-statistic* can be approximated by a *t*-distribution with a degree of freedom equal to $n_1 + n_2 - 2$.

For example, if $\bar{y}_1 = 30\%$, $\bar{y}_2 = 50\%$, $s_1 = 40\%$, $s_2 = 55\%$, $n_1 = 30$, and $n_2 = 30$, we calculate $s_p = 48.1\%$ and $t = -1.61$. For a degree of freedom of 58 (= 30 + 30 − 2), the corresponding cumulative (one-tailed probability) from the *t*-distribution is 5.63%. We can therefore reject the hypothesis that the two subportfolios belonging to the same population at a confidence level of 88.7% (= 1 − 2 × 5.63%).

The *t*-distribution is again a poor approximation of the distribution of the difference in same means when $n_1$ and $n_2$ are small. In those situations, we can again borrow the results of the Hoeffding inequalities to derive upper bounds for our tail probabilities. For both $y_1$ and $y_2$ bounded between zero and one and under the null hypothesis that the two subportfolios have identical population mean LGD, the probability that the difference in sample mean being larger than a certain critical value "$a$" satisfies the following inequality of Equation 3.12.

$$\Pr\left[y_1 - y_2 \ge a\right] \le e^{-2a^2/\left(n_1^{-1}+n_2^{-1}\right)} \qquad \text{(Equation 3.12)}$$

Applying the Hoeffding inequality of Equation 3.12 to the above numerical example, we can therefore reject the hypothesis of equal mean at a confidence level of *at least* 39.8% (= $1 - 2 \times \exp\{-2 \times 0.2 \times 0.2/[(1/30) + (1/30)]\}$). The power of the hypothesis test decreases when we do not impose the assumption that the sample means follow the $t$-distribution.

## Supplementary Analyses

### Examination of LGD Risk Drivers

In addition to examining the ultimate LGDs assigned, the individual LGD drivers can be another possible focus of analysis. For example, do exposures collateralized by marketable securities experience lower losses than do those backed by inventory, which in turn experience lower losses than do fixed asset–backed exposures? In order to focus on the mean of the distribution, LGD bands should be used to compare realized losses among LGD drivers. Possible segmentation includes:

1.  Margined versus unmargined exposures
2.  Secured versus unsecured versus subordinated
3.  The various collateral categories
4.  First versus second charge (real estate)

*Override Analysis*   Some LGD rating systems allow for overrides to accommodate special circumstances where it is believed the modeled LGD is not the best predictor of an exposure's potential loss. It is important to track these overrides and analyze them separately to ensure the overrides provided a net benefit. For those exposures upon which overrides have been exercised and LGDs are eventually realized, a comparison of the realized LGDs and predicted LGDs would be helpful in determining the benefit, if any, of the overrides. If it can be shown that the overrides indeed provided a net benefit (e.g., in terms of a smaller discrepancy between the realized and predicted LGD value), introduction of a new LGD driver may be warranted by investigation into the underlying characteristics of the overridden exposures. On the other hand, evidence of poor performance would warrant amendments of further controls in the use of overrides. It is expected that minimal data will exist meeting the required criteria, nevertheless, annual analysis of overrides is to be completed. Moreover, using all available information, all performing exposures with LGD ratings derived using the override feature of the LGD rating system are to be analyzed for any systematic bias. Evidence of systematic bias suggests that a group of exposures are not being adequately parameterized by the LGD rating system.

*Reestimation of LGD Factors*    "As more data become available over time, reestimation of LGD factors can also be conducted as a part of the annual validation process. The continuous validity of the high-level LGD drivers should be confirmed, for example via regression analysis, subject to data limitations." The analysis should be conducted on the accumulative dataset, not only including the new losses observed since the last validation exercise, but also all internal loss observations in the bank's database. The aim of this analysis is to ensure the LGD factors are still justified as new loss observations are added to the database.

The regression analysis should consider, but not be limited to, the following:

- Collateral-specific recovery cash flows to be used whenever available for classification of an LGD observation.
- Facility-level realized LGD to be used whenever available; entity-level realized LGD should only be used when facility-level information is not available.
- Check all regression results for goodness of fit using standard techniques.
- Collateral-specific regression analysis:
  - Regress all applicable realized LGDs against collateral type and coverage percentage to estimate collateral-specific LGD factors.
  - If data permits, repeat the above regression excluding multicollateralized facilities and compare to above for evidence of any interactive effect among collaterals.
- General regression analysis:
  - Regress realized LGDs against all applicable LGD risk drivers identified in the existing LGD rating system (i.e., seniority, collateral type, industry, etc.).
- Investigate new LGD risk drivers using regression analysis as data become available. External data sources may be better suited for data mining techniques until more internal data is accumulated.

- If the results from any of the above regression analyses are robust
  and reasonable, consider using regression results to set LGD
  factors.

## Case Study: LGD Backtesting

### Overview

In this analysis, the realized LGDs are compared with the predicted LGDs
(i.e., assigned LGD) one year prior to default to test the accuracy of the LGD
risk rating system. The reference point for LGD ratings is one year before
the respective default events, which is consistent with the economic capital
risk. Computations performed for the various analyses in the LGD backtesting of this case study are presented in the Excel spreadsheet "LGD
Backtesting" on the CD which comes with the book.

### Initial Examination of Realized LGD Data

Table 3.25 presents the basic statistics of the realized LGD of a sample data.
Predicted LGDs of the LGD segments (i.e., bands) are reported in the
second column.

    Initial examination shows the wide dispersion of realized LGD data,
as observed in very large ranges and standard deviations for all of the segments due to the typical non-normal bimodal behavior of LGDs. For example, for segment 1, the LGD observed ranges from 0% to 100% and the
distribution is presented in Figure 3.17.

**T A B L E  3.25**

Summary Statistics of Realized LGD

| Segment Ranking | Predicted Mean LGD (%) | Realized LGD | | | | |
|---|---|---|---|---|---|---|
| | | Minimum (%) | Mean (%) | Median (%) | Maximum (%) | Standard Deviation (%) |
| 1 | 80 | 0 | 75 | 97 | 100 | 35 |
| 2 | 55 | 7 | 65 | 78 | 100 | 32 |
| 3 | 45 | 13 | 39 | 40 | 58 | 15 |
| 4 | 35 | 31 | 46 | 47 | 68 | 11 |
| 5 | 25 | 7 | 19 | 18 | 40 | 11 |
| 6 | 15 | 0 | 8 | 7 | 32 | 10 |
| 7 | 5 | 0 | 3 | 1 | 17 | 5 |

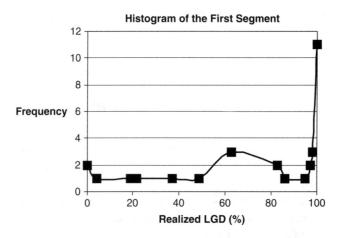

**Figure 3.17** Histogram of realized LGD values of the first LGD segment.

It should be noted, however, that the mean (and median) LGDs are reasonable close to the predicted mean LGDs for all segments, which should be considered as a positive outcome in this preliminary stage of assessment.

### Testing the Discriminatory Power of the Risk Rating System

Discriminatory power analysis assesses how well a model or rating system discriminates between different rating grades and tests for the ordinal ranking of the LGD ratings. The expectation is that the worst realized LGDs come from the higher LGD ratings (numerically higher). We therefore plot the CLAR curve of the above sample data (see Figure 3.18). The corresponding CLAR coefficient is found to be equal to 86%, which is an indication of a very high discriminatory power.

### Testing the Calibration

A number of tests have been performed to compare the level of predicted and realized LGD at individual facility level and at aggregated level.

*Tests at the Individual Facility Level*

1.  Using the example data, a simple scatterplot, with predicted LGDs on the horizontal axis and realized LGDs on the vertical axis, is presented in Figure 3.19.

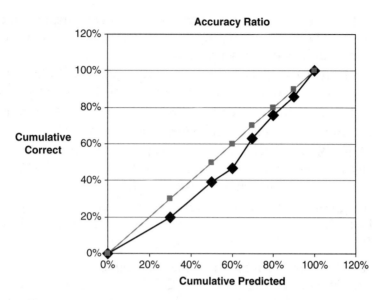

**Figure 3.18** CLAR curve of sample data.

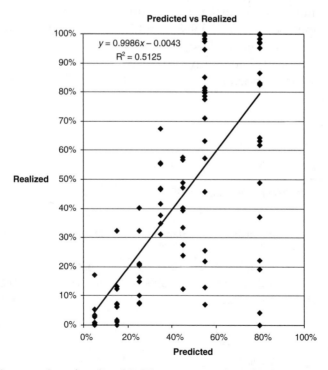

**Figure 3.19** Scatter plot of realized LGD versus predicted LGD at individual facility level.

The visual examination again confirms wide dispersion of realized LGD per segment, which is expected. There are two important positive observations, however:

- The realized LGDs are more heavily concentrated near the respective predicted LGD values.
- The trend line has high positive slope and small intercept.

2. In addition, the mean square error, calculated as

   MSE = Sum(Realized LGD − Expected LGD)$^2$/Number of observations, is found to be equal to 8%, which is considered to be quite low and thus a positive indicator.

3. A regression analysis between predicted LGDs and the realized LGDs has been performed, and the results are presented in Table 3.26.

The results from the regression analysis suggest the realized LGD is indeed well explained by the predicted LGD. The intercept of the regression equation is found to be equal to −0.00428, which is not significantly different from zero as judging by the corresponding $t$-statistic. It therefore suggests the predicted LGD can serve as an unbiased estimator of the realized LGD. The slope coefficient is 0.99861, which is not significantly different from unity. The adjusted R-square is high (0.51), which indicates a high goodness-of-fit. The highly significant $F$-statistic ($p$ value = 0.00000) also suggests the importance of the predicted LGD in explaining the realized LGD.

**TABLE 3.26**

Cross-Sectional Regression of Realized LGD

| Parameter | Estimated Value | Standard Deviation | Student's $t$ | Prob ($>|t|$) |
|---|---|---|---|---|
| $b_0$ | −0.004277615 | 0.053317359 | −0.08022931 | 0.936218493 |
| $b_1$ | 0.998605505 | 0.098373855 | 10.1511271 | 5.68827E−17 |
| Residual standard deviation | 0.256763299 | | | $y = b_0 + b_1 \times x_1$ |
| $R^2$ | 0.512547868 | | | |
| $R^2$ (adjusted) | 0.507573866 | | | |
| $F$ | 103.0453817 | | | |
| Prob ($>F$) | 5.68827E−17 | | | |

## Tests at the Aggregated Level

### Accuracy Ratio

We also compute the accuracy ratio at the aggregate level. As discussed above in the section on "LGD Backtesting," it is very similar to plotting the CLAR curve and computing the CLAR coefficient. The only difference is we do not establish a separate set of realized LGD segments (i.e., bands). We simply categorize the realized LGD observations based on the same set of predicted LGD segments. The accuracy ratio calculated in this fashion will always be less than the CLAR coefficient computed for the discriminatory power test discussed above. The accuracy ratio is found to be equal to 82% for the example dataset, which is considered to be very high. A graphical representation is given in Figure 3.20.

*Confidence Interval Approach*   We also conduct hypothesis tests based on establishing confidence intervals around the predicted LGD values. We compare the realized mean LGDs with the predicted ones for each of the LGD segments.

1.  As we have 30 data points (realized LGD) in the first LGD segment, we construct the confidence interval based on the *t*-distribution.[33] According to Equation 3.8, we have $\bar{y} = 75\%$

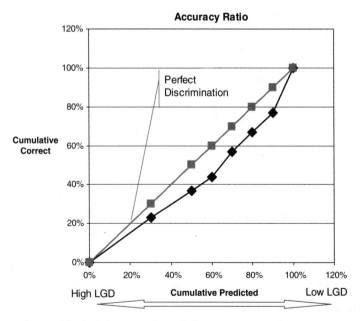

**Figure 3.20**   A graphical representation of the accuracy ratio.

(sample mean of realized LGDs), $s = 35\%$ (sample standard deviation of realized LGDs), and $n = 30$ (number of realized LGD observations) for the first LGD segment. Suppose the desired confidence level is 95%, it corresponds to a $t$ value of 2.045 with a degree of freedom equal to 29 ($n - 1$). Based on Equation 3.8, the corresponding confidence interval has a minimum LGD of 62% and maximum LGD of 88%. As the predicted mean LGD of 80% falls in between these boundaries, we cannot reject the hypothesis that the predicted mean LGD of 80% is in fact the population mean.[34]

2.  Testing segments 2 to 7 where we have less than 30 data points (realized LGD) in the segments: $t$-distribution becomes a poor approximation of the distribution of the sample mean when sample size is less than 30. We therefore used the Hoeffding inequality to derive confidence intervals for our hypothesis tests (Hoeffding, 1963). According to the Hoeffding inequality, the upper bound of the probability that the realized sample mean is larger than the predicted value by a positive value "$a$" is given by Equation 3.13.

$$\Pr\left[\bar{y} - E(\bar{y}) \geq a\right] \leq e^{-2 \times n \times a^2}, \qquad \text{(Equation 3.13)}$$

where $y$ = sample mean of realized LGDs of the segment, $E[\bar{y}]$ = predicted LGD value of the segment, and $n$ = number of LGD observations of that segment. To apply it in the setting of a two-tail hypothesis test, we need to derive the bound on the probability that the absolute difference is larger than a positive value "$a$":

$$\Pr\left[\left|\bar{y} - E(\bar{y})\right| \geq a\right] = \Pr\left[\bar{y} - E(\bar{y}) \geq a\right] + \Pr\left[\bar{y} - E(\bar{y}) \leq -a\right]$$

$$= \Pr\left[\bar{y} - E(\bar{y}) \geq a\right] + \Pr\left[-\bar{y} + E(\bar{y}) \geq a\right] \leq 2 \times e^{-2 \times n \times a^2}. \qquad \text{(Equation 3.14)}$$

We can therefore establish a lower bound for the confidence level in rejecting the hypothesis that the predicted mean LGD is in fact the population mean when we observe a difference equal to "$a$":[35]

$$1 - \Pr\left[\left|\bar{y} - E(\bar{y})\right| \geq a\right] \geq \max\left(0, 1 - 2 \times e^{-2 \times n \times a^2}\right). \qquad \text{(Equation 3.15)}$$

With a criterion of rejecting the hypothesis at a confidence level of *at least* 95%, we can solve for "$a$" for each of the segments such that

$\max(0,1-2\times e^{-2\times n\times a^2})=0.95$. For example, the threshold "$a$" value of segment 1 is equal to $(\{-\ln[(1 - 0.95)/2]\}/(2 \times 30))^{0.5} = 0.248$. The corresponding confidence intervals can therefore be established to check against the predicted LGD. The results are tabulated in Table 3.27.

As the predicted mean LGDs of all the segments fall within the corresponding confidence intervals, we cannot reject the hypothesis that the predicted mean LGDs are in fact the population mean at a confidence level of at least 95%.

*Using the Two Approaches Jointly*   We can use the two approaches jointly as suggested in the section on "LGD Backtesting" earlier in the chapter.

1. When $n > 30$ we use the confidence interval constructed with the $t$-distribution. We have only one segment (segment 1) with $n = 30$ and we cannot reject the hypothesis that the predicted LGD of 80% is in fact the population mean at 95% confidence level. The predicted LGD lies within the confidence interval of (62% to 88%).

2. When $10 > n > 30$, we use the Hoeffding inequality as the primary tool but also use the $t$-distribution in a conservative manner as below:

   a. If realized LGD falls outside of the Hoeffding inequality bounds, reject the predicted LGD.

   b. If realized LGD falls inside of the confidence interval of the $t$-distribution (and thus also within the confidence

**TABLE 3.27**

Confidence Intervals Constructed Based on the Hoeffding inequality

| Segment Ranking | $n$ | $a$ (%) | Confidence Interval | | Predicted Mean LGD (%) |
| --- | --- | --- | --- | --- | --- |
| | | | Maximum $(y + a)$ (%) | Minimum $(\bar{y} - a)$ (%) | |
| 1 | 30 | 24.8 | 99.8 | 50.2 | 80 |
| 2 | 20 | 30.4 | 95.4 | 34.6 | 55 |
| 3 | 10 | 42.9 | 81.9 | 0 | 45 |
| 4 | 10 | 42.9 | 88.9 | 3.1 | 35 |
| 5 | 10 | 42.9 | 61.9 | 0 | 25 |
| 6 | 10 | 42.9 | 50.9 | 0 | 15 |
| 7 | 10 | 42.9 | 45.9 | 0 | 5 |

interval of the Hoeffding inequality), accept the predicted LGD.

c. If realized LGD falls inside of the confidence interval of the Hoeffding inequality but outside of that of the $t$-distribution, exercise judgment in accepting or rejecting the predicted LGD.

For this example, this condition applies to segment 2. Specifically, the predicted mean LGD of 55% of segment 2 lies within both the confidence interval of the Hoeffding inequalities (34.6% to 95.4%) and that of the $t$-distribution (49% to 80%). We therefore accept the predicted mean LGD.

3.  When $n < 10$, we exercise judgment in accepting or rejecting the predicted LGD.

Not applicable to this example.

### Testing the Realization of the Risk Rating Philosophy

In our example, the stated philosophy of the bank is *acyclical* as LGDs are not adjusted with respect to LGD cycles (but only adjusted for the changes in collaterals). We examined the LGD transition matrices with the expectation of observing minimal mobility. This was indeed the case as the mobility metrics are calculated as 0.11, 0.19, 0.09, and 0.05 using last four years of data, which supports the stated acyclical philosophy of the bank.

### Homogeneity Testing: Subportfolio-Level Validation

*Significance Tests*   Because of data constraints, we can only check the homogeneity within the first segment using the results of the Hoeffding inequalities to derive upper bounds for our tail probabilities. The first segment, which has 30 observations, is composed of both U.S. and Canadian facilities. The first 16 observations are Canadian and the last 14 are U.S. facilities. The mean realized LGDs for the Canadian and U.S. subsegments are 85.78% ($y_1$) and 63.16% ($y_2$) respectively. We want to find out if the difference of 22.62% is in fact statistically significant. We need to assess the likelihood of both segments having the same population means despite having a seemingly large discrepancy of 22.62%. From the Hoeffding inequality, the probability that the sample mean $y_1$ is larger than the sample mean $y_2$ by a certain positive value "$a$" is given by Equation 3.16:

$$\Pr\left[\bar{y}_1 - \bar{y}_2 \geq a\right] \leq e^{-2a^2/\left(n_1^{-1}+n_2^{-1}\right)}. \qquad \text{(Equation 3.16)}$$

We want to test if we can reject the null hypothesis that the two sub-segments have identical population mean LGD. To apply it in the setting of a two-tail hypothesis test, we need to derive the bound on the probability that the absolute difference is larger than a positive value "$a$":

$$\Pr\left[\left|\bar{y}_1 - \bar{y}_2\right| \geq a\right] = \Pr\left[\bar{y}_1 - \bar{y}_2 \geq a\right] + \Pr\left[\bar{y}_1 - \bar{y}_2 \leq -a\right]$$

$$= \Pr\left[\bar{y}_1 - \bar{y}_2 \geq a\right] + \Pr\left[-\bar{y}_1 + \bar{y}_2 \geq a\right] \leq 2 \times e^{-2a^2/\left(n_1^{-1}+n_2^{-1}\right)}. \qquad \text{(Equation 3.17)}$$

We can therefore establish a lower bound for the confidence level in rejecting the null hypothesis that the two subsegments actually have identical population mean LGD when we observe a difference equal to "$a$":

$$1 - \Pr\left[\left|\bar{y}_1 - \bar{y}_2\right| \geq a\right] \geq \max(0, 1 - 2 \times e^{-2a^2/\left(n_1^{-1}+n_2^{-1}\right)}). \qquad \text{(Equation 3.18)}$$

Applying Equation 3.18 to the above example, we can only reject the hypothesis of equal mean at a confidence level of *at least* 6.8% (= 1 − 2 × exp{− 2 × 0.2262 × 0.2262/[(1/16) + (1/14)]}). In other words, we cannot reject the hypothesis at any reasonable confidence level.

Alternatively, with the criterion of rejecting the hypothesis at a confidence level of *at least* 95%, we can construct the confidence interval by solving for "$a$" such that $\max(0, 1 - 2 \times e^{-2 \times n \times a^2}) = 0.95$. = 0.95. The threshold "$a$" value is found to be equal to $(\{-\ln[(1 - 0.95)/2]\}/[2/(14^{-1} + 16^{-1})])^{0.5}$ = 0.497. Because the observed difference of 22.62% is smaller than 49.7%, we cannot reject the null hypothesis with a confidence level of at least 95%.

## EAD Backtesting

EAD backtesting is very similar to LGD backtesting. Some tests are performed at the individual exposure level and some at the group level. For the group-level tests, we need to group the expected EADs (assigned to the exposures one year before the respective default events) and the realized EAD (recorded at default) very much like the analysis performed on LGDs discussed above. An example segmentation corresponding with EAD risk ratings is presented in Table 3.28. Once this segmentation is constructed, the same tests discussed above for LGD backtesting are also applicable to EAD backtesting.

Similar to LGD backtesting, in addition to the above segmentation by EAD risk rating, EAD observations are often segmented by potential EAD

**T A B L E  3.28**

Example of Segmentation of Expected and Realized EADs

| Segment | Expected | | | Realized | | | No. of Observations |
|---------|---------|-----|-----|---------|-----|-----|---------------------|
|         | Minimum | Mid | Max | Minimum | Mid | Max |                     |
| 1 | 70% | 80% | 90% | 50% | 70% | 100% | 12 |
| 2 | 55% | 65% | 75% | 55% | 72% | 90% | 15 |
| 3 | 10% | 50% | 60% | 30% | 55% | 70% | 22 |
| 4 | 25% | 35% | 45% | 35% | 40% | 75% | 34 |
| 5 | 10% | 20% | 30% | 0% | 30% | 50% | 55 |
| 6 | 2% | 6% | 10% | 5% | 10% | 40% | 60 |

risk drivers for backtesting purpose. It is for us to better understand the behavior of EAD and to improve our EAD models accordingly. Some examples of potential EAD risk drivers are facility type (i.e., committed vs. uncommitted), vintage of exposure (<1 year, 1–2 years, 2–4 years, >5 years), and PD rating of obligor. More advanced banks also investigate the trends of undrawn amounts for similar exposures as obligors approach default (i.e., EAD at various time intervals prior to default). This allows for more homogenous segmentation in EAD modeling as we would like to segment EADs with similar time series behavior. In summary, following is a list of analysis for EADs backtesting.

- Graphical (visual) examination
- Discrimination:
  - Standard rank correlation measures (Spearman rank correlation and Kendell tau)
  - Cumulative EAD accuracy ratio
- Calibration test:
  - Mean square error
  - Regression analysis
  - Accuracy ratio
  - Hypothesis testing
- Confirmation of EAD philosophy
- Homogeneity: significance testing
- Downturn EAD and PD–LGD–EAD correlations

## VALIDATION OF MAPPINGS BETWEEN INTERNAL AND EXTERNAL RISK RATING SYSTEMS

As discussed, most FIs have a mapping between internal and external risk rating systems. These mappings are used in

1. Risk rating system quantification when external default rates are used in assessment of long-run PDs for the internal ratings.
2. Validation exercises.
3. Mapping different internal risk ratings within the same organization to each other (in particular, international FIs use mapping to external ratings as an intermediary step to map their different national internal ratings to each other).

Considering these uses, the correctness of the mappings between internal and external ratings is critical and should be validated. From a developmental evidence standpoint, we need to compare the following attributes of the internal and external systems:

1. rating methodologies[36]
2. risk drivers used and their weights
3. rating criteria
4. default definitions
5. qualitative descriptions of the ratings

From a backtesting standpoint, the following should be evaluated:

1. Are the long-run PDs calculated for the mapped internal and external ratings consistent? For example, suppose internal risk rating 5 is mapped to Standard & Poor's BBB. We calculate the long-run PDs using default rate time-series for both Standard & Poor's BBB and internal risk rating 5 and compare the two estimates. Large discrepancies indicate poor mapping. The methodology introduced for long-run PD estimation in the section on "Long-Run PD" in Chapter 2 allow us to account for the differences in correlations in internal and external data.
2. Are the externally rated obligors rated consistently by the internal and external rating systems? Large discrepancy indicates poor mapping. Table 3.29 present the results of an example of this analysis where we examined the Standard & Poor's–rated obligors. As seen, the exact match is 34.7% while the match improves to 78.4% within ±1 notch.

**TABLE 3.29**

Actual Standard & Poor's Ratings versus Internal Ratings

| Standard & Poor's on Internal Scale | Standard & Poor's Rating | Internal Rating | | | | | | | | | Number of Standard & Poor's Credits |
|---|---|---|---|---|---|---|---|---|---|---|---|
| | | 0 | 1 | 2 | 3 | 4 | 5 | 6 | 7 | 8 | |
| 0 | AAA | 1 | 0 | 0 | 0 | 0 | 0 | 0 | 0 | 0 | 2 |
| 1 | AA+/AA/AA− | 0 | 5 | 13 | 2 | 1 | 0 | 0 | 0 | 0 | 20 |
| 2 | A+/A/A− | 0 | 9 | 23 | 14 | 4 | 1 | 0 | 0 | 0 | 51 |
| 3 | BBB+/BBB/BBB− | 0 | 0 | 11 | 24 | 25 | 11 | 11 | 0 | 0 | 82 |
| 4 | BB+/BB | 0 | 1 | 0 | 5 | 14 | 10 | 7 | 7 | 0 | 44 |
| 5 | BB− | 0 | 0 | 0 | 1 | 4 | 10 | 4 | 1 | 0 | 20 |
| 6 | B+/B | 0 | 0 | 0 | 0 | 2 | 5 | 5 | 3 | 3 | 18 |
| 7 | B− | 0 | 0 | 0 | 0 | 0 | 1 | 3 | 0 | 1 | 5 |
| 8 | CCC+ and below | 0 | 0 | 0 | 0 | 0 | 0 | 0 | 0 | 3 | 3 |
| | Number of credits | 1 | 15 | 47 | 46 | 50 | 38 | 30 | 11 | 7 | **245** |
| | Percentage | 0.4% | 6.1% | 19.2% | 18.8% | 20.4% | 15.5% | 12.2% | 4.5% | 2.9% | 100.0% |

Exact match       34.7%

Within ±1 notch   78.4%

3. Are the ratings for the other obligors consistent? For those obligors without a Standard & Poor's rating, we can use the Standard & Poor's Credit Model, which produces Standard & Poor's ratings in lowercase to repeat the above analysis. Large discrepancy again indicates poor mapping.

4. Are the risk rating philosophies consistent? If the philosophies are not fairly consistent, for example if the internal risk rating system is fairly PIT, the mapping may not be stable over time. We can use the mobility metric approach to assess the difference in the internal and external rating philosophies (see the subsection on "Testing the Rrealization of the Risk Rating Philosophy" in the section of "PD Backtesting" earlier in this chapter).

5. Is the mapping stable overtime? We need to monitor the stability of mapping overtime as discussed in the section on "Benchmarking" earlier in this chapter).

## ANNUAL HEALTH CHECK

On an annual basis, the risk rating systems must be reviewed to ensure that they are operating as intended. This review is broad ranging in scope and the examination should incorporate the findings from all validation activities as discussed above. When necessary, it may be complemented by a qualitative assessment of the risk rating system's performance based on expert judgment.

Using medical health check as an analogy, individual validation activities performed throughout the year are like medical examinations, e.g., X-rays, blood tests, and so forth, performed on an individual throughout the year. Once a year, a full body checkup connects the dots among all the examination results and arrives at an overall diagnosis. This is what an annual health check intends to achieve. The final annual report, showing the overall performance of the risk rating system, issues raised, and remedial actions taken is circulated to top management including the board of directors. Considering the wide range of individual validation results, some qualitative requiring fundamental credit knowledge, some process oriented, and some very quantitative in nature, it is probability necessary that the annual health check analysis be conducted by a group of cross-trained risk professionals with different core areas of expertise.

## GOVERNANCE

The governance of IRRS operations and validation has been one of the most heavily discussed topics of IRRS implementation. Issues like the "independence of validation," the role of internal audit departments in validation, and what constitutes "effective challenge" have been globally debated. In this section, we discuss some of our observations with respect to these governance issues.

Many FIs have reviewed and refined their governance structure with respect to Basel II and established a governance framework including validation corporate standards and validation protocols.

**Governance framework** sets up the rules for how the individual pieces of validation fit together. It describes the validation activities at a high level and places validation within the bank's overall credit risk management framework. It covers the scope and timing of validation, roles and responsibilities—accountabilities, role of internal audit, independence, escalation procedures, ongoing education of senior management, continuous improvement, and so forth.

**Validation corporate standards** provides the "30,000-foot" view, starting with basic definitions, detailing the scope of validation, roles and responsibilities, frequency and timing of the validation activities, and how the different validation activities seamlessly fit together.

**Validation protocols guidelines** provide the validators with a detailed checklist of the validation activities that need to be performed and specify the tests and procedures at a detailed level.

An example organizational chart is presented in Figure 3.21 One common noteworthy observation is the unification between risk management and treasury (or corporate finance group). In pre-Basel days, regulatory capital was not risk sensitive, and thus, quite commonly it is considered a reporting function handled by treasury or corporate finance group. Basel II capital is much more risk sensitive than Basel I capital and accordingly the roles and responsibilities of the relevant parties have been redefined. Some large banks have been reorganized accordingly as illustrated schematically in Figure 3.21, merging risk management and finance/treasury group. It is much more common today to see that the same group is responsible for both regulatory and economic capital. This trend is expected to continue especially with Pillar II implementation requiring the demonstration of overall capital adequacy (see Chapter 4).

### Independence of the Validation Groups

Basel's "independence" requirement for the groups conducting validation has been debated heavily. Some of the earlier interpretations of the independence requirement were quite strict, even requiring that the validation groups be completely independent from the "profit centers" of the loan

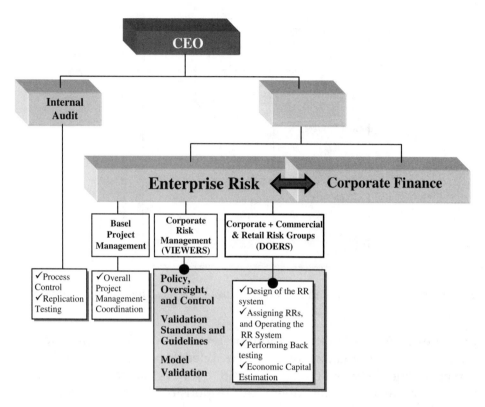

**Figure 3.21**  Example organization chart.

origination groups. Even if a portion of the validators' bonuses were driven by the performance of the origination group, this strict interpretation of the independence requirement would be violated. Later interpretations are much more lenient. One minimum requirement is quite certain that the same person(s) should not be responsible for developing the models and validating them (the same models).[37] Because *"structural independence"* would not always be cost effective, especially for the smaller organizations, *functional independence* of the validators and the validators ability to *effectively challenge* the model developers are deemed sufficient. One practical question with functional independence is at what level can the modeler and the validator report to the same person. After all, when we go high enough, everybody reports to the same person (e.g., CRO). From our observations, the modeler and the validator could report to the same person that is only a single level above, provided that this person is sufficiently senior (VP or higher) and functionally she or he has the dual responsibility of development and validation without an overwhelming conflict

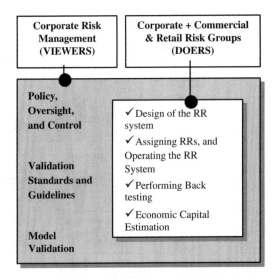

**Figure 3.22** Separated roles and responsibilities between "doers" and "viewers."

of interest.[38] An undoubtedly more preferable functional independence adopted by larger organizations involves a clear separation of the roles and responsibilities between the "doers" and "viewers" as depicted in Figure 3.22. In this structure, the "doers" are responsible for the design, implementation, and performance of the risk rating system and they are independent from the loan originators. The "viewers," on the other hand, are responsible for the policy, oversight, validation, and control aspects of the risk rating systems and as such they are independent from the "doers."

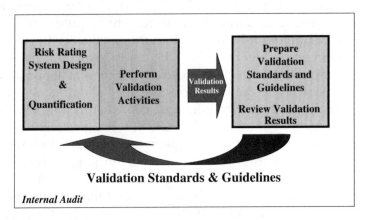

**Figure 3.23** First example of functional independence.

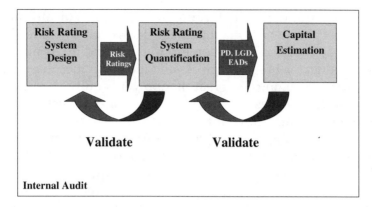

**Figure 3.24** Second example of functional independence.

Above are two examples of functional independence. In the first example (Figure 3.23), the doers develop the models, whereas the viewers prepare the validation standards and guidelines, according to which the doers "conduct" the required tests. The test results are then independently reviewed by the viewers. The fact that doers are the ones actually conducting the tests as required by the viewers makes this structure arguably cost-effective.

The second example of Figure 3.24 depicts a more clear-cut picture of functional independence. In this example, three different groups have different responsibilities in the capital estimation process, where the group "upstream" validates the one "downstream" of the process.

The role of the internal audit in validation has also been debated. In some countries, the regulators initially requested that internal audit (IA) attest to overall Basel compliance. While the regulators' intention is most likely to establish a single point of contact, some FIs has argued otherwise on the basis that:

1. IA is specialized in "process" validation and as such does not have the required set of skills for Basel validation;
2. IA does not confirm external compliance; and
3. IA itself is not supposed to be a "control function," but rather IA tests the effectiveness of the processes and controls against the relevant corporate standards.

We have observed that, to a large extent, the above arguments are received well. IA's responsibilities are confined to the validation of the effectiveness of the Basel II processes and their controls, whereas the validation activities are conducted by independent validation groups typically under the umbrella of corporate risk management. However, in some European banks, IA has become the validation group by extending its mandate and skill set to conduct the broad range of validation activities discussed here.

Regulators, realizing the great manpower required for conducting the validations themselves, are seeking *reliance-based validation* where regulators rely on organizations' internal viewers. These are, for example, internal validation groups, IA and corporate risk management as a whole. FIs would need to demonstrate to their regulators that their viewers can *effectively challenge* their doers. This naturally requires that the viewers have the necessary skills, experience, and, most importantly, the authority. It is important that a clear escalation mechanism is defined to cater for any unsettled issues between the doer and the viewers, as the doers may not necessarily agree with all of the viewers' conclusions. Senior management should also be well aware of the issues debated. Regulators would like to see that senior management is well informed and on top of the issues regarding the performance of the IRRS. It would be a very big cause for concern for the regulators to realize that the issues identified by the viewers are not known or acted upon by the senior management, which shows a weak risk culture for the organization. History repeatedly showed that losing the confidence of the regulators (and the external rating agencies) about the organization's ability to self-regulate can be very costly.

The example organization chart presented in Figure 3.25 shows how different business units are involved in different dimensions of the validation process (i.e., the validations of IRRS design and quantification, operations, and annual health check). Note that validation processes cross organizational boundaries, involving many different units, which poses a challenge from an auditing standpoint as it needs to be defined who "owns" which processes and thus is responsible for their effectiveness.

In the example organization chart of Figure 3.25, there are three layers of independence:

1. The designers and the operators of the risk rating systems are independent from lines of business.
2. Validators are independent from the designers (this is not always clear-cut in smaller organizations as discussed above).
3. Additionally, corporate audit, which checks the effectiveness of the relevant processes, is independent from all groups involved.

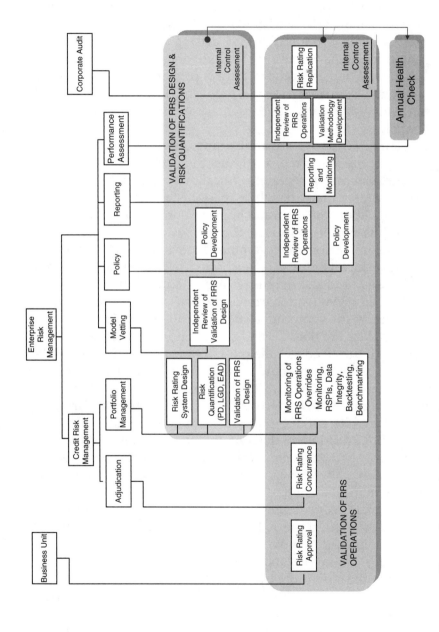

**Figure 3.25** Example organization chart.

## CONCLUSIONS

In this chapter, we have discussed IRRS validation. We notice that IRRS validation is much more comprehensive than model vetting or model validation exercises, which more advanced banks have been conducting for many years in order to manage the model risk arising from the use of their models (e.g., in pricing, market risk, VaR, credit and operational risk, economic capital, etc.). Whereas model vetting is primarily a technical function, IRRS validation is broader in scope, requiring different skill sets such as advanced quantitative skills, fundamental credit risk knowledge, and process validation.

As IRRSs are new, and we are all learning, it is only natural that FIs will not get it right the first time, and thus, the emphasis should be on continuous improvement. It is therefore critical that we do not consider the validation exercise as a black-or-white, pass-or-fail test, but rather an opportunity to learn about the IRRS and improve our practices accordingly. We can achieve this objective only if the validation exercise provides accurate diagnoses and actionable recommendations. The focus, therefore, is to make sure that sufficient tests are performed, test results are analyzed, issues are diagnosed, and the diagnoses are acted upon with remedial actions taken. Individual validation exercises discussed here are only tools helping us to identify the symptoms, such as realized default rates and LGDs are too high, PDs are not PIT, and so forth. Identifying these symptoms is useful only if they lead to a diagnosis. Some FIs discuss the validation results (sometimes as a part of the annual health check) in large forums with people from risk rating (i.e., rating analysts), operations, and risk management to diagnose the underlying issues. These forums, bringing people together from different disciplines, are extremely useful as these are the people using IRRS day in and day out and are thus able to offer valuable insights. The role of management is particularly important in creating a learning organization. The best validation teams cannot help if the issues are not known by management and remedial actions are not taken. With reliance-based regulations, regulators will need to be convinced that the bank has established a continuous learning and improvement process where issues are diagnosed, top management is informed, and corrective actions are taken in a continuous and timely fashion.

With respect to the individual tests discussed here, we need to realize that no one test is sufficient; we need to look at a *mosaic of evidence*. When comparing the performance of different IRRSs or for different years, an apples-to-apples comparison is essential: risk rating philosophy, portfolio composition, and portfolio risk characteristics should be taken into account in the interpretation of the results. Whereas backtesting and benchmarking are very informative, validation of conceptual soundness is especially important for low-default portfolios. Mapping to external PDs (or default rates), LGDs, and EADs needs to be well justified and validated.

## REFERENCES

Friedman, C. and S. Sven, 2006, "Utility Functions that Lead to the Likelihood Ratio as a Relative Model Performance Measure." *Journal Statistical Papers*, vol. 47, no. 2, pp. 211–225.

Hoeffding, W., 1963, "Probability Inequalities for Sums of Bounded Random Variables." *Journal of the American Statistical Association*, vol. 58, no. 301, pp. 13–30.

Hosmer, D.W. and S. Lemeshow, 2000, "Applied Logistic Regression, Second Edition." John Wiley & Sons.

Jafry, Y. and T. Schuermann, 2003, "Metrics for Comparing Credit Migration Matrices." Working paper, 03–09, The Wharton Financial Institutions Centre.

Miu, P. and B. Ozdemir, 2005, "Practical and Theoretical Challenges in Validating Basel Parameters: Key Learnings from the Experience of a Canadian Bank." *Journal of Credit Risk*, vol. 1, no. 4, pp. 89–136.

Saidenberg, M. and T. Schuermann, 2003, "The New Basel Capital Accord and Questions for Research." Financial Institutions Center, 03–14.

Tasche, D., 2003, "A Traffic Lights Approach to PD Validation." Working paper, Deutsche Bundesbank.

Van Deventer, D.R. and X. Wang, 2003, "Advanced Credit Model Performance Testing to Meet Basel Requirements," in *The Basel Handbook—A Guide for Financial Practitioners*. Edited by M. Ong, RISK Publications.

Vasicek, O., 1987, "Probability of Loss on Loan Portfolio." Working paper, Moody's KMV Corporation.

## CHAPTER 4

# Pillar II, Challenges, and Dealing with Procyclicality

## INTRODUCTION

Pillar II, the next frontier, extends Pillar I's internally estimated parameters into the full capital adequacy framework. Under Pillar II, FIs using different inputs as illustrated below within their risk appetite framework demonstrate their capital adequacy to their regulators.

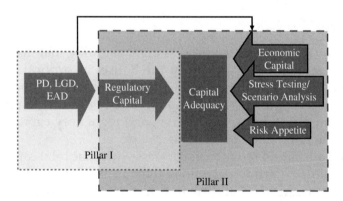

Pillar II implementation will include (but possibly not be limited to) the following tasks:

- **Designing a Framework to Manage Capital Adequacy:** Engineering a transparent, auditable, and replicable capital adequacy framework, through which the inputs are processed, alternative views of capital are reconciled within the organization's stated risk appetite, and capital adequacy is managed and demonstrated.

- **Risk Quantification:** Estimation of the inputs and parameters for the capital adequacy assessment framework, more specifically the effects of stress testing/scenario analysis, PIT versus TTC capital elements for different risk types.
- **Capital Allocation Management:** Reconciling different views of capital and managing the differences among them in the capital allocation process with respect to business cycles; incorporating the differences in a bank's different lines of business to incentify the correct business behavior in maximizing risk adjusted profitability.
- **Validation and Governance Framework:** Establishing a validation and governance framework around the whole capital adequacy process.

With the implementation of Basel II, regulatory capital will become much more risk sensitive resulting in changes in capital levels with respect to business cycles. This chapter will discuss some issues regarding Pillar II implementation and procyclicality from both the capital adequacy and the capital management perspectives.

## BACKGROUND DEFINITIONS

**Capital adequacy** refers to the process demonstrating that institutions are adequately capitalized at the top of the house, incorporating different concepts of capital: market value of equity, book value of equity, rating agency capital, economic or risk capital, and regulatory capital. Rating agency capital, economic or risk capital, and regulatory capital reflect the capital from debt-holders' point of view.

**Capital allocation** refers to the process where the total capital (usually the book equity) is partitioned among the business units, which is in turn used for risk-based profitability and pricing estimations and strategic decision-making. Usually, the partitioning is done based on (the usage of) economic capital (or risk capital).

With the implementation of Basel II, regulatory and economic capital will be much more closely aligned in comparison with Basel I. However, for example, if we look at credit capital, some disconnect remains due to the following issues:

1. Distortions due to the coverage issues: In the regulatory framework, some uncovered risks are embedded into the parameters for the covered risk.

2. Distortions due to Basel's shortcomings in capturing concentration risk: The Basel (credit) capital formula is an approximation assuming portfolios are infinitely granular, which is not always realistic.

3. Basel correlation assumption (i.e., asset correlation = f(PD)) is weak, as correlations are not driven by PD levels, but rather by the industry types and size of the obligors. As a result, more realistic correlation structures cannot be captured under Basel II.

4. Economic capital is likely to be more cyclical than Basel capital. The gap between them will be cycle sensitive, which has implications in both capital adequacy and capital allocations.

We can define three different views of the capital as seen below before we start our discussion:

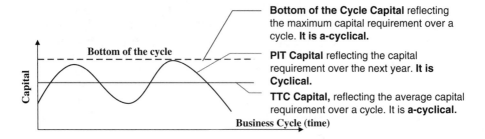

**Bottom of the Cycle Capital** reflecting the maximum capital requirement over a cycle. **It is a-cyclical.**

**PIT Capital** reflecting the capital requirement over the next year. **It is Cyclical.**

**TTC Capital,** reflecting the average capital requirement over a cycle. It is **a-cyclical.**

Under the point-in-time (PIT) view, capital is cyclical, reflecting the level of capital required (usually over the next year) given "current risk taking" and corresponding with where we currently stand in the cycle. Under the through-the-cycle (TTC) view, the capital is acyclical, reflecting the average of PIT capitals over the cycle. Bottom-of-the-cycle capital reflects the maximum of PIT capitals over a cycle. It is also acyclical.

If a financial institution manages its capital based on a PIT philosophy, the intent is to match the capital level with the current risk taking. As the risk fluctuates over the cycle, so does the capital. This view is often criticized as undesirable, since the financial institution would have to increase the level of capital to match the increased level of risk during downturns. Raising capital (i.e., equity) during downturns is expensive.

If a financial institution manages its capital based on a TTC philosophy, its intent is *not* to match the capital level with the current risk taking but to hold capital based on an average level of risk over a cycle. This view has the advantage that during downturns, the firm would *not* have to increase the level of capital to match the increased level of risk. However, the capital held does not match the current risk taking at any point in the cycle unless by coincidence.

Under the bottom-of-the-cycle capital philosophy, the capital level is always higher (or equal only at the bottom of the cycle) than the current risk taking. This view therefore results in excess capital at all times (relative to risk taking) for which the firm's shareholders are not compensated. In other words, this extra cushion of safety comes at the expense of the firms' shareholders.

We need to clarify one point here. It is sometimes thought that if we use TTC parameters (PD, LGD, EAD, and correlations) in capital estimation, the resulting capital would be TTC. This is not entirely true. TTC capital is the average of PIT capitals over the cycle. More formally, PIT capital can be expressed as Equation 4.1.

$$\text{PIT Capital}_t = f(\text{PD}_t, \text{LGD}_t, \text{EAD}_t,$$
$$\text{Conditional correlations}) \qquad \text{(Equation 4.1)}$$

where $\text{PD}_t$, $\text{LGD}_t$, $\text{EAD}_t$, are PIT probability of default, loss given default and exposure at default, respectively. The role of correlations in risk rating philosophy will be discussed later on. Now, TTC capital can be defined as Equation 4.2:

$$\text{TTC\_Capital} = \frac{\sum_{t=1}^{n} \text{PIT Capital}_t}{n} \qquad \text{(Equation 4.2)}$$

where $n$ is the number of the years in a cycle. We can interpret TTC probability of default, loss given default, and exposure at default being functions of their PIT counterparts. Unfortunately, TTC capital is sometimes incorrectly referred to as:

$$\text{TTC Capital} = f(\text{TTC\_PD}, \text{TTC\_LGD}_t, \text{TTC\_EAD}_t,$$
$$\text{Unconditional correlations}). \qquad \text{(Equation 4.3)}$$

Note that Equation 4.3 will not necessarily be a cycle-average capital and will not necessarily produce the correct TTC Capital as expressed in Equation 4.2. Nevertheless, it will be less cyclical than is PIT capital due to the use of TTC parameters in the capital estimation.

**Is cyclicality of capital a problem that needs to be dealt with?** *An excessively stable (thus, not risk sensitive) capital is not desired by the shareholders.*

Regulators appear to prefer the more stable TTC capital over the more cyclical PIT capital. They may have two motivations: *conservatism* (an extra safety cushion for potential undetected and unmeasured risk) and *aryclical capital* (to prevent the [systemic] risk of many institutions needing capital during the downturns). Given regulators' concern about systemic risk, these motivations are understandable. However, as discussed above, extra capital (in excess of the current risk taking) comes at the expense of shareholders (i.e., excess capital means institutions are not taking enough risk to generate the required rate of return for its shareholders). Thus, excessively ayclical capital should not be desired either, as it creates excess capital relative to the risk raking during good parts of the cycles.

We now examine how cyclical the capital will be when Basel II is implemented.

**How cyclical will Basel II capital be?** *There are built-in cyclicality dampeners already.* We can answer this question by examining the inputs to the capital estimation process. A quick look at the inputs below illustrates the built-in cyclicality dampeners.

| | | |
|---|---|---|
| ✓ | **PDs** | Either philosophy is acceptable. However pure PIT philosophy is not attainable |
| ✗ | **LGDs** | A-cyclical due to the interpenetration of the downturn LGD requirement (bottom of the cycle) |
| ✗ | **Correlations** | Unconditional |
| ✗ | **Stress Testing** | Appears to be pushing towards a-cyclical conservative measure: *"If a bank chooses a rating philosophy that is likely to result in rating transitions that reflect the impact of the economic cycle, its capital management policy must be designed to avoid capital shortfalls in times of economic stress – ANPR, July, 2003"* |

**PDs:** Institutions seem to be allowed to use different philosophies: PIT, TTC, or a hybrid. We, however, need to acknowledge that PDs *cannot* be purely PIT even though they are intended to be (as not all information is observable even when we had a frictionless risk rating process). Therefore, even if an institution's stated philosophy is PIT for PDs, in reality these PDs are from a hybrid philosophy, which reduces the cyclicality. The more TTC the PDs are, the larger the dampening effect. We observe that some large banks use two or three different sets of PDs. The most PIT PDs are used for pricing and risk management, less PIT PDs are used for economic capital, and the least PIT PDs are used for regulatory capital.

**LGDs:** It appears that most institutions adapt a fairly acyclical LGD philosophy where facility LGDs, once set, are not adjusted for any changes in expectations over the next year. LGDs are only adjusted for the change in collaterals rather than the change in LGD cycles. In other words, within the spectrum of *cyclical* and *acyclical* LGD philosophies, the philosophy of most banks seems to be closer to an acyclical measure. LGD ratings are not expected to change over the life of an exposure due to cyclical changes. Therefore, even at a good part of a LGD cycle, expected LGDs are not reduced, also creating a dampening effect.

Sometimes it is argued that because capital represents an extreme stress event, using bottom-of-the-cycle LGDs[1] rather than PIT LGDs would be more appropriate. This is not necessarily true. Interestingly, using an acyclical conservative LGD would be equivalent to increasing the risk horizon to beyond one year in calculating capital requirement. Suppose a bank adopts a PIT risk rating system and intends to measure risk *over a one-year risk horizon with respect to the current state of the business cycle.* If we use an acyclical conservative LGD, we effectively consider the same extreme LGD event irregardless of where we currently are in the cycle (i.e., whether we are one year or five years away from a downturn). Suppose we are at the *top* of the LGD cycle (e.g., point A in Figure 4.1, when LGD risk is generally low), and if things turn bad, it may actually take another three to four years to hit the bottom of the cycle. Thus, when we adopt an acyclical conservative LGD when we are at point A, we are effectively lengthening our risk

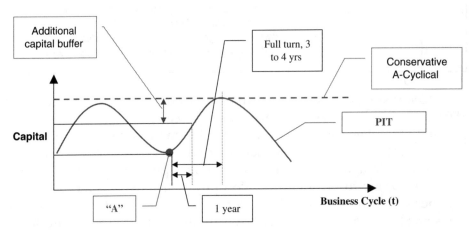

**Figure 4.1** Use of bottom of the cycle LGD effectively lengthens risk horizon.

horizon to beyond our intended one-year period. The net effect would therefore be a less cyclical capital but with a capital cushion that is likely to be above the PIT capital required during the booming stage of the economy. This appears to be consistent with the intention of creating an additional capital buffer for market downturns.

**Correlations:** Miu and Ozdemir (2005) explicitly showed that correlations are specific to rating philosophy; namely TTC correlations are unconditional, whereas PIT correlations are conditional and, therefore, materially smaller. These findings have interesting implications. In Basel II capital estimation as well as most internal economic capital models, unconditional correlations are used. Therefore, even if PIT PDs (as well as LGD and EADs) are used, the resulting economic capital will not be PIT but rather an overstated PIT.

**Stress testing:** Stress testing requirements, especially under Pillar II, are likely to prevent financial institutions from reducing their capital levels at the favorable parts of the credit cycle. Therefore, this requirement, too, is likely to dampen the procyclicality as well as creating an extra capital cushion. Because of the stress testing requirements, there will be an add-on to PIT capital during economic expansions. Thus, despite the low PDs during an economic expansion, required capital will not necessarily go down—at least not as fast. The role played by stress testing will be further discussed later in this chapter.

**Do we need to smooth out the procyclicality of capital?** There are some research papers suggesting that regularly capital requirement needs to be smoothed, citing that procyclicality (risk sensitivity) of the capital is a problem (e.g., Gordy and Howells, 2006). We need to be careful about this statement. It is true that adoption of PIT capital may require institutions to raise equity during downturns when it is expensive, but there are other considerations. First of all, as discussed above, there are already built-in elements smoothing the cyclicality of capital requirement. Second, excessive smoothing will result in capital in access of risk taking and, thus, will cost the shareholders. If further smoothing is indeed necessary, how much more smoothing is appropriate? This issue needs to be carefully studied and examined by the institutions themselves, regulators, and the industry as a whole. It would be highly appropriate for the institutions to incorporate (and document) their preferences with respect to cyclicality of capital as well as its justification within their stated risk appetite.

**How can we smooth the capital requirement?** If we were to further smooth the required capital, there appear to be two alternatives: we can smooth the output or the inputs. Smoothing the output involves translating the current (cyclical) capital requirement into some kind of cycle-neutral capital using a formulaic approach. This is not easy to do in a robust manner. The alternative is challenging as well. First of all, as discussed above, using cycle-neutral inputs will not necessarily produce cycle-neutral capital. Second, the transformation of PIT parameters to TTC parameters is not easy. As discussed, the only parameter that can be PIT is PD (as discussed, LGDs, EADs, and correlations are already acyclical to a large extent). This (PD transformation) is what some banks seem to be doing already. We should note, however, that smoothing the PDs in a theoretically robust manner is not easy and will not result in cycle-neutral capital as defined in Equation 4.2.

**An alternative (third) approach:** *One way to stabilize capital could be to use a cyclical solvency ratio/confidence level corresponding with the target rating. This approach has the advantage that despite using PIT PDs, the resulting capital will be relatively stable.*

Today, most institutions use a constant solvency ratio corresponding with their target debt rating when they calculate economic capital. For example, a bank whose target rating is AA– may calculate economic capital at a 99.95% confidence level (assuming the solvency ratio or default probability is 5 bps per annum for AA–). The common practice is to maintain a constant confidence level (and, thus, solvency ratio or default probability) regardless of where they are in the cycle. The underlying assumption is that being AA– requires having a 5 bps (for example) constant solvency ratio over the cycles. We can challenge this assumption. First of all, default rates of say AA– obligors do not remain constant but vary with the credit cycle. Second, there is no mention in the rating methodology adopted by external rating agencies (e.g., Standard & Poor's) that ratings are in fact assigned based on the one-year default probability. Instead, ratings are assigned based on a longer (usually three- to five-year) time horizon. As a result, for example during a downturn, the companies whose relative rankings (both within the sector and the larger universe) do not change are not necessarily downgraded despite the potential increase in the one-year default probability. Thus, maintaining an AA– rating does not mean having a constant one-year default probability of, for example, 5 bps. The one-year default probability may vary over a cycle while the rating is maintained. This nuance in definition of having a target debt rating has interesting implications in capital estimation.

Let us consider two cases. First, assume we use the former definition with the constant solvency ratio, say 10 bps so that we estimate capital at 99.9% confidence interval. As seen in Figure 4.2, during a downturn, PDs increase, and the tail of the loss distribution moves further to the right

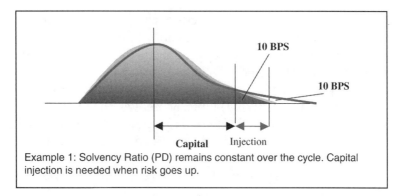

**Figure 4.2**   Use of constant solvency ratio.

(illustrated in red in the figure). Under the constant confidence level assumption, we would need to inject capital (equity) to maintain our target rating as illustrated in Figure 4.2.

Now consider that we adapt an alternative definition for our target rating, more consistent with the rating methodology of external rating agencies: our target rating can have a 3 bps solvency ratio (over one year) during an expansion and a 17 bps solvency ratio over a downturn. This means we use 99.93% and 99.83% confidence intervals during the expansion and downturn, respectively. As seen in Figure 4.3 (the darker line), during a downturn, PDs increase, and the tail of the loss distribution moves further to the right. But this does not translate into a need for capital injection as we now use a lower confidence level (99.83%). Similarly during an

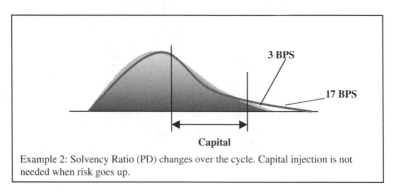

**Figure 4.3**   Use of cyclical solvency ratio.

expansion, no capital release is needed as we use a more stringent (i.e., higher) confidence level (99.93%). In adopting this strategy of varying confidence level, the financial institution can still maintain its target external rating of say AA– over the credit cycle.

The latter approach has the advantage that, despite using PIT PDs, the resulting capital will be relatively stable. Moreover, the institutions can use the same set of PDs for capital adequacy, capital allocation, pricing, and risk-adjusted return calculations (rather than converting one to the other). This is an advantage considering that most of the institutions prefer to use PIT PDs for pricing and risk-adjusted return calculations, and converting PIT PDs to TTC PDs in a robust manner is difficult.

## SOME PILLAR II IMPLEMENTATION ISSUES

### Background

Pillar I requires internal estimation of PDs, LGDs, and EADs, and under Pillar II institutions will need to demonstrate the adequacy of their capital. In the implementation of Pillar II, institutions, by utilizing Pillar I parameters, will estimate and use inputs like regulatory capital (TTC, PIT, stressed, and unstressed), economic capital (TTC, PIT, stressed, and unstressed),

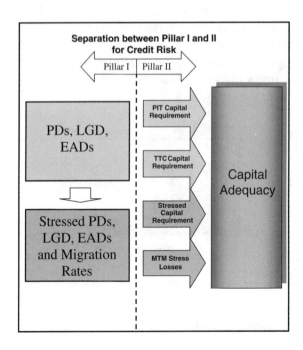

stress test, and scenario analysis. Currently, it is not clear how these different inputs will play out under Pillar II.

Pillar II regulations are "principle" based. Institutions will have to establish a *capital adequacy assessment framework,* the surrounding processes and methodologies to determine the adequacy of their capital. They also need to demonstrate to the regulators "why they believe their capital is adequate." This process will need to be transparent, auditable, and replicable and will need to be validated. This process also includes *capital allocation* among the institutions' different business units. It covers all types of risk (credit, market, operational, business, concentrations, liquidity, etc.). Most institutions already have a process for capital allocation, but it is not usually sufficiently transparent, auditable, and replicable (sometimes based on negotiations and not properly documented) and usually not validated adequately.

Institutions usually have a simple framework for *capital adequacy,* where they compare total regulatory, economic, and agency (Standard & Poor's and/or Moody's) capitals. This simple framework is not likely to be sufficient for Pillar II, which is much more comprehensive.

From our experience, the following is the most common deficiencies in the implementation of the capital adequacy assessment framework:

- *Parameter estimation/risk quantification:* Not all ingredients of the capital adequacy process (stressed, unstressed, PIT, TTC capital, and stress testing/scenario analysis) have been estimated to date. Stress testing and scenario analysis, if done, are usually not sufficiently robust.
- *Design of capital adequacy assessment framework*: The capital adequacy framework, which is required to process all these ingredients with respect to the institution's risk appetite, is usually not established for Pillar II purpose.
- *Organization risk appetite* with respect to capital adequacy is not sufficiently determined and spelled out (target rating under stress, earnings at risk, etc.). Procyclicality of the capital is not sufficiently examined and tied into the risk appetite.

Moreover, the following will need to be validated for both capital adequacy and capital allocation. This is much more comprehensive (both depth and breath) than Pillar I validation.

- Design of capital adequacy assessment framework
- Risk quantification: all inputs and parameters
- All models (in-house and third party)
- Governance framework

Considering all these, financial institutions most likely need to enhance their capabilities in the following areas:

- **Designing the capital adequacy assessment and management framework:** This includes engineering a transparent, auditable, and replicable capital adequacy framework where the inputs are processed with respect to risk appetite and capital adequacy is demonstrated and managed.
- **Risk quantification:** Risk quantification will involve the estimation of the inputs and parameters for the capital adequacy framework, more specifically stress testing/scenario analysis, PIT versus TTC capital elements for different risk types, including concentrations and liquidity risks.
- **Capital allocation management:** When allocating the total available capital (a formal definition is provided in a later section of this chapter) among its lines of business, financial institutions will need to reconcile different views of capital and manage the differences among them with respect to business cycles. In capital allocation, incorporating the cyclical differences in a bank's different lines of business will be critical to incentify the desired business behavior.
- **Validation and governance framework:** Financial institutions will need to establish a validation and governance framework around the whole capital adequacy and allocation process.

Among these tasks, the design of the framework and the methodology for both capital adequacy and allocation are perhaps the most challenging. How an institution will incorporate different views of capital and stress testing (and scenario analysis) and demonstrate that they are sufficiently capitalized with respect to where they are in the cycle and their stated risk appetite is an endeavoring task. Allocating the total capital among the lines of business (some of which are more cyclical than others) again with respect to where we are in the business cycles to motivate the right business behavior, while keeping the risk under control, is equally challenging and important.

As stated, Pillar II regulations are high level and principle based. The early indications show that regulators do not want to prescribe a formulaic approach to capital adequacy and allocation problems, but they prefer that banks themselves define the framework and demonstrate to their regulators that their capital is adequate and allocated appropriately. This framework will be engineered as Pillar II is implemented, and the role of stress testing warrants a discussion.

### The Role of Stress Testing and Scenario Analysis

Pillar I requires that risk parameters (PDs, LGDs, EADs) need to be stressed, and Pillar II requires that results of stress testing and scenario analysis be incorporated in the capital adequacy assessment framework. It is not clear how exactly stressed risk parameters will be used in Pillar I stress testing. Some indications suggest the following:

- Calculate the stressed parameters corresponding with a moderate level of stress (perhaps a mild recession).
- Calculate the regulatory capital according to the Pillar I formula using these stressed parameters.
- Demonstrate that it is less than the current capital level.

This approach might be reasonable given that Pillar I capital only sets the minimum capital requirement (albeit it still appears to be a placeholder until Pillar II is implemented).

Stress testing and scenario analysis play a more important role in Pillar II, which is demonstrated in the schematic below. See the section on "Stress Testing" in Chapter 2 for the generation of stress PDs, LGDs, and migration rates.

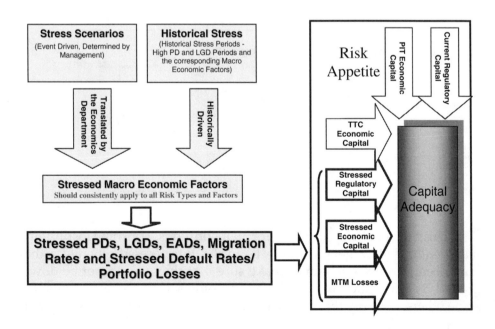

### How Do We Use Stressed Parameters in Pillar II's
### Capital Adequacy Assessment Framework?

There appear to be two options:

1. We can calculate (stress) economic and regulatory capital using the stressed parameters and demonstrate that the stress capital is less than the current capital level; or
2. We can estimate the marked-to-model (MTM) stress losses and demonstrate that they are less than the current (unstressed) capital level.

Naturally, the first approach is much more conservative resulting in much higher capital levels. We, therefore, need to consider conceptually what the first approach implies. Today's PIT capital represents the amount of equity we need to hold to maintain our target rating over the next year given current risk levels. When we conduct stress testing or scenario analysis, we estimate the increase in PDs, LGDs, and EADs given selected stress scenarios (historical or hypothetical). We, however, say nothing about when this stress event can take place, which, if it ever happens, can be many years away from today. Estimating the capital using these stressed inputs and allocating this stress capital today effectively means that we would like to maintain our target rating *even after* we were to be hit by such stress events. The idea is demonstrated in the following illustration:

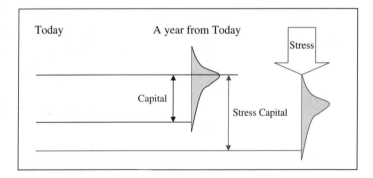

This may not be appropriate for all institutions. For some institutions, maintaining their target rating may be an absolute necessity, therefore, they may need an extra cushion to make sure that they would not be downgraded *even after* they were to be hit by some selected stress events. For some others, possibly for most of them, this may not be true and they may comfortably say that their capital is for the risk they are taking today, and if such unlikely stress events occur, they can live with a downgrade—*as the cost of holding this extra capital today outweighs the expected cost of downgrade.*

## The Importance of Risk Appetite

The proper place to address this trade-off is the risk appetite. Today, the risk appetite of most institutions is loosely defined, usually including only the target rating (current capital level) and some earnings volatility statements. Therefore, it is important that the cost-benefit analysis between the downgrade risk under stress and holding an extra cushion of capital (to avoid a downgrade even after the stress event) is well understood, carefully examined, and stated in the risk appetite.

Some institutions set *stress capital limits* (e.g., 10% more than their current capital level), and as long as their estimation of the stress capital is below the limits, their current level of capital is considered adequate. The rationale behind the stress capital limits is the following: As discussed previously, risk capital is intended to match an institution's risk taking. If an institutions suffers from some unexpected losses due to a stress event losing a portion of its capital, it would be subject to a downgrade, unless it either raises more capital (which is likely to be very difficult during a stress period) or reduces its risk taking or a combination of both. Setting a stress capital limit is tied more to the ability to quickly reduce the risk taking. If an institution carefully studies how much of its risk can be eliminated in a short period of time, even during a stress period, and justifies this capability and elaborates it within its risk appetite, this level (of justifiable immediate risk reduction) can be used as a stress capital limit (in our example, it is 10%). Example: assume an FI holds $100 billion of risk capital and has a target rating of A. The FI determines its stress capital limit as $110 billion, which means that FI can reduce its risk taking by $10 billion within a short period of time should it suffer from an unexpected/stress loss. Further suppose that this FI has no tolerance for downgrades. If the stress capital is estimated to be under $110 billion, FI does not need to increase its capital level of $100 billion (as the risk taking can be reduced up to $10 billion shortly after the stress event). If the stress capital is estimated to be $120 billion, however, the capital level would need to be increased by $10 billion.

We have used a simplified example here; however, we need to distinguish between *available capital* and *risk capital*. The former refers to the total capital available to the institution to support not only risk taking (plus a safety cushion) but also growth and/or acquisitions. It is usually measured in terms of book equity.[2] The latter refers to the capital supporting only the *risk taking* from the debt holders' perspective. It is measured in terms of economic capital and/or Pillar II capital (which is also risk-sensitive despite its shortcomings relative to economic capital).

Moreover, intended cyclicality of both risk capital and available capital (the former is more cyclical than the latter) also needs to be examined and tied into the risk appetite statement. The risk appetite with respect to both downgrade risk under stress events and the target cyclicalities will then need to be incorporated into the capital planning and capital adequacy assessment framework accordingly.

## CAPITAL PLANNING AND CAPITAL ADEQUACY ASSESSMENT FRAMEWORK WITH RESPECT TO PILLAR II

In this section, we would like to discuss how to design a capital management framework and capital planning process and to demonstrate capital adequacy as required by Basel II also incorporating stress testing results. In general, the framework should elaborate on and justify the strategies for dynamically matching an institution's risk taking and, thus, its risk capital to its available capital within the risk tolerances stated in risk appetite, including the following:

- *Procyclicality management:* Risk will increase/decrease following the cycles. What is the institution's capital management strategy to deal with cyclicality? The options are to hold some capital buffer (to absorb the increase in risk during the downturns) and/or balance available capital and risk taking dynamically with respect to the cycles (by increasing available capital and/or decreasing risk). The higher the capability for dynamic balancing, the smaller the capital buffer needed.

- *Dealing with unexpected losses:* Available capital will decrease after unexpected losses and stress events. What is the institution's strategy to replenish its capital level after unexpected losses? What is the tolerance to downgrades after unexpected losses and stress events? If the tolerance to downgrades is low, the options are again to hold some capital buffer (against the downgrade risks after the stress events and unexpected losses) and/or to rebalance available capital and risk taking (by increasing available capital and/or decreasing risk). The higher the capability for the rebalancing, the smaller the capital buffer needed.

The following is a flowchart of the dynamic capital adequacy management framework:

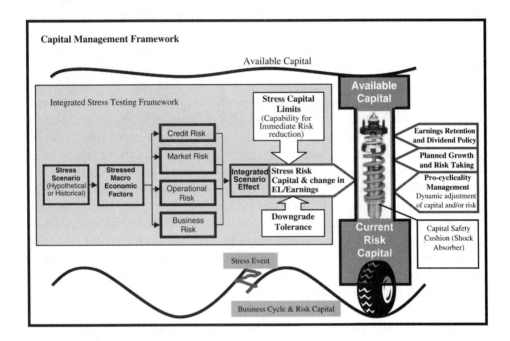

We would like to discuss the components of the framework above.

*Integrated scenario effect:* In this step, we determine and assess the effect of the Integrated Scenario Effect. As seen above, in the *integrated stress testing framework*, the selected (hypothetical or historical) scenarios are first translated into stressed macroeconomic factors, and then the effect is quantified in terms of credit, market, operational and business risk (including foregone revenues). These individual effects are then aggregated to determine the effect of the scenario on risk capital, future earnings, and expected losses.[3] First of all, we expect to see that the aggregated stress MTM loss is less than the current risk capital—a violation of which would imply that our current risk capital is underestimated. Second, we need to determine if our available capital needs to be increased. This depends on the safety cushion between available and risk capitals, our tolerance for downgrades, and our ability to reduce the risk immediately after the stress event, which are quantified in terms of stress capital limits as discussed above. If the stress risk capital is within the limits, implying that the institution can download some of the risk even after the stress event with reasonable certainty, or a potential downgrade is tolerable, or the current cushion between available and risk capitals can absorb the increase in risk capital, then there would be no need to increase the available capital level.

*Managing Procyclicality:* Regardless of our intended capital management philosophies, risk itself is cyclical (PIT), and, thus, we need to make sure that the risk capital corresponding with the PIT risk does not exceed the available capital at any point in the cycle. This means we need to have a good picture of both the current (PIT) and the planned risk taking, which incorporates the expected cycle effects, and then proactively manage the safety buffer between the available capital and the sum of current and expected risk taking. Those institutions that would like to keep this buffer smaller (to reduce the cost of capital) will need to demonstrate their capability to proactively manage it with respect to cyclicality. The management needs to be proactive because raising capital during downturns is not desirable.

The first requirement of this proactive management is to have an accurate PIT assessment of the (current and planned) risk taking and the corresponding PIT risk capital requirement. This should not be confused with the intention of some institutions to manage their capital in a TTC fashion, which is, in fact, based on their desire to keep their "available capital" stable, and is, by the way, consistent with the desire of the regulators. The point we are making here is that we cannot determine where we stand with respect to our available capital without knowing our current (PIT) and planned risk taking and thus the capital required to support that. Some U.S. regulators expressed their preference for those institutions having alternative (both PIT and TTC) assessments of their risk capital.

Organizations using TTC risk capital for capital adequacy are, in fact, blurring the line between available and risk capitals. In our view, knowing the current and planned risk taking in a PIT view and then managing the available capital in a more stable (less cyclical) manner through regulating the capital safety buffer should be desirable. Making the risk capital TTC would prevent us from having a clear picture of the safety buffer between the risk taking and available capital. Effective capital management and planning can be achieved by managing the safety buffer proactively by:

- Balancing risk taking and capital;
- Considering the effect of potential stress events (and making sure the buffer can absorb the potential impact); and
- Incorporating planned growth and dividend policies as illustrated above.

We noticed that some institutions calculate stressed PDs under stress events but then smooth them (by averaging them with their long-run PDs) before they calculate stress (economic) capital, based on the rationale that their economic capital policy is TTC. In our capital adequacy framework, this is nothing more than reducing the effect of the shock on the stress capital side and adding this shock to the procyclicality management side. At the end of the day, the effect of stress needs to be dealt with in either side.

In short, for capital adequacy management, having a PIT view of risk capital and managing the safety buffer by incorporating effect of cycles and potential stress scenarios should be a preferred approach. Nevertheless, adopting a TTC view of risk capital has merits in *capital allocation* (i.e., allocating available capital among an institution's lines of business) as discussed below.

### Impact of Procyclicality in Capital Allocation

Procyclicality also plays an important role in capital allocation. At the end of the day, available capital will be more conservative and less cyclical than is our internal view of capital (risk capital), as discussed above. Our internal view of capital is likely to be more PIT/cyclical and less conservative, which means we will have a cyclical gap between economic capital and allocated capital as illustrated below:

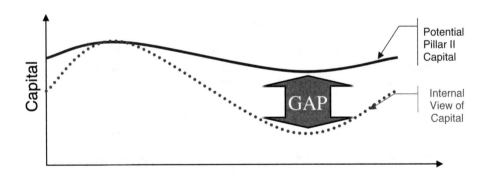

We define *gap* as available capital (usually refers to book equity) minus the sum of PIT risk capital (i.e., economic capital) allocated to lines of business. As discussed before, one way to stabilize the economic capital, and thus the gap, could be to use a cyclical solvency ratio/ confidence level corresponding with the target rating in estimation of economic capital.

The gap grows in good times and shrinks in bad times primarily due to the more cyclical businesses. When allocating the total capital to the lines of business, most institutions also allocate this gap.

### Allocating Available Capital among the Individual Business Units over the Course of a Business Cycle

If we look at the different lines of business under the umbrella of a financial institution, we notice that some of the lines of business are significantly more cyclical than are the others. For example, retail and midmarket portfolios are less cyclical than are corporate portfolios. The question is how to allocate available capital among the individual business units over the course of a business cycle. Let's consider the following example: Assume we allocate capital to the lines of business (LOBs) proportional to their economic capital (EC) usage based on the below formula:

$$\text{Capital allocated to LOB}_i = \frac{EC_{LOB_i}}{\text{Total EC}} \times \text{Avalible Capital (Total book equity)}.$$

Consider the following simple example:

|  | EC (PIT) | | |
|---|---|---|---|
|  | $LOB_A$ | $LOB_B$ | Total Book Equity |
| Downturn | $40 | $40 | $100 |
| Expansion | $20 | $40 | $100 |

|  | Capital Allocated | |
|---|---|---|
|  | $LOB_A$ | $LOB_B$ |
| Downturn | (40/80) × 100 = $50 | (40/80) × 100 = $50 |
| Expansion | (20/60) × 100 = $33 | (40/60) × 100 = $66 |

As seen above, $LOB_A$ is more cyclical than is $LOB_{A'}$ and as a result, $LOB_B$'s allocated capital is going up (from $50 to $66) during an expansion despite the fact that its risk capital (EC) remains unchanged. We can avoid this problem by allocating capital based on TTC risk capital (EC) as illustrated below:

| | EC (TTC) | | |
|---|---|---|---|
| | LOB$_A$ | LOB$_B$ | Total Book Equity |
| Downturn | $30 | $40 | $100 |
| Expansion | $30 | $40 | $100 |

| | Capital Allocated | |
|---|---|---|
| | LOB$_A$ | LOB$_B$ |
| Downturn | (30/70) × 100 = $43 | (40/70) × 100 = $57 |
| Expansion | (30/70) × 100 = $43 | (40/70) × 100 = $57 |

Usually, FIs prefer to allocate the gap separately to their LOBs. For example, if an FI has two LOBs:

Gap = Book equity − $\Sigma$ EC (PIT)
Capital allocated to LOB$_A$ = EC$_A$ (PIT) + $x$%Gap
Capital allocated to LOB$_B$ = EC$_B$ (PIT) + $(1 - x\%)$Gap

In reality, FIs have more than two LOBs, and they need more complex allocation of gap. For instance, once we have observed that gap is allocated the following way:

- **50% of gap is allocated based on regulatory capital**
  - The higher the regulatory capital, the higher the allocated gap
- **50% of gap is allocated based on EC volatility**
  - The more cyclical the EC, the higher the allocated gap

The first element gives LOBs incentive to manage their regulatory capital, whereas the second element provides, in effect, capital allocation based on TTC EC.

Cyclicality also plays a role in limit management for LOBs. If we use PIT EC for limit management, during good times, there will be risk-taking capacity for the cyclical LOBs. However, we need to be careful about the term risk. If these cyclical LOBs take too much long-term risk in good times, there can be implications later—as the institution is stuck with the term risk, which may be a problem when the cycle turns.

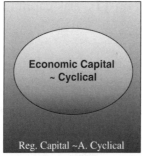

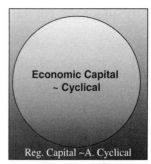

**Top of the cycle**                                  **Bottom of the cycle**

One way to deal with the issue is to allocate TTC capital to the lines of business for limit management purposes as well. Therefore, even during the good part of the cycle when PIT capital goes down, especially for the more cyclical businesses, these businesses will not be allowed to take extra risk as a bigger portion of the gap will be allocated to them, keeping their total allocated capital fairly stable. This may be an appropriate view, if the business has no or limited control over the terms of the deals. This way, the gap can be allocated to reduce/eliminate cyclicality.

If the business has reasonable control over the term of the deals, we may want to give them some control over the term of the new deals allowing them to grow their portfolios while managing the term risk. This can be done, for example, using a concept like capital holdback—where some capital proportional to the term of the deal is held back initially and released as the deals reach maturity.

### What Is the Role of Differentiated Cost of Capital (Hurdle Rate)?

If a business is cyclical, the required rate of return should be higher. Therefore, there is a theoretical basis for using a differentiated cost of capital/hurdle rate for different lines of business within a single institution. Sometimes it is argued that it would result in the double counting of risks, as cyclical businesses have already been allocated higher economic capital. However, this view is not correct, as economic capital represents the debt-holders' perspective. It is a constraint to maintain the target rating of the institution. The cost of capital, on the other hand, represents the share-holders' perspective. We expect shareholders requiring a higher return on capital for the more cyclical businesses, even though these businesses are mixed with some other less cyclical businesses under the umbrella of one holding company—a large bank. Thus, the use of differentiated cost of capital and economic capital allocation are complementary to each other reflecting both the shareholders' and the debt-holders' perspectives of risks.


## CONCLUSIONS

In this chapter, we discussed different approaches in dealing with the procyclicality of Basel capital and a number of issues with respect to Pillar II implementation. We discussed that whereas the procyclicality of Basel capital may be perceived as a problem, excessive smoothing of the capital is costly for the institutions' shareholders. We recognized that there are already built-in cyclicality dampeners in Basel parameters. We discussed that one way to stabilize capital, while maintaining PIT PDs, is to use a cyclical solvency ratio (i.e., cyclical confidence level). We examined the role of stress testing and scenario analysis in Pillar II implementation and their relation to risk appetite of organizations. While capital provides protection (like fire insurance), stress testing provides preparedness and awareness (like a fire drill). The risk appetite with respect to both downgrade risk under stress events and the target cyclicality will need to be incorporated into the capital adequacy assessment framework accordingly. For capital adequacy management, having a PIT view of risk capital and managing the safety buffer between PIT risk capital and available capital by incorporating the effect of cycles and potential stress scenarios should be a preferred approach. Having a TTC view of risk capital has merits however in allocating available capital among an institution's different lines of business. Allocated capital is more conservative and less cyclical than the internal view of capital—resulting in a cyclical gap between risk capital and available capital. We finally discussed how this gap can be allocated among an institution's lines of business to give them control over the term of the new deals while accounting for the term risk.

Financial institutions will need to examine these issues and incorporate them within their capital adequacy framework and risk appetite. For the regulators, it will be critical to understand a bank's capital adequacy assessment framework and risk appetite, place the bank's philosophy within a PIT to TTC spectrum considering all relevant elements (PDs, LGDs, correlations, EADs and stress testing) so that the bank can be appropriately benchmarked to its peers.

## REFERENCES

Gordy, M. B. and Howells, B. 2006, "Procyclicality in Basel II: Can We Treat the Disease Without Killing the Patient?" *Journal of Financial Intermediation*, vol. 15, no. 3, pp. 395–417.

Miu, P. and Ozdemir, B. 2005, "Practical and Theoretical Challenges in Validating Basel Parameters: Key Learnings from the Experience of a Canadian Bank." *Journal of Credit Risk*, vol. 1, no. 4, pp. 89–136.

# NOTES

# CHAPTER 1

1. In some cases, the template is further customized to incorporate new risk factors preferred by the particular FI.
2. With revenue of at least $50 million (¥10 billion for Japanese firms).
3. For example, the International Association of Credit Portfolio Managers (IACPM) has conducted a study on this issue. In this study, performances of commercially available private firm PD models are compared using data collected from 10 large U.S. commercial banks. The results are shared with the participating banks.
4. Agency ratings incorporate both quantitative and qualitative risk drivers.
5. For example, conditional on current stock price or the corresponding distance to default.
6. Typically, a three-month delinquency constitutes a default event.
7. The Standard & Poor's LossStats Model is a Web-based application. More information is available from the Web site http://www.lossstatsmodel.com.
8. For detailed discussions on the model, please refer to Friedman and Sandow (2003). Please also refer to Standard & Poor's Credit Market Services (2003) for the implementation details of the model.
9. See "Guidance on Paragraph 468 of the Framework Document," Basel Committee on Banking Supervision, July 2005.
10. See also Davis (2004).
11. Risk premium is discount rate subtracting the prevailing risk-free interest rate.
12. LGD can be estimated either by observing the market price of the defaulted instrument immediately after default or by computing the present value of future workout recoveries. Because the trading of most defaulted bank loans in the secondary market is illiquid, financial institutions typically have to rely on the latter approach in assessing their LGD. In the latter approach, LGD can be defined as one minus the recovery rate, which is the sum of the workout recoveries discounted at the *appropriate* discount rate divided by the total exposure at default.
13. In the context of this study, the risk premium is equivalent to the expected or required excess return (over risk-free rate) of the asset holders (or investors of defaulted instruments). These terms are used interchangeably throughout the paper.
14. See "Guidance on Paragraph 468 of the Framework Document," Basel Committee on Banking Supervision, July 2005.

15. See also Davis (2004).

16. In this paper, we focus on LGD risk rather than probability of default (PD) risk. The former measures recovery uncertainty after default has occurred. Moreover, the terms *LGD risk/uncertainty* and *recovery risk/uncertainty* are used interchangeably throughout the paper.

17. The data does not allow us to distinguish the level of security, only the security type. That is, we could have two loans listed as secured, but the first one may be 100% secured, whereas the second one may only be 5% secured. It is very possible that this limitation weakens the significance of the secured versus unsecured differentiation.

18. The October 2005 release v1.5 of the LossStats Database is used for this paper.

19. Pre-petition creditors are creditors that were in place prior to filing a petition for bankruptcy.

20. A total of 17 defaulted instruments with excess returns of more than 800% are removed from the original data set to ensure the results are not affected by these outliers. Moreover, among the remaining 1,139 defaulted instruments, 236 of them potentially represent near duplicated observations referring to similar instruments issued by the same obligor. They are however not identical instruments. For example, the 19 senior unsecured bonds in the Enron Bankruptcy are of different issuance characteristics and maturity dates, although they do share the same default date, recovery date, 30-day distressed trading price, ultimate recovery values, and therefore resulted in identical discount rate calculations. To check for the robustness of our results, we repeat the analysis but with all the potentially duplicated observations excluded (e.g., for Enron's 19 senior unsecured bonds, we remove all but one of these instruments from the analysis). The results are not materially different from those reported in this paper.

21. The classification is based on the earliest Standard & Poor's ratings of the instruments. Instruments from obligors that were not rated by Standard & Poor's are classified as "Others."

22. In a distressed exchange, both the default and recovery events happen simultaneously, and hence no discount rate would be applicable, and there would be no information uncertainty regarding recovery values at the time of default. Therefore, if we were to include these cases and use trading prices of the defaulted instrument 30 days after the default event, all information regarding the exchange would be known and there would be no uncertainty as to the recovery event.

23. The Global Industry Classification Standard (GICS) is an international industry classification system. It was jointly developed by Standard & Poor's and Morgan Stanley Capital International in 1999 as a response to the global financial community's need for one complete, consistent set of global sector and industry definitions. The highest industry sectors of GICS are found to be broader than those of the corresponding SIC codes.

24. Maclachlan (2004) proposes the use of a single-factor market model of asset value to study the systematic risk premium of defaulted debts. Unlike this study, the impact of market, firm, and instrument-specific characteristics on the required risk premium is however not investigated.

25. Cangemi, Mason and Pagano (2006) model the ultimate recoveries on defaulted debts using real options together with optimal stopping rules.

26. For illustration purpose, a single (net) recovery cash flow is assumed.

27. Although both Cangemi, Mason and Pagano (2006) and this paper are related to the pricing of defaulted instruments. Their objective is to explain the ultimate recoveries of these instruments with firm-level and instrument-specific information, while our objective is to estimate the discount rate parameter by matching the ultimate recoveries with the market prices of these instruments under the present value approach specified under Basel II.

28. Given the fact that the time-to-recovery of the instruments in our data set ranges from slightly more than a month to more than six years, the results can be significantly biased if we ignore the relation between LGD uncertainty and time-to-recovery. If we had assumed no time adjustment, the risk premiums would have been different from those presented here. However, the conclusions drawn in this study are robust whether we adjust for time or not.

29. Note that $\{1 - 2 \times [1 - \Phi(1.6449)]\} = 90\%$, where $\Phi$ is the cumulative standard normal distribution function.

30. In our sample, the majority of the default instruments have only single recovery.

31. In this analysis, $p_{i,j}$ are estimated in an iterative fashion such that they are proportional to the present values of the realized recovery cash flows $R_{i,j}$ discounted at the discount rate incorporating the most-likely risk premium $\hat{r}_x$.

32. As a robustness check, we also repeat the analysis in the section *Estimated Risk Premium* by directly using the *raw* unexpected recovery $\varepsilon_i$ rather than the *normalized* version of $\varepsilon_i / \sqrt{t_i^R - t_i^D - 30 \text{ days}}$ in Equations 1.5, 1.6 and 1.10. This alternative formulation is therefore consistent with an economy where the recovery uncertainty is time homogenous. The results are reported in the Appendix. The conclusions drawn in the section *Estimated Risk Premium* are essentially invariant to these two alternative formulations.

33. As an indication, using the full data set, when a flat $5 (i.e., 0.5% of the notional amount of $1,000), representing the collection cost, is subtracted from the ultimate undiscounted recoveries, overall risk premium decreases from 6.7% to 5.5%. It is more appropriate to assume a cost of collection as a fixed percentage of the notional amount rather than a fixed percentage of the actual recovery to accommodate the cases of zero recoveries.

34. The absolute priority rule, however, may not necessarily always be observed in practice.

35. It may also be due to the fact that the sample size of the secured debts is smaller than that of the unsecured ones (refer to Table 1.2). The precision of our point estimate is therefore lower for the secured segment.

36. The point estimate of zero risk premium for NIG is not economically intuitive. However, the corresponding confidence interval suggests that there is a 90% chance that the true risk premium lies between −5.6% and +5.6%. We therefore cannot rule out the possibility that the true risk premium is in fact positive. This argument is applicable to all subsequent zero or negative risk premium point estimates, where the confidence intervals always straddle the zero value.

37. It is important to emphasize that we attempt to measure *recovery risk* (i.e., uncertainty) rather than *recovery rate* (i.e., expected level). Only the former determines the size of the risk premium demanded by asset holders. The fact that the recovery

rate of defaulted IG debts might be higher than that of the defaulted NIG ones does not have any direct bearing on their respective levels of recovery risk.

38. In this study, Information Technology (GICS 40-45) and Telecommunication Services (GICS 50) are considered as technology-based industries, whereas others are non-technology-based industries.

39. It should be noted that risk-free rate tends to be lower during the stress periods, which by itself may lead to a lower discount rate. However, analysis (not reported) suggests that the increase in risk premium during the stress periods is more than able to offset the reduction in risk-free rate thus resulting in a higher overall discount rate.

40. Although the point estimate of the risk premium of "No DA and no DC" category is negative, the corresponding confidence interval suggests it is in fact statistically indistinguishable from zero.

41. Recovery cash flow always has a lower bound of zero.

42. The reader will find out later that the answers are "yes" for both of these questions.

43. To make sure the results will not be distorted by a few outliers, we only consider those subsegments with more than or equal to 50 LGD observations.

44. Within the "No DA, Some DC" segment, the risk premium of the unsecured instruments sub-segment is estimated to be equal to 26.8%, which is significantly different from the segment risk premium of 15.4%.

45. The data do not allow us to distinguish the level of security but only the security type. That is, we could have two loans both classified as secured, but the first one may be 100% secured, whereas the second one may only be 5% secured. It is very possible that this limitation weakens the significance of the secured versus unsecured differentiation.

46. The excess return on individual defaulted instrument is not the expected risk premium on the instrument, which we discuss in the previous sections. The former is the realized excess return and can be substantially different from the expected risk premium due to recovery uncertainty. A negative realized excess return, therefore, does not suggest investors price the instrument using a negative risk premium.

47. We ignore the degree of security (i.e., secured vs. unsecured), industry effect (i.e., technology vs. nontechnology), and marketwide stress condition, of which their relations with estimated risk premium are found to be weak or inconclusive in sections *Estimated Risk Premium* and *Validation of Results.*

48. Because there can be multiple recoveries paid out at different times during the recovery process, we use average time-to-recovery weighted by the nominal recovery values. Our analysis suggests that using the time-to-recovery of the final cash flow rather than the weighted average time-to-recovery does not affect the conclusions drawn in this study.

49. In this study, we consider various single-explanatory variable versions of Equation 1.12 together with a few multiple-explanatory variable versions involving various subsets of the independent variables.

50. In order to avoid multicollinearity, we do not consider DA, DC and the dummy variable of senior subordinate bond at the same time in any single regression.

51. Specifically, it is the average of all available prices from different sources during the period from day 15 to day 45 after the respective default event.

52.  It should be noted the market price naturally changes from the point of default to the point of emergence as more information is revealed over time during the workout process. This subsequent price movement should not be confused with the settlement of the market price during the first 30 days of default.

53.  For example, see Bos (2003).

54.  It represents the increase in opportunity cost of holding on to and working out defaulted instruments during a market downturn. The cost of capital and thus the opportunity cost (and hurdle rate) is typically higher during a recession. This increase in required risk premium also applies to instruments without a market.

55.  Regarding the appropriateness of emergence and settlement pricing in assessing the ultimate recovery values of the medium-size companies, the following should be noted. The method of using trading prices at the point of emergence is one that may not be the maximum or minimum value received but is one that can be consistently applied across different instruments, of which secondary markets exist. It ensures a uniform data set that we can perform analysis on. We recognize that the value based on the trading prices of the new or old instruments at emergence may not capture the maximum value the pre-petition security holder would have received had they held on to these instruments until some undefined point in time when they received the maximum return. However, it is impractical to measure and use such a return because the exact timing of this maximum return would not be known until after the event already occurred. This approach would assume the asset holders would be able to predict the point of maximum value and trade out of the security at that time, which would be a very unlikely scenario.

56.  Time-to-recovery of the instruments included in our data set ranges from slightly more than a month to more than six years.

57.  It should be noted that 82% of all defaulted instruments in our full dataset have time-to-recovery shorter than two and a half years.

58.  Our discussions with some banks indicate it is for the same reason why, when bank loan defaults are evaluated, a cutoff cohort year of close to three years prior to the current default year is utilized to avoid the exclusion of the yet to be resolved defaulted cases.

59.  To conserve space, the results are not reported here. They are however available on request from the authors.

60.  Most likely estimates reported in bold.

## CHAPTER 2

1.  Three- to five-year horizon is unlikely to cover a full credit cycle. Risk rating based on the entire credit cycle is not achievable given the limited ability to forecast over longer risk horizon.

2.  This issue will be further elaborated on in the section on "Long-run PDs" later in this chapter, when we attempt to infer long-run PD from the observed time series of default rates.

3.  We do not have a choice under Pillar I where correlation is simply a stated function of PD.

4. The authors would like to acknowledge the *Journal of Credit Risk* in granting the rights to reproduce the relevant sections of Miu and Ozdemir (2005).
5. A similar conclusion can be drawn by using the stylized model of Heitfield (2004).
6. At the extreme situation where all information about the systematic component is fully revealed, conditional asset correlation becomes zero.
7. These findings are also considered to be consistent with the empirical research on PD volatility and covariance. In trying to reconcile the different credit risk models, Hickman and Koyluoglu (1998) report that PD volatility of CreditRisk + corresponds with PD covariance in CreditMetrics and the Moody's KMV Portfolio Manager. They are positively related. The findings in another empirical study conducted by Rösch (2004) suggest that the volatility of TTC PD is much larger than that of PIT PD. These two pieces of empirical evidence together therefore suggest the TTC PD covariance is larger than that of PIT PD.
8. The Moody's KMV EDF is calculated based on the *distance to default* of the obligor, which is a function of the current stock price and its volatility. It should therefore contain timely information about the current state of the economy. Similarly, the Standard & Poor's CRT incorporates macroeconomic leading indicators and distance to default.
9. LGD cycles may be different from PD cycles.
10. For example, the increase may be defined by specifying a certain percentage increase (i.e., markup) from the current value of LGD.
11. For example, in constructing the confidence sets of the default (and transition) probabilities through bootstrap experiments, Christensen et al. (2004) assume credit risk is time-homogenous over the time windows. Also, Nickell et al. (2000) assume cross-sectional independence in computing the standard errors of their estimates of default (and transition) probabilities. Blochwitz et al. (2004) conduct a number of simulation exercises and conclude that the confidence intervals of the PD estimate established by ignoring the cross-sectional and time dependencies do not result in unacceptably high errors in the relevant hypothesis tests. The highest asset correlation scenario examined is, however, only 9%, which is believed to be less than those of most of the practical situations.
12. Please refer to Miu and Ozdemir (2008a) for detail illustrations.
13. A number of studies (e.g., Carling et al. [2007] and Chava et al. [2006]) suggest Pt covariates with macroeconomic variables. It is also likely to be positively serially correlated (the autocorrelation is observable in default rates).
14. We could have estimated both $R^2$ and $\beta$ together with LRPD by MLE.
15. The confidence interval of Equation 2.18 tightens up with increasing $T$. The degree of accuracy therefore increases with the length of the historical default rate data.
16. Sometimes they may be able to supplement their internal data with external default rate data compiled by the rating agencies. For example, Standard & Poor's default data for the United States go back to the early 1980s.
17. Numbers in bold represent the ones obtained from **LRPD**$_{MLE1}$ which is one of the proposed methodologies where both cross sectional and serial correlations are taken into account.
18. $CI_{MLE1}$ produces type I errors of the two-tail and one-tail tests very close to the theoretically correct values of 5% and 2.5%, respectively, even in these small sample settings.

19. For example, we can very easily do that using Standard & Poor's CreditPro.
20. In this approach, $R^2$, $R_x^2$, and $\rho$ are assumed to be known parameters. If they are unknown, we could have estimated $\Phi$ (DP), $\Phi$ (DP$_x$), $R^2$, $R_x^2$, and $\rho$ simultaneously by solving a set of simultaneous equations under MLE.
21. Here, we assume the two systematic factors $P_t$ and $P_{x,t}$ are i.i.d. through time (i.e., $\beta = 0$).
22. We typically have longer time-series of external default rate data than of internal data.
23. In this example, we assume the systematic factors are i.i.d. through time (i.e., $\beta = 0$).
24. Numbers in bold correspond with joint estimation.
25. Any direct and indirect costs associated with collection activities should be subtracted from the recovery cash flows.
26. For illustrative purpose, let us assume there are exactly eight defaulted facilities in each year.
27. Bold numbers represent LGDs from downturn years when speculative-grade default rates are higher than the long-term average default rate.
28. For detailed discussion on the model, please refer to Friedman and Sandow (2003). Please refer to Standard & Poor's Credit Market Services (2003) for the implementation details of the model.
29. Users also need to specify the "collateral type" if they choose to enter the "percentages of debt above/below."
30. Using 100% probability of default results in a loss distribution that is identical to the LGD distribution. An input is required for the probability of default, otherwise there will be an error message prompting an input.
31. The authors would like to acknowledge the *Journal of Credit Risk* in granting the rights to reproduce the relevant sections of Miu and Ozdemir (2006).
32. Beta distribution is commonly used to represent the empirical LGD distribution.
33. By construction, these residuals are, however, assumed to be independent among different borrowers.
34. In the subsequent estimation of Equation 2.31, we might need to incorporate an intercept term to accommodate for the fact that the unconditional mean of $l_t$ can be significantly different from zero.
35. Because $n_t$ is typically large in practice, it is more convenient to approximate function $\Omega(\bullet)$ with a Poisson distribution function with lambda equal to $n_t$ times $N(z)$.
36. Though we could have estimated both $R_{PD}$ and DP at the same time, here we assume a $R_{PD}^2$ of 0.25, which is consistent with our illustrations in the previous sections. The conclusions regarding the relation between the systematic PD and LGD risks drawn subsequently are found to be robust to changes in this assumed value.
37. The value of DP is found to be sensitive to the assumption of pairwise PD correlation. If we assume a $R_{PD}^2$ of only 10%, DP becomes $-2.0793$, which corresponds with a PD of 1.9%. Nevertheless, the subsequent analysis regarding the relation between the systematic PD and LGD risks is found to be robust to changes in the assumed value of $R_{PD}^2$.
38. Here, we normalize the two time series with their respective standard deviations. For visual illustration purpose, we present the negative of the values of $P_t$ in Figure 2.19. In our model, the lower the value of $P_t$, the higher is the PD risk.

39.  Numerically, the correlation between $P_t$ and $L_t$ is actually –0.53, which suggests a positive correlation between systematic PD and LGD risks.

40.  For example, in the Basel regulatory capital formula.

41.  Here, we consider a definition of economic capital at the 99.9% critical level. The required markup will be higher if the appropriate critical level is 99% rather than 99.9%.

42.  A higher threshold of 60 is used for the facility-level analysis given the fact that quite a number of the LGD data at the facility-level are dependent among each other.

43.  "Collateral type" is not specified in running the LossStats Model given that information on "Debt Below/Above" is not available in this example.

44.  Diversification of LGD risk across industries is therefore catered for by assessing the industry-specific default rates during the market-wide downturn periods rather than the industry-specific downturn periods. For example, the industry default rate during a market-wide downturn may actually be lower than its cycle-average counterpart if the particular industry under consideration were in fact countercyclical.

45.  Using 100% probability of default results in a loss distribution that is identical to the LGD distribution. An input is required for the probability of default, otherwise there will be an error message prompting an input.

46.  For more details, please refer to Miu and Ozdemir (2006).

47.  To ensure we can transform into a normal distribution, we have to impose upper and lower bound on the observed LGD. Any LGDs smaller (larger) than 0.01% (99.99%) are replaced by 0.01% (99.99%).

48.  We only compute systematic LGD risks for those years where we have equal to or more than five observations of LGD.

49.  We obtain Table 2.21 by trial and error (and interpolation). When we increase the mean LGDs, we maintain the original variances of the beta distributions as presented Table 2.17.

50.  For example, in the Basel regulatory capital formula.

51.  Alternatively, if prior information is available with regard to the values of some of these parameters (e.g., $R^2_{PD}$), we may assume they take on these known parametric values in conducting the estimation of the remaining parameters.

52.  Bold numbers represent conditional probabilities.

53.  Consider the following for further demonstration: if we were to produce two-year conditional cumulative default rates from the one-year conditional transition matrix, we can use Markov chain, that is, by multiplying the one-year matrix by itself. The resulting two-year default rates would be higher than those implied by the unconditional transition matrix because of the stressed transition rate.

54.  In general, default rate data are more readily available than are LGD data.

55.  In the following analysis, depending on the availability of individual explanatory variables, we are using different subsets of the full time-series (from 1990:Q1 to 2006:Q3).

56.  To avoid the possibility of overfitting, one should avoid using more than three to four explanatory variables in this analysis.

57.  The use of the quadratic functional form was not found to be value adding for the Industrial Sector.

## CHAPTER 3

1. For example, Standard & Poor's provides these estimates for unrated obligors on a fee basis.
2. The authors would like to acknowledge the *Journal of Credit Risk* for granting the rights to reproduce the relevant sections of Miu and Ozdemir (2005).
3. The dollar EAD amount represents the extreme case of default and should be distinguished from the expected usage amount, which is used under the normal course of business.
4. In the proposed methodology, the outstanding amount is captured only at two single points in time: at default and at one year before the default.
5. For example, see Saidenberg and Schuermann (2003).
6. EAD distribution is truncated at 0% and 100% to conform to the intended use of the EAD factors in the capital model. That is, the bank does not model the propensity to grant additional authorizations or the propensity to pay down revolving credits. However, there are numerous observations in the historical data where authorization levels increased in the time period analyzed.
7. A better way to capture the time variation of exposure is to construct three- or six-month windows, starting from two years before default to the default point, generating eight or four data points. The shorter the windows, the more the data points, the better the behavior is understood.
8. Because of the lack of historical data on refinancing and the difficulty in quantifying the effects of all these underlying characteristics, it is not uncommon to find commercial banks using simple rules-of-thumb to adjust for the fact that the expected maturity is different than the contractual maturity; for example, an across-the-board approach of shortening the contractual maturity by one year for loans with an actual term of maturity greater than one year.
9. Here, we are referring to those internal models, of which ETTM uncertainty is not explicitly modeled (e.g., in the Moody's KMV Portfolio Manager). In order to use these models, we therefore need to preadjust the contractual maturities of the loans before they can serve as input to the models.
10. It is only true if there are no grid pricing agreement (see below) and other factors that might affect the borrower's refinancing decision.
11. In other words, any loss from these loans can only be due to default rather than credit migration over the risk horizon.
12. In using this simulation tool, asset correlation among obligors is assumed to be given.
13. Neither Basel II correlations nor the correlations used for commonly used off-the-shelf economic capital estimation models make a distinction with respect to intended philosophy.
14. When we use economic capital correlations, we can, for example, use the average correlation for the risk rating being tested via Monte Carlo simulations above.
15. For example, KMV's implied transition matrix, which should score high on PIT scale, returns a mobility metric around 0.6.
16. Assets return correlations do not need to be the same.
17. Note that U.S. obligors in RR5 may have a different assets return correlation than those of Canada.

18. In this analysis, a relatively high confidence level (larger than 90%) is recommended.
19. Note: Accuracy ratio = (1 + Gini)/2.
20. The Monte Carlo Simulation Tool is provided in the Excel spreadsheet "Monte Carlo Simulation" on the CD which comes with the book.
21. Banks are required to disclose their risk rating philosophies under Basel II.
22. As discussed earlier in this Chapter, it is essential to have any mapping between internal and external risk ratings validated before it is used in the backtesting exercise. The validation should be based on both the methodological soundness and developmental evidence of the mapping. For illustration purpose, we assume this mapping has already been validated.
23. In this example, it could be the case that the "stated" philosophy of the bank calls for an even higher mobility metric (i.e., even more PIT-ness) than that of the "realized" philosophy. To address this discrepancy, the bank should therefore consider ways to, for example, reduce the friction in its internal risk rating process in order to improve its PIT-ness.
24. Note that this risk rating system is different from the one considered previously in this case study. This risk rating system has a total of 16 risk ratings.
25. In rare cases, above 100% LGD (losing more than principal due to good money following bad money or to collection costs, etc.) or below 0% LGD (practically a gain due to access collateralization and recovery) are possible.
26. The frequently observed U-shaped LGD distributions may indeed suggest the possibility of missing risk drivers.
27. As emphasized in the previously discussions, the predicted and realized values are not measured at the same time. Typically, the predicted LGD represents the predict value one year before the default event, whereas the realized LGD is measured on the default date.
28. It can be obtained by using the Excel formula TINV(1-CL,dof).
29. The Hoeffding inequality is valid in situation where the underlying random variable is bounded. In the application here, individual LGD observation is assumed to lie between zero and one.
30. We illustrate this example by using the Hoeffding inequality, even though we could have used the $t$-distribution (since $n > 35$) and obtained a tighter confidence interval.
31. LGD cycles may be different from PD cycles.
32. LGD cycles may be different from PD cycles.
33. The use of $t$-distribution is appropriate for sample data that contains at least 30 data points.
34. When we repeat the same calculation for segment 2 where we have 20 observations, we obtain $t = 2.093$, minimum LGD of 49%, and maximum of 80%. As the predicted mean LGD of 55% falls in between these boundaries, we cannot reject the hypothesis that the predicted mean LGD of 55% is in fact the population mean. This conclusion is however questionable given the fact that the t-distribution approximation might not be appropriate when $n < 30$.
35. The fact that probability is always non-negative ensures the lower bound of the confidence level cannot be negative.

36. As discussed before, if the FI is using a standard rating template of an external rating agency, methodological consistency is already established.
37. A model developer would need to provide *developmental evidence* for the models but this evidence needs to be independently reviewed by the validator.
38. Admittedly, this is not an ideal structure as the conflict of interest could be an issue.

## CHAPTER 4

1. A very likely motivation for the downturn LGD requirement is the fact that Basel capital formula as well as most commonly used off-the-shelf models do not capture PD and LGD correlations and thus underestimate the capital requirement.
2. Book equity is different from the market value of equity. The latter includes goodwill, although an important component of capital, is beyond the scope of this discussion.
3. Here, risk capital is the economic and Basel II capital requirements after the stress event, when these are estimated using stress parameters.

# INDEX

# A

Acyclical loss given default, 75, 286
Advanced internal rating-based
    approach (A-IRB), 1
Advanced-IRB treatment, 170
A-IRB. *See* advanced internal
    rating-based approach.
Average stress level, long-run prob-
    ability of default
    and, 90

# B

Backtesting, 208–209
    exposure at default, 267–268
    loss given default, 243–267
        calibration testing, 249–254
        case study, 259–267
        risk rating discriminatory test,
            244–246
        risk rating philosophy,
            254–255
        subportfolio-level validation,
            255–259
    probability of default, 208–243
        common observations,
            230–231
        discriminatory power empirical
            measurement, 209–210

risk rating philosophy
    confirmation, 220–225
risk rating system calibration,
    210–220
subportfolio-level validation,
    225–230, 239–243
probability of default case study,
    231–243
    risk rating system calibration,
        234–237
    risk rating system philosophy,
        237–239
    risk rating system testing,
        232–234
Basel II Accord, Pillar 1, 1
Basel II Accord, Pillar II, 1
    capital adequacy, 1
    regulatory capital requirements
        Cramer-Rao Lower Bound, 82
        long-run probability of default
            and, 79–82
        Merton's structural model, 79
Benchmarking, 203–208
    defaulted loans, 208
Borrower-level LGD data, 124

# C

Calibration testing, aggregated
    level, 263

# ABOUT THE AUTHORS

As a Vice President in Standard & Poor's Credit Risk Services group, Bogie Ozdemir is globally responsible for engineering new products and solutions, business development and project management, and he specializes in internal risk rating system implementation and validation.

Bogie has worked in different areas of risk management for more than 10 years. Most recently, as a senior director in the Risk Analytics group of the Bank of Montreal, he led teams in Economic Capital and Model Validation groups. As a thought leader, Bogie supported the bank-wide Basel implementation and validation.

Dr. Peter Miu is an Associate Professor of Finance at DeGroote School of Business, McMaster University. He teaches financial institutions and international financial management at both the undergraduate and MBA levels. His research has been conducted primarily in such areas as credit risk modeling and forecasting, pricing and risk management of credit portfolios, and Basel II implementation and validation. He has consulted on numerous Basel II implementation projects and is a frequent speaker in both academic and professional conferences on credit risk and Basel II. Dr. Miu obtained his Ph.D. and MBA in finance from the University of Toronto.

Bogie and Peter have coauthored the following papers:

- "Practical and Theoretical Challenges in Validating Basel Parameters: Key Learnings from the Experience of a Canadian Bank," Peter Miu and Bogie Ozdemir, *Journal of Credit Risk*, 2005.
- "Basel Requirement of Downturn LGD: Modeling and Estimating PD & LGD Correlations," Peter Miu and Bogie Ozdemir, *Journal of Credit Risk*, 2006.
- "Discount Rate for Workout Recoveries: An Empirical Study," Brooks Brady, Peter Chang, Peter Miu, Bogie Ozdemir, and David Schwartz, Working Paper, 2007.
- "Estimating Long-Run Probability of Default with Respect to Basel II Requirements," Peter Miu and Bogie Ozdemir, *Journal of Risk Model Validation*, 2008.

# CD-ROM WARRANTY